The Fragmented Dream

Multicultural California

Revised Printing

Howard A. DeWitt

Ohlone College

KENDALL/HUNT PUBLISHING COMPANY
4050 Westmark Drive   Dubuque, Iowa 52002

Copyright © 1996, 1999 by Kendall/Hunt Publishing Company

Revised Printing

Library of Congress Catalog Card Number: 95-82394

ISBN 0-7872-6287-0

Printed in the United States of America
10   9   8   7   6   5

Contents

Preface

Multicultural California, An Introduction

On November 2, 1769 the Spanish explorer Gaspar de Portola discovered San Francisco bay. At least this is what every major California history textbook suggests. A closer look at Portola's log and the copious notes he kept during the trip point to a different conclusion. San Francisco was discovered by a black Spaniard, thereby introducing a multicultural element to Spanish California.

While Portola led the party that named San Francisco bay, it was an obscure North African Moor, known simply as El Negro, who discovered the Bay which would make California a major trade center. Not only was El Negro an African but a large number of Spanish soldiers were mixed blooded. His name was lost to history and El Negro was no more than a footnote in Spanish California. Unfortunately, textbooks, monographs and major interpretive works have ignored El Negro. He is one of many people of color lost in California history. El Negro was one of many Africans who came to the New World as a fundamental part of Spanish exploration.

What does this mean in the broader context of California history? The answer is a simple one. All through the Golden State's rich and varied civilization there are impor-

tant ethnic figures who are missing from the history books. There is no conspiracy, no attempt to exclude multicultural figures and no plan to overlook ethnic history. It has neither been fashionable nor scholarly to include multicultural examples. For years historians have simply ignored multi-cultural contributions to the Golden State. Fortunately, this attitude has changed and for more than a decade multiculturalism has crept into California history.

One way to create new interest in state history is to demonstrate that it reflects the multicultural mix which dates from the earliest Spanish exploration to the present. By dividing California into three periods of history *The Fragmented Dream: Multicultural California* will analyze how important ethnic and multicultural turning points have been in the development of California civilization.

The Spanish and Mexican Era: Images of Ethnic Accomplishment Denied

When the Spanish settled California in 1769 they began a half century of creating a permanent civilization. Historians have failed to analyze the degree of conflict

v

amongst Spaniards due to skin color, geographical region or racial mix. Early in Spanish California the leadership class was the gachupines or men who wore spurs. Generally, the gachupines were pure blooded Castillians with ties to the King of Spain or the Viceroy in New Spain. They arrived in California and quickly became the leading rancheros, government officials and merchants.

In sharp contrast to the gachupines stood the criollos or creoles. They were mixed blooded Spaniards with a penchant for settling on the frontier and establishing an independent lifestyle. From California's earliest Spanish days there was conflict among the mixed blooded Spaniards and aristocratic Castillian officials.

When the Mexican Revolution was successful in 1821, the result was a multicultural California civilization. There were Moors, Indians and mixed blooded Spaniards who settled permanently in the Golden State and created its first sense of diversity. During the quarter century of Mexican California, there were two black governors. Not surprisingly, skin color was not an impediment to leadership. Both governors were accepted and respected leaders despite their black skin.

On March 8, 1830 Lieutenant Colonel Manual Victoria took over as Mexican California's governor and he wasn't hindered in any way by black blood. Not only was Victoria California's first minority political leader, he was also a strong supporter of Home Rule. Like most Californians, Governor Victoria believed that Spain and Mexico were wedded to outmoded political, economic, social, religious and racial ideas.

The result was the rise of the Californio or native son ruler. The long standing tensions over race exploded as Governor Victoria forced more equal treatment of the Native California Indian and the mixed blooded settlers. An attitude of racial equality permeated Mexican California.

By the time the last Mexican governor, Pio Pico, took office there were few problems between the mixed blooded settlers and those who considered themselves Mexican aristocrats. Few textbooks mention that Governor Pico was part African Moor and Aztec Indian. There was a subtle refusal to make this part of the official record. The color line that Spain had established crumbled in the development of a multi-ethnic Mexican Californian.

Yet, there is evidence that color consciousness did exist. In 1835, the novelist-historian Richard Henry Dana remarked: "Those who are of pure Spanish blood, having never intermarried with aborigines, have clear brunette complexions, and sometimes, even as fair of those of English women. There are but few of these families in California." What Dana failed to mention, or perhaps even recognize, was that the pure blooded Castillian Spaniard and the self styled Mexican aristocrat had abandoned California. It was now a mixed blooded civilization with a multicultural direction.

When the Mexican War broke out in May, 1846, the United States quickly moved in and annexed California by sea. There are only scattered mentions of African Spaniards and mixed blooded Mexican settlers, but they played a prominent role in the history of Spanish and Mexican California. Then the American period arrived and with the influx of new settlers there was a decided turn in patterns of immigration, settlement and ethnicity. The growth of business brought a new value system and ethnicity faded in the drive for economic success. Yet, ethnic groups and racial concerns remained an integral part of the California experience.

Early California Statehood and Economic Triumph, 1850-1900

The changes in California after the September 9, 1850 statehood ceremony were important ones. The prominence of African Americans, the rise of Mexican Americans and the influx of a wide range of white immigrant groups including the Irish Catholics, Jews, Italians and Yugoslavians created a great deal of change in the Golden State. The hostility to the Chinese and the racism directed toward the black population suggested the need for an ethnic leader.

When the Reverend Jeremiah Sanderson opened the all black St. Cyprian's elementary school in San Francisco more than one hundred students flocked to enroll and he became the acknowledged leader in the ethnic community. Soon Sanderson was instrumental in the civil rights activity of the United Colored People of California and he also helped former slaves at Sacramento's Hotel Hackett challenge pro slavery attitudes. Not only did the Reverend Sanderson foster a strong civil rights impulse, but he also helped to challenge the unofficial attitude which condoned slavery in the Golden State.

Although admitted to the Union as a free state, California's legislature, thanks to the leadership of pro slavery State Senator Thomas Jefferson Green, looked the other way when slaves were brought in to work the gold fields. When the Perkins case in 1852 and the Archy Lee case in 1858 challenged the employment of slaves in the gold fields, Rev. Sanderson was in the forefront of the civil rights battle. Cornelius Cole, a white civil rights attorney, helped to rally public support against white, racist attitudes in the California courts. Although the California Supreme Court protected slave owning rights, the civil rights issue was a dramatic one.

The Spanish speaking population declined in the first decade of statehood and was a decided minority by the 1860s. Yet, a San Luis Obispo Democrat, Romualdo Pacheco, ran successfully for public office. From the time Pacheco was elected a judge in 1853, until he became the lieutenant governor in 1871, he was the voice of the Spanish speaking voter. The key to Pacheco's political prominence was more than just the ethnic vote. He clearly understood the key changes needed in California politics and society.

In 1875, Governor Newton Booth was appointed to the United States Senate, and for nine months Pacheco was California's governor. His leadership skills were extraordinary. He built new prisons, created teachers' colleges, raised taxes for state services and began a system of libraries which increased California's literacy level.

Despite his leadership, Pacheco was not nominated by the Republican party as the gubernatorial candidate. Pacheco was bitter but he quickly returned to elective office. After serving in Congress, Pacheco was appointed in 1890 by President Benjamin Harrison as an Envoy Extraordinary and Minister Plenipotentiary to Central America. He retired to a ranch in Mexico shortly after holding this position and publicly declared his bitterness toward California politics.

Despite the success of African American and Mexican American politicians, businessmen and educators there was a legacy of disillusionment and second class citizenship which permeated the Golden State.

Much of the hostility to colored minorities came from the Irish Catholic settlers who moved into San Francisco and became a third of the population of that city by 1880. Since they were discriminated against so heavily in New York, the Irish Catholics led the way in the battle to exclude the San Francisco Chinese.

David Broderick, a New Yorker who had apprenticed in New York's Tammany Hall

Democratic political machine, organized the anti-Coolie clubs which helped to pass the Pig Tail ordinance of 1854. Not only did this San Francisco city ordinance harass the Chinese, but it created the public pressure necessary to pass federal exclusion bill. After Broderick will killed in an untimely duel with California Supreme Court Justice David S. Terry, the mantle of racial hostility passed on to Denis Kearney and the Workingmen's Party.

During the 1870s pressure was placed upon national politics and in 1882 President Chester Arthur signed the Exclusion Act which banned the Chinese from legally immigrating to the United States. This period of history was one which established strong feelings of nativism.

One of the great failings of California historians is their inability to recognize how effectively California's minority population was in resisting these early attempts to place permanent second class citizenship upon most immigrant and ethnic groups.

As B. Gordon Wheeler suggests: "the fight for rights and riches" was a major part of the late nineteenth century African American impulse. From the earliest days in the gold fields until the founding of an all black town, Allensworth, in the San Joaquin Valley, African Americans were part of the broader development of California society.

African American women were also significant in the nineteenth century. In 1851, Biddy Mason, who had been born a slave in Hancock County, Georgia in 1818, crossed the plains into Southern California and settled in Los Angeles. The thirty two year Mason had three daughters and quickly challenged her slave master, Robert Smith. She yearned for her freedom and found a way to accomplish it.

Because the California Constitution of 1849 outlawed slavery, Mason challenged Smith in the California Supreme Court and won her freedom. This is only the beginning of the story. Although she was thirty seven years old when she won her freedom, Biddy Mason had a vision.

She worked as a practical nurse for $2.50 a day and lived on no more than fifty cents a day. Soon she bought two parcels of Los Angeles land. It was about ten acres and she paid $250 dollars for it. When she sold this property five years later for $200,000 Mason was on the way to establishing her fortune. She had purchased land in what is now the downtown business center of Los Angeles.

Few text books mention Biddy Mason. After acquiring her fortune she began donating money for churches, schools and nursing homes. A deeply religious woman, Mason created the first African American charities. Why is Biddy Mason not a part of most textbooks? The answer is a simple one. She made her money in real estate, shrewd investments and through frugal living. Historians have been prone to discuss black entertainers, gamblers and speculators and not an African American woman with a business genius. By not concentrating upon the economic activities of black Californians major textbooks by John Caughey, Andrew Rolle and Walton Bean have ignored a fertile area. While these books are excellent texts by respected scholars, nevertheless, they leave out many key tales which would enhance the history of the Golden State.

The Twentieth Century and the Ethnic Impulse

Since the inception of the Progressive Movement there has been a rethinking of ethnic influences in California history. Prior to World War I there was a universal belief that Progressivism produced a new brand of equality. This was true. But for African Californians, Asians and Mexican Americans there was a double standard for jobs, housing, education and social needs.

By concentrating upon the ethnic attitudes of Governor Hiram Johnson, it is possible to examine how modern day racism developed. From his election as California's governor in 1910, Johnson was a model racist. He began this behavior when he convinced the California legislature to pass the Alien Land Law of 1913. Few, if any, textbooks concentrate upon the reasoning behind Johnson's anti-Asian attitudes. Generally, the major textbooks suggest that anti-Chinese rhetoric translated into votes. However, the Alien Land Law was aimed at the Japanese and the arguments used to pass it demonstrated a strong reaction against immigrants.

The San Francisco African American community worried that Governor Johnson's racism would extend to them. Although blacks were registered as Republicans, nonetheless, African American political organizations criticized the racial direction of Johnson's politics. San Francisco newspapers ignored this criticism and pictured the Golden State as a racial paradise.

After World War I ended and California returned to a semblance of normalcy, there occurred a period of hidden ethnicity. From 1920 to 1940 the hidden ethnic is a term which refers to the Chinese, Asian Indian, Korean, Japanese and Filipino who immigrated to the Golden State.

There was a demand for immigration restriction, and in 1924 changes in American immigration law slowed the influx of Asian settlers. Because they were an American protectorate, the Philippines had no restrictions upon their workers. They could migrated freely into San Francisco and Los Angeles. As a result, Filipinos became the major work force in California's farms and fields.

Most Filipinos came to California from the Hawaiian sugar cane fields. They arrived at San Francisco's Angel Island or in Los Angeles and were herded into buses by labor brokers. Until World War II broke Filipinos were one of the more stable and productive sources of farm labor. They also became increasingly urban between the wars and demonstrated skills in a wide variety of professions.

What separated the Filipino from Chinese, Korean, Asian Indian and Japanese workers was their command of the English language. Yet, like their Asian counterparts, the Filipino experienced a barrage of racism. When a series of race riots broke out in small California towns like Exeter and Watsonville there was concern about the Filipino. By 1930 Filipinos were organizing labor unions. C.K. McClatchy, the head of the California Joint Immigration Committee, remarked that "Filipinos were the state's next problem."

In 1934, the Filipino labor Union staged an important strike in the lettuce producing area around Salinas. It was during the Salinas Lettuce Strike of 1934 that the Filipino Labor Union won their first major strike and became part of the labor movement. By 1937, the F.L.U. was granted an American Federation of Labor charter.

The key to new ethnic influences in California began in the aftermath of World War II when the Japanese American Citizens League challenged Executive Order 9066 which set up concentration camps to house loyal Americans of Japanese descent. During and after World War II, Japanese Americans challenged the Federal Government's right in imprison a people because of their ancestry. Unfortunately, in case after case, the United States Supreme Court refused to recognize the basic disrespect for human dignity in the relocation camps.

Black Californians were equally incensed over the trial and court martial of black sailors at the Port Chicago Naval Facility in Mare Island. When African American sailors refused to load bombs, which had previously exploded and killed many people, the Navy quickly began court martial proceedings. Thurgood Marshall traveled to California to defend the sailors but they were still convicted.

What most California textbooks ignore is that degree of commitment to ethnic political organization which came from these events. From 1945 to 1995, because of the events described previously, California exploded into a cauldron of racial turmoil. The racial differences produced the fragmented dream and caused many to complain about California's commitment to equality.

Acknowledgements

During the course of writing this book, I have incurred many debts that I would like to acknowledge. The concept for *The Fragmented Dream: Multicultural California* resulted from a series of lectures that I delivered at the UCLA Asian American center in the late 1970s. These initial ideas were refined in papers delivered to the Pacific Coast Branch of the American Historical Association, the Organization of American Historians, the National Social Science Association Convention and the Popular Culture Association.

Conversations with Bradford Luckingham, B. Lee Cooper, Jim Kluger, H. Brett Melendy, Suecheng Chan, Hector Cordova, Hans Larson, Albert Acena, Fred Cordova, Belinda Aquino, the late Edwin B. Almirol, Peter Bacho, Richard Peterson, Jerry Stanley, Alexander Saxton, Harvey Schwartz, Rudolph Lapp, Charles Wollenberg, David Beesley, Ed Beechert, Lilian Galedo, Steffi San Buenaventura, Charles Reed, Dennis Roby, Ramon Quezada and Alex Fabbros helped to shape the manuscript.

The staffs at the libraries of Ohlone College, the Bancroft library, the Huntington library, the UCLA Special Collection, the Stanford Special Collection and the Los Angeles County Museum of Natural History provided assistance in completing the manuscript.

A wide variety of interviews with Filipino, Mexican American, Asian American and African American business people helped to shape many of my attitudes. Jimmy McCracklin, legendary Oakland blues singer, opened doors to the black community previously closed to researchers. Mr. McCracklin put me in touch with a wide variety of business people who helped me recount the African American experience.

The manuscript was edited with precision, skill and good humor by Ms. Amy Souders. She is a magnificent editor but the mistakes remain mine. Chuck Borgquist of Kendall Hunt facilitated the final preparation of the book and supported the constant delays with humor and enthusiasm.

At Ohlone College I am fortunate to work with three fine scholars with varying attitudes and viewpoints. Dr. Alan Kirshner provided excellent comments on civil rights and race, Professor Stacy Cole filled my mailbox with readings on ethnic history (I even read some of them) and our division chairperson, Professor Sheldon Nagel, facilitated a teaching schedule and academic atmosphere conducive to completing the book.

Professor Walt Halland provided lunch and encouragement and shared his vast knowledge of California's culinary past. Eleene Kraft and Luz M. Miller are former students who offered insights into the book.

A grant from the Sourisseau Academy at San Jose State University helped to establish the initial framework for this book. A number of my previous professors, notably August Radke, Keith Murray, Harley Hiller, Earl Pomeroy, Donald Swain, Irwin Unger, David Jacobson, Russell Ewing, and most notably my dissertation adviser Herman E. Bateman provided excellent research, teaching and writing examples.

Finally, my wife Carolyn and my children Darin and Melanie provided encouragement and endured long nights of computer clatter. Thanks for your support during this project.

During the last few months of this manuscripts preparation the Philippine Government extended an invitation to speak at the centennial celebration of Philippine Independence. This was an added plum as I finished the book and Dr. Salvador Laurel's gracious invitation made this work easier to finish.

Howard A. DeWitt
Ohlone College, Fremont, California

Introduction

The Fragmented Dream:
A Usable History for a Multicultural California

California's ethnic diversity is a commonly accepted phenomena. The California Division of Motor Vehicles hands out driver education pamphlets in twelve languages. Affirmative action is readily accepted as a part of the employment landscape. Women, minorities and the physically impaired can pursue jobs, schooling and loans without fear of artificial barriers. It has not always been this way. Nor does it appear that affirmative action will continue to dominate California. The Golden State is at a crossroads brought on by an inability to understand and accept a multicultural society. California is the fragmented dream.

The immigrant who arrives in San Francisco finds his or her expectations shattered by white racism. The long and tortured history of ethnic conflict in the Golden State is the product of a multicultural California history. When John C. Fremont traveled to Los Angeles in late 1846 to end Mexican resistance to the United States annexing California, he spoke of the Spanish speaking as the "foreign intruder." In 1995 Republican Governor Pete Wilson used the same demagogic language when he criticized the federal government for not closing the border to illegal Mexican immigrants. Both General Fremont and Governor Wilson were pandering to white racism. It is a popular and politically appealing means of garnering voter support.

Politicians often manipulate the system and the California legislature responds. When the California legislature elected John C. Fremont as one of California's first two United States Senators, State Senator Thomas Jefferson Green remarked that Fremont knew how to "handle the Mexicans." In 1995 Governor Wilson displayed attitudes similar to Fremont's regarding the Spanish speaking. Both politicians were crass opportunists who made the ethnic population a scapegoat for other problems.

A distinct and unique pattern of race and ethnic relations has taken shape during the span of California history from the earliest Native American era to the present. The differences among Californian's has gone a long way to explain the conflict inherent in the Golden State. From its earliest days, California has been marked by ethnic conflict and this has created turbulent periods of historical change. Hostility to ethnic groups is common and attempts to ban, exclude, control or classify the Chinese, Japanese, Filipino, Korean, Mexican American, African American and Asian Indian suggests the course of California history since statehood.

By the 1990s the ethnic composition of the Golden State reflected a Hispanic, African American and Asian influence upon public policy, education and business. Affordable public housing, bilingual education, affirmative action programs and enforcement of civil rights laws were demanded by multicultural California interests. The rise of advocacy groups or boards to implement fair treatment of the minority population continued to be one of the traits of California civilization.

Historians have gotten into the act. One Chicano historian, Juan Gomez-Quinones, in a 1977 paper, "On Culture," suggested that Chicanos were not assimilated into the mainstream of the Golden State. They resisted California values and this cultural resistance led to the strength of Chicano values. Chicano is a term used interchangeably to describe Mexican immigrants and those born in the United States, the Mexican American. Gomez-Quinones argues that Chicanos stand as a subculture resisting both Anglo America and the old values of Mexican life. Chicanos have created a new and vibrant Hispanic nationalism. But this has led to a "Schizoid Heritage," or a Spanish speaking world caught between two cultures. The result is a fragmented dream. One that is neither Mexican nor American. As ethnic groups strive for equality, fight institutional racism and produce new leaders there is a sense of gain.

But from these advances in the mid-1990s there were new problems. The fear of illegal immigration prompted Governor Pete Wilson to turn out television ads which blamed the problem on the federal government and the Democratic party. Governor Wilson's ads proudly proclaimed that he sent troops to the border. There has never been a governor whose administration has been so tainted with racism as that of Pete Wilson. He appointed few minority candidates to pubic office, he talked at length about Spanish speaking crime and he spoke of California being invaded from Mexico. Like the political bigots in the mid-to-late nineteenth century, Governor Wilson was building his political strength on fears of immigrant successes. He also hoped to become the 1996 Republican presidential candidate but quickly abandoned this notion due to lack of political support.

On television, Governor Wilson looks and sounds more like a Baptist minister than a conservative Republican. When the California voters overwhelmingly approved Proposition 187 to restrict immigrant rights, Wilson called it a voice of the California conscience. This statement placed Governor Wilson in the mainstream of such historical California bigots as Senator William Gwin who supported slavery in the 1850s, Denis Kearney who demanded the exclusion of the Chinese in the 1870s and Governor Hiram Johnson who helped write the Alien Land Law of 1913 restricting Japanese landowning rights.

Yet, Wilson and other California politicians seldom mention that much of California immigration is legal. The fear of illegal immigrants is a political tool. One which a demagogue like Governor Wilson can use to turn out the vote. Almost thirty percent of all legal immigrants arrive in California and the vast majority come from Latin America, India and Asia. They are often skilled labor, invest in businesses and take their place as respectable, middle class members of the community.

What is the significance of this immigration? The answer is a simple one. California's political, economic, social and cultural institutions have undergone dramatic change as a result of these ethnic influences upon California?

Since the reforms in federal immigration law in 1965 the increase of Vietnamese, Cambodian, Laotian and Asian immigrants, in general, has led to a boom in small businesses. From the Philippines, nurses, doctors and professionals stream into San Francisco and Los Angeles bringing a strong work ethic. In Daly City, California Filipinos form a potential voter majority. Yet, at the Serramonte Mall in Daly City it is common to see security guards roughly escorting young Filipino boys out of the mall. Violence. Intimidation. Harsh feelings. These are the words that the Filipino community often uses to describe local merchants. Immigration is a serious political problem. In 1994 Governor Pete Wilson focused much of his reelection campaign on the issue of stopping illegals. What Wilson's political ads failed to mention is that he did very little about illegal aliens until it was time for reelection.

Multiculturalism is the goal of most Californians, but the concept and the execution of it often gets caught up in politics. Multicultural aspects of California began to dominate the politics and culture of the Golden State in the early 1980s. The civil rights revolution of the 1950s and 1960s, the woman's movement in the 1970s, the rise of gay politics in the 1980s and, finally, the questions of equity, sexual harassment and reverse discrimination made multicultural history a significant part of the California experience.

What is the reason for this multicultural direction? The answer is a simple one; from its earliest inception California has had multicultural influences. Spanish troops were often of African Moor blood, the Mexican had Aztec blood and Americans were Irish Catholic, French, German and English. Soon Chileans, Peruvians and Chinese immigrated to the mines and the swing to a multicultural California began.

The major changes in California's multicultural society began taking place in the 1960s. When the African American Assemblyman, W. Byron Rumford introduced the Rumford Fair Housing Act of 1963. This law allowed African Americans to purchase homes. Then they found it easier to enter the job market and slowly they gained admission to major colleges and universities. In the more than three decades since Rumford's legislation became law the African American community has moved into a position of leadership. San Francisco based politician Willie Brown was the Assembly Speaker for years and as late as 1995 his power continued despite a Republican controlled state legislature.

The University of California Regents reconsidered their affirmative action program during the summer of 1995 and a major controversy broke out. Governor Pete Wilson used the issue for political purposes and held a series of well publicized meetings with the University Regents. The result was that affirmative action was taken out of the University of California system. The old blue football buffs in Berkeley were gleeful as were Neo Nazis, John Birches and disaffected whites.

California civilization is in a period of transition. As the Golden State debates its ethnic future there is raging controversy developing over whether or not quotas, special categories and diversification is the right path. Events of the next decade will provide the answers to questions of race and ethnicity.

1

California

Origin of the Term and Ethnic Contributions to the Golden State

Where did the name California originate? Historians believe that the term was popularized by Garci Ordonez de Montalvo's, *The Exploits of Esplandian*. The book, a piece of Spanish chivalric literature, was popular during the early sixteenth century. This was a widely read novel which told an uplifting tale of Christian conquest. Unwittingly, Montalvo characterized the Indian population as a black civilization in need of Spanish Christianity and cultural values. Somewhere in the New World, Montalvo warned, is an island filled with dangerous warrior women, the Isle of California.

The Spanish conquistadors who sailed into the New World, were the first generation of mass novel readers. Popular books like *The Exploits of Esplandian* were taken to sea to help Spanish navigators and soldiers pass the time. Since Montalvo's novel took place in the Isle of California, the use of the word California to describe exotic Indian settlements became a popular one. There were other books which developed themes centering around exploration, conquest and racism which created stereotypes about the pagan nature of Indian populations.

Amadis of Gaul, published in 1508, was the first in a series of romantic novels depicting the financial rewards and spiritual importance of conquest. *Amadis of Gaul* was Spain's best selling book in the early sixteenth century. The book so romanticized the common soldier that it persuaded volunteer military men to migrate to the New World. The book's main theme, serving the King of Spain and the Catholic Church by conquering the New World, centered around the main character, Amadis. In the novel, he suggested that wealth was the end result of his explorations. So *Amadis of Gaul* was a tale of Spanish Army volunteers which created a romantic vision of California and excited soldiers who volunteered to come to the New World. Gold was the motivating factor in their decision. The book was popular, and a sequel was published to satisfy the hungering thirst for knowledge on this exotic foreign settlement.

The Exploits of Esplandian was the sequel to *Amadis of Gaul*, and it continued to excite the popular imagination. The themes in this sequel were designed to encourage settlement of a mythical California. The son of Amadis of Gaul was the main character in *The Exploits of Esplandian*, and he warned future sailors about dangerous men with two heads, sexy Amazon warrior women, the Fountain of Eternal Youth and the potential treasure in the mythical Isle of California.

Spaniards agreed on one thing-California meant gold, wealth, adventure and an exciting civilization. As Spain explored and conquered the world, the name California was applied to the land from San Diego north. Spanish explorers called it High or Alta California.

Long before San Diego was settled, Spanish explorers wrote about the unique qualities of the mythical Island of California. Over the years, the myths associated with California—great wealth, an advanced population and a jumping off point for Far Eastern Trade—became reality.

The term California was popularized by a Spanish explorer, Fortun Jimenez. Who was Fortun Jimenez? Ironically, he was a common Spaniard. Jimenez was a crew member on the first ship to explore Baja California. Shortly after leaving Acapulco in 1532, he led a mutiny which killed the ships officers. By default, Jimenez became the expedition's commander and discovered Baja California. Since he had recently read the Garci Ordonez de Montalvo novel, Jimenez named the area Lower or Baja California

When Jimenez returned to New Spain, he exaggerated the agricultural potential of Baja California as well as the friendly nature of local Indians. In a moment of overstatement, Jimenez bragged about the local pearl wealth. In doing so, he created the first economic myths surrounding California. Potential riches, alluvial soil and friendly Indians were tales that appealed to Spanish greed.

As the Spanish discovered and explored Baja California, they created other legends. One tale , which was popular, was that Baja California was much like the Isle of Santa Cruz, populated by fierce, but primitive, Indians and possessing enormous wealth. A king with gold armor clothing ruled this land. The Gilded Man offered the potential for great wealth. This was a convenient myth to justify conquering the La Paz area.

Another tale centered around a hot, desolate island populated by Amazon warrior women. This mythical Isle of Santa Cruz was a hot desert. Calida Fornax was the Latin phrase the Spanish used to describe this island. The term meant hot furnace. Because of this Calida Fornax myth, the Spanish believed that California was not ready for permanent settlement. It was viewed only as a jumping off point to the China trade.

Since the Isle of Santa Cruz was also considered too dangerous to explore, Spanish military commanders, like Hernando Cortes, faced disciplinary problems with the troops. Before the Spanish explored and settled New Spain, there were tales of fierce Indian tribes, geographical obstacles and evil spirits. Rather than dissuading Spanish explorers from coming to the Western Hemisphere, these notions excited the popular imagination.

These myths were useful in attracting potential recruits. Wealth was a topic that every Spanish explorer discussed. Riches were rumored to be a part of Queen Calafia's mystical Isle of California. There were tales of hydra-headed monsters lurking in San Francisco Bay. The Shaman was described as a devil like religious figure who was the key to unlocking the door to another world. Eventually, the California Indian was viewed as independent and mysterious. All these forces helped to popularize the discovery and eventual settlement of California.

Chivalric Literature and California: Its Influence Upon Local Character

Another problem for the Spanish military leadership was finding a suitable place to settle the young troops. Amusement was at a premium, but the ships only carried a few books, and officers, not the crews, read these tales of Spanish conquest. Invariably, these books were pieces of chivalric literature. This was the literature of Spanish nationalism and these fictional tomes justified the conquest of heathen civilizations. The purpose of chivalric literature was not only to encourage conquest, but to pave the way for the mission system. So the themes in chivalric literature always pitted good versus evil to explain the Christian siege. The Indians were described in these potboiling and sensational volumes as pagan, uncivilized and in need of Spanish institutions. A chivalric novel with beautiful Amazon warrior women, lush fertile valleys and excellent ports became the model for Spanish explorers.

Why was Garci Ordonez de Montalvo's *Las Sergas de Esplandian (The Exploits of Esplandian)* so popular? This slender volume used the word California to describe a mythical island populated with warrior women who killed men and mated with large horned birds. Like other fictional laden chivalric romances, Christian knights were the heroes. Being a low-level chivalric tale, *The Exploits of Esplandian* told the tale of how a perfect knight, the son of Amadis of Gaul, conquered his heathen enemies. The book's popularity was increased by the appeal of the heroine, Queen Calafia. She was tall, buxom and a pagan. She ruled the Isle of California with an iron hand, and its perfect weather, excellent ports, abundant agriculture and gold and silver mines made it a garden spot. The lush and fertile valleys described in Montalvo's story caught the Spanish imagination. As Hernando Cortes suggested, it was the perfect catalyst to Christian conquest.

Montalvo's book gave the Spanish not only an excuse for conquest but a rationale for its success. Of course the tale had a happy ending. After Queen Calafia's Isle of California was conquered by the son of King Amadis of Gaul, a tranquil civilization with a Christian base was established. In the euphoric conclusion to this fictional potboiler,

there is not only a strong sense of Christian values but an indication that something is different about California. Once the female warriors were conquered, converted to Christianity and made into fine Spanish citizens, they were described as superior to other colonial Spaniards. So the myth is born of the hardy California pioneer. Unwittingly, this mythical pioneer is black, female and a symbol of strength.

For Spaniards, the term California was a slang term for a dangerous, unknown and uncharted land. Montalvo's book was at the peak of its popularity in the 1530s when Cortes planned Baja California's settlement. Like most Spaniards, Cortes was caught up in the myth of this land. He wrote the Spanish king that "an island of Amazons or women only, abounding in pearls and gold, lying ten days' journey from Colima waits to be conquered." These letters piqued the king's interest, and he gave Cortes permission "to explore California."

To Spaniards, California was a mysterious land. As Cortes suggested, they should both fear and love this new land. This attitude created a sense of awe and majesty about California and unwittingly fed the mythical notion of a "super area." The spiritual or magical side of Indian life caused the Spanish to experience historical hallucinations. As a result, much of what they reported was not only untrue but also derived from reading too much chivalric literature. The myth, not the reality, of California drew the conquistador. Sadly, the Spanish conqueror found that the term California was a misnomer.

California: Little Resemblance to Historical Reality

The earliest Spanish descriptions of Baja California bore little resemblance to reality. From the early 1530s to the 1540s, Baja and Alta California were explored by Spaniards who described the land they discovered as "glamorous," "daring," or "fearless." These were surprising conclusions considering that the settlement of La Paz was a disaster. In 1535, Cortes settled this area and two years later returned to New Spain for reinforcements. The Indians quickly ended this experiment in colonization by killing all the Spanish settlers.

What was the reason for the La Paz disaster? Cortes pointed out that the Bay of La Paz, located above the southern tip of the gulf shore of the peninsula, was more remote and difficult to bring ships into than other areas of Baja California. The Jimenez crew, Cortes reminded the Spanish king, had misrepresented the area. The Indians were fierce and not friendly. The rumors of pearl wealth were untrue. Agriculture was a difficult proposition. As Cortes suggested, these lies helped to delay Spain's future settlement for more than two centuries. From 1537, when the Indians massacred La Paz, until 1769 when Spain settled San Diego, there was very little official interest in settling California.

California: The Word in History

Thinking the word California was a piece of fiction is a delicious irony for many of the myths in *The Exploits of Esplandian* became reality. The Spanish never thought of settling California beyond the ports of San Diego, Santa Barbara, Monterey and San Francisco. The four governmental districts in Spanish California were located in these ports. Spanish settlers remained fifteen to twenty miles from the Pacific Ocean. Many Spaniards who elected to remain in California became large ranchers. With twenty-five Spanish land grants, California was a small, isolated Spanish colony.

Yet, the term California had a dramatic impact upon the Spanish mind, and the conclusion was that adventure and wealth awaited explorers and settlers. These were the words generally used to describe California. It also became a safety valve for the independently minded Spaniard who was tired of the King's arbitrary power and the restrictions of Catholic doctrine. A sense of personal freedom persisted in Spanish California.

From 1769 to 1821, Spanish California reflected the influence of *The Exploits of Esplandian*. It was a civilization fixated on harbors and finding a sea route to China. It also drew a casual rather than a permanent settler. Spain saw California as a pagan way station one which would allow the conquerors, the conquistadors as they were known, to work their magic on the heathen population.

Juan Rodriguez Cabrillo: The Discovery of California: The Racial Side of Conquest

Ethnic differences result from observations and conclusions about a people and a civilization that appear primitive in religious, economic and governmental direction. At least this is how the Spanish viewed the native Californian. No one provided more judgmental material on the California Indian than early Spanish explorers. In their diaries, journals and official reports, Spanish navigators presented a picture of a civilization that Spain was struggling to understand. They described the California Indians as "neophytes." Father Serra remarked: "they were like lost little children." The implication was that they needed to be conquered and civilized. At least this was the excuse to explore and conquer the California Indian from San Diego north. The earliest Spanish attitudes toward Native Californians began when Juan Rodriguez Cabrillo discovered San Diego and explored Alta California.

In New Spain, the port of Navidad was the predecessor of Acapulco and here, in June 1542, Juan Rodriguez Cabrillo in-

FIGURE 1-1. Juan Rodriguez Cabrillo. Courtesy California State Library.

structed his chief pilot, Bartolome Ferrelo, to prepare the San Salvador and Victoria for the voyage north. During the next nine month, Cabrillo's explorations set the stage for Spanish California exploration and eventual settlement of Alta California.

On September 28, 1542, when Cabrillo discovered San Diego, he commented on the Indian's behavior. They were frightened by his ship, and Cabrillo concluded that they were primitive and childlike. Cabrillo mentioned that the Indians were placated by simple gifts. After further observation, he commented that the local Indians were quiet or almost stoic in behavior. When an old Indian made signs to the Spaniards, he confused both Cabrillo and his men. Eventually, the Indians came on board ship with water and fish to display their friendship.

Soon Cabrillo changed his mind about the Indians. He saw them as a diversified and intelligent people. In his diary, Cabrillo commented on the diversity of the Indian population, and he warned Spaniards not to make hasty judgments. A perceptive observer of California culture, Cabrillo was the first explorer to comment on the remarkable diversity of the Native Californian.

By early 1543, Cabrillo's expedition had sailed north to Monterey and eventually landed near the Rogue River in southern Oregon. Unfortunately, Cabrillo caught the infectious gangrene when he broke his arm on the return trip home. When Cabrillo landed at San Miguel Island (near Los Angeles) to attend to his wound, he died unexpectedly. Buried off the coast of southern California, Cabrillo left a detailed diary of his exploits. From this diary, Spain selected San Diego and Monterey for eventual settlement. The lack of a cartographer prompted the expeditions new leader, Bartolome Ferrelo, to complain to the Viceroy in New Spain that it would be impossible to settle California without adequate maps.

Because of Ferrelo's widely publicized observations, Spanish explorers were opposed to settling California. It was simply too primitive, dangerous and unpredictable. There were other problems. California lacked wealth. Much of the land was not suitable for permanent agriculture. The ports were too difficult to develop. Once San Diego was settled in 1769, the Franciscan Order was brought in to create a mission system to civilize and Christianize the Indian neophyte.

Ferrelo, like most Spanish explorers, used the term neophyte to describe the Native American. This was an early indication of the low level of appreciation for the Native Californian. What impact did this have upon early Spanish settlers?

The logical answer is that the seeds of racism were sown by these early attitudes and continued to grow during Spanish California's turbulent half-century. But before Spain could settle California permanently, they needed an economic base. Trade with the Philippines, known as the Manila Galleon Trade, provided the earliest economic justification for eventual California settlement. Ferrelo wrote that the Indian didn't understand the profit motive and the subtle nuances of trade.

The Manilla Galleons and Racial Attitudes

In 1565, Spain began the occupation of the Philippine Islands. A Spanish navigator, Andres de Urdaneta, discovered a route from New Spain to Manila that landed for supplies either in Morro Bay near San Luis Obispo or Cape Mendocino above San Francisco. On the return trip home for de Urdaneta California once again became a supply stopover. This influenced Spain to settle Alta California.

It was Urdaneta's view that California was a primitive area that didn't deserve permanent settlement. He described the Chumash Indians around Morro Bay as primitive and "without civilization." Thus, for another two hundred years, Spanish navigators sailed past California and ignored the fertile valleys, the lush coastal areas and the rugged mountains. What is surprising about Urdaneta's observations is that the Chumash Indians were the most civilized tribe in California. To Urdaneta, however, they were like "wild animals."

The voyage from the Philippine Islands to California was one of the longest and most dangerous in the world. Despite their generally hostile attitudes towards the Indian, the contact that these people had with the California Indian were positive ones. The Indians provided supplies and understood commerce. Yet, the myth persisted that California was not important to Span-

ish settlement. Although the Spanish navigators and their soldiers witnessed the shaman or Indian medicine man at work, there was scarcely a mention of the potions or herbs used by the Indians to ward off disease. The Spanish used these herbs but failed to give the Indians credit for medical knowledge. The chief often guided the Spanish explorer safely out to sea and the Chumash met the Spanish at sea in sophisticated ocean going canoes. In order to settle California, Spain needed the perfect harbor. This set the stage for the explorations of Sebastian Vizcaino who created the myth of the Monterey Port.

Sebastian Vizcaino and the Monterey Myth: The Perfect Harbor

After the Manila Galleon Trade subsided, Spain commissioned Sebastian Vizcaino to explore California's coast. In mid-December 1602, Vizcaino sailed into Monterey Bay. Vizcaino wrote in his official government report: "...we found ourselves to be in the best port that could be desired, for besides being sheltered from the winds, it has many pines for masts and yards, and live oaks and white oaks, and water in great quantity, all near the shore." This description, as well as other flattering portrayals of the central coast, persuaded Spain to settle the area.

Vizcaino is credited with popularizing Monterey as the center of Spanish California settlement, and his voyage produced the first reliable map of the California coast. What has escaped historians is Vizcaino's harsh comments about the Indians. He viewed them as simple and primitive. On Vizcaino's voyage there were three elderly, white haired Jesuits on Vizcaino's ship who kept copious diaries. These religious men found the Indians in desperate need of civilization. They described the Indians as lustful and generally in need of civilization.

When Father Antonio de la Ascension was assigned a report on the California Indian, he turned in a detailed report to the Viceroy in New Spain which chided one California Indian chief for suggesting that he would provide ten women for every man on the Spanish ships. Morality was not one of the Indian's traits, de la Ascension reported, and this influenced early Spanish attitudes. When the chief complained that there were too many women in his thickly populated tribe, the Spaniards simply viewed this as uncivilized. Father Ascension lectured the chief as best he could on the concept of Christian morality.

In 1620, Ascension wrote his *Brief Report* which urged strong government action to convert the Indian to Christianity. The tone of Ascension's report is condescending and hostile to the Native Californian. Because he foresaw difficulty in converting the native population, Ascension included a detailed plan for conversion. In that plan, the seeds of Spanish racism were sown. It was an attitude, one which indicated that this primitive population simply could not be civilized.

The threat of pirates and foreign intruders, Ascension and Vizcaino agreed, may not be as great as Spain perceived. The reason not to fear foreign intruders, Vizcaino wrote, is because the California Indians are fierce and militaristic in the area from San Diego to Santa Barbara. Whether or not this was true is open to question, but a number of Spanish explorers worried about the potential for Indian violence.

In order to guarantee a docile Indian population, the Spanish began the process of religious instruction. When Vizcaino landed in Santa Barbara he set up a small chapel. There in a tent with a crude altar the Franciscans held a service. The Indians were curious. Vizcaino passed this off without thought, but, privately, he had a dim view of the Indian.

Despite these observations, Vizcaino didn't describe the California Indians as civilized. Even when Vizcaino was presented with evidence of advanced civilization, he ignored Indian accomplishments. After watching sea going Chumash canoes come to port with large boatloads of fish, Vizcaino refused to alter his opinion. Despite their impressive lifestyle, Vizcaino passed the Chumash Indians off as an aberration. When he returned to New Spain, Vizcaino had lost one third of his crew, but his maps, descriptions of local Indians and enthusiasm for port trade eventually led to the Spanish settlement of Alta California.

There is a common thread to these early discoveries. The native population of California is described as primitive and in need of Spanish civilization. This created the initial Spanish stereotype of the Native Californian, and the result was to create a negative picture of Indian civilization.

Spain, the Indians of Alta California and the Initial Spanish Stereotype

During the years prior to Spanish settlement, there was a vibrant California Indian civilization, despite what Spain thought. Spain paid little attention to this culture. Pagan was the word most often used to describe the California Natives. The initial Spanish stereotype of Indian civilization failed to take into account the elaborate hunting, gathering, trading, agricultural and political aspects of the various Indian groups. Spain instead described them as primitive, plodding, slow and lethargic, and these were the words most often used in official Spanish reports. The Franciscan friars, notably Junipero Serra, spoke of the Indians as "childlike." Governor Felipe de Neve wrote in a 1779 official report that the Indians "needed divine guidance." Governor Pedro Fages in the mid-1780s suggested that the Indian be placed in a "special citizen category." Clearly, Spanish officials, whether military or clergy, had a low opinion of the Native Californian.

Since California Indians often lived in small autonomous triblets, Spanish officials described them as uncivilized groups. Many early California history textbooks suggest that the Indian people were "primitive," "lacked social intercourse," "were provincial" or simply were a "Stone Age people." This is simply a modern and sophisticated version of an old myth—the Digger Indian.

While the Digger Indian stereotype no longer persists, there are still elements of it in recent historiography. As late as 1948 a popular history of the Mission San Jose suggested the primitive nature of the California Indian made the missions a "civilizing force." This book commissioned by a civic minded group of citizens in Warm Springs, California reinforced many existing stereotypes about the mission Indian.

It was because of popular histories that racist stereotypes continued to plague the California Indian. Some recent historians have compared the buffalo hunters of the Great Plains with California Indians and concluded that the lack of hunting, warfare and weaponry created a weaker culture, and the Spanish didn't believe that the Indians were capable of independence.

Independent Indians and the Spanish View of the Indios

When Spanish soldiers landed in Alta California, they brought food and religious objects to the native people. This troubled the Indians because one god, Qua-a-ar, secured food. This god provided not only the acorn to make bread but also deer, coyote, crow, berries and the roasted grasshopper. The Spanish bore gifts of corn and beans, which the Indians accepted with smiles, but they were not really welcomed gifts. The

smiles hid Indian anguish, and they were really very suspicious. The No Y-yo-ha-rivg-nain was the Giver of Life and the Indians believed that if they angered this life force they would pay for it. The Spaniards had no way of knowing that the Indians were suspicious of their intent and not particularly taken with the message of Catholicism and a Christian Spanish king. The Spanish renamed these Indians the Gabrielenos after the local mission which was founded to bring them ultimate Christian salvation.

As the mission system Christianized the Indians, the old ways often remained intact. Coyote tales were prominent in and around the California missions. Foremost, among these was a new tale of Franciscan brutality.

The Spaniards viewed the Indians as children. Fray Pedro Cambon wrote that the Indians stood "transfixed in wonderment." The Mission San Gabriel, Cambon lamented, was a place where the Indians "made themselves so scarce that even months later, one hardly saw a single Indio in the entire neighborhood..." Less than a month after the San Gabriel Mission was founded, the Indians united and fought a pitched battle against the outrages of Spanish troops. The picture of friendly missionaries who achieved limited, if successful, results with the California Indian is contrary to the Mission San Gabriel experience.

Not only did the Indians fight the Spaniards but they also protested the militaristic and inhumane attitudes of the military. "We awoke to find plumes of smoke signals along the entire horizon," Padre Cambon wrote. The Indians were angry and on the verge of war. In Cambon's correspondence there was a fearful tone. What his report failed to point out was that the Indians were fighting because their Chief had been beheaded by Spanish troops. Despite these differences between Spanish troops and the Indians, the Franciscan Order acted like all was going well with California settlement.

FIGURE 1-2. Native Californians: The Ravage of Anglo Civilization.

Father Junipero Serra, the founder and first president of the Alta California mission system, remarked that the mission offered a "promise of greater things both on the spiritual and temporal side." As Father Serra suggested, one day the Indians would be "gene de razon" or "people of reason" with all the sophistication of the native Spaniard. This was an erroneous conclusion. The depressing and backbreaking work schedule on the mission and the dehumanizing religious indoctrination destroyed Indian culture. While the Franciscans worked hard, they placed even stricter work schedules on the Native Californian. This prevented the Indian from adjusting to Spanish life.

The Spanish used words such as gentiles (heathens) or desgraciados (wretched) to describe the California Indian. When Viceroy Antonio Maria Bucareli traveled from Sonora to Monterey, California in 1774, he described the Indians as "fit subjects of the enemy of the human race."

Perhaps the severest judgments were made about the Gabrielenos and Fernandenos Indians. These tribes, named after local missions, occupied what is now Los Angeles County. The Yang-na village, in what is now downtown Los Angeles, was lined with thatched houses, and acorns, berries and grasshoppers were gathered. The Indians hunted for small game and lived seminomadic lives as they moved from the valley to the hills. To the Spaniards, these triblets were simple, primitive and without a concept of civilization. Father Serra urged that the concept of hell be

FIGURE 1-3. Pomo Indians: Mendocino. Courtesy of the A. E. Wilder Collections, Kelley House Museum, Mendocino.

taught with a missionary zeal. The richness and diversity of Indian culture was ignored. They were taught fear and humiliation through a Catholic god.

What aspects of Indian culture did the Spanish ignore? None of the Franciscan friars reported how the Gabrielenos defined their neighbors. They described the Paiutes as "mamajtan" or "dessert dwellers," and the Chumash were "pavajmkar" or "water people." The Luisenos and Juanenos called their creator Chingichinich and this god defined every aspect of their lives. The southern California Indian's life was rooted in custom. The Spanish didn't find this a sign of advanced civilization.

Along the central California coast, in the Chumash society, there were many customs. For example, small parcels of property were transferred from father to son. Among the Shoshonean Indians, the father decided when hunting and gathering took place. Many tribes paid the bride's family in exchange for her hand in marriage. Business was defined in terms of barter, trade and negotiation. The Spanish ignored the amassing of goods and social customs as simply the "response of a primitive people."

Indian customs were criticized by the Franciscan friars. Father Fermin Lasuen, president of the California missions from 1785 to 1803, stated that Indian women were "slaves to the men." The women worked too hard, Father Lasuen maintained, and they were not treated in a Christian manner. How this generalization emerged is a mystery. The Franciscan friars had little knowledge of Indian society and segregated men and women on the mission. There is no record of the Franciscan Order inquiring about family life. Yet, throughout the diaries of important Franciscans, there are statements of fact about Indian life which bear little resemblance to reality. There was a distant, emotional and rigid Franciscan response to Native California civilization.

Indian rituals bothered the Franciscan friars. The long list of Indian rules governing the balance of nature, the role of the gods, the importance of celebrations, such as puberty rites and the continual use of Coyote tales, frustrated the Franciscans. Everything beyond *topangana*, which meant the literal end of the world, was unimportant, but in their own world the Indians had rules that explained all aspects of their lives. Father Serra believed this impeded the conversion process.

The presence of ritual, rules and repetition made the California Indians a strange civilization to Spanish explorers. The Indians were too stoic in their judgments, too defined in their explanations and too passive in their understanding of Spanish life. As Father Lasuen wrote in a report to the bishop of New Spain: "the Indian didn't understand the Spanish way of life."

The Franciscans were also critical of the medicine man—the Shaman. Often times the Shaman was a woman who practiced a form of psychic healing. This appeared akin to witchcraft to the Franciscans. The medical practices of the Shaman was another oddity. A sucking Shaman would cure a snake bite. Father Lasuen noted that the shaman used powers for evil as well as good. The historical judgments in the diaries of Franciscan missionaries suggest the difficulty they had interpreting Indian's life. It also implies how racial attitudes created negative stereotypes.

A.E. Kroeber wrote that there was no evidence that the Shamans used their power

for either good or evil. Generally, the Shaman cured diseases, provided spiritual guidance and legitimized the chief's decisions. The Shaman combined political, social and economic advice to guide the tribe. He was also the chief spiritual figure. In the spring, spirits were plants and animals. During the winter, the spirits warded off the weather. The summer and fall saw the spirits provide food and protection from unseen forces. In Indian life, there was a strong belief that an animal spirit inspired the tribal men. This led to a belief among most Indians that the human spirit was no more or less important than the animal spirit. The spiritual side of Indian life was overlooked by the Spanish. Therefore, the Spanish had trouble understanding this concept and suggested it reeked of paganism. Father Serra chided the Indian for a belief in an other world religion because he believed that the belief destined the neophyte to hell.

Not only did the Spanish believe that the Indian possessed strange religious beliefs, but Spanish Government officials in numerous diary entries wrote that the Indian was inherently lazy. Juan Bautista de Anza, after observing California Indians, described them as "indolent by nature." Anza recommended that future Spanish governors monitor Indian behavior.

In 1794, Diego de Borica assumed the Governor's Office and remarked that the Indians lagged behind the Spaniards in "work tasks." They didn't have the same concept of time or a schedule as the Spanish, Borica maintained, and they had to be prodded to work. They were heathens, Borica suggested, who failed to understand the simple rules of life. Castilian assumptions about race, civilization, religion and family doomed the California Indian to fail as prospective Spaniards. In this way, the seeds of racism were sown and flourished for two centuries.

Spain and the Seeds of California Racism

When the Spanish settled San Diego in 1769 and Monterey in 1770, they cultivated the earliest seeds of racism. In the European mind all that was civilized was set off from that which was uncivilized by religion, social standing, education and government-economic achievement. The California Indians met none of these requirements and this caused the Spanish to conceptualize the initial seeds of California racism.

For centuries the Spanish had mixed with Northern African Moors and Indian women. By the time Spain settled Alta California, there were two types of Spaniards. One group was the Peninsulares or the Castilians who were considered pure blooded. The other settlers, the Creoles or Criollos, were the mixed blooded Spaniards who held a lower social status. The government, church and leading citizens pandered to the Peninsulares, thereby creating continual social strife. Inevitably, these differences were noted by the Franciscan friars.

The birth of mulatto children in California was another phenomena noted by Father Junipero Serra. In Serra's reports and those of his successor Father Lasuen, they documented the large number of black-Spanish troops. When black-Spaniards and Indians had children they were called *zambos*. He called them "half civilized" and urged Spaniards to approach them with caution. Father Lasuen, the president of the mission system in the 1790s, spoke out against the rise of *zambos*. The diaries of leading Franciscans contain hostile references to these children. Often the Franciscan friar would whip a zambo more severely to instill a sense of discipline.

While the barbaric cruelty of the Franciscan Order was confined to a small number of missionaries, there was mission genocide which caused 300,000 California Indians to dwindle to 50,000 by the end of Mexican California. Apart from the deaths, changes in food consumption, family patterns, the rise of European diseases and enslavement on the mission led to Indian disintegration. However, many historical texts suggest that Father Serra and the Franciscan Order brought civilization to the Indian. As a matter of fact, major California businesses created a public image of long suffering, caring Franciscan missionaries. The picture of a kindly priest holding a large cross over a knelling Indian decorates a bank in the San Fernando Valley. Too often these images destroy the reality of racial strife and personal difficulties brought about by the Franciscan Order.

It is impossible to appreciate the development of California civilization without a clear understanding of how the mission system altered the direction of the Golden State's history. When the Indians were brought into the Franciscan mission system it was because the Spanish considered them

FIGURE 1-4. The Cross and the Sword: Franciscans and Spaniards in California.

in need of civilization. Obviously, Father Junipero Serra and the Franciscan Order worked from preconceived ideas. When the Indians resisted conversion, this simply reinforced the notion that they were primitive and in need of re-education, a notion which persisted during Spanish California.

The interaction between the Spanish Iberian culture was tested by Coyote tales. It was common for the Franciscans, in government reports, to find Coyote tales fascinating. Often the Franciscan friars marveled at the manner in which the Native American population taught the Spaniards lessons from the land, the sea or the stars. In order to understand how these forces changed the direction of California history, it is necessary to examine the rise of Spanish California.

The Spanish Legacy in California

What is the Spanish legacy in California? The answer is a complex one. Normally, institutions are the legacy of a conquering people. California is no exception, the contribution of early Spanish explorers has left an enduring legacy for California.

The presidios and Missions of Spanish California are reminders of the legacy of Spanish conquest. The lay cities of San Jose, founded in 1777 and Los Angeles, founded in 1781, retained a Spanish character well into the twentieth century.

The early English, French and American travelers wrote accounts, memoirs and official government reports which praised the Spanish for settling California but condemned them for bringing in too many mixed blooded soldiers. The roots of racism can be seen in this behavior.

There was also a belief in the Black Legend or la teyenda negra as it was known. What was the importance of the Black Legend? For the Spanish it was an indication of the safety vale. The notion that California was settled more by the mixed blooded Spaniard of African and Aztec blood than by the pure blooded Castilian who had ties to the Crown. Mexican California governors suggested that the mixed blooded settler dominated the ranchos and indicated that there was an "African presence" in California. For Americans the Black Legend suggested that California was settled by the wrong type of Spaniards and Mexicans, and this brought out hostility to mixed blooded settlers.

The continual references to the mixed blooded settlement of Los Angeles created a racial controversy. In 1781, when Los Angeles was founded, more than fifty percent of its settlers were of African descent. The following year a Spanish governor with Aztec blood, Pedro Fages, began a governmental policy granting political and economic rights to mixed blooded settlers. During the Mexican California era, 1821-1846, there were also mixed blooded governors and strong feelings for equality. This created the concept of Aztlan which argued that the Spanish speaking could unite for the future. The Indian is the focus of Chicano historians who see Native Americans as a link with a Hispanic past.

Bibliographical Essay

Garci Ordonez de Montalvo's, *The Deeds of Esplandian* (Madrid, circa 1500) is an excellent chivalric novel that is important in understanding the Spanish attitude toward California. For a translation of key portions of Montalvo's work see Edward Everett Hale, *The Queen of California: The Origin of the Name of California* (New York, 1864, reprinted 1945). For the traditional historiographical view on matters of race and ethnicity in early California, see, for example, Sherburne F. Cook, *The Conflict Between the California Indian and White Civilization* (Berkeley and Los Angeles, 1943) and Robert F. Heizer and Alan Almquist, *The Other Californians: Prejudice and Discrimination Under Spain, Mexico and the United States to 1920* (New York, 1971).

Also see, Father Junipero Serra, *Writings of Junipero Serra* (editor, Antonio Tibesar, Washington, D. C., 1966) and Herbert Bolton, *Anza's California Expeditions* (volumes 1-2, Berkeley, 1930).

For textbook treatment of this period emphasizing ethnic issues see, for example, Julian Nava and Bob Barger, *California: Five Centuries of Cultural Contrasts* (Beverly Hills, 176) and Howard A. DeWitt, *California Civilization: An Interpretation* (Dubuque, 1979).

On problems of race see Philip Wayne Powell, *Tree Of Hate: Propaganda and Prejudices Affecting United States Relations with the Hispanic World* (New York, 1971) and David J. Weber, "Scarce More Than Apes: Historical Roots of Anglo American Stereotypes of Mexicans" in *New Spain's Far Northern Frontier: Essays on Spain in the American West* (Albuquerque, 1979).

For the earliest expression of historical racism see Hubert Howe Bancroft, *California Pastoral, 1769-1848* (San Francisco, 1888). Many of the basic books on California fail to analyze ethnic conflict but remain useful. See, for example, Henry R. Wagner, *Spanish Voyages To The Northwest Coast Of American In The Sixteenth Century* (San Francisco, 1929); H.E. Bolton, *Spanish Exploration In The Southwest, 1542-1706* (New York, 1916) and A Grove Day, *Coronado's Conquest* (Berkeley, 1940).

Robert F. Heizer, *Francis Drake and the California Indians* (Berkeley, 1947) contains the seeds of racism so prevalent in Spanish explora-tion. Also see, Warren L. Hanna, *Lost Harbor: The Controversy Over Drake's California Anchorage* (Berkeley, 1979) and the *California Historical Quarterly* (volume 53, Fall 1974) in which an entire issue is devoted to whether or not Drake landed in northern California.

For the best ethnic history of the United States see Ronald Takaki, *A Different Mirror: A History of Multicultural America* (New York, 1993). On Vizcaino, see, for example, Herbert E. Bolton, ed., "Diary of Sebastian Vizcaino," in *Spanish Exploration in the Southwest, 1542-1706* (New York, 1916); Herbert E. Bolton, "The West Coast Corridor," *Proceedings of the American Philosophical Society*, (volume 91, December 1947) and Henry R. Wagner, "The Voyage to California of Sebastian Rodriguez Mermenho in 1595," *California Historical Society Quarterly*, (volume III, April 1924).

An excellent re-evaluation of Indian civilization in relationship to Spanish attitudes is Daniel Garr, "Planning, Politics and Plunder: The Missions and Indian Pueblos of Hispanic California," *Southern California Quarterly*, (volume 54, Winter 1972) and Nancy Farriss, *Crown and Clergy in Colonial Mexico, 1759-1821* (London, 1968).

Tomas Almaguer, *Racial Faultlines: The Historical Origins of White Supremacy in California* (Berkeley, 1994) is a brilliant reinterpretation of racial attitudes upon California history. Also see James J. Rawls, *The Indians of California: The Changing Image* (Norman, 1984) and Albert L. Hurtado, *Indian Survival On The California Frontier* (New Haven, 1988) for the best recent studies of the California Indian.

2

Spanish California

Ethnic Settlement on the Frontier

The rise of ethnic differences in Spanish California resulted from the multi-cultural nature of the Golden State. The Spanish who conquered and eventually settled California were often of Aztec Indian or African Moor ancestry, and they volunteered to come to Spanish California. Freedom from church and government regulation motivated these early conquerors. They spoke of California as a safety valve. A place where they could establish a new society. The prevalence of mixed blooded settlers made California an independent and volatile civilization. However, the majority of the New Spanish population didn't want to settle California permanently.

As California settlement was planned, the Spanish Empire was in turmoil. The government sent Visitor-General Jose de Galvez to end opposition to California settlement from the corrupt New Spanish Government. An entrenched bureaucracy opposed the Crown's plan to settle California. In 1768 and 1769, Galvez prepared Spanish troops for California conquest and settlement. Increasingly, he depended upon mixed blooded troops. The majority of these soldiers were volunteers who hoped to escape the rigid class lines in Spanish society which had developed a rigid caste system that had

evolved in Spain and was carried to New Spain. The result was that in California the mixed blooded settlers were placed into a highly defined position: one which emphasized class differences. Mixed blooded Spaniards were at the bottom of the social-economic ladder, whether they were in Mexico City or Monterey.

Why did Spain's caste system place mixed blooded settlers below the Gente de Razon? The answer lies in Spanish history. The Spanish defined the Gente de Razon as those citizens who practiced Catholicism, spoke Castilian, lived in tax paying towns, worked in agriculture and were loyal to the King. The Spaniards argued that the Gente de Razon had a natural tendency to make rational decisions. The mixed blooded Spaniard was viewed as lacking civilization.

This attitude explains a great deal about Spanish California. Class consciousness was an integral part of the Spanish mind. So it is not surprising that the Spanish acted hostilely toward the Indian. The Franciscan friar, Father Serra, remarked that the California Indian shad to be broken of their addiction to liberty, independence and indulgence. Father Serra called the Indian a "simple, primitive people."

The Spanish weren't the only ones to make judgments. The Indians were often suspicious of the mission system, the nature of Spanish Government and the customs of the newly arrived settlers. Yet, they were intrigued by the mixed blooded Spanish troops. When the first African-Spaniards arrived in San Diego, as part of the Spanish thrust for empire, there was a sense of curiosity among the California Indians. The diary entries of the black-Spanish military men indicate that they felt at home in California. Eventually, many black-Spaniards settled permanently in California.

The interaction of Native Californians and African Americans is a neglected aspect of Spanish California history. Historians interpreting California have depended too heavily upon diaries, official government reports and pioneer historians, like Hubert Howe Bancroft and Josiah Royce, in presenting a picture of a pastoral society. Generally, these historians have ignored people of color. There are fragments of ethnic history but no clear definition of how the Indian and black-Spanish soldiers shaped early California civilization.

A myth that Spanish California grew up solely around Franciscan missions and Spanish presidios dominates much of the history of the Golden State. This is not surprising since many mission monographs were written by historically conscious Franciscan missionaries. The books they produced were not only well written, but carefully argued while achieving a remarkable degree of historical accuracy. Their bias, however, was in demonstrating more influence for the mission system than it deserved. These studies also ignore the repressive and often brutal Franciscan tactics. The reason for this historical direction is the heightened reputation of Father Junipero Serra.

A flood of biographies made Father Serra a virtual historical saint. This began a trend to glorify the missions. When Father Fran-cisco Palou's *Life and Apostolic Labors of the Venerable Father Junipero Serra* appeared, it was hailed as a major historical event. The renowned Spanish borderlands historian Herbert E. Bolton studied the contribution of a Franciscan, Father Juan Crespi, who worked closely with Father Serra and concluded that Father Crespi's career was another indication that the mission system was the most significant influence upon Spanish California.

Historians interpreting the Spanish borderlands agree that religious influences shaped local attitudes and institutions. The degree of civilization was related to Catholic influence, they argued, and the necessity of converting the neophyte justified the excesses of the mission system. People of color were not a part of this version of the Spanish borderlands.

Recently, revisionist Franciscan historians have studied alleged mistreatment of mission system Indians. Unanimously, they announced there was little abuse. The work of Father Maynard Geiger is instrumental in making a case for the mission as a civilizing agent. His thoughtful, scholarly work adds a great deal of knowledge to the history of the Santa Barbara Mission, and Father Geiger analyzed the friendly Spanish attitude toward the Indian with the eye of a seasoned professional. Geiger's work established the notion that while the Spanish soldiers and the Franciscan friars made mistakes, they had the Native Californians best interest at heart. This had led to a *softening history*. This is a form of history which ignores such questions as genocide and cultural castration. Historians are uncomfortable with the notion that a people could be systematically exterminated. Yet, the decline of Indians from 300,000 in 1769 to 50,000 in 1850 makes this theory plausible. The Spanish view of California was an important part of the reaction between the conquering armies and native Californians.

The Indian World: A View from the Spanish World

Spain never adjusted to the Indian concept of life. Coyote tales appeared pagan and troublesome. The Ohlone Indians were typical of California triblets who defined their life in a narrow and precise scope. For example, from puberty rites, which created bonds, respect for women and defined the importance of childbirth, to the Coyote tales, which preached respect for the elderly, the Ohlones precisely defined their way of life.

Because of the dominance of Coyote tales, the Indian world was one of laws. Coyote defined every aspect of Indian life. All tribal activities evolved around a list of laws. There were laws regarding coming of age, marriage, commerce and family rights. Coyote tales provided an answer to all of life's problems. Past experiences and attitudes created a sense of well being. Many anthropologists believe that Indians were governed by custom, but this ignores the strict nature of California Indian activity. Law is a better word to describe how the various triblets reacted. They were a conservative people who defined their rights.

When the Spaniard arrived in California, a well established civilization existed. Not only did the California Indian, live well, but they were also able to communicate with each other militarily, politically and economically. The Spanish had trouble recognizing this advanced civilization. They preferred to describe the Indians as diggers. The stereotype of heathen Indians digging for roots and berries was never a reality, but it provided the Franciscans with an excuse to brutalize the Indian. No myth was more brutal than that of the slow thinking Indian.

The sources for Indian myths include an impressive list of official Spanish Government reports, diaries of Franciscan friars and the observations of foreign travelers.

The historical record pictures the Spanish as conquering California against all odds. The California Indian is often not a part of this official record. As foreign travelers landed in California, few understood Indian civilization. Few had anthropological or historical training. The end result was a stereotypical picture of California's Native population.

The California Indian Before the Spanish Conquest

The early stereotypes surrounding Indian life resulted from the ease with which the Native Californian lived off the land. The California Indian created a simple world. Beauty, the abundance of food, the changes in environment and the way of the gods were conditions that Native Californians took for granted. A conservative people with a carefully defined lifestyle the California Indian lived in a narrowly defined world. They seldom migrated more than ten miles beyond their birthplace. They ate the same foods. They retained the same cultural patterns. They had little interest in change or innovation. When the Spanish arrived in California in 1769, they viewed this lifestyle as primitive.

Simple pleasures appealed to the Indian. The mission system had been made up of Franciscan friars who judged the Native Californian. Generally, they made negative judgments about Indian life. Typical of this attitude was Fray Francisco Garces who wrote that the California Indians were heathens. "Oh, what a vast heathendom," Garces exclaimed. "Oh! what lands so suitable for missions." What Franciscan friars failed to realize was that the California Indian had achieved a sophisticated level of civilization.

California history texts often suggest that the Native American population had little political interest, primitive economic institutions, few military alliances and virtually no weapons. War was seldom waged, and there was little interest in events beyond that of the day. This view fails to square with the facts. Professor Lowell Bean has found that Indian triblets often had alliances and political confederations. The Chumash Indians on the central California coast, Bean points out, had a surplus of fish which were used for trade purposes.

The most sophisticated aspect of California Indian society was food production. Not only were a great variety of foods available for the Indians, but they were often harvested by hunting or fishing. Some tribes employed sophisticated technological means of extracting food from plants. However, the planning and technology of Indian food production was all but ignored by Spanish, Mexican and American settlers. Yet, these same food sources and techniques were adopted by early Spanish settlers. Again the term digger Indian is misapplied.

The Establishment of Spanish California

When Spanish military leaders Pedro Fages, Juan Bautista de Anza and Gaspar de Portola established an Alta California settlement from 1769 to 1791, it was with the help of mixed blooded troops. The general feeling among Spanish commanders was that the African-Spaniard was a superior scout and Indian fighter. When San Diego was settled, the use of advance scouts, who were mixed blooded, was an indication of the high esteem in which they were held. But it wasn't just the average Spaniard who was mixed blooded, too often leading Spanish explorers were of African descent.

The Commander of the San Carlos, one of two ships which settled San Diego, was Captain Vicente Vila. He was a Spanish navigator whose father married a Bantu prin-

cess from the African Congo. In appearance Vila had, as one Spanish commander remarked, "a Negroid nose." The presence of black blood did little, if anything, to disqualify Vila from becoming a leading Spanish explorer.

After Vila landed in San Diego, he was instructed to wait for Captain Fernando Rivera y Moncado who was in charge of twenty-five Spanish-black soldiers traveling from Loreto in Baja California and forty-two Christian Indians who were journeying by land from Baja California. Rivera's predominantly African-Spanish soldiers, who were described in diaries as exceptional frontiersmen, were considered the vanguard of Spanish troops. Once these soldiers arrived in San Diego they were instructed to travel north in order to explore the future settlement site at Monterey.

When Captain Rivera rode into San Diego on May 14, 1769, his mixed blooded troops created a sense of security. The black-Spanish soldiers were unusually adept at establishing law and order on the frontier. They did this by setting up precise laws and

FIGURE 2-1. Gaspar de Portola Discovering San Francisco Bay. Courtesy Bancroft Library.

carefully understanding punishment for the Indian. After setting up camp at the foot of Presidio Hill, in San Diego's Old Town, the Spanish soldiers explored the countryside.

Once they settled in San Diego, the black-Spanish soldiers also used African work skills to survive the summer heat. Non-traditional food sources were found. The African Spaniards found fish, small animals and wild berries plentiful. They harvested these foods in accordance with African customs. African religious influences were obvious in special prayers which defined which foods to harvest. The search for Indian grown goods and a plentiful water source helped black-Spaniards establish permanent California settlement.

By cultivating small acres of land, black-Spaniards intrigued the Indian population. The ability to farm these small plots of land by using irrigation, special seeds and little shovels interested Native Californians. Soon the Chumash Indians practiced this form of irrigation. The Ohlones soon practiced as well as they searched out non-traditional food sources such as grasshopper, and the Gabrielenos, becoming adjusted too, planted small agricultural plots. These innovations introduced by African-Spaniards often went unrecognized in Franciscan diaries. If they were mentioned, it was often with derision and a sense of a primitive accomplishment. There was an uneasiness amongst Spanish military, Government and religious leaders. They didn't know how to place the Indian within the context of Spanish California society.

The Spanish Conquistadors Visions of California Indians: Scientific Racism of the Frontier

The conquistadors were a diverse group spiritually, and they shared a zeal to Christianize the Indian. This passion to convert, however, often provided comical incidents.

In the 1780s, the Viceroy sent troops to California to separate mixed blooded Creole priests from their Iberian counterparts. The soldiers and government officials complained about fist fists over who would convert the local Indians. Some years later a Franciscan mission leader, Father Jose Maria Zalvidea, learned the Gabrieleno language and rode into the village of Talihuilimit to convert the Indians. A psychologically unbalanced Franciscan, Zalvidea began whipping himself to keep the devil out of his body. He also drove nails into his feet to keep out evil spirits. Only one Indian was converted during Zalvidea's ill fated trip. The rest armed themselves.

Sexual excess was also a problem. There were a number of incidents of reported mental, sexual and alcohol abuse among the Franciscans. Fray Geronimo Boscana of San Luis Capistrano suffered bouts of lunacy, and his reports suggest that he had sexual relations with the Indians. Jose Eusebio Galindo, a local Californio, complained that the Franciscans had an easy life and worked at a "snail's pace." The Spanish needed to define where the Indian civilization fit into Spanish life, Galindo observed, "and they must try to understand the Indian."

Who Is the Native Californian? The Spaniard Defines the Local Population

Since the Spanish represented the Papacy and were engaged in a Christian siege, they were shocked that the Indian was not mentioned in the Bible. Early Spanish explorers viewed the Native Californian as a "neophyte" in need of civilization. Black-Spaniards had a much different view of the Native Californian. African religions cautioned people to be aware of "divinity" in strange forms. Quietly, the black-Spaniard believed that there was a mysterious side to California Indian life. Coyote tales, Captain

Fernando Rivera wrote, "exposed the mystical side of Indian life." Consequently, the mixed blooded Spanish soldier was more understanding about Indian ways. At least this was the perception of Juan Bautista de Anza. It was Anza who selected mixed blooded soldiers for the more dangerous tasks.

The Spanish may have been influenced by Indian religious tales which told of special warriors, but the mixed blooded Spaniards were more interested in the Coyote tales. The initial mention of Coyote tales or the spiritual side of Indian life is revealed in a number of Spanish Moor diaries. Black soldiers with names like Pico, Carillo, Yorba, Ortega, Alvarado and Soberanes left a wealth of information about the Indian, and their diaries and personal lives revealed a respect for the native population. These black soldiers also left place names such as Santa Margarita, Santa Ana, Carpinteria, Gaviota, Canada de los Osos, Pajaro and San Lorenzo.

Early Spanish travel was led by experienced black soldiers who were aware of the perils of frontier life. They often took along African good luck charms which the Indians associated with Kachinas. The Indian use of Kachinas provided a system of gods that explained everything and helped the Native Californian cope with the mysterious invaders.

The Sacred Expedition and California Settlement

When the first permanent settlement party left New Spain in the spring of 1769 there were a number of black soldiers who arrived in San Diego. The vast majority of these African-Spaniards remained in California and left a legacy of permanent achievement. The use of black soldiers was due to the belief that they possessed special skills.

When Don Gaspar de Portola was chosen to lead the military expedition to Alta California, he carefully selected his soldiers. Portola informed the Viceroy of New Spain that he needed a substantial number of Moors. These black-Spaniards would be advance scouts and deal with Indian problems. Like many Spaniards, Portola was a student of history. In Spain, Portola's family was a well known part of the Catalonian nobility, and his education was a broad one. Portola understood racial differences. For that reason, he included a number of black-Spaniards in his settlement party.

After Portola and Serra arrived in San Diego in the early summer of 1769, they made plans to explorer to the north and establish five missions. The journey north was a cumbersome one as church ornaments, vestments, instruments of worship and sacred vessels were combined with seeds, plows and craft equipment. Poor maps and bad weather further complicated the journey.

There were two ships, the San Antonio and the San Carlos, that supplied San Diego with goods. Captain Vicente Vila was the commander of this ship, and his African blood was not a concern for the Spanish. Vila commented that without the hard working African-Spaniard it would have been more difficult to secure Alta California. The Viceroy in New Spain asked for reports on the black soldiers and was given a glowing appraisal of their worth. Many were significant to California's discovery.

An African slave, Moreno, was an integral part of the Portola-Serra expedition. It was Moreno, for example, who suggested that vegetables be taken to protect settlers from disease. Moreno was also instrumental in the cultivation of traditional Spanish plants, such as shrubs and trees. With blacksmith skills and an understanding of veterinary medicine, Moreno was useful in nurturing the two hundred head of cattle which were brought from New Spain. As Portola suggested, Moreno had a sense of agricultural technology, horticulture and animal science which made him indispensable.

The primary reason for Moreno's presence was that he was a linguist who could interpret the various Indian languages. His presence intrigued the Indians who believed that he had special gifts. However, the Moors truly excelled as explorers. The Moors with their North African heritage not only were skilled explorers but introduced sophisticated African agricultural concepts.

El Negro and the Founding of San Francisco Bay

On the journey north from San Diego to Monterey, Portola and his men had geographical problems. They rode up the San Joaquin Valley into an area of tall trees they named Palo Alto. Then moving north, the weary and malnourished Portola party sent an advance scout out to look for water. It was this scout, known only as "El Negro," who discovered San Francisco Bay. The black-Spaniard who looked out at San Francisco Bay reported that it was the finest potential harbor in the New Spain area. Portola agreed.

The celebration on November 2, 1769, was one complete with mussels, wild duck, and geese which were abundant in and around the fertile bay. The malnourished and starving Spanish soldiers found the San Francisco Bay a haven for food. Therefore, had it not been for the exploration of a black-Spaniard, El Negro, Portola's army might have had trouble securing supplies and could have returned to San Diego a failed expedition.

The discovery of San Francisco Bay excited the Portola expedition. After this celebration they traveled south to Monterey. After finding the harbor that Sebastian

Vizcaino called "the best natural harbor in the world," Portola planted a cross and announced that a presidio would be built near the mission. This euphoria would have been impossible without "El Negro," but he was soon lost to history. The Spanish military simply identified "El Negro" as the African-Spaniard who discovered San Francisco Bay without identifying his Christian name.

Spanish California was not described as an attractive place to settle. It was isolated from the rest of the empire; it lured hostile foreigners, and the only good settlement areas, according to Spanish explorers, were San Diego, Santa Barbara, Monterey and San Diego. The Spaniards were also wary of foreigners and immediately came into conflict with the English and Russians. Despite these misgivings, Spain made a half-hearted attempt to settle California.

Once the Portola expedition established a foothold in Baja California, the Spanish began planning their "sacred expedition." This was the term used to describe the expedition which was sent to build the early missions and presidios in Alta California. There was a fanatical zeal associated with the Franciscan mission. Father Junipero Serra, a Spanish Franciscan priest from Mallorja, announced that it was a spiritual as well as a military mission, but the "civilizing of the heathen" was the primary focus of California settlement.

During Serra's decade and a half-tenure as the spiritual leader of Spanish California, he was the chief representative of the Spanish king and the Catholic Church. Because Serra believed that he personally represented the Pope, he was often an egotistical and testy leader. Serra's belligerent attitudes toward Spanish Government and nasty disagreements with the Bishop of New Spain obscured the manner in which he brutally treated the California Indian. Slavery was the end result of the mission system. James Rawls's pathbreaking book,

Indians of California: The Changing Image, suggests that slavery was not only a problem, but also one that the Franciscans didn't understand. While the Indians weren't slaves in the classic definition of the term, they did lead lives similar to enslaved people. They were cultural slaves as the California Indian submitted to a brutal and repressive mission atmosphere. Yet, historians find much to praise in the Franciscan system. Father Serra's leadership, in the view of many historians, was strong and farsighted.

From 1769 to 1784, Father Junipero Serra was the Father President of the upper California mission system, and he remains a controversial figure. Much of the historical record is laden with praise for Serra's work. Father Pedro Font's diary is often used by historians to suggest that slavery was non-existent. Since Font was essentially an employee of Serra, there is a great deal of skepticism about his conclusions. Font argued that Serra only allowed those Indians "who voluntarily commit themselves for baptism..." into the missions. Font's diary ignores the Indian revolts, the runaway Indians and the fugitives who terrorized the mission system. Others refused to work on mission lands. The Indian work ethic declined each year for the Indian on the mission. It was a form of protest. the Franciscans saw it as the act of spoiled children. The neophyte, according to the Franciscans, was still in need of civilizing. "He could not learn," Father Font remarked about the Indian field hand.

In 1772, Father Serra founded the Mission San Luis Obispo to control the most advanced California Indians—the Chumash. When the military leader, Pedro Fages, opposed this plan, Serra traveled to Mexico City and demanded that Fages be removed. Fages responded to Serra's charge by arguing that a proposed mission at San Buenaventura was located in a desolate and remote place. The Franciscans, Fages maintained, had no business setting up a mission in this remote spot. It was done solely to enslave the Indians. As a Spanish leader with Aztec blood, Fages was horrified with Franciscan attitudes.

When the Viceroy replaced Fages with Captain Rivera y Moncada, the message was clear. The Franciscan Order would settle and civilize Spanish California. Eventually, the popular Moncada was excommunicated in 1776 by Serra and critical Spanish soldiers. The immediate reaction was to intensify hostility to the Franciscan Order. Not only was Moncada a respected leader, but he wrote scathing reports on Serra's mistreatment of the Indians. Father Serra struck back by demanding married troops, because the incidence of rape was so high that the Indians were ready to go on the war

FIGURE 2-2. Father Junipero Serra.

path. This was not the type of behavior associated with California Indians. So Serra intensified his campaign against Moncado's soldiers atrocities toward the Indians. While the Spanish agreed that the Indians were mistreated, no statistics were available on Indian mortality. In later years, the historical figures were frightening. More than 85% of California's Indian population was dead by American annexation.

The worst indictment of the mission system comes from one of its contemporary defenders, Father Francis F. Guest, the director of the Santa Barbara Museum. Father Guest defends isolating (enslaving) the Indians in order to teach them morality. "In their native habitate," Father Guest writes, "the non-Christian Indians followed a number of customs and observances which did not conform to Christian morality..." These practices were divorce, remarriage and casual cohabitation. What is astonishing is that Father Guest suggests that when Indians visited these villages they were prone to sexual abuse. For that reason, they were not always allowed to leave the mission. But, as Father Guest suggests, this was not slavery it was simply re-education.

Another charge against the Franciscan leadership was that they whipped the Indians and used excessive corporal punishment. "This charge has no adequate foundation," Father Guest writes. But in the next sentence Guest states that the Franciscan Order "imposed a form of corporal punishment on the badly behaved, a practice that had been followed in the missions of Spanish America for two centuries."

Perhaps the most enduring myth associated with the missions is that the non-Christian Indian loitered around asking for Christian instruction. The source of this myth is Father Fermin Francisco de Lasuen, the second Father President of the upper California mission system who completed a lengthy diary justifying Indian conversion.

Surprisingly there is little mention of the non-Christian Indian in Father Lasuen's voluminous daily records. Father Lasuen was inventing a theory that all Indians loved the missions. Historians have taken Lasuen's observations and repeated them uncritically. Fathers Maynard Geiger and Francis Guest are professional historians with a series of brilliant articles and books on the Franciscan Order, but they are an example of uncritically lionizing Lasuen's reports.

Another dubious assumption is that the mission Indians and their ancestors remained loyal to the Catholic Church. The source sited for this conclusion is the scholarship of Sister Eileen Cotter, a retired English literature Professor at the University of the Redlands. She produced a series of dubious interviews in which the Indian appears as a defender of conversion. By depriving the California Indian of many of the basic necessities of life, the Franciscan Order believed that it was civilizing the neophyte. "The austerity of the missionaries was intended as a help in the spiritual life, " Father Francis E. Guest writes. What Guest fails to realize is that a bitter well of resentment was building in California Indian life.

Recent books cast a different view on Indian loyalty to the Catholic Church. Interviews with hundreds of Native Americans by Rupert and Jeannette Henry Costo cast doubt on this widely accepted notion of Indian loyalty. It also suggests the depths to which the well meaning clergy went to defend the mission system.

The inevitable question of genocide comes up, and Father Guest and Sister Cotter address this issue by pointing to similar death rates in European cities. The only problem is a two to three hundred year difference in history and conditions which were dissimilar. What Father Guest and others fail to address was the growing psychological abuse which led the Indian toward suicide, alcoholism and criminal behavior.

The tendency of Franciscan missionaries to report non-Christian Indians appearing for baptism has obscured many of the problems of mission life. Father Lasuen's widely circulated report that 130 heathen Indians showed up at the Mission San Francisco to be baptized has prompted other Franciscans to report non-Christian baptism. There is no way of verifying these stories. Father Jose Senan, who handled baptism procedures, reported in 1817 that 55 non-Christian Indians showed up for baptism. To justify his position, Senan may have inflated baptism figures. One wonders why these events didn't occur prior to Father Lasuen's widely circulated and much praised memo on the conversion of non-Christian Indians. After the memo, there was an avalanche of well meaning non-Christian conversion tales.

The mission system was a tragedy which destroyed Indian culture. The political and economic advances of California Indians went unrecognized, and the slow, but brutal, descent into mission slavery was inevitable. The notion that Father Serra and the Franciscan Order were nice men doing their best for the Native California population is a convenient myth of California history.

By 1790, the eleven Franciscan missions had approximately 7,500 Indian coverts. But only those Indians in the immediate vicinity of the missions were being Christianized. Indians did not flock to the mission system, as Father Serra and later Father Lasuen proclaimed; they were curious about the mission system but not eager to embrace it. The Indian remained legally free to select or reject salvation and the vast majority ignored the mission system. A decade later in 1800, Anastasio Carrillo wrote that the Mission San Fernando Indians "were very distant." Soon they ran away, and Spanish troops were sent to bring them back to the mission. Carrillo remembered "a vacant look in their eyes." She observed that they acted like "beaten animals."

In 1805, Luis Peralta, a bounty hunting Spanish soldier, was sent from the Santa Clara Mission to find Indians who refused to submit to Christianity. After Peralta killed five, all of whom were men, he captured twenty-five women and brought them to Santa Clara for conversion. Without the duplicity of the military, the Christianizing of the Indians would have failed completely. The problem of attracting and holding converts suggested serious problems between the Indians and the Spanish. Many early Spanish observers believed that it was because of the military leaders that the church survived.

The Military Leadership in Early Spanish California

The "sacred mission's" military leadership was entrusted to Gaspar de Portola, the former governor of Baja California. A respected veteran of European military campaigns, Portola was a visionary who warned his men about the "insidious" enemy. To make the California Indians aware of Christian rewards a group of converted mission Indians were taken from Baja to San Diego and Monterey. This display of the Christian life had little impact upon the Indian.

The spiritual leader of the expedition, Father Junipero Serra, was intent upon founding missions, Christianizing Indians and establishing a permanent Spanish California civilization. However, the government had less grandiose plans. One of Spain's colonial policies was to provide mixed blooded soldiers in the remote provinces. The government hoped these settlers would remain in California. As a result, Spanish California was filled with Africans, mulattos and the part white-part Indian mestizos.

The religious tone of the first California settlement party was hampered by the hostile racial attitudes of Captain Fernando Rivera y Moncado. Not only was he an important military figure, but he also had an eye to the future. Rivera believed that local Indians needed military discipline rather than religious indoctrination. Until 1781, he planted the seeds of fear and repression in the minds of local Native Americans. It was Captain Rivera who demonstrated the first important signs of Spanish racism, and he set a precedent which continued into Mexican California.

To implement his military policies, Captain Rivera employed black-Spanish troops. From March 1769, when he marched into San Diego with the first expedition of leather armored soldiers, until the summer of 1781 Captain Rivera terrorized the Indian population. Finally, in mid-July 1781, a carefully planned Yummy Indian assault killed Rivera, three Franciscans and more than thirty soldiers. Captain Rivera's legendary military feats ended. He remained alive as a legend in Spain's conquest of California. Unfortunately, racism was his legacy.

The Nature of Early Spanish California Settlement

California's early settlement was slow and painful for everyone. Although eight missions were completed from 1769 to 1777, there was little sign of permanent civilization. The reasons were simple ones: the Franciscan friars could not convert large numbers of Indians and Spanish military and Governmental officials had trouble creating workable institutions. The result was chaos and confusion. Spanish Governmental institutions didn't work very well and leadership was needed.

These difficulties were partially solved by Spanish California's first significant governor, Felipe de Neve. From 1775 to 1782, de Neve developed the institutions necessary for permanent civilization. The Reglamento of 1779 created laws designed to bring in families, develop new businesses, loosen the stranglehold of the church and, most importantly, fit the Native Californian into the mainstream of Spanish life. Governor de Neve implemented these policies and helped to create a more stable society.

When Governor de Neve left California in 1782, the number of married soldiers created a new stability. The mission and presidio at Santa Barbara not only helped to stabilize settlement on the California coast, but it also made the area an attractive place to live. When the last Presidio was completed at Santa Barbara in 1782, any thoughts of a successful Indian uprising vanished. While the Indians still had the potential to revolt, a calm settled over the previously volatile Spanish California countryside.

But what had the Spanish accomplished? California's first nine missions were completed in 1782 as the aged Father Serra was nearing death. The conversion of Indians was not a successful venture. With 300,000 Indians in California, only 5,000 were converted by Father Serra, and they showed little interest in the mission system. The Franciscan experiment was a dramatic failure.

What Spain created was a paternalistic mission system which warehoused the Native Californians rather than teaching them the fundamental beliefs of the Catholic Church and the Spanish nation. The Franciscan friars had to contend with Spanish governors who opposed the brutal mission system. Pedro Fages is the best example of a farsighted Spanish governor who recognized dangers of the mission system.

Pedro Fages came to California as one of the earliest Spanish explorers and returned from 1782 to 1791 to become a popular Spanish California governor. With Aztec blood in his background, Fages understood the people and tried to introduce elements of tolerance toward the native population.

FIGURE 2-3. Santa Barbara Mission, 1786.

A hard drinking military man with a fondness for Indian women, Fages was often seen with the Indian maiden, Indizuela. He smiled and mentioned that he was civilizing her. Fages's wife went to Father Serra and asked for a divorce. Serra could not grant a divorce, but he urged Governor Fages to meet his marital obligations. There was talk of removing Fages, but he changed his ways and returned to his wife. Once the scandal was settled, Fages emerged as one of the most popular Spanish Governmental officials. He was also an astute observer of local customs.

During his tenure in California, Fages observed the Chumash Indians on the mission at San Luis Obispo and in the area around central California. "The natives are well appearing, of good disposition, affable, liberal and friendly toward the Spaniard," Fages wrote. What is striking about Fages' observations is that he recognized that the Native Americans had moral principles. They took only one wife, families participated in funeral ceremonies and the Chumash lacked a tendency toward violence. These customs prompted Fages to search out the Indian's positive side.

But Fages was often critical of Chumash civilization. "They are addicted to the unspeakable vice of sinning against nature and maintain village joyas for common use." Joyas were men who dressed as women and fulfilled all the functions of the female in Indian society. To Fages, the spiritual side of the Native population lacked intellectual depth. Fages was bothered by the religious activity of the Chumash. "They are idolaters," he wrote. "Their idols are placed near the village...to protect the seeds and crops." Fages concluded that these primitive gods revealed a civilization in decline and one badly in need of Christian values.

By the 1790s, Fages's view was typical of Spanish Government officials. It was during this period that a new Franciscan leader emerged in California to replace Father Junipero Serra. When Father Serra died in 1784, he had established the concept of a twenty-one mission system connected by a day's travel between each mission. Since 1769, Father Serra had fostered the notion that California Indians were "idle and prone to feasts." As a result, he was driven to convert the heathen, and in his zeal, he established many of the initial stereotypes regarding Native Californians.

As Father Serra died, his legacy was a mixed one. When the Indians failed to listen to his sermons, Father Serra held a large burning candle with multiple wicks to his chest. He often stood at the pulpit and beat himself with a heavy stone while preaching. Before he went to bed, Father Serra lashed himself with a four pronged whip that brought him close to personal martyrdom. In the manner of Saint Francis of Assisi, the founder of the Franciscan Order, Father Serra would do anything to make the California Indians a part of the Spanish Empire. He was committed to a version of salvation which blended fanaticism with historical vision. It was an odd mix. His death brought the Franciscan Order to a crossroads. Serra believed throughout his life that converting the Indian was a difficult, if not impossible, task.

The end result was that by the 1790s the view of the typical Spaniard was that the Indian population had not adapted to conversion. This helped to explain why there was little apparent concern among the Spanish about the high death rate of Native Californians. It seemed to be God's vengeance for not accepting Spanish Catholicism.

The Spanish Invasion and Violent Cultural Conflict

Who were the Spanish speaking that invaded California in 1769? They were settlers from a cultural legacy quite different from that of Native Californians. The Spanish were citizens of an authoritarian state, a rigid Catholicism and a stiff moral code. These values made the California Indians appear uncivilized to the Spanish.

The Native Californian had another way of life. There was little warfare. The concept of permanent agriculture, the use of advanced technology and the personal rivalry of individuals so common in Spanish military and religious life were lacking in California Indians. The Native Californian lived in a state of nature. There was a stoic quality to Indian life. The use of a religious holyman, known as a Shaman, provided the answers to all problems. Coyote tales were a Bible or a litany of tales into the tribe's past, and these tales were often used to predict the future. The Shaman represented a link between the Indians and their past. A defined nationalism resulted from Coyote tales and gave the Indian a sense of history. The Spaniard vowed to end this culture.

Coyote tales were a pagan ritual to the Spaniards. They reacted in horror and lectured the Indian population on the dangers of pagan rituals. Such Coyote tales as Dance Madness in which a young boy can't stop dancing because he has had sexual thoughts were abhorrent to the rigidly moralistic Spanish. The simple idea of animal gods was also too much for the Spanish. Father Serra continually lectured the Indians on their lack of morality.

When the Ohlone Indians explained that a woman must be tattooed before going with a man, Father Serra announced he would break this pagan belief. By the mid-1780s, when Serra died, he had established the notion of the "Digger Indian." The primitive, uncivilized Native Californian who needed the Catholic faith. Unfortunately, Father Serra was so busy building his own legend that he had little time for the Indian. His legacy of nine missions was an important one, but it was his successor, Father Lasuen, who established the permanent stereotypes used to brand the California Indian as a subhuman digger Indian. When the term neophyte was adopted by the Franciscans to point out that the Native Californian was much like a young person training to be civilized, it was the first sign of institutionalized racism.

How did the Indians respond to the mission system? One answer is that the Indians avoided it by moving their villages, and sometimes they would attack foreign invaders. The myth persists that the Indians didn't revolt until the 1820s and 1830s. This is preposterous as Indian revolts were constant in Spanish California.

When Lieutenant Pedro Fages reported on November 30, 1775, that the Indians were compliant and meek, he created a stereotype; one which suggested that the mission system was doing its job of neutralizing the Indians and placing them into the job market. Fages also praised the military for maintaining law and order. In reality, just the opposite was true. Throughout California there were numerous Indian uprisings. These violent confrontations were often directed at the missions.

In October 1785, the Gabrielenos tried to destroy the San Gabriel Mission. They failed. The incident was not widely reported. Throughout central and southern California there was discontent among the native population, and Franciscan reports mention the problem of maintaining law and order. Often the freedom fighters were unlikely individuals. When Father Lasuen took over the mission system, he wrote a lengthy report expressing fears over potential Indian revolts. Lasuen suggested that charismatic Indians who "maintained the old ways" needed discipline.

A good example of a unique revolt was one led by a woman, Toypurina. She is described as a green eyed sorceress whose small army tried to kill the Spanish soldiers. She was captured and brought to trial. Toypurina screamed during her trial that she hated the Spaniard for moving on her land. For her insurrection, Toypurina was banished to the Mission San Carlos for the rest of her life. In effect, she was enslaved for practicing black magic. The reality is that Toypurina was a woman standing up for her rights. This was unheard of in Spanish California and certainly not tolerated from an Indian woman. Black magic was an excuse to end her independent attitudes and place Toypurina in prison.

Retired Spanish soldiers often were the cause of Indian revolts. Father Gonzalez de Ibarra of the San Fernando Mission complained that the invalidos (retirees) were consorting with the Indians. The result, according to Father Ibarra, was a rash of petty crimes, drunken behavior and attacks on church authority. The Indians often allied with discontented Spaniards to challenge local authority.

Father Lasuen: The Finalization of the Digger Stereotype in Spanish California

When Father Lasuen became the President of the mission system, Spanish California had grown into a civilization dominated by mixed blooded criollos. Business leaders, influential rancheros and lay settlers often had Aztec or African blood.

As Spanish California took shape, black-Spaniards dominated Los Angeles. On September 4, 1781 the second lay city or civil pueblo, Los Angeles, was founded with eleven settlers and their families breaking ground near the San Gabriel Mission. After a dispute with the Franciscan friars, the Spanish settlers moved a few miles away and established the Pueblo of Our Lady, the Queen of the Angels. Early Los Angeles settlers were predominantly African-Spaniards. Opportunity for land grants and the economic freedoms of the frontier attracted the discontented Spaniard. Many of these settlers were mixed blooded, and this suggests the degree of racial tension within Spanish society.

In just three years, visitors to Los Angeles remarked that well built adobe houses, a fine church and other government buildings made the city a favorite for settlers who arrived with goods from the Overland Trail. Soon trade with Los Angeles prompted the trappers to refer to the area as the end of the Old Spanish Trail.

One of the earliest African Spanish families, the Picos, dominated Los Angeles. When Santiago Pico arrived in Spanish California, with Gaspar de Portola, he was a formidable solider with an eye toward science and technology. He established a family home in Los Angeles, and his wife gave birth to five sons. An industrious rancher with a penchant for profitable business deals, Pico quickly became a rich and respected citizen. He was also a political force who emphasized equality and a sense of political independence.

In time, the Picos were the most important southern California Spanish surnamed family. The family intermarried with Spanish, European and early American families. In the 1780s, the Picos established business and government ties which caused them to become the leading family in and around Los Angeles. Eventually, in 1846, Pio Pico

became the last Mexican California governor while Andres Pico led the Native Cavalry opposing United States annexation of California. The Pico family established a tradition of leadership and formed a local nationalism which prompted many to call themselves *Californios*. This term refers to native born, Spanish speaking Californians and is the first significant expression of local nationalism. The Picos were one of the first families to speak out against Franciscan mistreatment of the Indian. They represented the well to do businessman and rancher who were concerned about the Indian. The reason for this concern was the hostile attitudes of the Franciscan Order.

The Franciscan Order and the Indian as Children

"They are our children," Father Serra wrote the Viceroy concerning California Indians. As a result, they were placed in dormitories, creating a physical and emotional dependence on the mission system and providing a Catholic education which made the Indian fearful of hell.

Pablo Tac, a Luiseno Indian, complained that the Franciscans were both loving and stern, but they forced the Indian to ask for even the basic necessities of life. It was in the educational process that the missions failed. Tac remarked that the "fear of hell" robbed the Indians of their culture. Constant complaints about the mission system prompted the Franciscans to answer the allegations of abuse. The Viceroy of New Spain asked the California Franciscans if the Indian could be civilized. The answer was invariably no.

In 1811, the Catholic Church provided each mission with a questionnaire about the degree of the Indian's Spanish language skills. The answer to this questionnaire varied. Most admitted that Spanish was taught in a crude and primitive manner. The average Spaniard would not recognize the language the Indians spoke. The Indian spoke a crude and often unrecognizable Spanish because the missionaries taught Spanish in a primitive and useless manner.

At the Mission San Jose, Father Narciso Duran suggested that the Indian couldn't assimilate Spanish language or culture. Duran was considered one of the most successful Franciscans, and his conversion rate for the Ohlone Indians was praised in numerous government reports. So Duran's opinions were important ones. "The Indian by nature is apathetic and indolent," Father Duran wrote. What Father Duran failed to recognize was that the Indians kept their own ways. Coyote tales dominated and Spanish culture was rejected. This was due to the low level of Franciscan teaching.

Spanish California: Some Conclusions

Spanish California began the multicultural direction which is critical to an understanding of the Golden State. When historians focus on the American West, they see that California is the laboratory for multiculturalism. Yet, much of early California history centers around the myths of Franciscan accomplishment. The earliest myths involving California were formed around Spanish religious figures, and for years the general public and historians glorified Father Serra. In 1934, a statue of Serra was donated to the Hall of Statuary in the Capitol in Washington D.C., and the finished product was a tall, lean and handsome Serra. There was no sign of the stooped body, the infected foot, the paunchy coun-

tenance of the venerable Franciscan or the abusive attitude toward the Native population.

The Native Sons of the Golden West, the Native Daughters of the Golden West and the fraternal society which romanticizes miners and early pioneers, E. Clampus Vitus, has for years financially supported historians who have an American view of California. The Mexican, the Chinese, the African American, the Irish and other immigrants are lost in the tendency to celebrate a perfect Spanish pioneer. The Herbert Bolton school of Spanish California Historiography emphasized the cross, the sword and the gold pan and trumpeted the virtues of frontier settlers. There was a sophistication and professionalism to Bolton's approach, but he ignored the ethnic contribution.

In 1966, this trend was reserved when Leonard Pitt's pathbreaking book *The Decline of the Californios* argued that the 15,000 Spanish speaking Californians, who survived during the first decade of statehood, felt like strangers in their own land. The Spanish speaking lost control of California almost from the moment that foreign intruders entered San Diego, Monterey, Santa Barbara and San Francisco. Foreigners were welcomed, and this turned out to be a mistake. Soon confrontations between the Spanish and foreign visitors created tensions which escalated into open racial conflict.

Once the last days of Spanish California began developing in the 1790s, the differences between the Spanish speaking and foreign settlers created new tensions, ones which altered the Hispanic nature of California civilization

Bibliographical Essay

Hauberk Howe Bancroft's multi-volume *History of California* (San Francisco, 1884-1889, 7 volumes) is an excellent starting point. Bancroft makes almost no use of ethnic history, but the wealth of detail and the richness of his research provides caveats of knowledge necessary to understanding ethnicity in California. Anne Loftis, *California-Where The Twain Did Meet* (New York,1973), chapter 1 and 2 provide useful information on the Indian and Spanish California.

This chapter depends heavily upon B. Gordon Wheeler, *Black California: The History of African-Americans in the Golden State* (New York, 1993), chapter l. Not only is Wheeler's book a pathbreaking study of California's Afro American population, but it is also an interpretation of the events in an even handed and historically sound manner.

For material on Father Lasuen see, for example, Francis F. Guest, *Fermin Francisco de Lasuen, 1736-1803: A Biography* (Washington, D.C., 1973).

On Spanish travel, see John Galvin, ed., *The First Spanish Entry into San Francisco Bay, 1775* (San Francisco, 1971); Francisco Palou, *The Founding of the First California Mission Under the Spiritual Guidance of the Venerable Padre Fray Junipero Serra* (San Francisco, 1934); Father Fray Pedro Font, *Diary of an Expedition to Monterey by Way of the Colorado River, 1775-1776* (edited by Herbert Eugene Bolton) in Ana's California Expeditions, Volume 4 (Berkeley, 1930).

The journal of Father Crespi is an important source because it details the black-Spanish soldiers and their contribution to San Diego's settlement. See, Herbert E. Bolton, editor and translator, *Father Juan Crespi: Missionary Explorer On The Pacific Coast, 1769-1774* (Berkeley, 1927) for this useful journal.

The tendency to view California Indians as heathens is demonstrated in Fray Francisco Garces and Garces Diary in Anza's Expeditions in Herbert E. Bolton, *Anza's California Expeditions* (Berkeley, 1930, Volume II, pp. 339-340).

Professor Lowell Bean of California State University, Hayward has corrected many misconceptions and attacked previously held stereotypes about California Indians. See, for example, Lowell Bean, "Social Organization in Native California," *Native California: A Theoretical Retrospective* (Menlo Park, 1976) and Lowell Bean and Harry Lawton, "Some Explanations for the Rise of Cultural Complexity in Native California with Comments on Proto-Agriculture and Agriculture" also in *Native California*. Also, see Lowell John Bean and Harry W. Lawton, "Some Explanations for the Rise of Cultural Complexity with Comments on Proto-Agriculture and Agriculture," in *Patterns of Indian Burning in California: Ecology and Ethnohistory* by Henry T. Lewis, pp. V-XLVII. Ballena Press Anthropological papers No. 1.

James J. Rawls, *Indians of California: The Changing Image* (Norman, 1984) is a revisionist history which adds a great deal to key questions of genocide, slavery, Franciscan and Spanish imperial attitudes toward Native Americans. Also see, Francis E. Guest, "Junipero Serra and His Approach to the Indians," *Southern California Quarterly*, Vol. LXVII (Fall 1985), PP. 223-261.

Sherburne F. Cook, *The Conflict Between the California Indian and White Civilization* (Berkeley and Los Angeles,1976) remains the standard and most balanced treatment. Also see, Rupert and Jeannette Costo, *The Missions of California: A Legacy of Genocide* (San Francisco, 1987) for a provocation revisionist look at the missions and Native Californians. The Costo's volume is particularly refreshing to point out how historians have mythesized the Franciscans and Father Serra in particular. There is also good evidence of uncritical acceptance of Catholic oriented books, reports and speeches.

The work of Franciscan trained historians is exemplary, and the best recent examples of this brilliant scholarship and lucid writing are Maynard Geiger, "Mission San Gabriel In 1814," *Southern California Quarterly*, volume 53 (1971), pp. 237-238 and Francis Guest, "Cultural Perspectives on California Mission Life, *Southern California Quarterly*, volume 61 (1983), pp. 1-77.

3

The Last Days of Spanish California

Foreign Intruders Alter Local Civilization

The last days of Spanish California were dominated by class differences and the racially slanted opinions of foreign traders. The British sailed into California to trade, the Russian American Company built Fort Ross north of San Francisco and French ships conducted scientific research off the Monterey and San Francisco ports. Invariably, these foreign intruders filed reports with their governments which were racially insensitive. Although a capitalistic rancho system had evolved, the observations of foreign travelers seldom mentioned the depth and success of Spanish California business.

The journals of Comte de la Perouse during the mid-1780s condemned the Spanish for imprecise scientific observations and described government officials as being slow and lacking ideas. In September 1791, an Italian explorer and geographer, Alejandro Malaspina, landed in California for two weeks and had dinner with Father Francisco Lasuen. This dinner was a turning point in how foreign explorers viewed Spanish California. Malaspina was convinced that California had many sources of wealth but he was most persuasive about agricultural possibilities. After recording his observations, Malaspina remarked that he

was not impressed with the economic future of the rancheros. This attitude was echoed by a wide variety of foreign observers.

A decade later, Captain George Vancouver wrote of wasted economic opportunities. Then just after the turn of the nineteenth century, the Russian American Company made the final plans to build Fort Ross. The Spanish opposed Fort Ross, but it was completed in 1812, and Russian officials began criticizing Mariano Vallejo and other Spanish speaking businessmen for their inability to complete "intelligent commercial transactions." These attitudes irritated Spanish Government officials and created a great deal of conflict. Soon foreigners complained of harassment.

Consequently, Spanish California from 1790 to 1820 was a quagmire of petty bureaucratic political bickering, fighting rancheros and insensitive foreign traders. In this atmosphere, the conflict over economic success divided local citizens into warring classes who fought one another over the future of Spanish California. But it was the activity of foreign settlers that upset the delicate balance of local society.

In the midst of this period of change, Spanish Californians also fought with one another over class origins. As foreign intruders explored and settled Spanish California, they were critical of existing values. This led to an increased emphasis upon class and race. Foreigners viewed the Hispanic population as slow and lacking ambition. Since ranchos didn't operate at a full level of economic profitability, most foreigners judged the rancheros harshly.

In their diaries, foreign visitors mentioned the class differences dividing Spanish California. They spoke of poorly constructed houses, scrawny cattle herds and simple product at the market. However, the pure blooded gente de razon were described as "noble, civilized and aristocratic." Since the majority of Spanish Californians were mixed blooded, this attitude created hostility. As a result, local settlers urged government action against the aggressive English, Russian and French visitors.

The upper class Castilian Spaniards and the mixed blooded Moors and Aztecs carried on a debate over land grants and political appointments. As Spaniards fought each other over policy decisions, a volatile political and economic atmosphere emerged and created a civilization that made land grants and trading rights the dominant factors. Inevitably, there were complaints about the power of the rancheros. Not only were the large ranchos economically influential, but they also meddled in political affairs.

The liberal ranchero modified Spanish California's governmental institutions in order to control the economy. He set up an advisory council which increasingly forced the government to recognize the rancheros as they provided money and protection for the poor paid Spanish officials. Soon government influences declined. This was largely due to the fact that rancheros paid bribes which caused government officials to look the other way. California's healthy economy centered around favors to rancheros, traders and government officials. A pluralistic society emerged into one in which

economic and political forces shaped Spanish California.

The end result of this new society created a Californio. This person was a native born, Spanish speaking citizen who identified with local nationalism. The Californio invariably owned a large rancho, resented the intrusion of Catholicism in business matters and spoke out against the King of Spain's policies. Californios were independent politically, economically and socially, and they challenged Spanish California settlers to develop a separate Hispanic nationalism. As a result of the Californio mentality, the volatile final three decades of Spanish California were filled with class differences, ethnic arguments and the increasing emergence of a multicultural civilization.

Governor Diego de Borica: Liberalism and Ethnicity

Governor Diego de Borica, serving in office from 1794 to 1800, spoke of the ranchero class as dominant. He had good reason to develop liberal governmental policies and to pander to the rancheros. The twenty-five Spanish land grants resulted not from agricultural skill but from close ties to the Crown. The rancheros were wealthy, politically influential settlers who constantly had the king's ear. As a result, Borica not only granted these rancheros special privileges, but he publicly emphasized their pure blooded, Castilian heritage. Race and class, as well as economic success, was the barometer for success. The mixed blooded Spaniards protested this attitude and used economic pressures to oppose Borica's policies.

Spanish California achieved a dramatic revolution as the mixed blooded settlers complained about the prerogatives of the gente de razon. Not surprisingly, a year after Governor Borica took office, he revised his attitudes and began an alliance with the prosperous mestizos. Mixed blooded ranchers and businessmen then donated large sums of money to help Borica govern. The result was that Borica was praised for recognizing local business initiative. By working with the mulattos and mestizos, Governor Borica drove a wedge into the racially defined Spanish California society.

Governor Borica recognized that the mission system had a problem with the Indians. In the summer of 1796, Borica discovered that two hundred Indians had left the Mission Delores. The San Francisco based mission with 872 people was known for its abusive treatment of the Indian. As a result, Governor Borica launched an investigation into the mission's Christianizing process. He found out that Fathers Antonio Danti and Martin Landaeta were not only mistreating the Indians, but also sending out small armies of mission Indians to search for runaways. However, one night when Father Landaeta sent out a group of mission Indians to find runaways, seven Christian Indians were killed in a massacre by non-mission Indians. Suddenly there was a law and order problem.

The massacre of seven mission Indians prompted Governor Borica to write Father Lasuen and demand a change in Franciscan policies. The result was a liberalization of the conversion process and an increase in free Indians. There were a small number of mission Indians who were citizens and lived like any other Spaniard. However, the free Indian was critical of the mission system and worked for land and civil rights for the native population. Governor Borica was pressured to control the criticism of the free Indians. But Borica stood up to Father Lasuen and refused to punish the Indian for verbal indiscretion.

The missionaries, given the worldly task of civilizing and Christianizing the Indian, were criticized for their ineffectiveness. Father Pedro Font remarked that once the Indian was clothed, educated and converted to Christianity, a new California would emerge. Father Junipero Serra was another prophet who predicted that a new order would result from the mission system. After Serra's death in the mid-1780s, there was a renewed questioning of the Franciscan mission system. This resulted in an internal California revolution which gave rise to a liberal, capitalistic society.

Governor Borica's conversion to liberal capitalism may have been due to his concern with smugglers. He was worried that American ships would engage in illegal trade with the missions and local businessmen. Thus, Borica attempted to establish a local economy, with the missions and rancheros participating equally in the profits. William Shaler, a Connecticut trader, observed that American ships were in search of the lucrative sea otter furs. "The missionaries are the principal monopolizers of the fur trade," Shaler wrote, but he also remarked that the rancheros and city businessmen were increasingly taking part in the fur trade.

From the 1790s until Mexico achieved its independence, Spanish California governors, like Diego de Borica, were liberal and critical of the mission system. Diego de Borica was the first of a long line of governors who recognized that mixed blooded settlers were dominating the economy and dictating political change. Because of the growing power of the rancheros and city businessmen, California was rapidly developing into a lay society where religious, military and governmental ideas were secondary to economic success.

California: Far from a Racial Paradise

After more than two decades of settlement, however, Spanish California was far from a racial paradise. Charles Chapman, a noted historian, observed that: "The officers and missionaries were for the most part of pure white blood, but the great majority of the rest were Africans, mulattos and mestizos..." The social differences between Californians were based on blood, military rank, government position and clerical privilege. It was a society torn apart by class tensions. Mixed blooded soldiers were not appointed to key government positions. The living standard for racially mixed soldiers was lower, and they were also more vigorously disciplined.

The best land grants were awarded to the Castilians. Initially, the commerce and trade, which increased was the exclusive right of the gente de razon, created an elitist economy. Soon the economically independent mixed blooded settlers began to refer to themselves as Californios. This term defined the native born, Spanish speaking and was used with a sense of local pride. The Californios led the drive for political, personal and financial independence. They formed an advisory council and pressured Governor Borica for specific economic privileges. The growth of the lay city, as well as the rancho, was foremost in the new California. The prospect of not having to combat religious influences, governmental interference and petty bureaucrats appealed to Spanish California settlers. Eventually, three lay cities-San Jose, Los Angeles and Branciforte-were founded and large numbers of lay-minded Spaniards migrated to California.

When San Jose was established in 1777, as Spanish California's first lay city, it was a sleepy pueblo populated by farmers who hoped to make a good living. A few years later, Los Angeles was established as a pueblo by black-Spaniards. The lifestyle in Los Angeles was so attractive that it soon became populated by a wide variety of settlers.

The Founding of Los Angeles and Racial Turmoil

When Los Angeles was founded in 1781, its population was 56.5% African-Spanish, but the earliest Los Angeles settlers were wracked with dissension. The gente de razon or pure blooded Spaniards who moved into Los Angeles abused the Indian population and created strong class lines. The lowest part of the social order was the Indian gentile. These Indians were unconverted workers who had not been part of the mission Indian Christianizing process. They became casual workers who were literally slaves.

During the 1780s, Los Angeles was a city in conflict not only because of the abuse of Indian gentile labor, but also due to the public outcry from mixed blooded Spaniards. As this system of forced labor emerged in Los Angeles, the Indian workers were jailed, beaten and cheated out of wages by the gente de razon. The Indian was so poorly treated that a Los Angeles city ordinance was passed which banned sex between Indian women and the gente de razon.

The crisis between Los Angeles citizens and the local Indian population was so severe that a series of laws were established regulating working conditions, social relations and there was even a law banning extreme cruelty toward the Indian. However, the Indian was required to live in designated neighborhoods and forbidden to congregate in large groups. Indian amusement was regulated. There was an unwritten code among the government bureaucrats and Franciscan friars to supervise Indian excesses.

Franciscan missionaries complained that the gente de razon were lazy and exploited Indian labor. But there were other factors influencing Indian labor. The spread of venereal disease was the key in decimating the Indian population. By 1803, there were only

200 Indian gentiles able to work for the 359 gente de razon. Foreign visitors complained about the "blight and degradation" of the Indian. The mixed blooded Spaniard was the earliest cause of racism in California.

The Rise of the Native Californian: The Argument for a California Culture

The Californio ranchers, businessmen and casual workers had a vision of an independent California. Their freedom oriented philosophy centered around hostility toward the church and its restrictions on California life. The Telemachus List, which banned dangerous books, was a cultural restriction that the Californios complained about constantly. They also resisted tithing and talked of establishing a representative assembly.

This resulted in the Native son, the Californio, taking over local leadership. Spanish soldiers and government officials often took up permanent residence in California. Santiago Pico, who was part of the Portola expedition, moved his family to Los Angeles where his wife gave birth to five sons who were successful southern California business pioneers. Pico was a mestizo who was part Aztec, part Moor and part Italian. The Picos and other pioneer settlers were of Moorish descent, but they had recognizable African features. As the Pico Family prospered and matured in and around Los Angeles, the offspring intermarried with wealthy Spanish and European families. When the Picos married into the Alvarado and Carrillo Families, they became southern California's dominant land owners.

The prominence of mixed blooded Spaniards in Alta California was mentioned constantly in the diaries of foreign visitors, and there was a nasty racial tone to these well read reports. The underlying feelings of racial hostility were developed during the last days of Spanish California when English and French ships sailed into San Diego, Monterey and San Francisco. As the British and French explored the California coast, they left behind a body of literature which praised the Castilian Spaniard and condemned the mixed blooded settler.

Spain had no real interest in Alta California; this made it easier for the Californio to rise to positions of authority, wealth or social prestige. Since California was a small and seemingly insignificant part of the Spanish Empire, the mixed blooded settler had little difficulty assuming positions of authority. As a result, Spanish California color was less of a barrier to success than in other parts of the Empire. Jobs were plentiful for mixed blooded pioneers and land grants were available. The African-Spanish ethnic population gravitated to the major cities. In 1790, Spanish Government census records indicated that 14.7% of Yerba Buena's (San Francisco) population was African-Spanish while San Jose had a 24.3% black settlement. The trend continued throughout California as Monterey registered 18.5% black settlers, Santa Barbara 19.3% and Los Angeles 22.7%. The local alcaldes (mayors), the major businessmen, the successful rancheros and the Franciscan friars were more often mixed blooded Spaniards.

Spain had a strong concept of race and class. The observations of foreign observers, particularly the English, explains a great deal about how racial differences create tensions. When diaries and official reports were completed by English officials, they wrote a great deal about the relationship between British and Spanish officials. The career of British naval commander George Vancouver offers a case study in how one British explorer developed his racial attitudes.

The British and Captain Vancouver's Explorations: The Seeds of Early Racial Conflict

On New Year's Day 1790, an elaborate ceremony in London christened a new British ship, the Discovery. This British vessel was launched to expand British influence along the Spanish California coast. George Vancouver was instructed to explore the northwest coast of America, and begin what the English envisioned as a lucrative trade with the California missions. As the British proudly looked on, they stood in awe of the 340-ton vessel resting majestically in the Thames River. When he first arrived in Spanish California, this young British first lieutenant, George Vancouver, supervised the outfitting of the ship, and he was a seminal figure in the three year journey. At the end of his voyage, Vancouver was a famous explorer who wet the appetite of English imperialists to conquer California. He was made a captain and became a famous British explorer.

The three year, world wide voyage saw Vancouver enter the California coast and explore it extensively. In the process, he wrote voluminously about Alta California and established English attitudes about the area. The Spanish were of particular interest to Vancouver because of his respect for their military tradition. Not only did Spain possess a fine navy, some of the best trained soldiers and a wealth of knowledge about navigation and commerce, but it was also on a mission for the Catholic Church. Fanaticism led to conquest, Vancouver warned, and the Spanish should be taken seriously.

When Captain Vancouver finally landed in San Francisco in November 1792, he described the commandant's house as being little more than two rooms with earth floors, not boarded or even leveled. Vancouver was repulsed by the primitive nature of the home. He condemned the commandant's home by writing a derogatory report on the windows with no glass and the decrepit furniture. Although Vancouver had a low opinion of how Spanish Californians lived, he still found much to praise in the Spanish lifestyle.

In a letter to the British admiralty, Vancouver spoke with respect for the Spanish mission. Divine inspiration made Spanish soldiers formidable, Vancouver wrote, and the military leaders were fanatical because they believed they were fighting for the Pope. Vancouver warned the English Crown that it would be difficult to seize California, and he urged caution in dealing with the Californios.

The thirty-two year old Vancouver's November 1792 visit to Spanish California was greeted by friendly Franciscans, and surprisingly he was allowed to travel freely as far inland as the Santa Clara Mission. Father Tomas de la Pena greeted Vancouver and his men, and they were treated to a sumptuous banquet of fish, fruit and sweet meats. Initially, the Spanish were eager to get to know the British.

At Monterey and Carmel, numerous banquets were held for Vancouver, and he kept track of everything by taking copious notes in his diary. The tragedy of this visit is that Vancouver was a pompous observer who judged Spanish California as an economic success but an uncivilized place to dine. After all, cultural superiority was still the mark of the English.

After his initial visit, the Spanish were suspicious of Vancouver's intentions. His name quickly became synonymous with British intervention. In 1793 when Vancouver sailed back into Monterey, he was met with hostility. The Spanish were aware of his intentions to conquer the area. A pompous and often condescending man, Vancouver viewed the Indians as nothing more than a laboring population, and this brought the immediate wrath of the Franciscans. Father Lasuen cautioned Spanish Government officials to be wary of the English explorer.

This prophecy rang true in the fall of 1794 when Captain Vancouver returned for a third visit. He boasted to Californians that the British were militarily in charge of the Pacific Ocean. The recent settlement of the Nootka Sound controversy led Spain to give up any intention of settling north of California. This agreement also gave the British trade rights in Spanish California. These concessions to the British angered the Californios and led to hostile feelings between the English and Spanish.

By sailing into California and writing a popular diary, Vancouver created worldwide interest in the area. In his diary and explorations, he revealed the complicated and divided nature of Spanish California society. Europeans were thirsting for knowledge about Monterey and San Francisco. Rumors of exotic products from local missions circulated among traders. This prompted other explorers to visit California.

A French Visitor in California: The Comte de la Perouse

When the French scientist the Comte Jean Francois de la Perouse visited Monterey for ten days in 1786, he commented on the possibility of extensive trade with this new and formidable civilization. Although Spanish California was only a few decades old when Vancouver, la Perouse and other foreign visitors analyzed its successes and failures, the conclusion was that the area was ready for world trade and multinational settlement.

On a social-cultural level, la Perouse was not impressed. He found the Californios "stultifying," and he complained about their food, manners and morals. Like the English

observers, la Perouse's attitudes were shaped by European values. He often found the Californios "coarse," "excessively competitive" and "without traces of the gentleman's life." These conclusions told a great deal about the foreign reaction to Alta California civilization.

Perhaps la Perouse's most important insight was that the Spaniards fought with one another over class status. They were a divided people settling in an unfamiliar frontier, but, as la Perouse wrote, "the Spanish had a strong penchant for developing their own society."

The popularity of Comte de la Perouse's book *A Voyage Round the World, Performed in the Years 1785, 1787, and 1788* made it a four volume best seller which created some of the earliest stereotypes surrounding both Spanish and Indian settlers. "The Indians say," la Perouse wrote, "they loved the open air, that it is convenient to set fire to their house when the fleas become troublesome, and that they can build another in less than two hours." Purporting to be a scientific observer, la Perouse chided the California Indian for "sexual indiscretion" and "poor judgment" in matters relating to family.

When la Perouse landed in Monterey, he commanded two ships, and the Franciscans welcomed him. La Perouse called the Franciscans: "men truly apostolic, who have abandoned the idle life of a cloister to give themselves up to fatigues, cares and anxieties of every kind." This was la Perouse's way of praising the Franciscan friar and setting himself up to trade with the mission system. By implication, la Perouse suggested that the Indian was a second class human being. This attitude persisted into the era of Mexican California. What la Perouse and the Spanish ignored was the fierce independence of the Native Californian. La Perouse remarked that there was a sense of local independence which permeated Spanish California. The frontier created opportunities for a new civilization. There was a sense of independence, la Perouse wrote, which set Californians apart from the rest of the Spanish Empire.

Spanish California: Addicted to Independence

As one Spanish Californian remarked, "we are addicted to independence." There was a sense of local freedom. Because Spanish Californians were mixed blooded, they had a penchant for liberty. Local citizens questioned government action and demanded local rule. Soon law and order problems arose, and there were constant conflicts. The rise of the pronunciamento (a device designed to bring compromise) and the first signs of a well developed, local nationalism made it difficult for Spain to control California.

This sense of independence was due to the mixed blooded settlers who migrated to California as a safety valve area of settlement. The frontier offered a place to settle which was free of restrictive Spanish religious, political and economic conditions. A place where they could develop economic freedom and ignore the dictates of the Catholic Church. The unyielding Catholic Doctrine, the arbitrary rule of the king and the strict social-economic class lines drove the young and mixed blooded to Spanish California.

The presence of African and Aztec mixed blooded citizens created a new political-business aristocracy. In Los Angeles, the Pico Family dominated the local economy and influenced political decision making. The Picos were not only of African heritage, but they also arrived in California with the earliest Spanish explorers. Jose Maria Pico often complained about the color consciousness of the Spaniards, the Monterey citizens and later the Mexicans. When his son, Pio, was born on May 5, 1801 at the San Gabriel Mission, Jose Maria had no way of knowing that his son would be the last Governor of Mexican California.

Jose Carrillo, Pico's brother in law, was an important figure who taught reading and mathematics to local Spanish Californians. Carrillo was also a leading southern California politico who criticized the Spanish Government for its inability to support local settlers. In his comments, Carrillo intimated that race conscious attitudes were causing problems. During the Mexican California era Carillo's influence grew, and he represented the local citizen who was "addicted to independence." Carrillo urged Spaniards to retain an independent local culture.

The Mission System: The Main Attraction in the Last Days of Spanish California

The mission system was the main attraction for the English and other foreign visitors. As Father Junipero Serra and later Father Fermin Francisco de Lasuen built the missions, there was little doubt regarding their profitability. Everyone benefited from the mission's vast agricultural riches. Forced and converted Indian labor made it unnecessary to recruit agricultural workers; therefore, production costs were low and profits high.

The purpose of the mission system was economic gain for the church. Food and meat were necessary to the local economy. Fathers Serra and Lasuen were not above using foodstuffs to gain concessions from the Governor and local citizens. Indian craft products quickly found a world market, thereby guaranteeing high profits. The colonial mentality was ingrained into the Spanish, and Indian labor was what attracted them to California.

Visitors often complained that the mission system was primitive. The crudely constructed missions bore little resemblance to the tourist attractions of the modern day. The huts of sticks were crudely plastered with mud or clay and roofed with tule. They were primitive, and there was a sense among the Indians that the Franciscan Order eventually would abandon these missions. These buildings unwittingly became a source of foreign prejudice. la Perouse found them primitive and lacking in the rudiments of civilization, and he complained that they were lacking even the simplest comforts. Another scientific expedition under the command of Spain's Alejandro Malaspina also found the missions lacking in "civilized appearance." The conclusion was that the Franciscans had little interest in religious conversion. But the British had praise for the economic side of the mission. However, these kind words went unnoticed.

When Vancouver reported on the California mission's economic system, he did so with reverential awe. Since Father Serra's death, Father Lasuen, president of the California missions from 1785 to 1803, ran a tight ship and profits increased. Indian labor was available in greater abundance. Captain Vancouver remarked that he had witnessed a number of primitive Indian civilizations in his world travels, but the California Indian had well developed work habits. As a result, Vancouver wrote, "the Indian helped the Franciscans turn a substantial profit." But Vancouver believed that the Indians were not ready for Christianity, and this made them a life long source of available labor. They were made for servitude, Vancouver argued, as they were "like children with skills."

Indian technology was badly misjudged. When Captain Vancouver encountered the Chumash Indians, he made fun of their conical reed houses and tule reed boats. Not only were these central coast Indians culturally California's most advanced tribe, but they were also able to explain to Vancouver how their ocean going canoes remained so long at sea. Rather than viewing these sophisticated elements of technology as advanced, one Spanish explorer remarked that the tule boats were "the most...sorry contrivances" on the water.

In the final analysis, the mission system created stereotypes about the California Indians, the limited nature of Spanish California civilization and led many explorers to recommend that settling in San Francisco or Monterey and developing ports for trade with the Far East was all that was in Spanish California's future.

The Indian's were a curiosity to the foreign visitors who wrote extensively about their habits. Comte de la Perouse described the Natives houses as little more than long poles stuck in the ground. These houses around Monterey, la Perouse wrote, possessed crude arches covered with a thatch that were primitive and poorly engineered. Clearly, la Perouse, like Vancouver, observed Indian culture as non civilized. La Perouse wrote that the California Indians were "the most miserable...among many people."

The physical size of the California Indian, the complexion and facial characteristics and the manner of walking prompted the Russian explorer Nikolai Rezanov to conclude that the Native Californian was "brutish and stupid." This observation was reflected in other early travel accounts as well.

What importance did these early racial stereotypes have to the larger course of California history? One obvious conclusion is that mixed blooded Spanish California settlers feared that these hostile racial attitudes might hinder their economic and political power. Consequently, during much of Spanish California's existence there was a great deal of success by the mestizo settlers. They established ranchos, were prominent in Los Angeles, Santa Barbara and San Francisco city life and led a cultural movement to create Californio values. However, the notion of Moors, with their African ancestry, having economic success was repugnant to some Spaniards.

Black Californians in the Last Days of Spanish California

During the last forty years of Spanish California, African Spaniards rose to positions of prominence. Many successful rancheros were Spaniards of African descent. The Rancho Rodeo, was owned by Maria Rita Valdez, an African, who was among Los Angeles' original settlers. He was a pioneer who recognized a lucrative settlement area. Rancho Rodeo eventually became Beverly Hills. Present day Rodeo Drive is a reminder of this pioneer black family.

As a leading Spanish citizen, Valdez was a political voice who complained continually about Spanish rule. Valdez was critical of Spain's inability to develop southern California, and he was one of the first rancheros to note the tendency to favor Monterey. Sectionalism was emerging in the last days of Spanish California, and Valdez charged that mixed blooded Los Angeles citizens were poorly treated. As a businessman, Valdez had few peers; thus, he formed an alliance with other Los Angeles ranchers. The result was an increasingly vibrant local economy.

Soon other southern California rancheros complained of the preference to favor northern ranchos. The Picos were the most virulent critics of Spanish Government, and they urged local citizens to form a new territory. A divisionist mentality arose which created hostility toward anything identified with Monterey and northern California. Foreign intruders, Pio Pico warned, have turned the heads of the Spanish speaking and new attitudes threatened local rule.

Another black rancher, Francisco Reyes, owned much of what is now the San Fernando Valley. In 1790, when Reyes became the alcalde (mayor) of Los Angeles, he urged Spain to grant more land grants in southern California. He charged that Governor Pedro Fages was a "man of limited vision." His criticism of Fages was instrumental in the Governor's attempt to placate the mixed blooded population.

In 1790, prior to leaving Spanish California, Governor Pedro Fages completed a special census. The results were surprising to Spanish Government officials as 18% of California's population was black. Since 1769, when El Negro discovered San Francisco Bay, there had been a steady influx of black-Spaniards to Alta California. Most of whom settled permanently in the Golden State. Governor Fages promised to grant more land to the mixed blooded, but he never fulfilled this promise. Yet, Fages unwittingly did publicize the contributions of mixed blooded California settlers in the census of 1790.

What was the significance of the census? The 1790 census indicated some important changes. The growth of black settlers was demonstrated with 15% residing in San Francisco, while San Jose had 24.3% Afro-Spaniards and Santa Barbara had 19.3% black settlers. There was an urban tone to black settlement. What did the black presence mean to California? The answer is a complex one.

Business in Los Angeles had a decidedly Afro-Spanish leadership. This was reflected in the large number of shops, import export traders and small farmers. The Saturday markets and trade with ranchos was conducted almost exclusively by black pioneers. The Gabrieleno Indians worked closely with the mission system, local rancheros and the small shopkeepers who marketed their goods. But it was the black-Spaniards who were the local business leaders. One prevailing myth of Los Angeles history is that the Gabrieleno Indians were happy with the mission system. Nothing was further from the truth. While they farmed, worked independently and interacted with African-Spaniards, they also had strong feelings about their economic abilities. The abundance of Indian craft goods, agricultural products and simple trading items suggested the independence of the Gabrieleno Indians and their economic contribution to Los Angeles. By the early 1790s, there was a multicultural atmosphere in and around Los Angeles. Black-Spaniards and the Gabrieleno Indians created an economically prosperous society. However, this cooperation quickly ended and black settlers faded from sight.

B. Gordon Wheeler's book, *Black Californians: The History of African-Americans In The Golden State*, argues that African features began to disappear at the turn of the nineteenth century due to intermarriage. This popularity of intermarriage virtually absorbed African features. By 1825, Wheeler writes: "Ignored, distorted, deliberately concealed or innocently omitted, the fact is that men and women of African ancestry played a significant and honorable role in populating and developing California's colorful, romantic pastoral era."

Black Californians were Spaniards who came to the Golden State for business and personal freedoms. They stayed on to forge a new civilization; one which was free of religious restraints, governmental interference and emphasis on skin color. Unwittingly, Spanish settlement planted the first seeds of freedom from the tyranny of race.

The Homefront During the Last Days of Spanish California

The reaction to the changes in Spanish California was a liberal one. Economic, personal and religious freedom evolved. The mission system was hit hardest by this liberalism. By 1790, the eleven missions had a population of 7,500 converts. Since there were 300,000 Indians in California, this was a clear indication that the mission system was a failure. Only Indians in the immediate vicinity of a mission were baptized. Clearly the Spanish religious message was a hollow one.

When the initial attraction of clothing, food and religious trinkets wore off, the Indians vanished from the mission. Governor Pedro Fages ordered soldiers to stop giving the Indians religious articles. The Spanish governors didn't coerce the Indians. They were free to choose or reject the Franciscan offer of salvation, and invariably, they rejected it.

By the 1790s, Father Lasuen announced that he had created a strong mission system. The Franciscan Order was excellent in self-promotion. This helped to hide the independent nature of the California Indian and local Spanish settlers. The church released statistics on its accomplishments. These figures pointed out the large livestock herds, the abundant agricultural production and the profit making craft industry. The Franciscans seldom mentioned the conversion of Indians to the Catholic faith. This was because those numbers were inordinately small.

From 1810 to 1820, the European population of Spanish California nearly doubled, but there were still only 930 European settlers in California. The Indian population was stable, but the thirty-nine Franciscan missionaries were still fighting a losing battle to bring the Indians onto the mission. When Father Dumetz retired to Mexico City, he complained that the California Indian had never accepted Christianity. "Catholicism," Father Dumetz remarked, "was foreign to the neophytes."

In the last days of Spanish California, there was a rigid social structure, religious uncertainty and a rising local nationalism. The result was to place the California Indian deeper into a position of second class citizenship, prompt the local born Californio to demand Home Rule and to force the church into a position of defending what little was left of its mission system.

As the Mexican War for independence raged from 1810 to 1821, Californians continued to form their own ideas. They thought independently and didn't share Mexico's attitudes. Governor Pablo Vicente de Sola convened a group of Franciscans, large rancheros, foreign businessmen and Californios to discuss the Golden State's future. Should they pledge their loyalty to Mexico or consider becoming an independent republic? Many Californios favored the Home Rule idea. The question of loyalty and the dominance of church wealth created the major issues in Mexican California.

Bibliographical Essay

Douglas Monroy, *Thrown Among Strangers: The Making of Mexican Culture In Frontier California* (Berkeley and Los Angeles, 1990) is an excellent starting point for the emerging Californio culture. Also, see H.H. Bancroft, *History of California* (San Rafael, Ca., 1886), volume II (1801-1824); H.E. Bolton, ed., *Historical Memoirs of New California* (Berkeley, 1926), 5 volumes; C.E. Chapman, *History of California, The Spanish Period* (New York, 1921) and A. Ogden, *The California Sea Otter Trade, 1784-1848* (Berkeley, 1941).

For the black contribution to Spanish California see B. Gordon Wheeler, *Black California: The History of African-Americans In The Golden State* (New York (1993).

Captain Vancouver and other foreign explorers are included in George Vancouver, *Vancouver In California, 1792-1794: The Original Account of George Vancouver*, ed. Marguerite Every Wilbur (Los Angeles, 1953-1954) and George Vancouver, *A Voyage of Discovery to the North Pacific Ocean and Round the World* (3 vols., London, 1798). Also see, F.W. Beechey, *Narrative of a Voyage to the Pacific and Berrings Straight* (sic) (London, 1831), volume 2; Alexander Forbes, *A History of Upper and Lower California* (London, 1839). Also see Jean Francois de la Perouse, *Voyage de la Perouse autour du Monde* (4 volumes, Paris, 1797). Also see Francisco Antonio Maurelle, *Journal of a Voyage in 1775 to Explore the Coast of America, Northward of California* (London, 1781) for an intriguing early view of Spanish California.

On Indian policy see Florian Guest, "The Indian Policy Under Fermin Francisco Lasuen, California's Second Father President," *California Historical Quarterly*, 45 (September, 1966); James J. Rawls, *Indians Of California: The Changing Image* (Norman, 1984) and Sherburne F. Cooke, *The Conflict Between the California Indians and White Civilization* (Berkeley, 1976).

C. Alan Hutchinson, *Frontier Settlement in Mexican California: The Hijar Padres Colony and its Origins, 1769-1835* (New Haven, 1969) is important in analyzing the force of Spanish and Mexican land settlement in Alta California. This book examines one particular settlement party that was instrumental in attempting to take over mission lands.

On Spanish California society see William Heath Davis's books *Sixty Years in California* (San Francisco, 1889) and *Seventy Five Years in California* (San Francisco, 1929). For an excellent analysis of ethnic attitudes see Moses Rischin, "Continuities and Discontinuities in Spanish California," in Charles Wollenberg, ed., *Ethnic Conflict In California History* (Los Angeles, 1970), pp. 43-60.

4

Foreign Intruders

From Mexican California to the Early Stages of American Annexation

The presence of foreign intruders in Mexican California created new problems. As foreign merchants grew more powerful, there were trading controversies and arguments over the fairness of Mexican California government, and racial tensions resulting from these differences created a volatile civilization.

Class and race dominated Mexican California. The growth of the local aristocracy was due to the increase in large land grants. The Mexican National Congress enacted a liberal land grant policy which opened up new land to settlement. More than 700 land grants of eleven square leagues (approximately 49,000 acres) created an economically prosperous local aristocracy. With two hundred Spanish speaking families owning 14 million acres of land, Spanish California had an entrenched aristocracy which was financially well off and politically influential. Early foreign intruders failed to note this economic success. Mexico also refused to acknowledge California's economic advances.

Don Pablo de la Guerra's family bought up most of the land around Santa Barbara. The fourteen land grants owned by the de la Guerras totaled 488,000 acres and Don

Pablo became an important and respected local citizen. It was Don Pablo who remarked that the term "white" was used to describe Europeans. The term, Don Pablo remarked, indicated that money, ancestry and social standing were the keys to local success. While Don Pablo had the monetary base necessary for being an aristocrat, he complained that ancestry and social standing made foreigners look down upon him.

At the bottom of the Mexican California social structure, the Indian and the mestizos were unable to find employment. The extensive use of Indian labor created a second class position for them in Mexican California society.

Indians worked on large ranchos, took odd jobs in the cities and generally were a people adrift. The Yorba Family of Los Angeles was typical of local families. They employed twenty-six Indian servants to keep their twenty five room house in order. Another one hundred Indian laborers worked on the Yorba farm. Mariano Vallejo hired six hundred Indian cowboys and day laborers to maintain his 66,000 Rancho Petaluma and his 99,000 acre Rancho Suscol. This was a pattern repeated throughout Mexican California.

Mexican California: The View from Mexico

Mexican California was, in the eyes of the Mexican Government, one of its more isolated and insignificant provinces. Influenced by Spanish myths, the Mexican Government viewed California as little more than an area of excellent ports settled by a few people who could not find a home in Mexico. Unwittingly, Mexican officials created stereotypes when they concluded that the local population was slow and lazy. Governor Jose Echeandia reported that Californians lacked the capacity to develop a vibrant economy. He was also critical of the differences between northern and southern Californians. Because of Echeandia's lack of leadership, Mariano Vallejo, Jose Castro and Juan Bautista Alvarado controlled local markets and continually pressured Mexico for more rights.

This combative, legalistic side of California's population bothered Mexico. For a quarter of a century there were sporadic attempts to punish the wayward Mexican Californians. When Los Angeles was made the capital in 1836, it was as a punishment, not a reward, for independent political action. This further agitated the Californios who pressed on for Home Rule.

Independent attitudes were one reason that Mexico had trouble controlling California. The local legislature, the Diputacion, soon created an economic-political alliance with the governor. Because governmental funds were scarce, the Californios controlled the governor.

It was the strength of local nationalism which made the rancheros leaders. There was a sense of excitement over the economic opportunities available in Spanish California, and as a result, the civilization was attractive to foreigners. In this success, however, the seeds of ethnic differences grew into full blown racism.

California's Foreign Trade Impulse and the Books Fostering Racism

Traders and trappers arrived in California to seek out the lucrative hide and tallow commerce. During the early days of Mexican California, the sea otter and the fur seal were all but extinct. New England whalers exhausted the sea otter supply and soon trading interest shifted to cowhides and tallow.

The hostile racial attitudes of foreign traders created ethnic problems. The success of black Spaniards and mixed blooded Mexican settlers was not easy for race conscious foreigners to understand. The English, French, American and Russian settlers displayed signs of racial intemperance. The frontier's freedom made conflict inevitable. Law and order was a temporary and uneven phenomena, and the result was that commerce and trade often led to ethnic, as well as economic, disputes.

When Mexican rancheros complained that the American firm of Bryant and Sturgis overcharged them for goods, William Gale, the representative for Bryant and Sturgis, charged that Mexicans controlled the economy and set prices. Acting on Bryant and Sturgis's behalf, Gale criticized Mexican ranchers for gouging foreign traders. Vallejo laughed at this charge and pointed out that the American company lacked fundamental fairness in its business practices.

As foreign immigrants arrived in California, they were critical of local life. Europeans and Americans found little to praise in California. They talked about the "cultural void" and the "lack of full economic development." The reaction to local politicians and rancheros was uniformly hostile. Pio Pico, the last Mexican California Governor, was derided for his lack of leadership, and for generations historians have ignored Pico's extraordinary achievements.

Pio Pico: A Mixed Blooded Mexican Californian Governor and Home Rule

In the waning days of Mexican California, Governor Pio Pico characterized foreign intruders as economically lustful. When the Pico family arrived in Spanish California they were one of a handful of leading citizens who were mixed blooded. Since the Pico family had a long history of African blood, they were aware of racial strife and cultural differences. By 1846, Governor Pico presided over a civilization in conflict and disarray. His lengthy political career highlighted the problems within Mexican California.

Because he was a leading figure in southern California's economic and political life, Pico was named in 1827 the secretary to Captain Don Pablo de la Portillo, the Attorney General of San Diego. In this position, Pico realized that foreign traders were not only condescending but dishonest in dealing with Spanish speaking government officials and local businessmen. He urged more control over foreign intruders. Pico lobbied for restrictions on the foreign traders. As a result, Mexican California's legislative powers expanded, and Pico began his political career.

In 1828, Pico was elected to a legislative body, the Territorial Chamber of Deputies. Governor Jose Echeandia consulted with the deputies, and eventually they became a permanent legislative body known as the Diputacion. Pico quickly became a voice for Home Rule. This was a program designed to force Mexico to appoint a native born, Spanish speaking governor. Monterey was to be the permanent capital and the Diputacion the recognized legislative body controlling local affairs. Pico argued that a native born ranchero with political strength would control the excesses of foreign merchants and create a stronger economy.

The drive for Home Rule was far from successful. Mexico resisted it. They informed the Diputacion and the large rancheros like Vallejo, that Mexican law and authority was supreme. This began a half-decade struggle which Mexico lost in 1836 when Juan Bautista Alvarado was appointed the first Home Rule governor.

But for some time Mexico resisted California's demands for local rule. The Mexican Government made it clear that it would not bend to accomodate Californio demands for Home Rule. In 1831, when Mexico appointed Manuel Victoria as governor, he suspended the Territorial Diputacion. As Mexican governors, like Victoria, ruled in a dictatorial fashion, they unwittingly helped Pico increase his power. In 1831, Pico, along with Mariano Vallejo and other leading Californios, signed a statement complaining of Governor Victoria's spiteful leadership. It was Victoria's job, Pico argued, to provide law and order. In the legislative records of the Diputacion there are speeches in which Pico complains that Governor Victoria all but ignored southern California and didn't challenge the actions of foreign merchants.

Governor Victoria was noted for his heavy punishment. Simple disagreement often resulted in a long prison term. He liked to cut off one hand for petty theft and publicly flog prisoners were minor indiscretions. Victoria was cruel, barbaric and laughed at the locals. He helped to build a groundswell of support for California freedom. The first time that Mexican Californian's used the term a Pacific Republic it was to describe their desires for freedom.

Not only was Governor Manuel Victoria an impossible tyrant, but he had no sense of his own failures. When Pico criticized Victoria, the Governor responded by declaring that Mexican California was in a state of rebellion. The militia, Victoria announced, would expel all troublemakers. As he poised his army for battle, Governor Victoria had trouble finding an enemy. Since he could not locate a common foe, he invented one. The discontent settlers, Victoria stated, were a group of mixed blooded rancheros who were plotting to overthrow the Mexican Government. They hoped to return a form of Spanish rule, complete with Moorish or African Spaniard influences. In a comic opera battle, Governor Victoria attacked a small band of men he believed were about to seize the San Gabriel Mission. On December 5, 1831, near Los Angeles, Victoria and his fourteen soldiers dispersed a group of settlers he believed were intent on seizing mission land. This action made him look like a fool. They were simply local settlers.

The Mexican Government removed Victoria when a petition signed by Pio Pico, Juan Bandini and Jose Antonio Carrillo made it clear that the Diputacion would send Jose Castro and the Native Cavalry to expel the Governor. This was too embarrassing for Mexico, and they recalled Victoria. Although Home Rule was still a few years away, the movement was gaining strength.

Ecomonic Questions in Mexican California: The Racial Side of Capitalism

Economic questions were as important as political ones. Pico delivered a number of speeches in the Diputacion criticizing California's negative direction. Foreign intruders were not always positive influences, he warned, and something had to be done about economic poaching.

The hostile attitudes of foreign intruders and the rise of racial antagonism was tied to economic questions. When American and foreign ranchers and businessmen moved into California, they had no trouble displacing the Indian and the African blooded settlers. But the Mexican ranchero offered a stiff challenge to the European American

migrating into California. Anglo capitalists were continually at odds with Mexican rancheros and businessmen.

Not only could the upper class Mexican rancher resist American capitalism, but they also criticized the lack of ethics and morality in the Anglo business community. The success of Sonoran miners and businessmen was a bone of contention with American settlers. The success of the Mexican peddler created a small group of Spanish speaking businessmen who challenged the foreign intruders in their own markets. Pio Pico suggested that American businessmen manipulated prices and did everything in their power to destroy local peddlers.

Pico based his hostile attitude toward foreign traders on the experiences of his Rancho Santa Margarita y Las Flores and other small cattle ranches that he owned in and around Los Angeles. Pico's criticism of the business tactics of the Bryant and Sturgis Company began in the early 1820s when Governor Luis Arguello offered William Gale special trading privileges. Pico then charged that Mexican officials took bribes from foreign traders and acted as self interested businessmen.

Gale was hated by Mexican Californians because he began his career as a smuggler. But soon he became a legitimate businessman. His business with the missions was suspect, and once he began representing Bryant and Sturgis, Gale created ill will. His attitude toward Mexican and Californio citizens was pompous and condescending. There was a subtle racism to Gale which did not go unnoticed by the Californios.

The Boston based Bryant and Sturgis Company, the first American firm to compete for Mexican California goods, was constantly charged with unfair business dealings. While the price of the California sea otter and related good doubled in the 1820s, the cost of goods purchased from Bryant and Sturgis exceeded reasonable limits.

Foreign traders brought a wide variety of attitudes and some obvious prejudices to California. As a British visitor, Sir George Simpson, remarked: "Nature doing everything, man doing nothing" was the cornerstone of the Mexican California economy. Generally, European Americans believed that the Spanish speaking were indolent and backward.

Richard Henry Dana, Alfred Robinson and Literary Racial Stereotypes

When Harvard educated Richard Henry Dana, the author of *Two Years Before The Mast*, visited California in 1834-1835 as a sailor on a Boston ship, he described Californians as "an idle, thriftless people" who "can make nothing for themselves." Dana called the Californio a flamboyant dresser and wondered about his unwillingness to work. To Dana the rancheros "were very much given to gaming." Gambling, drinking, laziness and promiscuity were the themes running through Dana's book.

Although Dana is described in many textbooks as "California's first great literary writer," his attitudes were based on emotion and not fact. He described Californio's, like Mariano Vallejo, as settlers who could produce little for themselves. Dana charged that Indian servants produced the labors of Mexican California's economic success.

Dana's writings set the tone for future American attitudes. When Americans came west, they looked upon the Mexican and California as indolent settlers who had done little to capitalize on California's enormous land potential, sea and port resources and proximity to the China trade. Dana was typical of foreign intruders who criticized the tendency of Californians to celebrate holidays and create an atmosphere which was more social than economic.

Alfred Robinson, a foreign merchant, who married into the de la Guerra Family, settled in Santa Barbara and produced an autobiographical tome critical of California. *Life In California*, published in 1846, described local citizens as "generally indolent" and addicted to gambling, drinking and pleasure. Robinson, like Dana, became a major source for early historians and popular writers who interpreted Mexican California.

There was another side to Robinson's book when he described the dress of the wealthy rancheros. Jose Arnaz, a local ranchero, during a fiesta wore: "shoes of deerskin embroidered with gold or silver threads, breeches of cloth, velvet, or satin reaching to the knee..." Robinson also found the women to be pretty "but plain." Perhaps the strangest comment Robinson made on local dress was that some rancheros "of the higher class dress in the English style..."

FIGURE 4-1. Mariano Vallejo.

Many European American travelers found little to praise in Mexican California. This simplistic view obscures achievements in trade, politics and religion. There were also differences over skin color, economic privilege and political rights, but these were subtle ones. As a result, historians have interpreted Mexican California as a pastoral historical era, one of Halcyon Days.

Halcyon Days and the Foreign Intruder

Mexican California's relaxed atmosphere has been described as "Halcyon Days." What Leonard Pitt defines as "Halcyon Days" is simply a calm, relaxed, prosperous period where there was no need to engage in competitive capitalism. This tendency to ignore capitalism bothered many foreign visitors and they commented upon "a different business climate." The reality was that Mexican California had a strong business impulse with foreign traders and local businessmen engaging in regular commerce. There was also a strong internal economy directed by the rancheros and a select group of city businessmen.

The Pastoral Era in Mexican California was a period of slow but steady economic growth. It was also a time in which aristocrats, like Mariano Vallejo, had the wealth to create a luxurious lifestyle. Visitors to the Vallejo home remarked that his wife, Benicia, had a household staff which she directed with grace and elegance. She made sure that each of her children had a servant. School was an important function. Literature, music and the arts occupied the Vallejo's life. There was an aristocratic side to Mariano Vallejo's family which impressed foreign visitors.

Unfortunately, the foreign visitors who didn't witness Vallejo's successes were the most widely read observers. Sir George Simpson, Governor in Chief of the Hudson Bay Company, visited California in 1841 and wrote that "the population has been drawn from the most indolent variety of an indolent species." In a classic example of the colonial mentality, Simpson concluded that "Californians are a happy people, possessing the physical pleasure to the full..." The implication was that the ranchero, the city merchant and the common worker had no desire to earn a respectable living. Drinking, gambling and personal pleasure, according to Simpson, were the primary traits of the Californian.

The reasons for these stereotypes are complex ones. The past had an extraordinary influence upon Mexican California. Beginning in the 1770s and 1780s, the initial California settlers were the gente de razon or the Castilian Spaniard. They were the pure blooded Spaniards who observers like Simpson believed had a special understanding of Hispanic values. With strong ties to the king, a degree of wealth and a lifestyle which emphasized privilege they were not typical settlers. By the 1820s, the gente de razon were in the minority. They were less than 20% of the population, but to foreign visitors, like Simpson and Vancouver, they represented the typical Californian.

FIGURE 4-2. Mexican California: A Pastoral Scene.

It is ironic that the first stereotypes resulted from French, English, American and Russian observations. The literate government official, the scientist and the writer all reflected the prejudices of foreign observers. None understood the Hispanic influences upon California.

The constant conflict in Mexican California challenges the notion of a calm society, and the tensions among local citizens were invariably racial ones. These tensions were due to the complex relationship between local settlers and the economy. Often foreign traders exaggerated the differences between ranchers and businessmen. However, economic goals were most important. Since the Franciscan missions were the major source of wealth, Californians hoped to share in the sale of church wealth. The secularization of the missions was ordered by the Mexican Government in the mid-1820s, and from this point, the sale of mission land, livestock and craft industries was the key issue in Mexican California.

Governor Jose Echeandia and Mexican California: A Cultural Crisis and the Missions

In 1825, the arrival of the first Mexican Governor, Jose Echeandia, created a crisis in California culture and politics. The native born, Spanish speaking Californios had created a defined society. One that was neither Spanish nor Mexican. The primary thrust of Mexican California was land settlement and local commerce. Californios immediately urged Echeandia to open mission lands to lay settlers, and they suggested foreign merchants and skilled American artisans be granted citizenship.

The new Governor hesitated, thereby beginning two decades of dissatisfaction with Mexican governors. Echeandia failed to recognize the power of the Diputacion and temporarily suspended it. The result was

that a few years later, Echeandia had to beg the Diputacion's leaders, Juan Bautista Alvarado, Jose Castro and Mariano Vallejo, for funds to govern Mexican California. The rise of local influences was dominant and Mexican authority never took hold. Part of the problem was Governor Echeandia's personality and style of government.

Jose Maria Echeandia was a tall thin Lieutenant Colonel in the Army Corps of Engineers who had ambitions to become the Director of Engineers in Mexico. He was a petty bureaucrat with strong ambition. But he was a bland, ineffectual administrator. He was careful not to offend the church at a time when there was universal hostility toward the Franciscan Order and the mission system. He quickly lost the respect of local citizens.

Echeandia lacked common sense. Among his worst blunders was his decision to make San Diego the capital of Alta California because of its excellent weather. There was almost a religious feeling for maintaining Monterey as the capital.

When the secularization plan was announced, Governor Echeandia handled it clumsily, and many suspected that he opposed breaking up church wealth. It took Governor Echeandia four years to implement a small part of the initial secularization plan. Local rancheros were supposed to buy up the hide and tallow trade, but Echeandia refused to take this trade away from the church. He criticized the Californios for being too aggressive economically and politically.

Mariano Vallejo and others complained that Echeandia was working with the Franciscans. The best example of the Governor's sympathy for mission economic activity was his Indian policy. Indian labor on the missions, Echeandia argued, had to be maintained for Alta California's well being. This idea was contrary to the power and influence of the large ranchos. It also violated the government mandated secularization plan.

Mission secularization was a twenty year process which emphasized the low opinion that most Franciscans had for the Indian. Father Narciso Duran at the Mission San Jose was particularly venal. He wrote: "The Indians want the freedom of vagabonds." Implicitly, Father Duran charged that the Native American was unwilling to work. This was a common perception amongst the Franciscan Order. The Indian's hostility to the mission system was evident in a number of well publicized incidents.

When Father Sanchez, the president of the mission system, freed a group of Indians at the Mission San Gabriel they accosted him for the Franciscan's years of hostility. He was verbally abused by the Indians and some even made threats of physical violence. Father Sanchez died broken hearted a few months later. By the mid-1840s, secularization was part of the transition of race relations in Mexican California. There was an attempt to mainstream the Indian population into California society. This instant citizenship was a dramatic failure. How did the Indian fit into the fabric of Mexican California society?

The Indian's Progress in Mexican California

The Indian was almost forgotten in Mexican California. From 1821 to 1846, as the missions fought with Mexican officials, foreign settlers and the newly empowered ranchero worked hard to make California society socially and economically vibrant, and the Indian was an important, if ignored, member of society.

The Mexican Government recognized problems between the Indian and the mission system, and they attempted to reform local attitudes. In 1823, Secretary of State Lucas Alaman reported to the Mexican Government: "It is necessary to consider other interests than those of the missionaries..." He urged the Mexican Government to try to understand the Indian culture, and to consider some economic reforms in order to bring the Indian into the mainstream of local society.

Mexican California settlers complained about the lack of Indian culture and religion. As a result, there was a tendency to view the Indian as a practitioner of black magic or witchcraft. In 1826, at the Mission Santa Inez, an Indian, Tomas, was accused of witchery. He cast a spell on the Indian wife of a soldier by touching her hand with a stick. She became ridden with pain, made sounds like a pig and had little black hairs growing from her mouth. The local alcalde (mayor), Adriano, testified extensively about this tale, and a frightening folklore of Indian witchcraft emerged.

A few years later, another sorcery case occurred when a group of sick Indians were taken to a dancing house and cured by offering glass beads to the devil. In both cases, the strength of Indian religion overwhelmed the Franciscan leadership and caused the rate of conversion to dwindle. Coyote tales resurfaced and the missions failed to Christianize the Indian. Mexico recognized this problem and attempted to legislate a place for the Indian in local society.

When the Mexican Constitution of 1824 was forwarded to California, the Indian refused to swear loyalty to the new government. California was now a territory governed by the Mexican Congress. But Mexico found it difficult to control California because of institutions established by the early settlers and the Indians. These institutions included the Diputacion which began as an advisory council and became a legislature, the Reglamento of 1779 which created local laws and the increasing power of the alcaldes who governed the lay cities. The rise of local democracy also influenced the

California Indians as they became independently minded during Mexican California.

By the 1820s, as Coyote tales resurfaced, there was talk of the old tribal ways. The Indian revolts of 1824 were the final blow to the belief that the Indian was happy with the mission system. Santa Barbara was one of the missions seized, and this act symbolized the defiance of the California Indian. Not only was Santa Barbara the most prosperous mission, but the myth persisted that the Indian converts were happy. However, nothing was further from the truth. Franciscan friars throughout California complained about the lack of Indian commitment to the mission way of life. Father Gonzalez de Ibarra wrote to Jose Antonio del la Guerra that the Indian didn't feel an obligation to the mission system, and the great experiment in Christianity was over.

As the mission decline continued in the 1830s, there was immediate approval from the Indian population. Secularization was a process where from 1826 to 1842 one or two missions a year sold off its land, livestock and craft industries to the rancheros and went permanently into the business of saving souls. Once secularization was complete, the missions faded into oblivion. The Indians, according to Father de Ibarra, were not interested in having their souls saved. By the mid-1830s, baptisms were a fifth of what they had been during the Spanish period.

The cause of Indian revolts varied. The series of well publicized Indian rebellions at the Mission Santa Cruz, the Mission Santa Barbara, the Mission Purisma Concepcion and the Mission Santa Inez were the result of oppressive discipline. There were also charges of sexual abuse and punishment for infanticide. These revolts highlighted the brutal attitudes of the Franciscan Order.

In 1831, Indians burned the small Franciscan settlement near San Bernardino. The Indians were furious when the Franciscans ventured away from their mission and attempted to extend their influence into San Bernardino. This extension of the Mission San Gabriel was attacked by the Paiutes under the leadership of Perfecto. The message was clear; the mission system was not in the realm of Indian life. Perfecto was typical of Indian leadership; he suggested that any act of expansion by the Franciscans would be viewed as an unfriendly one.

Indian Revolts and the Foreign Settler: William Hartnell and the English Impulse

By the 1830s, the Indian revolts made foreigners suspicious about California's future. "Many soldiers ...do not know how they are going to settle with their growing families," one settler remarked.

The influx of foreign settlers had a strong impact upon Mexican California. Not only did foreigners employ Indians as paid labor but they also treated them with kindness and dignity. When the Russian settlement at Fort Ross hired contract or day Indian labor, it had great success. The Indians showed up and spent the day working. As one Russian field supervisor remarked: "The Indian is without peer in the fields." This is exactly the opposite of what the Franciscans found on the mission system. The Indian refused to work on the mission because it was little more than a sophisticated system of slavery.

When Mariano Vallejo visited Fort Ross, he was shocked by how hard the Indian worked. He noted that the Indian not only put in a full week's work but understood that the money earned them had to be spread out over a week. Vallejo wondered what made the Russians such excellent employers. He also had trouble understanding the Indian's superior work ethic.

The Russians were not the only foreigners settling in Mexican California. In the summer of 1822, a young Englishman, William Hartnell, landed in San Diego in search of a trading agreement with Mexican California officials. The road to California began for Hartnell in Lima, Peru where he worked with the English merchant John Begg. Eventually, Hartnell and two business partners launched an enterprise in Mexican California.

The hide and tallow trade was in its infant stages when Hartnell landed in Monterey and met with Father Mariano Payeras, the president of the mission system, and Governor Pablo Vicente de Sola. Hartnell's proposition was a simple one. He would create a flourishing cattle industry and develop a lucrative trade in hides and tallow. Governor Sola and Father Payeras were impressed with Hartnell's sincerity and intrigued by his manner of dress and language. Hartnell's clothes were Latin American, not English, and he spoke a fluent and idiomatically correct Spanish. He seemed to be a businessman who would help the local economy. The local reaction to Hartnell was cordial and suggested that business minded foreigners were welcome in Mexican Californian.

Although foreign visitors integrated themselves into the social order, they were not immediately accepted into Mexican California. But William Hartnell was a different breed of foreign settler. He built a rancho near Monterey and called himself Don Guillermo. He married into one of the most influential local families, the de la Guerra family, and he adopted the life of the Californio aristocrat.

Not only was Hartnell a wealthy rancher but he also became one of California's most influential foreigners. The Californio leader, Mariano Vallejo, frequently sought his council, and when the Diputacion met, it asked Hartnell's opinion on business matters. Hartnell gave his children Spanish names and he adopted the manners and culture of the Californio.

From 1825 to 1831, in his dealings with Governor Jose Echeandia, Hartnell was careful not to alienate the Mexican Governor. Echeandia believed that Hartnell was the best person to market mission goods. Hartnell urged Governor Echeandia to trade with Fort Ross and take advantage of Russian goods. The English businessman suggested that Fort Ross was a potentially lucrative market for Mexican California goods. The economic successes of Echeandia's half-dozen years as governor owed a great deal to Hartnell's advice.

For more than a decade Hartnell made a substantial living selling mission goods, and, as a result, he became a defender of the mission economy. There was little Hartnell could do to prevent the disintegration of the economic system. In 1835 and 1836, as Governor Jose Figueroa secularized eleven of the twenty-one missions, Hartnell did what he could to make the process economically fair to the church.

Because of his friendship with leading Californios, Hartnell was a strong supporter of Juan Bautista Alvarado's Home Rule program. Since the mid-1820s, when Mariano Vallejo formed the Monterey Secret Society, there was a movement to secure a local governor. The notion of a native born governor was a controversial one and did not sit well with the Mexican Government. For a decade, turmoil swirled in Mexican California. Hartnell wrote the Mexican Government indicating that it could bring peace to California through the appointment of Alvarado as the new governor. In 1836, when Alvarado became governo, one of his first acts was the appointment of Hartnell as the mission tax collector.

The position as mission tax collector prompted Hartnell to travel to the missions and exact only a small tax. Soon Don

Mariano Vallejo considered Hartnell a meddler, and when Hartnell showed up at the San Rafael Mission, Vallejo arrested him. The honeymoon was over between Hartnell and local Californios. The issues were ones of religion, race and business, and they boded ill for the future.

Hispanics and Anglos: An Adjustment on the California Frontier

The first American Overland Party arrived in California in 1841. Its leader John Bidwell asked John Sutter how many Americans were in California. He was surprised that fewer than one hundred non-Mexican settlers lived in California. Those who did wore the clothing of the Californio vaquero and spoke fluent Spanish. Thomas Oliver Larkin was the most prominent American to fit this mold.

Larkin, a native of Charlestown, Massachusetts, immigrated to California in the early 1830s and became a respected businessman. Not only did Larkin remain a Protestant and an American, but he also opened stores laden with goods from incoming vessels. His personality was a mild one, and he was noted for his good sense and even temper. He counted Mariano Vallejo and Governor Juan Bautista Alvarado as his closest friends. In appearance, Larkin was a Californian. He dressed in the leather outfit of the vaquero, rode a horse with an elaborate saddle and portrayed the manner of the Californian. It was in his personal attitudes that Larkin differed from Mexican Californians.

In Larkin's view, the Californio wasn't a sophisticated businessmen. It was a subtle form of racism that Larkin practiced as he lectured his good friend Mariano Vallejo on the "responsibilities of capitalism." In addition to taking a dim view of local business attitudes, Larkin believed that Mexi-

can Californians lacked the proper work ethic. The rancheros, in Larkin's view, didn't drive a hard bargain. They needed to learn the lessons of American capitalism and democracy. Because of his viewpoint, Larkin became a strong proponent of American annexation.

In 1843, Larkin was appointed the American consul in Monterey. He reported regularly to the United States War Department. Larkin's dispatches were filled with facts about the weakness of Jose Castro's Native Cavalry, the ineptness of former Home Rule Governor Juan Bautista Alvarado and, finally, Larkin concluded that the Californians were an indolent lot. His reports praise the manners, lifestyle and cordiality of Mexican California, and he urged the U.S. War Department to recommend annexation.

Larkin was motivated by his view of the Californios. He believed that they could not accommodate themselves to the advancing technology, the wave of world trade and the concept of competitive capitalism. Despite his close personal ties to Alvarado, Castro and Vallejo, Larkin believed that American annexation would benefit Mexican California. The reasons were largely racial ones. The Californios were simply too slow in formulating economic attitudes, Larkin argued, to maintain local growth.

The American Consul Thomas Oliver Larkin played a key role in annexation. For three years he lectured Vallejo on California's advantages in becoming an American province. When President James Knox Polk took office in March 1845, Larkin found the man who would annex California. He began flooding President Polk's office with letters and reports. Larkin's message was a simple one. California was an untapped economic frontier and necessary for a stopping off point to the Far East.

In October 1845, Larkin was appointed a "secret agent" to advise the President on how annexation might be accomplished.

Eventually, Secretary of State James Buchanan wrote Larkin about annexing California: "The interests of our commerce and our whale fisheries on the Pacific Ocean demand that you should exert the greatest vigilance in discovering and defeating any attempts which may be made by foreign governments to acquire a control over California." Buchanan instructed Larkin to speak negatively about the Mexican Government but should not appear to take sides.

Larkin's appointment as a secret agent was the catalyst to southern California's hostility toward American control. The last Mexican California Governor, Pio Pico, remarked from his Los Angeles home that

Larkin was a Yankee who was overly critical of local authorities. Pico charged that Larkin's economic interests often destroyed his judgment. When Larkin appointed a Los Angeles American, Abel Stearns, as his confidential assistant, Governor Pico suggested that they were attempting to foment a revolution.

In a letter to Stearns, Larkin suggested that: "The fate of this Country...must... change by some means." Juan Bandini, a Los Angeles ranchero, warned Pio Pico about American intentions. Pablo de la Guerra, a Santa Barbara ranchero, was another critic who believed that the gringo political advice was self-serving. Southern Californians

FIGURE 4-3. French Pirates in California. Courtesy Library of Congress.

complained to Vallejo that the presence of foreign settlers was too vast. They worried about the large ranches, the private armies and the penchant for trouble making from foreign settlers. However, no one was more troublesome than John Sutter.

In 1839, John Sutter's New Helvetia was settled and quickly became the focal point for foreign settlers. In the spring of 1846, an American, Lansford Hastings, arrived at Sutter's Fort,and he noticed that 250 new Americans had settled in California. The hostility toward the Spanish speaking was overwhelming as the increasingly bellicose American population armed itself to ward off Jose Castro's Native Cavalry.

In Monterey, the Mexican California Government warned Sutter's Fort about its aggressive, anti-Mexican behavior. On April 17, 1846 an order from Governor Pico reminded government officials that foreigners who were not naturalized citizens would be liable for expulsion.

What bothered Governor Pico was the extensive criticism of his rule. The abuses in land settlement by Americans was also a problem. American land law created different attitudes and concepts of settlement, and the foreign visitors didn't recognize the sanctity of the rancho. Sporadic violence by American settlers and business interests was another problem.

Bibliographical Essay

Douglas Monroy, *Thrown Among Strangers: The Making of Mexican culture in Frontier California* (Berkeley and Los Angeles, 1990) is a study of Spanish and Mexican California which corrects many past misconceptions of race relations. Also see, Rudolfo Acuna, *Occupied America: A History of Chicanos* (New York, 1981) and Tomas Almaguer, *Racial Fault Lines: The Historical Origins of White Supremacy In California* (Berkeley, 1994).

Most myths and stereotypes regarding this era result from Hubert Howe Bancroft, *California Pastoral, 1769-1848* (San Francisco, 1888). Also see Theodore Hittel, *History of California* (San Francisco, 1897) for another view of Mexican California. An attempt to correct some of these early views is James D. Hart, *American Images of Spanish California* (Berkeley, 1960). The best brief corrective to these views is Albert Camarillo, *Chicanos in California: A History of Mexican Americans* (San Francisco, 1984).

See James R. Gibson, *Imperial Russia In Frontier America* (New York, 1976) for the background to Fort Ross.

Contemporary observers add a great deal to Mexican California's history. See, for example, Jose Bandini, *A Description of California In 1828* (Berkeley, 1951). Also see Richard Henry Dana, *Two Years Before The Mast* (New York,1840).

On the economic side of the missions, see Robert Archibald, *The Economic Aspects of the California Missions* (Washington, 1978). For a dated but useful look at the missions see, for example, Fr. Zephyrin Engelhardt, *The Missions and Missionaries of California* (San Francisco, 1908).

Manuel Servin, ed., *An Awakened Minority: The Mexican American* 2nd edition, (Beverly Hills, 1974) remains an indispensable book detailing the rising of political activism among the Spanish speaking.

Del Wilcox, *Voyagers To California* (Elk, Ca., 1991), chapters 9 and 10 offer some interesting sidelights to Mexican California and annexation. Contemporary diaries are also useful in establishing conflict between Mexican Californians and foreign intruders. See, for example, George Simpson, *An Overland Journey Round the World, During the Years 1841 and 1842* (Philadelphia, 1847).

For American traders see Richard Batman, *James Ohio Pattie's West* (Norman,1986). James J. Rawls, *Indians of California: The Changing Image* (Norman, 1984) and Robert F. Heizer and Alan F. Almquist, *The Other Californians: Prejudice and Discrimination Under Spain, Mexico, and the United States to 1920* (Berkeley, 1971) are important in placing the Indian within the context of Spanish and Mexican California.

5

Spanish Speaking Foreigners in California

From the Mexican War to Statehood

Americans viewed Mexican California as a land incapable of creating an efficient and effective government. In the observations of American settlers, there are constant references to the rancho system as an archaic form of capitalism. The Manifest Destiny which Anglos brought to California suggested that progress, capitalism and democratic values were possible only with American rule., thus, embracing the notion of Anglo Saxon superiority. In 1845, an American magazine editor, John L. O'Sullivan, coined the term Manifest Destiny in the *Democratic Review*. Suddenly, a national passion to seize California emerged.

This carefully defined Anglo attitude surfaced during the last days of Mexican California. Thomas Oliver Larkin, the American Consul in Monterey, predicted economic advances through Anglo capitalism. It is not surprising that conquerors like John C. Fremont believed that nonwhites were inferior and this notion eventually justified the war to seize California.

When the Mexican War broke out in May 1846 it was the result of the larger forces of American expansion. For years Texas and California were Mexican possessions that the United States hoped to annex. Prominent Americans coveted Texas for its natu-

ral resources and geographical location. But California was considered the bastard stepchild of the empire. An American Government envoy to Mexico, Nicholas Butler, spoke of the "backward nature" of Mexican California. Few Americans recognized the economic force of the ranchos.

Although California was the least significant Mexican possession, it still held an intriguing place in the American mind. The earliest Yankee attitudes were racially oriented ones. Anglos believed that the Mexicans were not only "indolent" but had a penchant for extravagant behavior. Because Mexican California was an isolated society, race conscious Americans believed that it was populated by half civilized settlers.

On the eve of the Mexican War, President James K. Polk suggested that commercial penetration of Mexican California would result in instant riches. In Polk's comments, the notion that Mexican Californians had somehow waved a magic wand and created a strong economy was an idea that many Americans shared. It is not surprising that President Polk promoted the war to seize California ranchos. If this did not work out, Polk counseled, the San Francisco port would offer a potentially lucrative world trade.

The leading American military figure in California, John C. Fremont, emphasized that the Spanish speaking people needed civilization. From 1844 to 1846, as he explored California with the Army Corps of Topographical Engineers, Fremont created many stereotypes about Mexican California. He suggested that the Mexican rancheros were lucky and not particularly skilled. Fremont labeled the Native American population as a "ready source of cheap labor."

Historians have overlooked Fremont's language. He insulted Jose Castro's Native Cavalry; he urged settlers at Sutter's Fort to take Mariano Vallejo a hostage, and Fremont charged that Mexicans kill all American settlers. Fremont's language was personally insulting, and his derogatory descriptions of local ranchos angered Vallejo and Castro. However, it was the economic side of American annexation which demonstrated the most significant racial attitudes which established and nurtured the idea of Yankee superiority.

The earliest European American hostility toward Spanish speaking settlers developed during the first half century of American trade. Throughout the late eighteenth century, American sea captains developed negative attitudes which they imparted to race conscious newspapermen and government officials. In 1796 when the first American ship, the Otter, sailed from New England into California, the rich trade in hides and tallow prompted one sailor to remark: "Californians are a slow lot who don't deserve their land." This statement was typical of those uttered in the next half century. What was it that Americans coveted about California? The answer was simple-land, commerce and the control of an economically sound civilization.

The agriculturally rich lands, the fine ports and the available Indian labor prompted Americans to urge the conquest or purchase of Mexican California. Ameri-cans coveted the region for almost two decades prior to annexation. The rise of Manifest Destiny prompted American newspapers to suggest that there was "a moral mission to occupy Mexican land."

The Spanish speaking population developed a Mexican capitalism very similar to its American counterpart. This proved to be a bone of contention to the American conqueror who needed to establish Mexican stereotypes to denigrate the capitalistic advances during Mexican California. The Spanish and Mexican land grants were a model of sophisticated business activity, but the racially conscious Anglo would not recognize this profit making enterprise.

Mariano Vallejo was typical of the Californio ranchero. He employed a large group of workers, but he failed to pay a daily or weekly wage. Although Don Mariano was a fair man, it was customary to pay the employees a share of their work effort. The concept of wages was alien to Vallejo, and this practice ran counter to American capitalism. Vallejo's Petaluma Adobe was a self-sufficient community with small landowners and a communal lifestyle. To American and other foreign settlers this was an uncivilized way of life. So foreign intruders, led by Americans, hoped to purchase California as a Pacific Republic and eventually make it into an American state. For more than a decade there was intrigue and outright American conspiracy to seized Mexico's northern most possession.

President Andrew Jackson and the Early Spirit of Manifest Destiny

As early as 1829, American expansionists hoped to persuade President Andrew Jackson to purchase Mexican-California. During the next seven years, Jackson read everything he could about the San Francisco port. As a result, he believed that Mexican

California had an unlimited economic potential. But there was a racially insensitive side to Jackson's view of Mexican California.

President Jackson suggested that the Californios lacked the skills and intelligence to develop their economy. An old friend, Colonel Anthony Butler, urged Jackson to "trick the Mexicans." The land could be bought, stolen through diplomacy or simply seized in war. Butler believed that Mexican Californians were unsophisticated people who could easily be exploited.

In 1835, Colonel Butler traveled to Mexico and offered to purchase Northern California. Butler admitted that the port of Yerba Buena (San Francisco), the rich lumber lands and the fishing industry were attractive to American investors. However, Southern California, Butler informed the Mexican Government, was a wasteland. Butler was fixated on the San Francisco port trade. Tales of port and agricultural wealth were exaggerated by American travelers. These stories were a catalyst to Butler's zealous attempts to annex California. The Mexican Government was suspicious of him, and the ensuing negotiations created bitter feelings.

On a trip to Mexico City, Butler reviewed his mission from President Jackson. He was instructed by Jackson to bribe the Mexican Government, if possible, and steal California via a sophisticated agreement. Butler was pompous and officious when he met Mexican officials. This attitude paved the way for failure.

When the Mexican Government formally received Butler with a lavish state dinner, government officials were incensed by his condescending attitude as he spoke disparagingly of local food and labeled Mexican customs as "primitive." Mexican culture, Butler remarked in a letter to President Jackson, was "base" and "tasteless." He also concluded that Mexicans were "slow and lazy." By offering bribes to Mexican officials,

Butler alienated the government. When Butler told General Antonio Lopez de Santa Anna that the United States would purchase Northern California to develop the San Francisco port for Far Eastern trade, Santa Anna predicted war.

The Mexicans were incensed that President Jackson hoped to purchase not only California but Texas and New Mexico. Who did the Americans think they were and why did they display such a haughty attitude? As Professor Andrew Rolle suggested: "Butler returned home in disgrace." Not only was the Mexican Government incensed by the superior American attitude, but it threatened to fight in order to keep Texas. War was inevitable.

Who Supports American Annexation?

There were many Mexican Californians who sympathized with the Americans. Long before the Mexican War broke out there was sentiment for American annexation. In 1844, Juan Bandini, a Southern California ranchero, argued that Yankee business was important to California's future. He remarked to Pio Pico that American Government certainly couldn't be any worse than that of Mexican Governor Manuel Micheltorena. The Mexicans, Bandini argued, were tyrants while the Americans were at least economically motivated. Perhaps of the two evils, Bandini informed Pio Pico, the Americans were the easiest to understand. There were other leading Spanish speaking Californians who supported American annexation.

Mariano Vallejo admired the industry and tenacity of American settlers. A few months before the Mexican War broke out, Vallejo publicly lamented the lack of effective Mexican Government. This explains why Vallejo was so supportive of American settlers. Vallejo and his brother, Salvador, helped Yankee settlers who moved into Petaluma and Sonoma. Soon a small group of Yankee ranchers lived peacefully in Vallejo's domain. They traded with the Vallejos amidst an atmosphere of friendship and economic cooperation. Vallejo was commissioned to make land grants and continuously granted land with the provision that it be settled within a year. He warned that speculation was the worst influence and would bring in the wrong elements.

When the large land owner American Consul Thomas Oliver Larkin called a meeting at his home in Monterey to announce support for American annexation, Vallejo not only attended but delivered an impassioned speech favoring American rule.

However, not all Mexican Californians supported annexation. There were many rancheros and businessmen agitated by American sentiments. The Yankee attitude, Jose Castro argued, was based on a false assumption that Mexico had no interest in the local economy. Californios were angry over rumors that stated Mexico was going to sell California. This promoted a boisterous local nationalism.

Mariano Vallejo, Jose Castro and Juan Bautista Alvarado developed Home Rule to let Mexico know that Californios had the right to decide their own future. For a decade they petitioned Mexico for a native born, Spanish speaking governor. Vallejo organized the Monterey Secret Society and urged Californios to become economically self-sufficient and politically sophisticated. The results were immediate, and Mexico recognized the strength of local nationalism.

Finally, in 1836, Alvarado was named governor and six years of Home rule ensued. Although Home Rule was not due to Jackson's expansionist politics, it did provide a rationale for local controls amidst Jackson's bellicose expansionism. The rise of strong local controls was due to pressures from the American Government.

President Jackson angered Mexican California. His self-serving comments did little to endear Americans to the local population. Colonel Butler never traveled to California, but his presumption that the land was for sale caused a ground swell of local nationalism.

Colonel Butler and other Manifest Destiny enthusiasts believed the Mexican Government would give up California in return for $3.5 million dollars. This offer only insulted Mexico. As a result, relations between the United States and Mexico were strained until an official declaration of war took place. Since the Mexican War didn't break out until May 1846, this made for more than a decade of acrimonious bitterness.

There were other nations that coveted California. France's Eugene Deflot de Mofras sailed into California and suggested a French protectorate. "A French protectorate," Mofras informed Jose Castro, "offers to California the most satisfactory way of escape from the angers that threaten its future." In 1841, Mariano Vallejo wrote Governor Juan Bautista Alvarado warning him of France's interest in Mexican California. Vallejo believed that foreign intruders, whether French, English, Russian or American, had little interest in the future of the Californio ranchos. The preservation of local land, the maintenance of profitable businesses and the continuation of Hispanic culture was paramount in Vallejo's thinking. He argued that American interests would be more sympathetic to the Spanish speaking, and he pointed to settlers like Thomas Oliver Larkin to justify his pro-American viewpoint. But Vallejo was critical of some foreign settlers.

Meddlesome foreign intruders like Johann August Sutter, a Swiss German merchant, angered Vallejo. Every action taken by Sutter was self-serving, Vallejo argued, and he pointed to Sutter's lifestyle to prove his contention. When Sutter arrived in Monterey he had fled Europe in debt, abandoned his wife and children and failed in business ventures in Latin America, Hawaii and along the Santa Fe trail. Sutter was typical of the frontier businessman. He looked for economic fads to exploit. A plan to develop a lumber industry brought Sutter to Monterey. Soon he was weaving tales of economic success while requesting a large land grant from Governor Juan Bautista Alvarado. An argumentative and self-centered man who asked for special favors, Sutter created strong anti-foreign feelings.

His character was also questionable. A tall, thin man with a penchant for dramatic dress, Sutter traveled with an entourage of Indians dressed in colorful French military uniforms. When making a formal entrance, Sutter was proceeded by bevy of young women throwing flowers at his feet. The nubile, nearly naked young Hawaiian and Indian women who traveled with Sutter made him appear like a prince. To Vallejo and other Californios, Sutter represented the worst excesses of the foreign intruder. He was vain, pompous and hostile to the Californios. But he did have some economic success. After just two years of settlement in 1841, Sutter began negotiations which resulted in the purchase of Fort Ross from the Russian-American Company. Not surprisingly, Vallejo hoped to purchase Fort Ross. The personal differences between Vallejo and Sutter reflected an intense racial hostility. Sutter frequently called Vallejo "a greaser with business interests." Vallejo responded by questioning the Swiss-German's character.

Sutter, like many foreign intruders, judged Mexican California's economy harshly and stereotyped the Californio as "indolent." Soon Americans and other foreigners fomented the Bear Flag Revolution which set the stage for the United States to annex Mexican California.

California's unique and distinctive history of ethnic relations took shape during the Mexican War. From the initial thrust of American interest, there was a systematic exclusion of Mexicans and Californios from American economic, political and social institutions. There were few new businessmen with Latin roots; the school systems were segregated and Latin surnamed politicians weren't asked to run for political office.

Once California was annexed, the property owning Mexican ranchero class was destroyed with the passage of the Land Law of 1851. This federal law forced Californio rancheros to defend any disputed land claim. When an American settled on his land, the Mexican American rancher took the case to the land commission. Invariably, the Spanish speaking rancher won in court. However, the cost of successful litigation often forced rancheros to sell their land to pay attorney's fees. It was a sad situation.

Americans defended the Land Law of 1851 and proclaimed that it was not biased or prejudiced. Despite these self-serving pronouncements, the Land Law of 1851 destroyed the Mexican American aristocracy and placed the Spanish speaking in a position of second class citizenship.

The road to second class citizenship began long before the Mexican War. Tensions between Californio and foreign settlers built from the time Lansford Hastings brought the first American settlers into Sacramento in 1842. Another American, Thomas Oliver Larkin, helped to alloy these fears by talking about the positive contribution of Yankee business. At Sutter's Fort there was constant agitation against the Spanish speaking. With less than a thousand Americans and other foreigners in California, few took these troublemakers seriously. But the Americans were organized and determined to form an independent Pacific Republic or to be annexed by the United States Government. They feared the Spanish speaking population and hoped to set up a separate pro American government. This led to the infamous Bear Flag Rebellion.

FIGURE 5-1. Thomas Oliver Larkin. Courtesy Bancroft Library, University of California, Berkeley.

Prelude to the Mexican War: The Bear Flag Revolution

In May 1846 when the United States and Mexico went to war, it was over Texas. Initially, the Mexican War had little to do with California. The remote California province was not considered a settlement plum and its small population, uneven economy and multi-ethnic settlement made California a curiosity to foreign observers.

Mexican California was a divided settlement when war broke out, and immediately, there were law and order problems. At Sutter's Fort settlers were concerned about Jose Castro's Native Cavalry. As he left for Oregon in the spring of 1846, John C. Fremont stopped at Sutter's Fort and told the residents that the Californio army might strike at any moment. When he stopped at Sutter's Fort, Fremont created paranoia among American settlers. He talked at length about Castro's plan to attack Sutter's Fort. Not only did Fremont act rashly, but

he spent an inordinate amount of time writing letters which justified his behavior. "I was but a pawn, and like a pawn, I had been pushed forward...." This is how Fremont recalled his role in California's annexation. This statement from Fremont's *Memoirs Of My Life*, published in 1887, was one of many justifications for his cowardly presence in Mexican California

Other Americans made the local population anxious. A U. S. Marine spy, Archibald Gillespie, rode into Mexican California quietly taking notes on Castro's troop strength, the fortification of the Monterey harbor and the general feeling concerning American annexation. Everyone knew that Gillespie was a spy, and that his disguise as a spa builder or a pots and pans salesman was simply a ruse to cover his true identity.

At Sutter's Fort there were discussions about the intentions of Castro's Native Cavalry. William Ide, a Mormon who led a group of Americans who hoped to establish a Pacific Republic, argued that the pro-American faction had to foment a revolution and form a free and independent republic; then request American annexation of Mexican California. The supporters of this idea called themselves Bear Flaggers, and they quickly made up a flag with a bear on it. They were determined to take an important Californio ranchero as a symbolic hostage to guarantee the safety of Sutter's Fort. The decision was made to seize Mariano Vallejo.

The sun was not shining but the birds were singing in Sonoma, California on the morning of June 6, 1846 when General Mariano Vallejo rose to drink his strong coffee. Vallejo was smoking a large cigar and thinking about his family when suddenly, the kitchen door burst open and thirty armed Americans rushed into the house. They were from Sutter's Fort and informed Vallejo that he was the prisoner of the newly formed Bear Flag Republic.

Ironically, Vallejo invited the men to stay for breakfast. He broke out large jugs of wine and a cook began making tortillas and eggs. The wine quickly vanished and Vallejo brought out three more bottles. The Americans explained that Jose Castro had driven horses through Sutter's Fort and they feared for their lives. The American population was small. There were perhaps two hundred American settlers and the Mexicans numbered more than seven thousand. The Bear Flag leader, William Ide, was made the spokesman because he was the only sober person, and he informed Vallejo that he was being held hostage for their security.

Dona Francisca Benicia Carrillo Vallejo, Don Mariano's wife, remembered the Bear Flaggers as "uncouth, dirty and confused." They were also dangerous. But Vallejo was the local Commandant and represented the power and prestige of the Mexican Government. If the Americans wanted to arrest him, Vallejo reasoned, he had no choice but to stand up to them. There were no Mexican troops nearby and Vallejo's duties were ceremonial. Pride, however, dictated that he would not shrink from the challenge. He demanded that the Americans declare themselves in a state of rebellion.

The Bear Flag Revolution was a classic example of ethnic conflict on the Mexican California frontier. Sutter's Fort, soon to be Sacramento, was not only the center of American settlement, but the Yankees had lobbied for some time for American annexation. For years Jose Castro, the commander of the Native Cavalry, intimidated and threatened American settlers. Castro was not violent; he simply demonstrated who was in charge. So the Bear Flag revolt was a means of answering Castro's militarism.

Two months passed before Vallejo was released from Sutter's Fort. His health had suffered and his rancho was in a precarious state. Surprisingly, Vallejo was not hostile to American annexation efforts, but he hoped to retain elements of Spanish and Mexican culture. Vallejo was never openly hostile to foreign settlers.

Throughout his career Vallejo welcomed leading American businessmen to Mexican California. In 1832 when Thomas Oliver Larkin began doing business as an importer-exporter in Monterey, he was intrigued by Vallejo's friendly nature. William Hartnell, the English merchant who settled in Salinas, spoke of Vallejo's kindness. When John Bidwell led the first large scale American wagon train into California, he wrote the Mexicans "had a custom of never charging for anything...." This hospitality intrigued American settlers. Larkin took advantage of it in his business dealings and he became a wealthy man. Vallejo had no idea that his kindness would be viewed as the sign of a weak leader and encourage John C. Fremont and others to urge the immediate conquest of Mexican California.

The Mexican War: Racism and Manifest Destiny

The Bear Flag Revolution was an excuse for California's immediate annexation. As John Bidwell suggested, the Bear Flaggers prompted the American Navy to occupy Mexican California. Racial differences dominated Anglo attitudes. At Stutter's Fort, Americans spoke disparagingly of the Spanish speaking. In 1849, an American magazine, the *Southern Quarterly Review*, wrote that "conquest was inevitable." Despite these boastful statements there was little fighting in Mexican California.

The United States conquest came by default. On July 2, 1846 an American ship sailed into Monterey and Commodore John Drake Sloat easily annexed Mexican California. There was no opposition to American annexation and no one seemed concerned about Sloat's presence. The only casualty was a woman who broke her leg by running down to the Monterey Harbor to watch the Americans land. Sloat quickly left California and turned it over to a new American military leader. The new American military leader, Commodore Robert F. Stockton, who on July 29, 1846 issued a proclamation announcing American annexation became the occupation commander. But Stockton was a racially insensitive and militarily inept leader. His annexation proclamation was a clumsily worded document that made harsh judgments about General Castro and Governor Pico. Not surprisingly, Californios, who had previously accepted the inevitability of American annexation, began to arm themselves. In Southern California there was a noticeable resurgence of Mexican loyalty. So an American military force, under the leadership of John C. Fremont, was dispatched to end Mexican resistance to conquest.

FIGURE 5-2. Kit Carson and John C. Fremont. Courtesy Brown Brothers.

As Fremont prepared his rag tag California Battalion of Volunteers to march on Southern California to quell the rebellion, there was criticism of Fremont. Since December 1845 when he first visited San Francisco and later Monterey in 1846, Fremont was a meddlesome force in Mexican California. He referred to leading local citizens as "greasers" and conspired with others to seize local land. A few years later, Thomas Oliver Larkin helped Fremont purchase the Rancho la Mariposas. Vallejo charged that Fremont was an evil man with a penchant for grabbing Spanish speakers' wealth.

On the eve of Mexican California annexation one of the most important foreign settlers was a young black man named William A. Leidesdorff emerged. In Leidesdorff's career, it is possible to see how the forces of Manifest Destiny and American business conspired to take over Mexican California. As a co-conspirator with Fremont, Leidesdorff was instrumental in California's conquest.

William A. Leidesdorff: A Black California Pioneer and the Seizure of Mexican California

In June, 1841 William A. Leidesdorff sailed into Monterey. He arrived from a six months sea journey, so the handsome young traveler spent a week relaxing. Then he continued on to Yerba Buena (San Francisco). Everyone wondered about Captain Leidesdorff. There was an air of mystery surrounding him.

Leidesdorff was a native of the Danish island of St. Croix and the son of a Danish sailor and a mulatto woman, Anna Marie Spark. After his birth in 1812, Leidesdorff was raised by an English plantation owner and provided with a classical education. An urbane, sophisticated man, Leidesdorff was fluent in German, French and English. He learned Spanish within three months after

FIGURE 5-3. William Leidesdorff.

arriving in Mexican California. In personal conversations, he quoted English poets, talked about Italian artists and lectured on the virtues of the French enlightenment. A tall, handsome well dressed man, Leidesdorff was a dashing figure with the ladies.

Leidesdorff was a highly successful man with an education, and his skin was so light that he appeared to be of the white race; thus, because of his education and background, race was not a question. This soon changed when Leidesdorff visited New Orleans and fell in love with a young woman. After proposing to the young girl, Leidesdorff revealed that he was of mixed blooded ancestry. The girl broke off the engagement and this is when Leidesdorff migrated to Yerba Buena. Crushed by the ro-

mance, Leidesdorff vowed to make his fortune.

Once he settled in Yerba Buena, Leidesdorff became an important merchant. It was in the economic realm that Leidesdorff excelled. He was a pioneer figure in the world cotton trade. Leidesdorff introduced trade between Yerba Buena and Hawaii. His ship, the Julia Ann, filled with silk stockings, tobacco and dried food, traded with the Hawaiians. In five years, Leidesdorff became a rich man from this trade.

The hide and tallow trade was in its infancy and through his wise economic decisions Leidesdorff made enough money to purchase some key waterfront property. He built the largest local house at California and Montgomery Streets and constructed a huge warehouse to store his trading goods. In 1843, Leidesdorff built the City Hotel which was California's first luxury hotel. The City Hotel, at the corner of Kearny and Clay, was distinguished by fine rooms and included a library, reading and billiard room, an elegant dining hall and a lobby suitable for formal entertaining. Leidesdorff personally selected the finest mahogany for the dining room and had a hand carved bar brought in by ship from New York. The furniture and motif had a decided European flair. Visitors marveled at the sophisticated and elegance of the City Hotel.

Recognizing the value of property around Yerba Buena, Leidesdorff bought land on what is now the city of Lafayette. Another key economic decision was to purchase the 35,000 acre Rancho de los Americanos, which was on the southeast bank of the American River and later became the town of Folsom. Leidesdorff had to become a Mexican citizen to purchase the rancho. As his wealth and position increased, he became friendly with John A. Sutter. Soon the two men were business partners and conspiring secretly to promote

American annexation of Mexican California.

After making a series of loans to John Sutter, Leidesdorff realized his mistake. He had lent money to Sutter that would never be repaid. To check on his money Leidesdorff rode to Sutter's Fort where he met John C. Fremont and Kit Carson. They all had dinner with Sutter and talked about the rumored war with Mexico. Initially, Fremont didn't trust Leidesdorff and he mentioned to Carson that a black man with money was suspicious. In time, Leidesdorff won Fremont's trust and impressed the American explorer with his detailed knowledge of Mexican California military defenses. Soon they became good friends. Race became a question when Leidesdorff was wealthy and able to invest wisely. Suddenly Fremont, Carson and Sutter considered Leidesdorff "a Negro."

While he engaged in political intrigue, Leidesdorff continued his well developed business genius. His shipping runs between Honolulu and San Francisco on the Julia Ann, made him a rich man. But he was more than just a brilliant businessman, Leidesdorff had a penchant for science. He introduced California's first steam ship, the Sitka, and he talked incessantly about technology and developed engineering projects.

Because of his financial wizardry, Leidesdorff was selected by President Polk to be Yerba Buena's vice counsel. In this position he issued credentials to U.S. citizens and represented the interests of the American Government in Yerba Buena. He also kept in close touch with Monterey's Thomas Oliver Larkin, and maintained voluminous files on the differences between the United States and Mexican government. There were some who believed that Larkin and Leidesdorff were conspiring to bring about California's annexation.

During a meeting with Larkin on January 24, 1846, Leidesdorff discussed the Mexican Government's decision to restrict foreign settlers. Leidesdorff and Larkin agreed that war with Mexico was imminent. For three months rumors of war dominated Mexican California. Soon Leidesdorff was in the middle of a conspiracy to annex California. One of the co-conspirators was Archibald Gillespie.

In late April 1846, U. S. Marine Lieutenant Archibald Gillespie rode into Yerba Buena with a request from Counsel Larkin to brief Leidesdorff. Gillespie met Leidesdorff for dinner and confessed that his mission was to collect intelligence on Mexican California's military strength. This would prepare John C. Fremont's California Battalion of Volunteers for the final conquest of California. The military intelligence passed on to Fremont was that the Mexican army and the Californio Native Cavalry was weak and unable to protect California. This made it easier for President Polk to seize California because he would not need a large army or navy.

When Yerba Buena became San Francisco in 1847, Leidesdorff was one of its leading citizens. He had not only purchased large parcels of local real estate, but he also developed this land into a sizable fortune. Leidesdorff had a number of other thriving business and was an established name in city politics.

But a series of unforeseen events changed Leidesdorff's life. He became involved in the first organized horse racing business venture and was arrested by Alcalde George Hyde. The real reason for Leidesdorff's arrest was that Hyde hoped to dominate local horse racing. Leidesdorff protested to Governor John McDougal who ordered Hyde to resign and then proceeded to introduce and develop horse racing.

Then gold was discovered on Leidesdorff's land and he was on the verge of becoming wealthier than any man in California. With both economic and political power there was talk of appointing Leidesdorff to public office. This never materialized as he died suddenly on May 18, 1848. Leidesdorff was only 36 years old, and he had never married nor had children and he left no will. The $60,000 estate was taken over by the court.

A U. S. Army quartermaster, Lt. Joseph L. Folsom, found Leidesdorff's mother, Ann Marie Spark, and she sold her son's estate to Folsom. When Folsom returned to San Francisco he quickly renamed the ranch near Sacramento and set up a town to supply miners in the Sierra Nevada region. Folsom became the gateway to gold country. Although William Leidesdorff spent only seven years in California this African American pioneer created an economic and political legacy. Today only a small alley named after him remains in San Francisco, but despite what little remains of his name, he was a dominant force in the transition to American California.

John C. Fremont and the Mentality of Conquest

No one symbolized the mentality of conquest more than John C. Fremont. Once the Mexican War broke out, Fremont lurked in the background with sinister intent. Because of financial and logistic problems, the United States couldn't send an army to California, so Fremont became the commander of a makeshift military unit, the California Battalion of Volunteers. Due to Fremont's excesses, Southern California armed itself and for a time resisted American annexation. The reason was a simple one. Fremont's racial attitudes were barbaric. He had executed the venerable ranchero Nicholas de los Reyes Berryesa and then pompously called it a mistake. Bernardo Garcia, Berryesa's foreman, had witnessed the attack, and he alerted the Californios to Fremont's lies.

FIGURE 5-4. John C. Fremont.

In Los Angeles, Pio Pico warned Californios and Mexicans about Fremont's intentions to enslave Californians. Although Pico may have been too hard on Fremont, he did influence the Los Angeles native cavalry leader Serbulo Varela to issue a proclamation in which he accused the American Government of attempting to "oppress and subjugate" Californians. Varela stated that the Americans were putting "us in a condition worse than that of slave, are dictating to us despotic and arbitrary laws." For three quarters of a century Spaniards and Mexicans controlled their own destiny. They had formed a Diputacion (legislature) to govern themselves, a Reglamento (Code of law) to enforce law and order and they had secularized Franciscan mission wealth. Now, suddenly, American institutions took these advances away.

The last Mexican Governor and the leading Los Angeles citizen, Pio Pico, wrote to leading rancheros urging them to bring together local cavalry units. By August 1846, Southern California was armed and ready to fight. There was no other solution for the Americans but to impose strict law and order. Captain Archibald Gillespie, commander of the American occupying force in Los Angeles, announced a curfew. He jailed anyone who spoke out.

Varela organized a local army and planned his attack. He threatened to drive Gillespie out, and three hundred men joined Varela. This was three times the normal native cavalry. In order to achieve military precision the Californios selected a Mexican army officer, Jose Maria Flores, to lead them into battle. Two respected Los Angeles military-political figures, Antonio Carrillo and Andres Pico, were placed as the second and third in command. It was difficult to find guns and ammunition, but a sympathetic wife of a wealthy ranchero, Rafaela Cota, emptied her store of guns so the rebels could defend themselves.

What amazed the Americans was the precision and valor of the Californio army. Andres Pico took command of the Californio Native Cavalry and trained it to defeat American troops. The Californios won some spectacular victories against the U. S. troops. From August to October, 1846 the Spanish speaking army won a victory at Chino and then one at the Rancho Dominguez. By October 8, Gillespie and his troops were driven from Los Angeles. However, as Californios took charge in Southern California, there was concern about Spanish speaking rights in American California. Pio Pico was the strongest critic of American annexation and he suggested that second class citizenship and servitude to "Yankee ideas" was a possibility.

The major battle which delayed American annexation of California took place on

FIGURE 5-5. Pio Pico: The Last Mexican California Governor. Courtesy California Department of Parks & Recreation.

December 8 at San Pascual just north of San Diego. Although it was a brief skirmish, the Americans lost eighteen men and suffered a psychological defeat. What made the Californio victories so devastating was their ability as horsemen. They surrounded American troops and cut them to shreds with their guns and swords. A series of quick, decisive victories was as important for psychological reasons as it was in delaying the total conquest of California. When American conquest of California was complete, Fremont turned into a bully.

Fremont let it be known that Andres Pico would be arrested. This created even more tension. Pico recognized Fremont's self serving comments as an attempt to bolster American power. The Californios made it clear that they would rearm and once again resist American annexation if they were not granted full citizenship.

John C. Fremont sent a short note to Pico suggesting a compromise. The spirit of the pronunciamento was well and alive in California. On January 13, 1847, Fremont and Pico met at Cahuenga Pass and negotiated a treaty ending California resistance to American annexation. The Californios were allowed to keep their guns, horses, property and were pardoned for all crimes real and imagined. The Treaty of Cahuenga was negotiated without authorization from the President. What was even more outrageous took place in mid-January, 1847 when Fremont informed local citizens that he was the new governor. Fremont simply usurped this power and had no authority from President Polk. As Vallejo suggested, Fremont was pompous personality blended with outright fraud. But he still became a national hero. The Great Pathfinder, as Fremont was known, was credited with conquering Mexican California.

Because of his abuses of power, Fremont was recalled from California and subjected to court martial proceedings. He was a popular national hero and this forced the President to accept Fremont's resignation from the army. Eventually, he returned to California and became the first United States Senator. To the Spanish speaking, however, he was the embodiment of Anglo racism. His legacy was one of suspicion and repression.

California was now formally a part of the United States. For the next two years there was a tenuous peace in Southern California. Then in January 1848 James Marshall discovered gold and attention was diverted to the gold fields. The Southern California ranchero was able to sell full grown steers for thirty to forty dollars a head. This was a tenfold increase in price since the hide and tallow days. Thus, cattle and agriculture became Southern California's gold in the years prior to statehood.

On September 9, 1850 when California became the thirty first state, a system was in place which set up second class citizenship for the minority population. The next group of ethnic settlers would find an American California and a new set of racial attitudes. Conflict in the mines, agricultural areas and the cities intensified ethnic difficulties.

Bibliographical Essay

H.H. Bancroft, *History of California* (volumes 1-4, San Rafael, Ca., (1886); Robert G. Cleland, *The Cattle On a Thousand Hills* (San Marino, Ca., 1951); A. Ogden, *The California Sea Otter Trade, 1784-1848* (Berkeley, 1948); W.W. Robinson, *Ranchos Become Cities* (Pasadena, 1939).

John William Templeton, editor, *Our Roots Run Deep: The Black Experience in California, 1500-1900* (San Jose, 1991) is an interesting collection of non-traditional materials on the African American experience. Rudolph Lapp, *Blacks In Gold Rush California* (New Haven, 1977) is an invaluable source on William Leidesdorff and the general ethnic atmosphere surrounding the Mexican War. Also see, Donovan Lewis, *Pioneers of California: True Stories of Early Settlers In The Golden State* (San Francisco, 1993), chapter 28 for a treatment of Leidesdorff. Useful in analyzing the attitudes of local settlers are Richard A. Dillon, *Fool's Gold: A Biography of John Sutter* (New York, 1967) and Harlan Hague and David J. Langum, *Thomas O. Larkin* (Norman, 1990).

Ronald Takaki's, *A Different Mirror: A History of Multicultural America* (New York, 1993) contains an excellent chapter on the Mexican War and California's role in this pivotal event. Equally important is Douglas Monroy, *Thrown Among Strangers: The Making of Mexican Culture in Frontier California* (Berkeley, 1990) for its study of Indian and Mexican influences. Also see, for example, Myrtle

McKittrick, *Vallejo: Son of California* (Portland, 1944) for the role of this Californio pioneer in the Bear Flag Republic.

See David J. Weber, ed., *Foreigners In Their Native Land: Historical Roots of the Mexican Americans* (Albuquerque, 1973) for an interpretation of the Spanish speaking as foreigners in their own land. Also see Carey McWilliams, *North From Mexico: The Spanish Speaking People of the United States* (New York, 1968). For a contemporary view of Mexican California see, John Bidwell, "Life In California Before The Gold Discovery," *Century Magazine* vol. 41, no. 2 (December, 1890). Richard Griswold del Castillo, *La Familia: Chicano Families In the Urban Southwest 1848 To the Present* (Norte Dame, 1984) is an excellent book on the social side of the Mexican American experience.

For Mariano Vallejo's role see Alan Rosenus, *General M. G. Vallejo And The Advent of the Americans* (Albuquerque, 1995).

Kenneth Goode's, *California's Black Pioneers* (Santa Barbara, 1974), pp. 21-34 provides an excellent history of early black governors and their role in Mexican California and annexation.

One of the most revealing contemporary articles showing the influence of Manifest Destiny is "The Conquest of California," *Southern California Quarterly*, vol. 15 (July, 1849), pp. 411-415. Also see Rodolfo Acuna, *Occupied America: A History of Chicanos* (New York, 1981).

For the forces of Manifest Destiny see, for example, Reginald Horsman, *Race and Manifest Destiny: The Origins of American Racial Anglo Saxonism* (Cambridge, 1981) and Ronald Takaki, "Reflections on Racial Pattern in America,' in *From Different Shores: Perspectives on Race and Ethnicity in America* (New York, 1972).

For biographical information on key figures in the Mexican California era see, Donovan Lewis, "William A. Leidesdorff," in *Pioneers of California: True Stories of Early Settlers In The Golden State* (San Francisco, 1993), pp. 313-321. Also, see Richard Dillon, *Fool's Gold: A Biography of John Sutter* (New York, 1972) and Harlan Hague and David J. Langum, *Thomas O. Larkin, A Life of Patriotism and Profit In Old California* (Norman, 1990).

The concept of white supremacy is developed in George M. Frederickson, *White Supremacy: A Comparative Study In American and South African History* (New York, 1981). Frederickson believes that the term white supremacy is preferable to racism because it allows one to see how and why the dominant group discriminates.

To understand John C. Fremont's seminal role in California annexation see, Andrew Rolle, *John Charles Fremont: Character As Destiny* (Norman, 1991) and Allan Nevins, *Fremont: Pathmarker Of The West* (rev. ed., New York, 1961, 2 vols).

6

Ethnic Differences

From the California Gold Rush to San Francisco, 1848-1856

In late January, 1848, James W. Marshall was sent to the south fork of the American River, roughly thirty miles from Sutter's Fort, to build a sawmill. With a crew of Indians, a few Mormon settlers and some casual Indian labor, Marshall began constructing a sawmill. During the early morning hours of January 24, Marshall rode his horse down to the construction site. A sluice box had been built to catch the logs. During the night the crew drained the river bed. The next morning Marshall noticed small shiny flecks in the riverbed. He smiled. There appeared to be small nuggets of gold in the ground.

When Marshall discovered these gold flakes he remembered the Indian legends. For years Indians regaled Marshall and his boss, John Sutter, with stories of large veins of gold. Most people ignored these Indian tales. But two Californios, Mariano Vallejo and Jose Castro, had told similar tales of gold found by Indian, Mexican, Chilean and Peruvian miners. Walter Colton, Monterey's Alcalde, wrote that he had witnessed numerous small gold finds. Rumors of Franciscan gold hoards abounded. But despite the stories and legends no one had witnessed a large and permanent gold find.

Many Californians heard the rumor of a gold strike near Coloma, but it was months before Sam Brannan, a Mormon merchant, drove a huge wagon into San Francisco with large glass jars filled with painted sand to resemble gold. As he rode down San Francisco's streets, Brannan hollered, "Gold! Gold! Gold from the American River!" This brazen publicity device in mid-March, 1848 was designed to attract customers to Brannan's mercantile stores. He hoped to make his fortune by selling goods to prospective miners.

As Americans, Mexicans, Latin Americans and other foreign nationals heard about the gold strike, they descended upon the Sierra Nevada. Few knew how to identify gold and even fewer knew anything about the actual mining process. The gold rush of 1848 was a social romp, complete with heavy drinking, gun fights and vigilante action. In this atmosphere ethnic differences escalated into open conflict because oftentimes foreign miners were more skilled than their American counterparts.

The impact of the gold rush changed California's character and direction. The influx of American miners, businessmen and lawyers altered Hispanic social, economic and political institutions. Food, clothing, music and social interaction took on an American character. Suddenly the Spanish speaking were in the minority. However, it was only in the Sierra Nevada that the Spanish speaking became second class citizens.

In Southern California the discovery of gold created a demand for beef. This allowed local rancheros to retain their economic position and social-political power. The new millionaires included the Pico, Carrillo and de la Guerra families who retained their power and influence due to business success. The price of cattle soared to seventy five dollars a head in the half dozen years after the gold rush began. This created an immediate prosperity, but it also prompted American settlers to stream into the cow counties. Soon Los Angeles, San Diego and Santa Barbara became predominantly American towns.

Enterprising Americans recognized that food was a concern. In Southern California William Wolfskill began to grow oranges. In 1841, he planted his first orange grove but had little success marketing the new product. Once the gold rush began, Wolfskill was able to make his fortune. By the early 1850s he grew two thirds of California's oranges. In his writings and comments to other ranchers, Wolfskill preached about the problem of finding good labor. He described the Spanish speaking as "slow learners who didn't understand agriculture."

Wolfskill, like most Americans, failed to recognize the skill of foreign miners. The gold rush led to an influx of Chilean, Peruvian and Mexican miners who quickly dominated the gold fields. There was instant racial conflict and demands for laws and taxes to exclude foreign miners. A racially sensitive atmosphere emerged; the end result was that the Spanish speaking left gold country for the agricultural areas and large cities. The migration to the fields and urban centers was due to a lack of employment opportunities in the mines.

Chileans in the California Rush: The Genesis of the First Race Riot

Once gold was discovered the only skilled miners were Mexicans from Sonora and a few Chileans and Peruvians. Initially, Chileans and Sonorans migrated north in such large numbers that a local camp became a major gold rush city-Sonora. The 5,000 Mexicans who lived in Sonora were not only skilled miners but they had defined political ideas. They believed that land claims belonged to the person who established and worked the mine. Chileans who moved into the area found that race conscious Americans lumped them all into a Latin category. The Chileans were talented miners with a strong capitalistic impulse who provide an excellent example of the work ethic that foreign miners brought into California.

The Chilean miners also believed in a liberal land policy. In Mexican California the Colonization Act of 1824 allowed for liberal land grants. This created more than 800 ranchos and more than 700 of these grants were up to eleven square leagues or approximately 49,000 acres. The Chileans pointed out that they had the same right to mining land as they had to ranch property. The American miners quickly let them know that they would not tolerate large ranches in areas of heavy American settlement. Yet, many early American settlers had positive attitudes towards the Chileans.

When T.T. Johnson, an American miner, met a group of Chilean workers on Weber Creek in April 1849, he marveled at their entrepreneurial attitudes. They were not only skilled miners but they had an economic vision of California's future. A Chilean newspaper advertised for two hundred young girls willing to immigrate to California for marriage. The ad described the fortunes made by Chilean miners in the Golden State, and the California dream was written into the advertisement. This type of advertisement led to an influx of Latin American settlers. But there was conflict.

By April 1849, Chileans and Mexicans fought over mines and soon Americans complained about Latin violence. This term was little more than a stereotype to blame the Spanish speaking for law and order in the mines. Conflict in the mines prompted a large portion of the Spanish speaking population to settle in San Francisco. In May, American miners near Jamestown took offense at the Mexican flag and tore it down. They fired shots at Mexican miners, and one was killed. Much of the hostility to foreign miners was the result of their fortunes. Therefore, a few Chileans and Peruvians with substantial gold moved to San Francisco.

Soon tensions in San Francisco escalated between the Chilean population and local settlers. On July 4, 1849, the first race riot in California history took place in an area of San Francisco known as Little Chile. This enclave of foreign settlers at the foot of Telegraph Hill saw race conscious American and British settlers burn the Chilean settlement to the ground. The Regulators, a private police force, attacked Chilean families in tents on one of the city's sand dunes. Racial slurs were shouted as the Chileans beat off the intruders. Once the riot subsided the legacy of fear and repression reminded the Chileans that they were strangers in a strange land. But not all Americans found the Chileans a threat.

The Mexican Gold Rush: A Business Impulse and Racial Exclusion

One of the prevailing myths of the gold rush is that Mexican Californians had little

interest in business and no means of merchandising their gold discoveries. Nothing is further from the truth. There were a large number of skilled Mexican miners who found their fortune in California during the early days of John Sutter's gold bonanza. There were more than 1300 Spanish speaking miners, many of whom came from the Mexican state of Sonora, who were as skilled as any American miner.

The anti-Mexican attitudes which dominated the gold rush were due to the professional nature of Spanish speaking gold miners. Americans were also critical of the Mexican use of Indian and mestizo labor who worked for half of their gold find. Americans miners called this slavery. The irony is that this charge was often made by Southern miners who brought in African American slaves. The overlord or patron, as the Mexican labor contractor was known, hired the Indian and mestizo to the chagrin of Americans. The *Columbia Herald* published a series of articles indicting the Mexicans for abusing their labor supply.

The hostile attitude toward Mexicans was fueled by the moralistic Baptist preachers who roamed the Sierra Nevada looking for sin. Slavery was a sin to the fanatical anti-slavery zealot, and it was much easier to criticize the Mexican than the American slave owner who operated a nearby mine.

It was the business success of the Mexican which infuriated Americans. To cut into the profits of Spanish speaking miners, freight companies began charging Sonoran traders higher rates by raising the $7 standard rate to $75. An enterprising Mexican trader brought 10,000 pack mules into California and sold them to the "Sonoran Peddlers" for from $150 to $500 a head.

Don Antonio Coronel, the Mexican-born Los Angeles businessman and school teacher, made a fortune in the gold fields. He helped Francisco Lopez near Newhall from 1842 to 1846 and then he secured another fortune on the Stanislaus River. But when Coronel went to Hangtown (Placerville) it was a mistake. One Sunday he saw a notice which requested all non citizens to leave California within 24 hours. Coronel laughed at the notice and ignored it. A few days later, Coronel was one of a number of French and Spanish speaking miners who were seized by vigilantes. Coronel quickly posted bail or a bribe, as he called it, and he moved to another mining camp. But the same problem persisted. The Spanish speaking were seized and thrown out of the camps.

By 1850, the vast majority of Spanish speaking men settled in Sonora. When the Foreign Miners Tax Law of 1850 was proposed it was the direct result of this hostility to foreign miners. The Sonora miners protested the law and for a moment there was a crisis. Sonoran miners were armed and knowledgeable, and they had developed good relations with the California born Spanish speaking miners. There was a temporary fear that they might united to protest the American presence.

The conflict which erupted in the mining regions during the Gold Rush pitted white and foreign miners against each other. The Anglo miners protested that the Sonorans were "unfair competition." Soon Americans began equating the

Spanish speaking miner with black slaves. This made for an atmosphere of racial insensitivity.

Since the annexation of California, the rush of American settlers were critical of Mexican society. From the initial conflict with John C. Fremont there had been bad blood, and the use of the term "greaser" to describe the Spanish speaking was the ultimate racial slur.

Santa Barbara as a Spanish Speaking Enclave and the Ascent of the Yankee Intruder

The only California settlement to escape American control was the Mexican pueblo of Santa Barbara. From 1846 to 1850 Santa Barbara was an amalgamation of Indian, Mexican, Spanish colonial and mestizo influences. The mestizo was the main influence in Santa Barbara, and they had migrated to California from small towns in Mexico. The Catholic Church, the Spanish language and the Hispanic culture survived in Santa Barbara while American influences dominated elsewhere.

Although Mexican society did not experience the same traumatic change as other cities, nevertheless, it did undergo important social and institutional changes. The presidio and mission buildings appeared as relics as new homes and settlers moved into Santa Barbara. Ex-soldiers and their families, as well as itinerant citizens, came into California and settled around Santa Barbara. Soon 200 one story adobe dwellings with red-tiled roofs were scattered throughout Santa Barbara. The presidio and mission no longer controlled Santa Barbara as a group of local settlers dominated the town.

By 1850, Santa Barbara retained a dominant Mexican character. Charles E. Huse, an early American lawyer, settled in Santa Barbara and wrote in Yankee prose that the locals were "negligent, rude...and to a certain degree discourteous." Huse complained that there wasn't a Protestant church in town ,and he called Catholicism "a barbaric form of worship." Huse was one of the growing number of Anglos who made up 20% of Santa Barbara's population by 1855.

The *Santa Barbara Gazette*, a local four page weekly newspaper, was founded by a New England journalist who began criticizing local Hispanic culture. The *Gazette* was instrumental in the Anglo settlement of Santa Barbara as it reflected not only the growing racial tensions but the ascent of Yankee business interests as well.

American settlers did not settle easily in Santa Barbara. There were frequent disagreements over land supplies, business transactions and lifestyle. The *Santa Barbara Gazette* contributed to this growing rift between Anglos and Mexicans because of its editorial attacks on Hispanic culture. The tension between the Spanish speaking settler and the recently arrived American saw both sides arm themselves. An American pioneer, William Streeter, organized a Committee of Vigilance to protect the non-Mexican population. By 1856, the Gazette reported a "racial crime wave," and this newspaper raised fears of increased lawlessness. The tensions in Santa Barbara society were a microcosm of California's racial difficulties.

The Foreign Miners' Tax Law of 1850 and the End of Spanish Speaking Mining Influences

Much of this controversy was a reaction over the Foreign Miners' Tax Law of 1850. This law required a twenty dollar a month permit for foreign miners. When State Senator Thomas Jefferson Green, a Texas slave owner, proposed that the tax be used for state government purposes, the pro slavery Democrats extolled the virtues of the law. Supporters of the Foreign Miners' Tax Law of 1850 argued that it produced almost 75% of the money needed to operate state government.

This statistic hid the racist nature of the California law. The tax was collected by the sheriff and indiscriminately applied. The Spanish speaking miner, rather than applying this exorbitant tax, simply left the mines. Many former boom towns turned into ghost villages. Mining related businesses declined and there were constant complaints about Anglo law and order. The sheriff helped to collect the tax and used it to consolidate his power.

The Foreign Miners' Tax Law of 1850s helped to single out Mexican, Chilean, Peruvian and African American miners for harassment. The Spanish speaking and black miners often found themselves outside the newly established Anglo-American laws. Since Spanish law was based on Roman law, the Mexicans found it difficult to understand American law. African Americans could not vote or testify in court, so their rights were abridged. Mexicans were also not citizens and could not participate in American democracy.

Pablo de la Guerra summed up the Spanish speaking attitude when he protested the land law in a speech before the California State Senate. "They are strangers in their own country," de la Guerra charged in reference to Mexican miners. "They have no voice in this Senate...." de la Guerra concluded. Mariano Vallejo requested that Americans consider Californio rights and end the force Yankee culture.

When American culture and law imposed itself upon California, blacks and the Spanish speaking were excluded from the courts and denied the material rewards of the gold rush. Mexican miners protested the tax as discriminatory. After a near riot took place in Sonora when 5000 Spanish speaking miners protested the tax, the Mexican miners began comparing their plight to that of black slaves. This set up violent confrontations between irritated Yankees and prosperous Spanish speaking miners. Through mob action or vigilante organizations, white throngs ejected the Chinese, the African-American, the Chilean, the Peruvian and the Mexican miner. During these disputes there was continual violence.

The reason for the violent white reaction was a simple one. The Sonorans were skilled miners who made more money than Anglo miners in an openly competitive society. White racism reared its ugly head and the result was arbitrary enforcement of the Foreign Miners' Tax Law of 1850.

Don Antonio Coronel remarked that violence was directed against Sonora miners. According to Coronel these miners were skilled and achieved quick profits. "The Mexican miner," Coronel remarked, "arrived first and understood mining." So the Foreign Miners' Tax Law of 1850 was used as an excuse to expel non-Americans. The Mexican and Chinese were especially singled out for harassment. Finally, the foreign miner simply gave up. Often vigilante mobs and threatening local citizens drove out foreign miners. Sometimes the sheriff would collect the tax five or six times in a month.

In the California gold fields there were often classic confrontations between American values and Mexican working class ethics. The Americans viewed the Sonoran miners as opportunists who were temporarily taking advantage of the gold fields. Since Sonoran miners were more productive than their American counterparts, this further exaggerated the hostile feelings. When a group of Sonoran businessmen brought in 10,000 pack mules and sold them at an immense profit to local miners, a Committee of Vigilance was organized to systematically rid the Sierra Nevada of Spanish speaking miners

As ethnic miners left the Sierra Nevada there was an increase in violence. A small portion of the displaced Mexican, Chinese and English miners often turned to crime. Newspapers created the impression that this was a typical career move. Thus, the stereotype of ethnic crime reared its ugly head. Still there was a problem. Bandits did surface and used race as an excuse for lawlessness. This trend can be traced to the negative impact of the Foreign Miners' Tax law of 1850.

The absence of jobs, land opportunities and political equality created a new class of entrepreneur—the bandit. Soon the outlaw became a noticeable part of California. The Spanish language weekly *El Clamor Public* noted that there was an increase in violence and robbery. There was also a controversy over the place of African Americans in California. Since slavery was still a recognized part of American history, the Golden State was involved in a prolonged battle over the place of blacks within the state.

African Americans and the California Gold Rush: There Is More Opportunity Than Just in the Gold Fields

In September 1848, a young black man was walking near San Francisco's Embarcadero. Smiling at the cool blue water, he savored his freedom. Slavery was rampant in the United States. The North and South were beginning to quarrel over the legality of slavery. In California there was a sense of freedom. Suddenly, this African American found his tranquillity broken. He was approached by a white man who asked him to carry his bags. The black man walked away. After taking a few steps, the black man whirled around and shouted: "Do you think I'll lug bags when I can get that much in one day in the gold fields." The young black man smiled and held up a pouch of gold dust.

This story appeared in a number of American newspapers, and it acted as a catalyst to the migration of the free Negro to California's gold fields. Tales from miners in the Golden State soon found their way into newspapers. The *Albany Argues* printed a letter from a black soldier which suggested that in the mines: "The merest Negro could make more than our present governor." Not surprisingly, free blacks migrated to California in large numbers. By 1850, an abolitionist publication, the *Liberator*, carried a letter from 37 black Californians who had formed a mutual aid society. They demanded economic, political and social equality. But, as they suggested, it was the business impulse of black Californians which created a strong African American community.

Soon an all black mining company was formed and a large group of New York African Americans sailed for San Francisco. The *New York Tribune* reported that Reuben Ruby, a black man and a well known antislavery crusader, was headed to California to make his fortune. In general, the African American's who migrated to California were politically active and economically aggressive settlers.

The reason for the African American interest in California was due to the politics of slavery. It wasn't until October 1849 that California declared itself a free state. This was a catalyst to African American migration and created the illusion that California was free from racism. There was also progress in leading California cities. The social and economic freedom in San Francisco helped early black settlers to become prominent in business and settle in their own homes without incident.

Black seamen who jumped ship in San Francisco were among the first Americans into California's gold fields. One of the eastern cities which sent black settlers to California was New Bedford, Massachusetts which was a haven for fugitive slaves. By 1851, slave hunters were so prevalent in New England the *New Bedford Mercury* advised fugitive slaves to migrate to California. Unwittingly, the fugitive slave debate was brought to California because of this appeal.

Although the Californians drafted a State Constitution forbidding slavery, they still allowed the devices of second class citizenship to intrude on their constitution. The California Constitutional Convention of 1849 relegated African Americans to second class citizenship. The earliest draft of the California constitution limited suffrage to "white male citizens." African Americans were denied the right to vote, to hold public office, to testify in court against white people, to serve on juries, to attend pubic schools, or to homestead public land. This injustice attracted black ministers who moved west to challenge the prevailing myths about African American settlers.

T.E. Randolph, a Marysville minister, was one citizen who heeded this plea to go west. Born a Virginia slave, Randolph fled to New Bedford. By 1851, he was in California and quickly became a leader in the African American community. Marysville was a small, northern California town settled by liberal Democratic party voters who came west to find total freedom. In this environment Randolph safely pursued his antislavery political agenda. Randolph, a staunch supporter of a free state constitution, crusaded for black education. He launched a series of law suits to challenge segregated education. Johnson equated education with the right to vote. He joined David Ruggles, a free Negro, in urging African Americans to donate a dollar a month for free schools. They were supported by another San Francisco black businessman, William Henry Hall, and the state set up an excellent, although still segregated, San Francisco school system. Because of these advances, there were those who hoped to legally restrict black rights.

In 1858, assemblyman J. B. Warfield introduced a bill to bar African Americans from entering California. Immediately, T.E. Randolph waged a relentless campaign to defeat the Warfield Bill. It failed to pass the California legislature despite being introduced on four separate occasions. The United Colored People of California organized a campaign to defeat any laws restricting African American rights. The bill did have its effect as half of California's black population moved to Victoria, British Columbia.

But the gold mines and lucrative farm land continued to lure large numbers of black settlers. They saw it as a chance to achieve economic equality. There were two important black leaders who emerged during the gold rush. The Reverend Barney Fletcher, a former slave, arrived in Sacramento and proceeded to earn enough money to purchase his wife and children from the slave owner. Barney then organized Sacramento's first black Methodist Church. Morality, economic independence, education and responsible citizenship were Rev. Fletcher's themes in his popular Sunday sermons. Soon, other preachers arrived to challenge the dominant white population.

In 1853, James R. Starkey arrived in San Francisco after purchasing his freedom in North Carolina. Starkey, a businessman, was a leader in the San Francisco black community. He worked tirelessly to secure the right to testify in court for African Americans. In 1863, when full court privileges were granted for blacks, Starkey was ecstatic. Due to African Americans like Barney and Starkey the black population doubled from 1850 to 1853. Yet, African Americans were only about one percent of California's population.

Black Californians had opportunities other than in the gold fields. Black cooks in San Francisco were paid $125 a month at the height of the gold rush. A Kentucky born free black, known simply as John, earned his passage to California by cooking for a group of German miners. The Hagerstown Indiana Mining Company traveled to California with a young, free black cook Harry Whithe.

How Withe fit in with the Indian miners suggests that there was an element of equality on the California frontier. He was referred to on the company list as "Harry Whithe: Coloured Boy-cook." Once the Hagerstown Mining Company began operation, Withe was an equal member. He was paid a fair salary, he had good living conditions, and there were few signs of overt discrimination. Withe saved his money and settled on a farm.

The social relationship between whites and blacks was in some cases a solid one. One California gold miner remembers: "Negro songs being sung....dancing...good food." These comments ran heavily through the journals of 49ers. While many slaves were brought into California by their masters, there were also a large number of free African Americans who made their way into the Golden State.

As hundreds of blacks crossed the United States and entered California a steady stream of East Coast newspapers advertised for steamship travel to California. Soon large numbers of free black men were sailing into San Francisco Bay. These early African American settlers were free men of means who often had a marketable skill.

The black leaders who migrated to San Francisco quickly became community leaders. Abner H. Francis arrived from Buffalo, New York and wrote a series of letters describing the freedoms in California. Francis remarked that he didn't experience one racial slight, and these letters widely circulated among African Americans which led to another large influx of black settlers.

African Americans in the California Mines: The Economic and Cultural Changes

It was in the mines during the gold rush that black Californians made their strongest impact. When James W. Marshall discovered gold in January 1848 there were less than 30 blacks in California. By the census of 1850 there were almost a thousand African American settlers. The majority of African Americans lived in small gold mining communities. San Francisco and Sacramento had noticeable, if small, black communities. What role did African Americans play in the gold fields?

The answer is a complex one. Most blacks were free people who mined or worked for wages. They came primarily from New York, Pennsylvania and Massachusetts. The presence of runaway slaves made most black miners politically active. They strongly argued against making California a slave state. By example they often changed racial attitudes by breaking down stereotypes abut African American work habits, living patterns and social life.

In small gold mining communities with names like Negro Hill, Negro Bar or Negro Flat, groups of free African American miners worked much like anyone else. Tales of black gold mining successes quickly surfaced. A young African American, known simply as Dick, took $100,000 from a mine in Tuolumne County.

The *Alta Californian* reported that four miles from Mormon Island in California's first major gold find, a group of African Americans were making a fortune. There were two African American gold mining communities known as Negro Hill. The tale of these two settlements and the differences between them tell us a great deal about the ethnic history of California.

The first Negro Hill, located on the American River near the spot where James W. Marshall discovered gold, provided a fortune for proud and resourceful black pioneers. Negro Hill's wealth was necessary to overcome the disadvantages of bondage and discrimination. High wages and plentiful jobs made early African American settlers prosperous. Negro Hill was exclusively black and this challenged the prevailing stereotype that African American's lacked

good work habits. Since 1849, black miners have frequented the area and found large sums of gold. The tales of gold spread, and soon enterprising black eastern businessmen began the journey west to open a series of black businesses.

This settlement was the work of a Massachusetts African American, known simply as Kelsey and a black Methodist minister. They were responsible for the influx of other black settlers. Initially, this area was known as "the hill" and soon everyone referred to it as Negro Hill. But it was only one source of gold. Another vein was quickly discovered and a second black community known as Little Negro Hill sprung up.

In 1852 two African Americans from Massachusetts opened a boarding house and general store. Soon the large mining community known as Little Negro Hill was organized. Three years later Little Negro Hill had a population in excess of 400. As Chinese and Portuguese miners moved in, Little Negro Hill became the first truly multicultural settlement in the California gold fields. It was in Little Negro Hill that the first signs of ethnic political organization took place as the local residents staged a well organized protest against state laws and local ordinances which discriminated against them. They posted signs protesting proposed state laws which discriminated against African Americans, and they lobbied to defeat unequal laws.

African American Mining Success and the Rise of Racism

Once African American miners established their roots in a Sierra Nevada mining town, there was invariably conflict. In January 1852 California Assemblyman Henry A. Crabb, a southern aristocrat, introduced the Fugitive Slave Bill, and he announced that it was to keep the slave from the gold fields. Crabb argued that the Foreign Miners' Tax Law of 1850 failed to keep the "colored miners from the fields." So he urged the better white settlers to use any means possible, legal or illegal, to maintain a white presence in gold country.

As a result, the Foreign Miners' Tax Law of 1850 and the California Fugitive Slave Act of 1852 were the focus of African American protests. In Negro Hill the example of strong, black politics was an imposing one. When Southerners brought their slaves to work in the nearby mines, there were public meetings denouncing this practice. Unfortunately, the power of the slave holder didn't diminish. The California Fugitive Slaw Law contained a provision which made slaves pay off any debt claimed by their owner. Although California was a free state, slaves were sold openly in public auctions.

Negro Hill protested these sales and made it difficult for the sheriff to overlook this violation of state law. The *Alta Californian* and other leading newspapers quickly became critical of Negro Hill leaders. The idea of an all black California mining town bothered local citizens. This attitude accounts for the hostility to the predominantly African American settlement in Negro Hill. The *Alta Californian* had no problem with the residents of Little Negro Hill and most whites were comfortable with a mixed town.

The differences between Negro Hill and Little Negro Hill were vast. Because Negro Hill was exclusively black, race conscious whites descended upon it and racial problems ensued. There was constant conflict from right wing, pro-slavery organizations, and the American Party complained about the lawless nature of Negro Hill. As proof of this charge they pointed to a young African American who was killed by vigilantes. The Coloma Sheriff was notorious for arresting black miners although most were eventually freed.

Contemporary observers agreed that there were racial tensions. But there were fewer problems in the mixed ethnic atmosphere of Little Negro Hill. Black and white abolitionists co-existed in Little Negro Hill and fought against slavery. The church was also stronger in Little Negro Hill with both black and white preachers urging peace. But there was still occasional white harassment in Little Negro Hill. Although California had an advanced racial climate with a reputation for fairness, there was still constant pressure to prevent the African American population from achieving full economic independence.

As black miners became economically successful violence increased. In Fort John, Benjamin Bowen, a young white Iowa miner, leased land to both white and black miners. After three years of multiracial land leases, a dispute arose between white and black miners. Black mining claims were more prosperous and better developed, and as a result, a group of whites attacked local black miners. When Jack Kimball, an African American, left the area he dropped off a bag of books he had borrowed from Bowen and complained about white racism. When Bowen tried to unsuccessfully talk Kimball out of leaving, a town meeting was called. Local miners addressed the racial problems but one no offered a solution to the brutal beatings black miners experienced at the hands of local vigilantes. So Kimball left for San Francisco. However, there were attempts to work together.

There are a number of cases of white-black business partnerships. When the Reverend Sherlock Bristol left New York, his traveling companion and business partner was an African American, Isaac Isaacs. They opened a mine near Downieville. This small, northern California mining community was the site of the first woman executed by a vigilante mob and the town had a well deserved reputation for eccentric behavior. So a mixed business drew little attention. They tried to quietly work their mine until it was discovered that Isaacs was a boxer. Soon a brawny Kentucky fighter challenged Isaacs to a fight. But when the black boxer agreed, the match turned into a near riot. After the fight began the Kentucky miner pulled a knife in the ring and attempted to kill Isaacs. With a roundhouse left, Isaacs knocked the white fighter cold. Only the calming influence of Reverend Bristol prevented this situation from turning into a full scale riot. The Reverend Bristol calmed the crowd by jumping into the ring and delivering an impromptu sermon on Jesus the boxer who saved souls. The crowd murmured approval and dispersed.

Since not all blacks were free, the slavery issue continually resurfaced. There were a small number of slaves brought into the gold mining towns. Generally, Californians were egalitarian, and the slaves were treated like any one else. Yet, there were still slaves brought into California and no attempt was made to free slaves. The pro slavery Democratic Party faction which followed the ideas of United States Senator William Gwin did everything it could to maintain slavery. The antislavery David Broderick faction challenged slavery. The result was institutional confusion and a California Government which failed to meets its obligation under the law. Even thought the California Constitution of 1849 forbade slavery, the presence of enslaved blacks indicated that authorities winked at the law. This allowed slaves to be brought into the state.

In the spring of 1851, a slave owner used the National Fugitive Slaw Law to jail an African American slave named Frank in San Francisco. The runaway slave had escaped in a Sierra Nevada mine and found housing in the city. The slave owner petitions the court to take his property back to Missouri. S.W. Holliday, a local lawyer, submitted a petition for Frank's freedom. This decision

stunned the pro-slavery community because Judge Roderick N. Morrison ruled that the National Fugitive Slave Law of 1850 had no impact on the case. Judge Morrison stated that Frank had taken his freedom in California and had not crossed state lines. So, Frank was a free man.

The debate over bringing slaves into the California gold fields heated up after statehood. A small group of slave owners challenged the anti-slavery state constitution. In 1850, a Texas Ranger brought thirty-two middle aged slaves into California to work a mine along the Sacramento River. This helped pro slavery propagandists who suggested that the slaves who dug between $15 and $20 a day from the mines were a contented lot.

For example, the settler who identified with the Southern way of life widened racial differences. Colonel William F. English, a Georgia planter, sold his large plantation and moved to Nevada City where he set up a profitable mining venture. An elegantly dressed man with pompous statements on the Southern way of life, English was an aristocrat who so angered the locals that they began making fun of his lifestyle. English owned black slaves who did his mining while the slave women took in washing and hired out for domestic chores. As a result of this forced labor, English became a wealthy man.

Soon there was a level of discontent in and around Nevada City and the turmoil was over the slavery issue. There was a sense of democracy for black Californians. They were excellent miners and blended into the frontier with ease. Most white miners were not threatened by their black counterparts. As J.D. Borthwick, an Englishman, observed: "In the mines the Americans seemed to exhibit more tolerance of Negro blood than is usual in the states...." The California frontier setting was the reason for this liberalism. It also began a trend in race relations in the Golden State.

Ethnic Diversity in the Gold Rush: Some Conclusions

The black miner viewed the California gold fields as a chance to buy his freedom. For that reason, he was a serious and hard working miner. He avoided confrontation, whenever possible, and was a model citizen. "I saw a colored man going to the land of gold," an Ohio miner wrote in his diary. Thus, the gold fields offered this African American a chance to make a new life for his wife and children.

This story was typical of African American miners who hoped to being a new life. The problem that black miners faced was that local authorities did not prosecute the slave owner for violating African American rights. The vigilante committees which sprung up all over the sierra Nevada were intolerant of black miners. This further complicated the quest for equality.

While there was an atmosphere of equality, it was common for white miners to drive off some competing African American miners. The Sweet Vengeance Mine in Brown's Valley was a successful black venture which made Fritz Vosburg, Abraham Holland and Gabriel Simms well to do businessmen. One day Vosburg was jumped by a gang of white miners and in a wild fight the African American stabbed one of the gang members. A national African American newspaper, *The Liberator*, reported that Vosburg was simply defending himself. Some race conscious whites charged that "Negro crime" was becoming a problem. The Sweet Vengeance Mine continued to operate until 1854 and it serves as an example of the success that African Americans had in the California fields.

The legacy of ethnic diversity in the gold rush, however, was to create hostile white attitudes toward African American business success. This would lead local politicians to force the sheriff and the law enforcement community to look at black rights. This began the long road to second class citizenship which dominated the next century of California civilization.

Bibliographical Essay

Rudolph Lapp, *Blacks In Gold Rush California* (New Haven, 1977) is the standard work on the subject. Also see, Richard Dillon, ed., *The Gila Trail* (Norman, 1960) for information on the African Americans who traveled west.

Delilah L. Beasley, *The Negro Trailblazers of California* (Los Angeles, 1919) is an excellent, if often overlooked, source on African American history. Also see, P. Sioli, *History of El Dorado County* (Oakland, 1883) for a contemporary account of the area in which back miners prospered.

The major work on the California gold rush is J.S. Holliday, *The World Rushed In: The California Gold Rush Experience* (New York, 1981). Holliday's excellent book ignores racial issues but contains a combination of biography and epic narrative which makes it a valuable reference tool. Equally important is Rodman W. Paul, *California Gold* (Lincoln, 1947) and Paul's, *Mining Frontiers of the Far West, 1848-1890* (New York, 1963). W.W. Robinson, *Land In California: The Story of Mission Lands, Ranchos, Squatters, Mining Camps, Railroad Grants, Land Scripts, Homesteads* (Berkeley, 1948) is an unusually valuable source. The best book on mines and land is Leonard Pitt's, *The Decline Of The Californio: A Social History of Spanish Speaking Californians, 1846-1890* (Berkeley, 1970).

For Mexican influences upon the Gold Rush and land grants see, Leonard Pitt, *The Decline Of The Californios: A Social History of Spanish Speaking Californians, 1846-1890* (Berkeley, 1970); David J. Langum, "Californios and the Image of Indolence," *Western Historical Quarterly*, 9 (April, 1978); Paul Gates, "California's Embattled Settlers," *California Historical Society Quarterly*, 13 (June, 1962) and Richard H., "Anti-Mexican Nativism In California, 1848-1853: A Study In Cultural Conflict," *Southern California Quarterly*, 62 (Winter, 1980).

Ronald Takaki, *A Different Mirror: A History of Multicultural America* (Boston, 1993), chapter 8 provides an excellent view of the Gold Rush. Also see Tomas Almaguer, *Racial Fault Lines: The Historical Origins of White Supremacy In California* (Berkeley, 1994) for another view of racial attitudes. Howard A. DeWitt, *California Civilization: An Interpreta-tion* (Dubuque, 1979), chapter 6 suggests the importance of ethnicity in the Gold Rush.

For the emigration of the Chinese to California and their early role in the Gold Rush see, for example, Robert Irick, *Ch'ing Policy toward the Coolie Trade* (San Francisco, 1982) and Sing-wu Wang, *The Organization of Chinese Emigration, 1848-1888* (San Francisco, 1978).

7

The Irish-Catholic, African-American and Mexican American

Nineteenth Century Rising Ethnicity

During the nineteenth century the Irish-Catholic, African American and Mexican American in California experienced racism, a closed society and a double standard in housing, employment and public attitudes. Their experiences were different but they had many common traits. Ethnic advancement in the 1850s depended upon politics, economic success and maintaining cultural unity. The Irish-Catholic dominated San Francisco politics; African Americans had a visible economic success, and Mexican Americans retained the Hispanic culture necessary in celebrating California's past. The rise of ethnic voter blocs, special interest newspapers and challenges by groups like the United Colored People of California to offensive laws via the courts helped to establish the power of these ethnic groups.

Once some degree of political power was achieved, each ethnic group carved out a section of the employment market, established a cultural heritage and acted as a watchdog over government challenges to their freedoms. The influx of diverse ethnic groups created changes in the economy. The Irish immigrants left their homeland and New York because of economic opportunity in the American West. When they migrated

to San Francisco it was often because of mechanization and other labor saving devices. The introduction of labor saving techniques in the spinning and weaving trades brought the Irish to America and they left New York when these devices and the general labor condition placed them at the bottom of the job market. As a result, the Irish were a working class population migrating to San Francisco to work on the docks as day labor and in the burgeoning industry in the Golden State. Many Irish workers had a small business mentality and entrepreneurial skills which were unachievable in New York. They quickly became an integral part of San Francisco's economy, because of Irish Catholic politicians like David Broderick. By 1851 Broderick controlled patronage in the California legislature. As a result, patronage political appointments employed large numbers of Irish Catholics in the San Francisco Bay area and the Irish were in political control of the Golden State.

In sharp contrast, the Mexican American worker was gravitating to the expanding agricultural fields and taking service jobs in the cities. In the racial hierarchy, the Spanish speaking retained some power because of the ranchero elite. A large segment of the Mexican American population, the gente de razon or the people of reason, were economically strong and able to ignore Yankee racism. The European descent of the gente de razon impressed class conscious Americans and allowed the old Californio families to retain positions of prominence and power.

Despite their position, Californios and Mexicans still faced a great deal of hostility from American settlers. The hostile reception that Mexican nationals and Latin Americans received was the first indication of Anglo California racism. By 1900 the Mexican American experienced increased hostility as the ranchero elite vanished. The Mexicans were tied to the pastoral economy and this is one of the reasons that Americans believed that they were not suitable as skilled labor. This economy emphasized producing just enough to live on and it failed to live up to the American capitalistic model. As a result of this belief, the Mexican American was placed into a position of second class citizenship.

African Americans often found themselves in direct competition with the Irish because they both occupied the lowest rung on the labor ladder. While the Irish-Catholic opposed the introduction of slavery in California, they didn't have a positive view of African American labor. As the mines declined, black workers left for San Francisco and Sacramento. They also settled in Stockton and Marysville where African Americans were employed as unskilled labor. By 1860, San Francisco had 1176 African Americans and Sacramento 468 residents, and, not surprisingly, both cities were a hot bed of black political and economic progress.

Although there was racial hostility, the Irish-Catholic, the African American and the Mexican American experienced gains in the job market, found housing and began to experience some of the advantages of American democracy. When New York Tammany Hall Democratic politician David

Broderick migrated to California, his political actions guaranteed strong advances for Irish-Catholic settlers. The Irish-Catholic experience suggests how one ethnic group was able to control San Francisco politics by creating a strong political machine, then use this power to gain economic concessions.

The Irish Catholic Experience: San Francisco and White Ethnicity, 1850-1880

In January, 1848 San Francisco was a city with almost 200 buildings and less than one thousand people. The gold rush brought a flood of new settlers, unlimited economic opportunity and a spate of get rich schemes. The influx of Irish workers and the rise of a Democratic political machine under David Broderick created opportunity for the newly arrived migrant.

On March 17, 1851 the first San Francisco St. Patrick's Day parade was held with an air of celebration. The following year a small group of Irishmen organized the Hibernian Society and they approached California State Senator David Broderick for help in promoting Irish causes. Soon another society, the Sons of the Emerald Isle, was organized to find jobs, housing and social activities for recently arrived Irishmen. The result was an immediate Irish-Catholic middle class who controlled much of downtown business while dominating the city and police departments. The Irish were the first to realize the potential for political power by employing their own in city, county and state government.

During the 1850s visitors to San Francisco noted the economic and social success of the Irish. The building industry and many small businesses were Irish owned. They also had a strong influence upon city politics as San Francisco State Senator David Broderick was the resigning Irish-Catholic boss in the California legislature. Later in the 1850s,

Broderick became a United States Senator and developed pork barrel political projects to line the pockets of Irish business interests. This combination of political influence and economic aggressiveness created a strong Irish-Catholic business community.

By 1870, San Francisco was the tenth largest city in the United States and one third of San Francisco's population was Irish-Catholic. The majority of Irish-Catholics were American born and they had a strong sense of their own destiny due to anti-Irish riots in New York and a history of discrimination in eastern American cities. They formed benevolent associations to help each other while they developed a strong economic and cultural presence.

The Hibernia Savings and Loan Society was founded in 1851 and began to help Irish-Catholics invest their funds. From 1860 to 1880, Irish-Catholic economic influences dominated San Francisco. The rise of Irish owned manufacturing companies made San Francisco the ninth largest manufacturing city in the United States by 1880. In the cigar and boot and shoe making industries the Irish ruled California. As craftsmen the Irish were recognized by foreign merchants and tourists.

When an English visitor arrived in San Francisco in 1871, he compared the activity of local commerce to that of England's prosperous Liverpool port. On the docks, Irish-Catholic workers dominated the waterfront and the early labor unions which grew up in San Francisco often had Irish-Catholic leaders. The House Painters' League, the Eight Hour League, the Boot and Shoemakers' Union and the Cigarmakers' Association of the Pacific Coast were unions filled with Irish-Catholic members. They were also led by shrewd Irish unionists who weren't above using their political connections to create advantages for the union.

Unlike African Americans or Mexican Americans, the Irish-Catholic didn't face a closed system of discrimination. Since they were white ethnics, the Irish had fewer doors closed in their faces. The Irish were not poor immigrants when they arrived in San Francisco. They had saved money for the passage west and they had small sums to invest in business enterprises. They spoke the same language and shared the culture of other Anglo-Americans. They simply took over the political and economic institutions in San Francisco and created their own equality. Yet, despite this material success, they faced many obstacles while trying to achieve equality and acceptance.

The early hostility to the Irish-Catholic was blunted by David Broderick. He set up a Ward political system in San Francisco where the Irish were employed in a wide variety of occupations. By the 1860s, the police and fire department were controlled by Irish workers. National magazines and newspapers angered the California Irish-Catholic community by constantly comparing them to Chinese workers. *Scribner's Monthly* examined the Chinese and Irish and concluded that the Irish were lazy. This was a stereotype that Broderick did his best to combat. The Irish made excellent social and economic strides in San Francisco and by the late nineteenth century they controlled the skilled labor market. Irish dominance in the skilled labor market was largely due to Broderick's political influence.

African-Americans in California: An Introduction

The African American experience in California was influenced by the Spanish and Mexican California experiences. Since both Spain and Mexico recognized mixed blooded settlers, there was a historical sense among members of California's black community. There was a strong black presence since the Mexican California era.

As local Californios fought for Home Rule during the 1830, the first African

Americans arrived. On the commercial ships which sailed in from New England, black Americans came west to find their fortune. The prospects for skilled workers was much better in California than anywhere else in America. Consequently, the earliest black settlers were people of extraordinary skill.

African Americans, however, often found it difficult to make their way successfully in California. There was an intense animosity toward blacks in San Francisco and this atmosphere created a number of nasty incidents. In September 1848, a young black man was walking by a San Francisco dock. A white man coming off the ship asked him to carry his luggage. The black man looked indignantly at the white man and walked in the other direction. Then the enraged African American spun around and hollered: "Do you think I'll stoop to lugging trunks when I can get this much in one day?" Holding a large sack of gold in his hand, the black man shook his head and walked away. That same month the *Alta Californian* reported that restaurants, cleaning establishments and small stores were being opened by African Americans who had arrived from in and around Boston.

African Americans invariably came to California on whaling vessels, and the early migrants were accomplished work men. The whaling vessels were filled with skilled seamen and one of the first Afro-Americans to arrive in California, Allen B. Light, married, raised a family and became a respected Santa Barbara citizen. Light was not restricted by attitudes regarding color, because he lived and worked in Santa Barbara, and there was little concern over color in this sleepy Mexican California town.

In town meetings, Light was articulate and suggested programs for maintaining Santa Barbara's natural beauty. Something of an environmentalist, Light was a strong voice against illegal otter hunting along the Santa Barbara Coast. He complained about foreign traders who poached or hunted illegally along the California coast. He was an obscure figure who seldom ventured from Santa Barbara and fit nicely into Mexican California life.

Daniel Rodgers was an African American slave who traveled overland from Little Rock, Arkansas in 1849 in company of his master. Rodgers was promised his freedom if he worked in the gold fields and paid his master $1000. But after paying the money for his freedom, Rodgers' master broke the agreement, and he was sent back to Arkansas. But Rodgers had had a taste of California freedom and made plans to return. A decade later in 1859, he left Arkansas and settled in Watsonville. Located north of Monterey, Watsonville was a liberal, antislavery community. He was readily accepted by local citizens and purchased land. With one other African American family, the Derricks, Rodgers petitioned the local school to admit his children. The school district refused to integrate but did hire a teacher for the two African American families and their children were educated properly. This unfortunate incident is one indication of the lingering influence of slavery in the Golden State. Although California was admitted to the Union on September 9, 1850 as a free state, it was plagued by the slavery debate.

Slavery and California Statehood

In 1849, the national debate over slavery dictated that California would be a free state. This led African Americans to migrate to California. From 1849 to 1852, more than two thousand free blacks arrived in California. Most lived in the mining regions, the farming communities or out of the way rural areas. A few settled in Southern California but no more than half a dozen initially lived in Los Angeles. But there was a large Spanish speaking population with African ancestry and mixed blooded settlers dominated the political-economic structure.

In Los Angeles, Antonio Pico, of African descent, represented Southern California during the Monterey Constitutional Convention of 1849. Not only was Pico an aristocratic rancher, but he was a leading political figure. He recognized that Anglos had hostile racial attitudes. Consequently, Pico was a staunch supporter of a free state. He argued that California's heritage was one of freedom. Certainly slavery would not be tolerated. Pico pointed out that Southerners had brought in only a few slaves and suggested that the individualistic character of Californians precluded the institution's success.

Despite the small number of Afro Americans in Los Angeles, there were some economic successes. For example, Peter Biggs was the leading barber and he invested his money in other businesses. The most successful African American entrepreneur, Robert Owen, had the title to several blocks of property on Broadway near Third Street. In time, locals referred to the area as the "Owens Block." Economic opportunity drew a select African American population.

In the 1850s, the black population was largely male. But by 1854 there were enough families for black children in San Francisco and Sacramento to go to private schools. In San Francisco, the African Methodist Episcopal Church gained a reputation for advanced or progressive teaching. In Marysville and Stockton, black churches and segregated schools sprung up and there was a demand for state tax money to support education. However, it wasn't until the late 1850s that the segregated black schools received California tax money. The California legislature remarked that the tax support was due to the school's "fine educational achievements."

These advances were due to the Rev. Jeremiah Sanderson who was California's first prominent black educator. After migrating from Massachusetts, where he had built a fine reputation as an educator, Sanderson opened Sacramento's first black school and approached the city council for approval to integrate the school. The city council approved but Mayor William English vetoed the politically controversial idea. Then Sanderson took his campaign to other parts of California and was instrumental in black schools opening in Stockton and San Francisco. Sanderson's significance is that he fought for integrated education. He believed that African American children must go to school with their white counterparts. His ideas fell largely on deaf ears because of the racial atmosphere in the 1850s. However, Sanderson created California's first ethnic political controversy.

Afro-Americans and California's Racial Politics: The 1850s

Although California was a free state, the pro-slavery secessionist wing of the Democratic party, led by United States Senator William Gwin, interfered in state politics. Gwin and his political followers constantly pushed for racially defined laws to discourage African American settlers. In the fall of 1850, the first sign of Anglo-American racism occurred when Senator Thomas Jefferson Green of Sacramento began to complain about the presence of blacks in the Golden State. A Texan and a slave owner, Green was not only a bigot but a scientific racist who spouted negative statistics on black abilities. To combat Senator Green, black Californians congregated at the Hackett Hotel in Sacramento and organized an embryo civil rights movement. They wrote newspaper articles, handed out pamphlets on equal rights, set up schools and found jobs for black settlers. A tight knit African American community emerged and challenged the prevalent racism. What amazed foreign visitors like France's Alexis deTocqueville was that favorable attitudes towards slavery were strongest in areas where slaves didn't live in large numbers. In his writings, deTocqueville found the attitudes of Californians negative on race.

In California there was a strong Jim Crow attitude. Jim Crow was a term which identified those who believed that African Americans should be segregated or restricted in eating establishments, social situations, schools and the job market. As one Californian remarked: "We desire only a white population in California." This attitude helped create the United Colored People of California, an African American civil rights group that fought for new laws to outlaw discrimination.

The large number of pro-slavery Democrats who sat in the California Legislature attempted to pass laws prohibiting the entry of blacks and mulattos into the state. In 1849, Antonio Maria Pico, a man with one-eighth black blood, listened at the Constitutional Convention of 1849 to arguments that were white supremacist in nature. Quietly, Pico led a movement to defeat a provision in the California Constitution which would have barred blacks from migrating to California. Pico complained of a "hidden racism" and suggested that "questions of race" occupied many Californians.

When the California Legislature passed a Fugitive Slave Act, it provided a one thousand dollar fine or six months in jail for harboring a slave. Whites were known to drive free black miners from important mining areas and then take their claims away by stating that these men were slaves. Senator Thomas Jefferson Green's bill set the tone for the debate over slavery for the remainder of the first decade of statehood. For a free state to debate slavery meant that race

and class were its primary concerns, and so they were for the Golden State.

It was the large scale employment of African Americans which created these tensions. The California mines were filled with black men who worked in the mining towns as waiters, barbers and deliver men. The mining camps and small towns of northern California had separate churches, newspapers and schools for blacks. There was continual and often violent controversy over the small number of interracial marriages which took place in the gold fields and small towns. Eventually, this forced the African American population to move to the major California cities.

It was the minuscule nature of the African American population that prevented major problems. From 1850 to 1900, black Californians were less than one per cent of the state population. As a result, African Americans were not considered to be an important part of California history. When blacks migrated to California the homestead laws offered a chance for them to claim land. The federal land law system, according to the California Legislature, was meant for white people and in 1860 the legislature passed a concurrent resolution which declared that "a free white person over twenty-one years and a citizen of the United States" was the only person eligible for homestead land.

Black Californians had anticipated this reaction. In 1852, the Franchise League was formed to allow blacks to testify in court and fight attitudes regarding land settlement. However, it was more than a decade before the law was changed to allow for black testimony. Land ownership was another matter, but by the late 1860s, there was a substantial degree of black land ownership. Free blacks could own land and there was an increased willingness to sell farms and city plots to African American settlers. Then the Franchise League organized a campaign to turn out the black vote and garner some political power.

Gordan Chase, a San Francisco black barber, organized a group of political activists after he was robbed by a white man and couldn't testify in court against him. The goal of this activist organization was to create a strong African American political presence in California. In 1855 and again 1857, the Convention of Colored Citizens sent petitions to the legislature asking for the rights to vote and testify in court. The convention also passed resolutions condemning the Dred Scott decision by the U. S. Supreme Court in 1857 which essentially defined slaves as property. But the Franchise League eventually admitted defeat; its members dissolved the organization, and the African American population dwindled in the face of repressive racism.

In 1858, many Afro-Americans left for Victoria, British Columbia and the Fraser gold rush. Canada offered a racial atmosphere free from color prejudice, Gordan Chase remarked, and his comment echoed the feeling of many black Californians.

However, not all blacks left the Golden State. Some African Americans remained in California to live their lives and fight for educational, economic and social reform. The American Civil War and the political changes in California since statehood helped to grant black voters minimal rights. These early successes created an African American political movement which continued to agitate for change.

African Americans and Settling into California: The 1860s

By 1860, there were almost five thousand Afro-Americans living in California. Despite some restrictions, blacks bought property while continuing to press for the right to vote. It was not until 1863,when African-Americans were granted full voting privi-

leges and civil rights, that property ownership was no longer questioned. Full rights were extended in 1870 when the Fifteenth Amendment to the U. S. Constitution prevented the states from denying blacks the right to vote.

In the aftermath of the American Civil War, there was a small, but steady, black migration to large ranches. On the cotton growing farms in the San Joaquin Valley, black field hands were hired. The *Sacramento Daily Union* and the *Stockton Weekly Independent* noted the arrival of field hands who quickly became an important part of the work force. But there were also skilled African Americans. In matters of technology, there were many blacks who excelled in the mines. An ex-slave Mose Rodgers became a respected hydraulic mining engineer and was the superintendent for a company in Mariposa county.

It was in education that the most significant changes took place. The first state sponsored public school education for black children began in 1865 when California law was revised to allow African Americans to attend public schools. Jeremiah Sanderson's crusade for integrated education was successful. In Oakland, an African American school was opened in an old house in what is now East Oakland. Black Californians fought segregation in the courts, and in 1872, African American political activists submitted a test case to the California Supreme Court which led to the admission of blacks students to all public schools. The court ruled in favor of black students and in 1875 segregated schools where closed once and for all. Unfortunately, many school districts ignored the court decision.

It was during the 1860s that Afro-Americans made their biggest gains in California. This was largely due to the emergence of two black newspapers-the *Appeal* and the *Elevator*. Suddenly, personalities, rather than issues, dominated black history. The *Eleva-*

tor argued black Californians had to be more militant about getting the vote. They opposed the election of Democratic Governor Henry H. Haight because he was hostile to African Americans. He won, but the major parties courted the black vote after this election.

Mammy Pleasant: The Mother of California's Civil Rights Movement

Mary Ellen "Mammy" Pleasant was one of California's most mysterious African American pioneers. A Georgia born slave, Pleasant migrated to San Francisco in 1849, and at age thirty-seven found herself in a free state. By 1857, Pleasant through hard work and scrupulously money management secured her freedom.

For a black woman, there were few normal business opportunities. So she went into the entertainment business. In San Francisco, Pleasant quickly became a successful madam who operated a series of high class houses of prostitution. She moved into legitimate business, as the opportunity presented itself, and Pleasant became one of San Francisco's first successful business women. She was very shrewd with her money and quickly became wealthy.

Once Pleasant was worth a large sum of money, she took up the anti-slavery cause. As efforts to defeat the insidious institution of slavery increased in the 1850s, Mammy Pleasant was in the forefront of the civil rights struggle. She provided financial assistance to abolitionists who were arrested for working for African American rights. In 1858, she traveled east and met with famed abolitionist John Brown. The meeting took place in Windsor, Canada and Pleasant presented a $30,000 check to two other abolitionists to support their defense against government charges of illegal activity. When John Brown was arrested after his attack on

Harper's Ferry, a letter from Mammy Pleasant was in his pocket. He acknowledged her support, and Mammy Pleasant became a national figure.

Upon her return to San Francisco, Pleasant became one of the leaders of San Francisco's African American community. Her earliest concern was segregated city services. After delivering a number of speeches on the evils of segregation, Pleasant filed a law suit against a San Francisco streetcar company for refusing her a seat on one of its streetcars. She won the landmark law suit in 1866 and a $500 award.

Two years later, Pleasant once again sued the streetcar company. This time she challenged the conductor who refused to pick her up. In court, Pleasant charged that the conductor stated: "colored people would not be taken aboard." She won another case as well, and the San Francisco streetcar company changed its racial policies.

In 1876, Pleasant built a mansion on Webster Street and continued to work for expanded educational, occupational and political rights for black Californians. Cooks, waiters, chambermaids and African American bellboys dominated the San Francisco hotels. Most were recommended for employment by Mammy Pleasant.

Mammy Pleasant was an extremely generous person. She placed more than 600 black Californians in jobs and another hundred were employed in her own businesses. She also lent money to newly arrived African American settlers. She also began some speculative investments to create a fund to continue the fight against racism.

From 1862 to 1890 Pleasant was an outstanding businesswoman and a strong advocate of African American civil rights. She helped the most important black families to settle in and around San Francisco. Unfortunately, in 1903 Mammy Pleasant died broke. An economic recession, declining land values and the inability to collect her loans made Pleasant's later years poverty filled ones. However, during her years in California Pleasant helped establish the African American middle class and developed a strong civil rights impulse.

African Americans in Southern California: Cow County Gains

In Southern California the black population was drawn to the fields and the ready employment in and around Los Angeles. The climate was another obvious reason for African Americans migrating to Southern California. Some arrived with money and proceeded to create new businesses. Thus, despite negative racial attitudes, black Californians found opportunity in the white dominated Los Angeles area.

One of the earliest black newspapers, the *California Eagle*, provided a sense of community. By 1852, a small African American settlement of twenty-five black Mormons sprung up in San Bernardino, and they lived quietly in this small desert community. One Riverside settler remarked: "They are so unusual; we leave them alone." One of the black Mormons, Robert Smith, was seized and brought into court and charged with being a slave. A local judge freed Smith and lectured pro-slavery forces on the immorality, as well as the legality, of slavery.

Biddy Mason was Southern California's best known African American. In 1851, Mason, a slave from Hancock County, Georgia, settled in San Bernardino. She was thirty-two and the mother of three young daughters. Legend has it she walked across the desert to reach California, and then her owner demanded that she work for him.

In 1856, Mason sued and won her freedom. She quickly moved to Los Angeles and went to work as a practical nurse for $2.50 a day. After saving a small sum of money she purchased a ten acre parcel and sold it five years later for $200,000. Mason's plot was

the center of the new downtown business district. She continued to invest in real estate and quickly became a multi-millionaire.

A religious woman, Mason began visiting jails and reading to prisoners. Soon she donated money and land for schools and churches. When a flood hit Los Angeles in the 1880s, Mason opened an account at her grocery store for any victim who needed food. When she died on January 15, 1891, Biddy Mason was a seventy-three year old African American woman who became a millionaire and a philanthropist. The *Los Angeles Times* described Mason as: "a pioneer humanitarian who dedicated herself to forty years of good works."

However, segregated housing, unequal employment and a feeling that the South's doctrine of white supremacy ruled local attitudes and made it difficult for black Californians to make important strides in the late nineteenth century.

FIGURE 7-1. Biddy Mason.

African Americans and California, 1870-1900

During the last three decades of the nineteenths century, the completion of the transcontinental railroad, the growth of agriculture in the San Joaquin Valley and the hostility toward the Chinese obscured the role of African Americans. By the 1880s, San Francisco with 1,628 blacks and Alameda County with 686 African American residents dominated the black population. Between five and six thousand blacks lived in California and all but two counties in 1880 listed black resident s in their census.

It wasn't until the 1870s that blacks began to vote in California. Once they did, black Californians attacked the segregated and dilapidated facilities which African American children were forced to attend. In 1871, a California law provided separate schools for black children. Because of the woeful condition of these schools the Rev. Jeremiah Sanderson organized the Education Convention of November 1871 in Stockton. It was Sanderson's view that the schools perpetuated a legal form of second class citizenship.

The work of the Education Convention was a major breakthrough in African American education in California. The delegates to this convention requested that the state's educational code be amended to end segregating black children. State Senator S. J. Finney of San Mateo introduced a bill to make segregation illegal for Afro-American children. However, the bill was defeated. This didn't end the controversy as African American leaders pursued segregation in the courts.

Consequently, during the summer of 1872 black civil rights advocates prepared a court case challenging segregation. John W. Dwinelle, a prominent lawyer, argued the case of a young black girl named Mary Frances Ward who had attempted to enroll in the Broadway School and was denied admission and then proceeded to sue the principal, Noah Flood, for admission into the school. Because black Californians resided in large numbers in San Francisco, Dwinelle reasoned that the case would be successful. The controversy erupted when Mary Francisco Ward attempted to attend the Broadway Grammar School, a public school that educated only white children. The California State Supreme Court agreed to hear the petition for Mary Frances Ward's admission in order to settle the controversial question of integrated education.

The Ward v. Flood case began its journey in a San Francisco court but went all the way to the California Supreme Court. Finally, after eighteen months, in 1874 the Supreme Court ruled that Mary Ward's right was not denied because she had access to an all black school. The African American school, the Court maintained, was the equal of the white school. This decision recognized the right of segregation. However, not all Californians were refusing to break down racial barriers. As early as 1872 the Oakland school district permitted black children to attend elementary schools with their white peers.

The *Appeal*, a black newspaper, noted that the 1870s was a time when many segregated schools closed and there was a trend toward desegregation. However, this move to integrate the schools was more dependent upon financial constraints than liberal political ideas.

During the 1880s California's black population almost doubled as it rose from 6,018 to 11,322. African American workers were dominate in the service industry and on unskilled laboring jobs. Increasingly, in the late nineteenth century black Californians migrated to Los Angeles where land prices were inexpensive, jobs plentiful and concerns about color not as strong. In Fresno and Kern counties, black farmers increased enormously from 1880 to 1900.

The railroad was one reason for the growth of Southern California's black population. Redcaps and bellman porters stayed in Los Angeles hotels while eating and drinking in clubs with names like the Bellman and Waiters or the Bakers and Porters. But, job discrimination remained a problem. In San Francisco, a Jamaican, J. Alexander Somerville, left town to find a new home in Redlands. After working in this Southern California city, Somerville saved enough money to attend dental school. After graduating from the University of Southern California, he became the Golden State's first black dentist. After all his hard work, Somerville was not recognized as an African American. When he graduated from dental school with highest honors he was listed in the graduation program as "West Indian." In his autobiography, *Man of Color*, Somerville lamented the inability of white Californians to recognize "colored achievement."

San Francisco was the first liberal haven for African Americans. From 1870 to 1900 a feeling of equality and a sense of progress dominated the city by the bay. By 1893 more than 30,000 African Americans lived in California and a convention of the African American League of San Francisco was held at the California Hall at 620 Bush Street with delegates attending from all over the state. Eula Mason, Biddy's daughter, was a delegate, and in a keynote address, she talked at length about "the Negro's progress."

While racism still persisted, there were signs of advancement. One of the obvious areas of progress was the food industry. In Los Angeles, San Jose and Placerville food service was an African American monopoly. Harriet Foster's Southern Delights operated the best cooking school in Sacramento, California and helped to create a generation of cooks who made excellent wages.

As the twentieth century dawned, black Californians were in a decided minority. Yet, there were gains in jobs, education and population growth. By 1900, 2,841 African Americans lived in Los Angeles County. To the north in San Francisco the Fillmore district was home to the rapidly growing black population, and the twentieth century would offer changes and strain the Golden State's reputation for racial equality.

Mexican Americans and the Mid Nineteenth Century

In 1855, twenty year old Francisco P. Ramirez developed the political side of Mexican American politics in *El Clamor Publico*. This weekly newspaper expressed the outrage of Californios over the racist direction of California civilization. Not one to mince words, Ramirez described California as a lynch mob Democracy. "The often praised liberty of Americans," Ramirez wrote, "is imaginary."

The reason for Ramirez's anger is a simple one. Ranchos were on the decline, thereby ending the power and economic influence of the Spanish speaking. The Land Law of 1851 caused many Californios to lose their land claims. Ramirez also charged that the Native American was treated in an equally poor manner. American law also forbade court testimony by Indians. Manuel Dominguez, a mestizo who had signed the California State Constitution of 1849, was a respected ranchero who could not testify in court because he looked more like an Indian than a European. His protests went unheeded when he attempted to take a land case to court. He wound up losing a large portion of his rancho.

Juan Bandini, a Californio, complained in 1855 that "our inheritance is turned to strangers, our houses to aliens...." The gold rush had changed the population balance as more than a 100,000 Americans entered California by 1850 and the 13,000 Mexicans found themselves a minority. But land was still owned by the Mexican ranchero. This was soon challenged through American land law.

Senator William Gwin, a pro-slavery Democrat, pushed the Federal Land Law of 1851 through Congress with the intention of legally seizing Spanish and Mexican land grants. Senator Gwin's attacks on the Spanish character prompted newspapers like the *San Francisco Bulletin* to demand that disputed family claims be settled immediately.

A three man Board of Land Commissioners was set up to hear the cases. After more than eight hundred disputed land claims were heard, the board upheld more than six hundred. On the surface this seemed fair. A closer examination of the cases, however, revealed that the two hundred plus ranches taken away belonged to the Spanish speaking aristocracy. The six hundred ranches ruled as valid land claims were one section or 640 acres. So the Land Law of 1851 disenfranchised the most prominent Mexican American families. Once the Spanish speaking aristocracy declined, so did Mexican American political influence.

Since the burden of proof was placed on the Spanish or Mexican landowner, who paid exorbitant fees to lawyers, the Land Commission frequently found the evidence of ownership "weak" or "imprecise." Length of time living on the land didn't seem to matter.

Bandini summed up the Land Law of 1851 when he suggested that families who had lived for forty or fifty years on their land were certainly the owners. "They have reared themselves homes," Bandini wrote, "and their children were born there-and there they lived in peace and comparative plenty." But, as Bandini suggested, all this changed due to the new American laws. He called the Americans "pinche gringos."

Mexican Americans were angry because the Land Law of 1851 violated the basic tenets of the Treaty of Guadalupe Hidalgo. Not only were hundreds of legitimate land owners forced from their homes, but aspiring Mexican-American ranchers were forced to move to the city. Suddenly the Spanish speaking population owned less property, fewer businesses and had decreased economic opportunities. This placed them in a position of second class citizenship. But it was the large, prosperous ranchero who suffered the most financial damage.

When Vicente Peralta's Rancho San Antonio, the site of present day Oakland, Berkeley and Alameda, began to confront American settlers, he had no idea that a land law had been passed. Peralta didn't speak English. He was generally friendly to Americans, and he loved to share his wealth. Eventually, an American lawyer, Horace Carpentier, persuaded Peralta to sign an agreement in which the lawyer would lease some of the Peralta land grant. This agreement turned out to be a quick claim and Peralta lost the Rancho San Antonio to his lawyer. The rise of American laws perplexed settlers like Peralta who didn't understand the new system and couldn't figure out how to fight it.

The loss of Spanish and Mexican ranchos and the influx of Anglo-American settlers created a new California. Law and order was a problem. A number of famous bandits arose as a protest against the changes in the Golden State.

Joaquin Murieta became a notorious bandit. He was known as the "Robin Hood of El Dorado" and defended his actions by suggesting that the Foreign Miners' Tax Law of 1850 and the Land Law of 1851 robbed him of his economic means. Murieta was a legitimate folk hero who protested the inequities of the new California. When Captain Harry S. Love finally captured the bandit, Joaquin Murieta, the bandit craze ended.

A lesser known Mexican bandit, Tiburcio Vasquez, was also a symbol of resistance to Anglo rule. Vasquez, a native Californian, was the son of an influential ranchero near Monterey, and he mainly robbed cattle ranchers. Not surprisingly, state authorities declared Vasquez a career criminal and he wound up in California's most notorious prison, San Quentin. Unfortunately, Murieta and Vasquez were described in Anglo newspapers as part of the Spanish speaking crime wave.

The decade following the annexation of California was a period of economic opportunity and population growth for American ranchers, business people and itinerant settlers. The economic decline of the Spanish speaking population was immediate as American laws placed the Mexican American in a position of second class citizenship. As Anglo-American economic successes soared, the decline in Spanish speaking fortunes was obvious. This decline was strongest in Mexican Southern California. No one suffered more from the Anglo American onslaught than the Los Angeles based Pico family. They had dominated Southern California's economic, political and social affairs since the early 1800s. Suddenly the Pico empire was subject to American approval.

In Los Angeles the Pico family fell on hard times after American annexation. The *Los Angeles Star* reported on September 18, 1852 that Andres Pico bet a thousand dollars on a horse race. As Pico's gambling and business losses unfolded during the decade, he headed straight for bankruptcy court. This reinforced the stereotype that Californios and Mexicans were unable to manage their money. Unfortunately, this was a myth aided by stories in the American press. By the late 1850s, both Andres and Pio Pico were broke and depended upon friends and family for money. It was an ignominious end for two great men.

As the last governor of Mexican California, Pio Pico granted more than 600 last minute land grants and this created hostile Anglo feelings which were still prevalent in the Golden State. For the next decade there was antipathy toward the Picos.

What happened to the Picos was the product of economic and population shifts. When James Marshall discovered gold at Sutter's Mill there were large numbers of skilled Mexican, Chilean and Peruvian miners. By the mid-1850s the Spanish speaking miners were migrating to the larger cities. Sonora, a mining town of 5,000 Mexicans, quickly turned into a ghost town after the local sheriff used the Foreign Miners' Tax Law of 1850 to indiscriminately and unfairly collect a $20 monthly mining tax. Rather than fight the corrupt sheriff, the Sonorans went home or to the San Joaquin or Sacramento Valley. If they failed to find adequate employment, they migrated to San Francisco, San Jose, Santa Barbara or Los Angeles, because these towns still retained a Hispanic character.

The average Mexican miner believed that by leaving the Sierra Nevada gold fields he would escape the racial and economic hardships that the new American Government placed upon the Spanish speaking. Nothing was further from the truth.

The Decline of Mexican Southern California: The Early Years

The Southern California cow counties became increasingly Anglo in the first decade of statehood. During the 1850s and early 1860, there was a business-land revolution. The result was a dramatic increase in American settlers. The census of 1860 reported that Los Angeles was only 46.1% Spanish speaking and by 1880 it was 19.3%. In Los Angeles and Santa Barbara, ethnic tensions between Anglo-American and Mexican residents increased each year as Yankee settlers and businessmen prospered. There was a subtle, yet pervasive, feeling that the old way was in decline. The Spanish speaking ranchos no longer dominated the local economy and the pioneer families declined in importance.

By the early 1860s, Anglo politicians had taken over Los Angeles government. In Santa Barbara the Spanish speaking vote continued to elect the mayor. Yet, tourists and land speculators changed the landscape of these towns. Eventually in both cities there were decidedly anti-Mexican political decisions.

In Los Angeles, the school system was reorganized to force Spanish speaking children into a small number of select schools. By setting up schools in the Spanish speaking neighborhoods with poor facilities and teachers, Mexican American children were doomed to a second rate education.

The best example of change occurred north of Los Angeles in Santa Barbara and Ventura. As tourists and new American settlers flooded into Santa Barbara, the town changed and the Spanish speaking vote weakened. By 1880, Councilman Caesar Lataillade and Sheriff Nicolas Covarrubias withdrew from Santa Barbara politics. It was never made clear whether they resigned voluntarily or left out of sheer frustration. Whatever the cause, tension between Anglo-Americans and Mexican Americans was high.

In Ventura County, Jose Arnaz complained about the American presence. For thirty years, Arnaz remarked, the Yankee had bullied and ignored the Spanish speaking population, thereby mining a legacy of racial hatred. But much of Ventura's land was lost through indebtedness to Yankee merchants. The large Californio rancheros were notorious for making extravagant and needless purchases and American business-

men were eager to sign them up for extended credit. By the 1880s, much of the original Spanish and Mexican settlement in Ventura County was owned by Anglo-American interests.

The revolution in agricultural employment in Ventura County was another indication of the changes throughout California. The Mexican American, Native American, African American and Chinese men who worked in Ventura County were overwhelmingly part of the unskilled strata of the working class. As Anglo land owners took charge of the fields, new employment patterns emerged. Only 17.6% of the white population worked as unskilled agricultural labor. The significance of race is demonstrated by statistics which show that 60.2% of Mexican Americans, 90.5% of Native Americans and 100% of the Chinese males worked in the fields. Nearly all of the minority population in Ventura County in the late nineteenth century worked in servile agricultural jobs.

By 1880 Mexican Americans were moving into Los Angeles as the large ranchos declined. There were no Spanish speaking politicians of any significance by the 1880s, and Mexican American businesses were on the decline. The beginning of a long slide into second class citizenship began the cataclysmic events of the first three decade of California history came to a close.

Race was a key factor in the changes surrounding California in the mid to late nineteenth century. The rise of Anglo businesses, the decline of the Spanish speaking ranchero and the rise of a minority job market with unskilled employment accentuated the minorities drift into second class citizenship. "We desire only a white population in California," a Southern California rancher remarked. His words were prophetic as the Spanish speaking nature of the Golden State was dramatically curtailed by 1880.

Bibliography Essay

Leonard Pitt's, *The Decline of the Californios: A Social History of the Spanish Speaking Californians, 1846-1900* (Berkeley and Los Angeles, 1966) is instrumental in understanding late nineteenth century Mexican Americans. Harris Newmark, *Sixty Years In Southern California, 1853-1913* (New York, 1916) is an interesting look at the formative years in and around Los Angeles and Robert Glass Cleland, *The Cattle on a Thousand Hills, 1850-1880* (San Marino, 1975) for a look at the importance of land. Michael Weiss, "Education, Literacy and the Community of Los Angeles in 1850," *Southern California Quarterly*, volume 60, no. l (Summer, 1978) is important in placing the citizenry into context.

Richard Woolsey, "Rites of Passage: Anglo and Mexican American Contrasts In Times Of Change: Los Angeles, 1860-1870," *Southern California Quarterly*, 69 (summer, 1987) is an important article on the evolution of Los Angeles. Also see, Richard H. Peterson, "Anti-Mexican Nativism, 1848-1853: A Study In Cultural Conflict," *Southern California Quarterly*, 62 (Winter, 1980) for an unusually perceptive analysis of anti-Mexican movements.

An excellent analysis of Mexican Americans is Albert Camarillo, *Chicanos In California: A History of Mexican Americans in California* (San Francisco, 1984). Also see Camarillo, *Chicanos in a Changing Society: From Mexican Pueblos to American Barrios in Santa Barbara and Southern California, 1846-1930* (Cambridge, 1979) for an in depth study of a major Mexican American settlement.

Mario T. Garcia, "The Californios of San Diego and the Politics of Accommodation," *Aztlan: International Journal of Chicano Studies Research 6* (Spring, 1975) and Charles Hughes, "The Decline of the Californios: The Case of San Diego, 1846-1856," *The Journal of San Diego History*, 21 (Summer, 1975) are important in analyzing the changes in Southern California after annexation and statehood.

On bandits see Pedro Castillo and Alberto Camarillo, editors, *Furia y Muerte: Los Bandidos Chicanos* (Los Angeles, 1973). For Ventura County, bandits and general land and mining problems see the brilliant analysis in Tomas Almaguer's, *Racial Fault Lines: The Historical Origins of White Supremacy in California* (Berkeley, 1994).

For African American influences in California see, for example, B. Gordon Wheeler, *Black California: The History of African Americans in The Golden State* (New York, 1993); Delilah Beasley, *The Negro Trail Blazers of California* (Los Angeles, 1919); Kenneth G. Goode, *California's Black Pioneers: A Brief Historical Survey* (Santa Barbara, 1974): Rudolph Lapp, *Blacks in Gold Rush California* (New Haven, 1977) and Jack D. Forbes, *Afro-Americans in the Far West: A Handbook For Educators* (Berkeley, 1966).

On David Broderick see David A. Williams, *David C. Broderick: A Political Portrait* (San Marino, 1969). The dominance of the Irish-Catholic political machine is analyzed with little reference to ethnic concerns.

For the problems of California agriculture see, Sucheng Chan, *This Bitter Soil: The Chinese in California Agriculture* (Berkeley, 1986). This seminal study brilliantly analyzes the mid and late nineteenth century Chinese contribution to agricultural development.

8

The Chinese in California History

An Introduction

"His dress, if judged by our standards, is ridiculous...his head is shaven...there hangs a tuft of hair as long as a spaniel's tail," Erasmus Doolittle, an American trader, wrote after seeing his first Chinese merchant. Few people paid attention to Doolittle's comments because they were made in 1830 when there were no Chinese in America. The irony is that Doolittle compared the Chinese to animals and labeled them uncivilized, and in twenty years, Californians would make the same generalizations. But the Chinese were welcomed to California by most people because of the need for unskilled labor.

Once California was annexed, American expansionists looked toward Asia. A ready market for goods and a cheap labor supply made China a potential source of wealth. When the Central Pacific Railroad connected to San Francisco's port in 1869, hopes for a lucrative world trade intensified. But the Golden State's fixation with China was apparent during the final negotiations for the Treaty of Guadalupe Hidalgo in 1848 when a government official, Aaron H. Palmer, spoke glowingly of Chinese labor. In the following year, the first Chinese immigrants arrived in California.

The history of the Chinese in California is a long and complex story filled with violence, racially motivated state laws and newspaper and magazine articles designed to produce anti-Chinese feelings. Although the two month voyage from China cost as little as fifty dollars, most immigrants could not afford it. The hui or credit association created an elaborate contract which made it difficult to repay the sum. But the Chinese eagerly entered into agreements with labor contractors to come to America. The reason was a simple one. Gold created fortunes, and the Chinese believed that the California gold fields were a sure source of wealth.

The Chinese in California: The Reasons for Cheap Labor and the Reaction to It

The California reaction to the Chinese was a negative one. Because white workers were brought into competition with the Chinese, they were susceptible to demagogic politicians who pictured the Chinese as a "heathen people" intent upon "mongrelizing California." From the election of 1852, anti-Chinese politics helped to determine electoral victories. As a result, a strain of anti-Asian politics entered California's electoral arena and persisted as a major influence in the Golden State.

Yet, there were three advantages to Chinese labor. First, the Chinese were a large labor pool. The anti-slave California constitution prevented the use of slaves; thus, there were few free Negro, Indian or Mexican workers who would accept the lower paying jobs. Prosperity made it easy to find work. Second, the Chinese worked at approximately two thirds the cost of other workers. Professor Alexander Saxton of the University of California, Los Angeles estimated that the Central Pacific Railroad cut its construction costs by a third by not feeding, clothing or housing Chinese laborers. Third, American employers had great success with the Chinese work ethic. The absentee rate and work productivity was higher than that of other unskilled workers.

Unfortunately, it was these strengths in the labor market which created the negative reaction to the Chinese. European Americans were hostile to the Chinese largely because of their physical appearance, language, manner of dress, food, religion and social customs. These were the excuses for the brutal racism and the repressive laws which humiliated the Chinese well into the twentieth century.

As Professor Stuart Creighton Miller has shown in *The Unwelcomed Immigrant: The American Image of the Chinese, 1785-1882*, the nineteenth century Californian viewed the Chinese as "ridiculously clad, superstitious, dishonest, crafty, cruel and marginal members of the human race." These vicious attitudes were transferred to politics, the job market and the educational arena. However, the "Heathen Chinee," as they were known, persisted because of economic reasons.

The Chinese who migrated to California were a working class people from the Kwangtung Province who found the mines

FIGURE 8-1. Anti-Chinese Cartoon, 1870s.

suitable to their skills. The main reason for their immigration, however, was a belief in the Golden Mountain Myth.

The Myth of the Golden Mountain: The Chinese in the California Gold Fields

By December 1849, there were three hundred Chinese miners working marginal mining claims. Only a few Chinese were visible, but there were already racial problems. During the Tuolomne County July 4th celebration an anti-Chinese riot broke out against sixty laborers who worked for a British mining firm. This riot was the work of independent, self-employed white miners who believed that the Chinese were unfair labor competition because they worked cheaply and quickly. Anti-Coolie clubs argued that the Chinese used gang laborers. This was a labor system in which the Chinese worked in groups at a lower wage than white laborers. The Tuolumne riot of 1849 was the earliest attempt to drive the hard working, marginally paid Chinese from the mines.

The Tuolumne County riot of July 4, 1849, is often referred to as an isolated incident, but it was the beginning of a general trend. What the riot reflected was a fear of other cultures, ones that Californians couldn't understand. Despite white hostility, Chinese miners grew to nearly 35,000 by 1860. So race riots didn't end Chinese population growth in gold country; it simply made it more difficult for them to find independent work. Yet, the Chinese continued to immigrate in large numbers.

There were a number of factors bringing the Chinese to California. The most important one was China's internal rebellion. Many sought refuge from the British Opium Wars. Others left due to the lackluster economy. The Quing Government imposed high taxes on the peasants, and the strife between the Punti (local people) and the Hakkas (guest people) also helped to drive workers to California.

In 1851, the Taiping Revolution broke out against the Manchu Dynasty and fifteen years of civil turmoil wracked China. The resulting poverty and social-economic disorder created conditions that led workers to immigrate to San Francisco. The Chinese formed companies, known as a Kongsi, under the leadership of a merchant contractor and solicited workers. These merchant creditors controlled the supply of workers streaming into California.

Although Chinese labor was exploited by unscrupulous merchant contractors, there was a ready supply of Chinese workers. The lure of the gold rush provided images of wealth. The Chinese term for California, "Gam Saan Haak," literally meant "travel-

FIGURE 8-2. Chinese Railroad Laborers, 1866 in the High Sierras.

ers to the Golden Mountain." The myth that instant wealth was available to anyone was a catalyst to this immigration. In some respects, there was a golden mountain.

In the Stanislaus County town of Knight's Ferry, the Chinese settled in the river crossing and mill town, because it was on the direct route from Stockton to the southern mines. It was in this part of the Sierra Nevada that the early Chinese settled. It would be another two decades before the Chinese preferred to settle in San Francisco.

When William J. Knight founded Knight's Ferry, it was the best river crossing on the route between Stockton and Sonora. It was a natural migration point to Chinese Camp in Tuolumne County. From Chinese Camp labor gangs were hired out in groups from as few as four to as many as four hundred. The presence of large numbers of Chinese workers made Knight's Ferry one of the first anti-Asian bastions in the Golden State. Because of the hostile attitude toward the Chinese, the newly arrived Asian immigrants tried to avoid Americans or European immigrants.

Abraham Schell owned the Red Mountain Vineyard and preferred Chinese workers because they were hard workers. He had liberal racial attitudes and leased town lots to the Chinese for home sites and businesses. As a result, there was a small Chinese business community. The reaction from Anglos was swift and predictable. Anti Coolie clubs emerged to drive the Chinese out of Knight's Ferry and into San Francisco. By the late 1860s, the Chinese were streaming into the city by the bay, and, initially, they found wonderful working conditions.

San Francisco wages were the highest in the world. Common labor received a dollar an hour; carpenters were paid fourteen dollars a day and specialized services were costly. A dozen laundered garments cost twenty dollars. But once they crossed the Pacific, the new immigrants felt isolated.

They needed a broker to make their way in the Golden State. Tongs and other community organizations helped this adjustment.

As the Chinese settled in California, they lived in Dai Four or Big City, as San Francisco was known, as well as Yee Fou or Second City, Sacramento, Sam Four or Third City, Stockton. Los Angeles and Marysville also had a representative Chinese population. The large numbers of Chinese in the Golden State created a strong reaction. It was the labor importer and Chinese community organization that brought the xenophobic Anglo reaction.

As Professor Robert W. Cherny of San Francisco State University has shown, San Francisco was not tolerant or civil to the Chinese. Politicians courted the working class vote with anti Chinese slogans; the school system was segregated; laws and public officials created second class citizenship and miscegenation laws prohibited whites and Chinese from marrying. So the Chinese were forced to depend upon the contract labor importer, the Chinese Six Companies and the tongs for patterns of community organization necessary for an independent life.

The Chinese Six Companies, Tongs and Community Organization

The Chinese Six Companies, a group of contract labor importers, working with American businessmen lured Chinese workers to California. The young contract laborers were duped by outrageous descriptions of California wealth. A large number of circulars and brochures were distributed to create the illusion of economic abundance. "It is a nice country without mandarins or soldiers," one brochure remarked. "Money is in great plenty and to spare in America," was a phrase from a popular pamphlet. Advertising was everywhere for the Chinese, complete with pictures of a golden mountain next to lush, fertile valleys and bubbling streams.

When Chinese immigrants searched for transportation to California, they fell into the clutches of their own people. The Chinese Six Companies created a credit ticket system. This was a business in which an individual borrowed money from a broker to cover transportation costs to California and then paid off the loan over many years. Soon, however, Californians complained about Coolie labor and charged that it was a form of slavery. Low wages and poor working conditions, local politicians argued, created new problems. State Senator Creed Hammond introduced a bill in the California Legislature in the early 1850s, attempting to ban Coolie labor. The bill was defeated but was a popular issue with voters. Soon politicians routinely used anti-Chinese slogans to win close elections. The Chinese Six Companies were invariably painted as the villain.

The Chinese Six Companies served as more than just labor brokers. Since Chinese workers had no influence with government or business officials, the Chinese Six Companies acted as a quasi-government and helped to negotiate housing, employment and social freedom. Even though they exploited the labor market, they lobbied for Chinese rights. The Chinese Six Companies hired San Francisco attorney Daniel Cleveland to argue for federal laws to protect Chinese rights. In 1853, representatives of the Chinese Six Companies testified before the California Legislature and urged the defeat of proposed anti Chinese laws. Political action was a strong part of the Chinese Six Companies' strategy. Soon they prevailed upon national politicians to grant the Chinese free immigration privileges.

When the Burlingame Treaty of 1868 was signed, it included provisions recognizing the "free migration" of the Chinese to the United States. In 1870, the Civil Rights Act provided that immigrants, regardless of whether or not they became naturalized citizens, would be protected under American law. So while the Chinese were prevented from becoming naturalized citizens, they still maintained all the legal rights of American citizens. To the Chinese, the merchant contractors were friends who aided their countrymen.

The Chinese Six Companies also acted as an arbiter in disputes between Chinese workers. In San Francisco, disagreements between Chinese associations were often referred to the Chinese Six Companies, and the police recognized their quasi-legal justice. Critics of self-imposed justice charted that Chinese labor was "servile." They were described as "Coolies" rather than free labor.

American businessmen worked in unison with Chinese labor contractors to create the "Coolie Myth." As Professor Ronald Takaki of the University of California, Berkeley has argued, the Chinese were not forced to immigrate to California. The Chinese came voluntarily as free labor. The servitude or virtual slavery which often resulted was due to the high cost of transportation. The positive environment for Chinese workers and the chance for economic gain overshadowed the dangers.

San Francisco was a tolerant city and the Chinese eagerly embraced it. Professor Sucheng Chan of the University of California, Santa Barbara argues that the Chinese readily adapted to American capitalism, cut profitable business deals with white merchants and established a small group of wealthy and influential families. Ronald Takaki points out that Chinese immigrants brought three social organizations to California: the Huiguan (district associations), the tongs (secret societies) and the fongs (clans). The tongs and the fongs were engaged in importing and selling illegal goods. The opium trade, prostitution, gambling and forbidden goods made the tongs and fongs an easy target for race conscious Americans. The criminal activity associated with these organizations created the stereotypes about Chinese crime, drug use and general immorality which hindered their progress in the Golden State.

Initially, among these groups, the tongs were the most important part of the Chinese experience. The Chinese Six Companies were a consolidation of six tongs. They were known as the Chinese Consolidated Benevolent Association, and they quickly became a major force in San Francisco. The vast majority of tongs were secret societies. Americans failed to understand that in China these organizations challenged the established power. In California, the tongs were secretive and had both a criminal and political function. Despite their shortcomings, the San Francisco tongs negotiated effectively with local authorities for limited rights.

Some tongs had enormous influence. In 1852, the Kwang-tek-tong was founded in California. It was an underground anti-government organization in China, but in San Francisco it became a social and economic club. In time, the tongs developed their own police force, businesses and hidden Chinatown government. Some tongs organized gambling, prostitution and the opium trade. As a result, tongs were a means by which American newspapers and politicians could characterize the Chinese as gangsters. The fighting between Chinese organizations was a problem because of the negative reaction from employers. Chinese merchant contractors often fought with each other over the San Francisco market.

To end the differences between Chinese merchant contractors the Hop Wo Wui Kun, known as the Company of United Harmony, was formed to employ contract workers and provide them with adequate housing, a fair wage and protection from anti-Chinese

FIGURE 8-3. A Chinese Laundry: 1870s.

forces. But when the Hop Wo Company applied for a California corporate charter, a San Francisco court rejected the request. As a result, the Hop Wo controlled Chinese workers through an elaborate and ritualistic underground society. The weekly payoffs to the police helped to establish a separate social life, and this new freedom helped Chinese immigrants adjust to California life. Because they were excluded from the mainstream of California society, the Chinese attempted to influence the political system. As the number of Chinese grew in the Golden State, so did their political influence.

The Early Politics of the Anti-Chinese Movement: The Forced Labor Debate and Civil Rights

By 1852, there were almost 25,000 Chinese in California and pressure from Nativist groups, like the American Party, prompted the California Legislature to debate a bill to ban Coolie labor. The issue of forced Chinese labor was a heated one and politicians used this debate to incite racial hatred. In San Francisco, Anti-Coolie clubs organized and publicized the "Yellow Peril." Once jobs became scare in San Francisco, there were public demonstrations against the Chinese. The popular belief was that the Chinese held the lower paying, unskilled jobs. The poor white worker could not compete with them. At least that was the prevailing stereotype.

Some politicians recognized the broader implications of the Chinese question. In January 1852 when Governor John McDougal left office, he warned Californians that discrimination against the Chinese might result in serious racial problems. The Governor predicted a lengthy and divisive debate over race. As McDougal pointed out, there was a need for cheap, industrious labor, and he urged acceptance of Chinese labor. The public outcry over McDougal's farewell address influenced incoming governors and state legislators who were increasingly anti-Chinese.

In April 1852 the newly elected Democratic Governor, John Bigler, delivered a fiery speech to the California Legislature demanding the exclusion of Chinese labor. Bigler spoke out relentlessly against the Chinese and developed xenophobic fears of Chinese workers. As a result of this hysteria, California politicians introduced numerous laws and city ordinances limiting Chinese rights. Many of these laws had been directed toward the Spanish speaking and then rewritten to control the Chinese.

A good example was the Foreign Miners' Tax Law of 1850. The $20 monthly tax was initially levied on Mexicans. However, this law was amended in 1852, and the Chinese were required to pay a $3 to $5 monthly mining fee. The sheriff could collect the money at his discretion and this gave him the perfect opportunity to harass the Chinese who believed in civil rights. Some miners complained of paying the tax as many as ten times monthly. This law was specifically directed at the 16,000 Chinese miners who were making a good living in small, out of the way mines. The Foreign Miners'

Tax Law was a means of social economic control. It put the Chinese in their place.

In 1854, a state law was introduced to prevent the Chinese from testifying in court. After some delicate lobbying by the Chinese Six Companies, the proposed law failed to pass the California Assembly and Senate. This didn't daunt anti-Chinese agitators. They searched for a legal precedent to exclude Chinese testimony in California courts.

Strangely, it was a murder case that defined Chinese rights, or the lack of them, in the California courts. When a working man, George W. Hall, and two others were tried for murdering a Chinese worker, Ling Sing, a guilty verdict was returned after three Chinese witnesses and one white observer testified for the prosecution. Once the jury returned a guilty verdict, Hall was sentenced to hang.

Hall's lawyer appealed the verdict. He took the case to the California Supreme Court. In 1854, in the People v. Hall, the Court ruled that the Chinese could not testify. A twenty-nine year old Justice, Hugh G. Murray, reasoned that California's original settlers, the Indians, had immigrated from Asia, and the fact that Indians could not testify meant that the Chinese were also prohibited from testifying against whites in court. This equation which linked the Indians with the Chinese defied the most elemental logic, but there were few voices raised in protest.

Murray was a member of the American Party, and his politics gave rise to the popular phrase that Chinese defendants didn't have "a Chinaman's chance" in court. He also considered himself a historian. More than once Murray lectured Californians on their history. He not only saw the Chinese as nonwhite, but he urged the to restrict other minority groups. The People v. Hall excluded African American and Native American citizens in court as well.

FIGURE 8-4. The Illustrated WASP, 1877.

The People v. Hall had an impact upon other areas in California. By 1859, the California Superintendent of Education applied this color line to the public schools. In 1863 and 1864, there were revised laws on the entry of nonwhites into the public schools. In 1870, the California educational system was overhauled to segregate white students in a complex system of schools which reflected racial stratification.

But the People v. Hall had its greatest impact upon the Chinese. It not only restricted Chinese civil rights, but also provided race conscious whites with a justification for their behavior. Soon anti-Chinese Californians found a provision in federal law that they used to prevent Asian immigrants from obtaining citizenship. A 1790 federal law provided that only "free white persons" could become naturalized citizens. This provision guaranteed the Chinese permanent second-class citizenship since they could not be naturalized. However, by the mid-1850s, San Francisco had a well organized Chinese community. As a result, San Franciscans demanded ordinances to control the Chinese.

In 1854, the San Francisco Board of Supervisors passed the Pig-Tail Ordinance which required any Chinese person convicted of a minor crime to have his/her pig-tail shaved. This was simply harassment because it intended to humiliate the Chinese. Another means of controlling the Chinese was the Cubic Air Ordinance which fined the Chinese for living in a small space. This was intended to discourage communal housing and make it too expensive for the Chinese to live in San Francisco.

The Chinese Enter the Political Arena in California: The Politics of the 1850s

The traditional image of the Chinese Six Companies was that they exploited contract labor. This ignores their political side. Be-

ginning in the early 1850s, the Chinese were extraordinarily political. In August 1850 Chinatown leader Norman Assing wrote to San Francisco Mayor James W. Geary and thanked him for inviting important Chinese merchants to a ceremony commemorating the death of President Zachary Taylor. During the July 4th, 1852 celebration a group of prominent Chinese merchants rode in a downtown parade. Although the Chinese couldn't become citizens, they formed wards or neighborhood political clubs.

In San Francisco, two Chinese merchants, Nissum and Norman Assing, who claimed to be Christians from Charlestown, South Carolina, became prominent local businessmen. In reality, the two men were exploiting their own people. They talked of opening boarding houses, setting up Chinese stores and catering to the needs of the Asian community. The Assings were articulate, well dressed and had the ability to form partnerships with American businessmen. The two men became so successful that they were listed in the San Francisco City Directory.

A San Francisco merchant, Lai Chun-Chuen, noted in 1855 that there was little hostility toward Chinese workers or business. Lai wrote: "The people of the flowery land were received like guests." The increasingly hostile racial atmosphere was not recognized by Lai and other Chinese immigrants. The term "John Chinaman" quickly became a popular derogatory remark. The main reasons for these tensions were economic ones. As the Chinese settled in the mining regions, they were economically successful and by the early 1860s, more than two-thirds of California's Chinese population still worked in the mines.

The Chinese in the 1860s: A Degraded and Distinct People

Once the Chinese emerged as an economic force, they gained minor political concessions. San Francisco mayors regularly consulted with Chinese leaders. There was an unofficial policy of listening to Chinese concerns and acting on some of them. This official interest in the Chinese was because the merchant contractors who dominated the China trade brought in goods that were profitable to Anglo merchants.

In the mid-1860s the Chinese Six Companies in a strongly worded letter to President Abraham Lincoln complained that the Chinese were not welcomed as freely as other foreign laborers. Although the Chinese Six Companies lobbied for protection for the Chinese immigrant, they were only marginally successful. Since the 1850s, when California State Senator Creed Hammond sponsored a bill to exclude the Chinese, there was little trust or public faith in Chinese business organizations.

As early as 1855 Governor John Bigler asked the California Legislature to limit Chinese immigration and business activity. Even though previous measures had failed and immigration restriction was a federal prerogative, the California Legislature passed an act to "discourage the immigration to this state of persons who cannot become citizens..." The one dissenting vote against the proposal was so unpopular that a shot was fired at the balking legislator. When the California Supreme Court voided the law, the issue continued.

In 1858, the California Legislature passed two bills to "prevent the further immigration of Chinese or Mongolians to this state." The first of many school segregation laws were passed, and when California's first Republican Governor, Leland Stanford, was inaugurated in 1862, he suggested that the Chinese were "a degraded and distinct people." The California Legislature immediately passed a "Chinese police tax" which allowed the police to impose a special tax. This tax was struck down by the California Supreme Court, but once again politicians found it an important vote getting issue.

As the Chinese miners left the gold fields, they were a ready source of labor for railroad barons and large scale agriculturists. The *Alta California* editorialized that the Chinese were no longer entrepreneurs but wage earners.

In 1868 the Federal Government ignited the flames of anti-Chinese sentiment when it negotiated a treaty with China. The Burlingame Treaty of 1868 provided the right of free immigration from China. It was intended to ease the flow of Chinese businessmen and capitalists who hoped to make their fortune in America. After the Burlingame Treaty was signed, Californians protested, and the San Francisco anti-Coolie associations held well publicized parades. The stage was set for the violent, anti-Chinese protests of the 1870s.

The Chinese in the 1870s: Violence, Racism and the John Chinaman Stereotype

As the Chinese became an economic force, racism reared its ugly head. The 1870s was a decade in which the term John Chinaman became a popular slogan. In July 1870 a series of anti-Chinese parades and public rallies featured large signs with slogans: *"THE COOLIE SYSTEM LEAVES US NO ALTERNATIVE—STARVATION OR DISGRACE,"* and for the politically conscious: *"MARK THE MAN WHO WOULD CRUSH US TO THE LEVEL OF THE MONGOLIAN SLAVE-WE ALL VOTE."*

Because of Chinese job skills and growing economic independence, there was a well organized movement to limit Chinese civil rights. But just the reverse occurred as a federal law extended Chinese rights. In 1870, a federal civil rights act protected foreigners from discrimination and discouraged state governments from using unequal treatment. As the Chinese arrived in America, they could not become naturalized citizens. However, due to federal law, they had many of the same rights as Americans. This intensified racial feelings in California and created systematic violence against Chinatown residents.

Under the Civil Rights Act of 1870, the federal courts invalidated most of California's anti-Chinese laws. So violence became the accepted method for discouraging future immigrants. Anti-Coolie clubs joined with labor unions and the Eight Hour Day League to demand an end to Coolie labor. Californians had a confused, emotional attachment to the term Coolie. In all probability, the word came from kuli which meant muscle in Tamil, a language in southern India. The British used Coolies, and in the Chinese language a Coolie was identi-

fied by two characters which meant "bitter strength." The primary labor importer, the Chinese Six Companies, advertised that their contract labor was the strongest, smartest and most reliable in the world. California employers agreed, and they hired Coolies in large numbers.

In many industries, notably cigars, tinware and clothing the Chinese were extraordinarily skillful. When they performed agricultural labor tasks or were domestic servants, the Chinese had few protesters. By the 1870s, however, the Chinese increasingly began to own key businesses. It was the rise of the economic power of the Chinese which created organized hostility toward the Chinese presence. Another contributing factor was the wealth and power of the Central Pacific Railroad.

FIGURE 8-5. Pulling the Chinese, 1879.

The Building of the Central Pacific Railroad: The Racial Side of Chinese Labor

The Chinese who immigrated to California's gold fields were fond of using the term "gam saan haak"—the Gold Mountain. The *El Dorado Mountain Democrat* expressed the opinion of most gold country newspapers when it described the Chinese as miners who could "buy a claim and pay liberally for it." This reputation for hard work, thrift and intelligence was not lost on Californians. When the Central Pacific Railroad began construction, there was an immediate labor problem. The Irish workers were too slow and unproductive.

As a result, in February 1865 Charles Crocker hired fifty Chinese workers to help build the Central Pacific. The President of the Central Pacific, Leland Stanford, praised the Chinese as people who were "quiet, peaceable, industrious, economical—ready and apt to learn all the different kinds of work." What Crocker and Stanford hoped was that the Chinese would not strike or delay construction. The first four years of Central Pacific Railroad construction were so slow that some doubted that the railroad would ever be completed.

Would the Chinese be able to replace the Irish-Catholic worker? This question was on everyone's mind. Since 1861, when the transcontinental line began building east from Sacramento, Crocker had employed a large, but ineffective, Irish-Catholic work force. When the Chinese began working on the Central Pacific, the *Alta Californian* reinforced Irish-Catholic stereotypes. In the first two years, the Chinese built no more track than Irish workers. Once technology took over, however, the Chinese worker appeared to be superior. It was advanced technology, not their labor skills, that led to Chinese labor superiority.

In less than two years, 12,000 Chinese were employed by the Crocker Construction Company. This was 90% of the work force. The Chinese were excellent workers, but they were not docile ones. They formed unions, they conducted wildcat strikes for higher wages; and they also negotiated for fringe benefits.

As Ronald Takaki suggested, the building of the Central Pacific was "a Chinese achievement." The actual labor of building the railroad was only a small part of the Chinese contribution. They provided the first experienced workers who handled power drills, and their skill in planting nitroglycerine helped blast a tunnel through the Donner Summit. Technologically the Chinese were superior to other workers, but race conscious Californians failed to accept these skills.

Racial attitudes were hard to break. Even Charles Crocker was uncertain about the scientific and technical aspects of Chinese labor. So he hired a group of English miners from Cornwall. These miners had proven their skills in the rugged Cornish mine, and they possessed extraordinary skill in cutting tunnels. Crocker placed the Cornish and Chinese miners side by side and at the end of each day the Chinese usually completed more work. The Chinese were so skilled in the use of hammer and drill that the Cornish miners began adapting their techniques. The Chinese realized their worth and complained about low wages and oppressive working conditions.

The Crocker Construction Company had taken such advantage of Chinese labor that the workers carried out wildcat strikes. Once the Chinese realized that they were paid the same wage as the Irish, but not given a food and housing allowance, they called a strike.

In the spring of 1867, a Chinese railroad strike occurred at an opportune time. The Central Pacific was building track for the first time at a consistent rate. However, when 5,000 skilled Chinese workers walked out demanding a $45 a month wage and an eight-hour work day, the Crocker Construction Company refused their demands. The previous wage had been $30 a month and included a twelve-hour work day.

When Crocker offered a $35 a month wage the Chinese called themselves: "One Man." The symbolism behind this term was to suggest that the workers were united in one, strong union. So the strike continued. The *Alta Californian* called the strike a "conspiracy to destroy the railroad." The only way to beat the strike, the *Alta Californian* editorialized, was to employ armed guards and cut off food, water and shelter, whenever possible, to the striking Chinese workers. It worked. The strike quickly ended.

Humiliated by the Crocker Construction Company the Chinese returned to work. Although the strike was beaten within a week, it was important in demonstrating the sophisticated labor techniques employed by Chinese workers. When scab workers were brought in to replace the Chinese, they had neither the working skills nor the drive to complete the railroad.

As the Central Pacific Railroad met the Union Pacific in Promontory Point, Utah in 1869, there were fifteen hundred people on hand to celebrate the completion of the transcontinental railroad. The irony was that the Central Pacific spike which completed the railroad, was driven into the ground by a Chinese worker. The *Overland Monthly*, the magazine covering this event, suggested that this was a fitting tribute to Asian labor. Once the transcontinental railroad was completed, a skilled and large Chinese work force had no place to go. Thus began the transformation of the urban Chinese. In 1860, only 2,179 Chinese lived in San Francisco, and they represented less than 8% of the Chinese population.

During the 1860s, the Chinese helped transform San Francisco into a major manufacturing city. As the boot and shoe, woolen, cigar and tobacco and sewing industries flourished, the Chinese grew into 46% of the work force. Because of myths surrounding their labor on the transcontinental railroad, Chinese workers were granted preferential treatment by some employers. But the reality was that low wages and poor working conditions persisted. The Chinese were often hired first because they were quiet, worked cheaply and had few employment alternatives.

By 1872, the *San Francisco Call* observed that almost half the workers in city factories were Chinese, and the *Call* praised their contribution to the California economy. As the Chinese left the mines and the railroad construction sites, they opened their own businesses. In the cigar industry, 92% of the workers were Chinese and their cigars were the best in America. Rival Irish companies printed small cigar wrappers: "This cigar made by white men for white men." The Irish made cigars were bought for the wrapper and they were placed above the superior Chinese cigar. But Chinese labor success provoked a vicious reaction. As the Rev. O. Gibson suggested: "The Chinese were taking jobs from Americans."

The Chinese as the Indispensable Enemy: The Road to Exclusion

During the 1870s, a series of events took place that made it difficult for the Chinese to escape the California hysteria which turned into a national campaign for a federal exclusion law. During the "Terrible Seventies," the fledgling labor union movement received a series of setbacks. The union found it difficult to organize as cities and counties passed ordinances restricting labor and the depression prompted wage cuts.

The Great Depression of 1873 to 1877 was a catalyst regarding the movement to ban the Chinese. By the early 1870s, the transcontinental railroad brought in settlers who envisioned the Chinese as a menace. The fear of mongrelization or race pollution was a growing trend.

As the Chinese ban became an integral part of California politics, journalists wrote long, detailed descriptions of the Chinese problem. Much of this writing was racist and used by demagogic politicians to win elections. A well known California writer, Bret Harte, sent a poem, "The Heathen Chinese," to one of America's most prestigious magazines, the *Overland Monthly*. They quickly published it and the editor sent Bret Harte a letter congratulating him for alerting Americans to the Chinese danger. Soon the phrase "the heathen Chinese" was part of American slang.

A scarcely known political writer, Henry George, migrated to Oakland to edit a local Democratic Party newspaper. He also hoped to begin a mainstream writing career. Frustrated with his lack of commercial success, George looked for an issue to make his writing a household word.

Prior to leaving New York, George wrote a front page article for the *New York Tribune* on the dangers of the "Yellow Peril." When he settled in California, George wrote strongly and in a pseudo scientific manner alleging that "the Mongolians on our Western coast...." were destroying the Golden State.

George, a shrewd political analyst, realized that there was tremendous discontent over Chinese labor. So he began writing newspaper columns about the dangers of Chinese workers. George stated that they were too efficient, too businesslike and sent too much money home. It didn't matter that George's writing bore little truth; he was suddenly an authority; a revered one who had caught the pulse of the Chinese problem in America.

George was such a popular writer because he had the ability to place complex arguments in simple terms. He appeared to be a serious scholar reflecting on the "Asiatic hordes." In reality, George was a sophisticated demagogue who raised concerns about the prodigious Chinese work habits and a penchant for hard work.

As early as 1869 when George published an article, "The Chinese on the Pacific Coast," in the *New York Tribune*, he became an authority on the Chinese. Like many journalists, George played loose with the facts. He ascribed questionable traits to the Chinese. Their health status, their penchant for hard work, their unwillingness to assimilate and their inability to participate in the American dream, George argued, made the Chinese dangerous.

For almost a decade George wrote about land, labor and industrialization. In 1879, George's book, *Progress and Poverty: An Inquiry into the Cause of Industrial Depressions and of Increase of Want with Increase of Wealth*, became a best seller. The United States had just recovered from a major depression and George's argument that the railroad and the Chinese were responsible for the recent depression appealed to conspiracy minded Americans. George appeared to have answers to the economic doldrums that inflicted America. Profits from Chinese labor, George argued, created enormous profits. The monopolistic businesses resulting from these empires ended the dream of the common settler.

The popularity of *Progress and Poverty* was due to changing economic conditions. As the Comstock mining boom collapsed, there was a vague notion that it was due to the Chinese. Journalists pointed out the dangers of Chinese labor. So Henry George's book which used sophisticated pseudo scientific arguments about increased land prices, inflation, monopoly and cheap labor, warned Californians about the dangers of contract labor.

Another direction of George's polemical writing explained that the advances in steamship transportation created a mass migration of Chinese to San Francisco. The Pacific Mail Steamship Company, a Central Pacific owned corporation, controlled the docks, purchased key downtown business sites, established new industries and built luxurious hotels. These economic advantages, according to George, resulted solely from the profits derived from Chinese labor. Politicians quoted liberally from *Progress And Poverty*, and soon this force turned into a political party.

In 1877, the Workingmen's Party was founded and helped to write a new California constitution. When 153 constitutional delegates met for six months to write a new California constitution, fifty of them were members of the Workingmen's Party. After voters approved the California Constitution of 1879 with its numerous anti-Chinese provisions, national politicians recognized the trend and began to support exclusionist legislation.

Only three years after the publication of *Progress and Poverty*, President Chester Arthur signed the Exclusion Act of 1882. This federal law culminated thirty years of anti-Chinese agitation. Initially, this law applied for only a decade. In 1892, however, the Geary Act extended the ban on new Chinese labor until 1902. Then the ban on Chinese immigration was made permanent, and this ban didn't fully end until the 1950s.

FIGURE 8-6. The Chinese Must Go.

The Chinese Six Companies hired lawyers to fight the Geary Act and to challenge the provision that Chinese workers register with the Federal Government. The Geary Act forced Chinese labor to prove that they were legal. By May 1894 more than 100,000 Chinese had registered as legal residents.

The Chinese Exclusion Act of 1882 was the triumph of white working class values. But as the 1880s and 1890s progressed, the decline in Chinese farm labor hurt the Golden State. As a result, white racism fostered economic problems, and Mexican and Japanese workers were brought into the fields in larger numbers. Soon ethnic problems associated with these minority groups dominated the last two decades of the nineteenth century.

Select Bibliography

Ronald Takaki, *Strangers From a Different Shore: A History of Asian Americans* (New York, 1989) is the best source on Chinese labor in California. Takaki's volume combines solid history with serious ethnic analysis. A brilliant view of the rural Chinese is Sucheng Chan, "Chinese Livelihood in Rural California: The Impact of Economic Change, 1860-1880," *Pacific Historical Review*, volume 53 (1984) and Sucheng Chan, *This Bitter Soil: The Chinese in California Agriculture, 1860-1910* (Berkeley and Los Angeles, 1986).

Elmer S. Sandmeyer, *The Anti-Chinese Movement in California* (Urbana, 1939) is the standard starting point on the subject. Gunther Barth, *Bitter Strength: A History of the Chinese in the United States* (Cambridge, 1964), Mary Roberts Coolidge, *Chinese Immigration* (New York, 1909); Stuart C. Miller, *The Unwelcomed Immigrant: The American Image of the Chinese, 1785-1882* (Berkeley, 1970) and Ping Chiu, *Chinese Labor in California* (Berkeley and Los Angeles, 1963) are standard references on the topic. An excellent comparative study is Roger Daniels's, *Asian America: Chinese and Japanese in the United States Since 1850* (Seattle, 1988). An excellent analysis of toleration and discrimination is Robert W. Cherny's, "Patterns of Toleration and Discrimination in San Francisco: The Civil War to World War I," *California History*, LXXIII (Summer, 1994), pp. 130-140.

Some tales of early Chinese visitors to California are contained in Hamilton Holt, ed., *The Life Stories of Undistinguished Americans as Told by Themselves* (New York, 1906).

For the Chinese and labor unions see, for example, Alexander Saxton, *The Indispensable Enemy: Labor and the Anti-Chinese Movement in California* (Berkeley, 1971). On the Foreign Miners' Tax Law of 1850 see Richard H. Peterson, "Anti-Mexican Nativism in California, 1848-1853," *Southern California Quarterly*, 62 (Winter, 1980), pp. 309-327. On nativism see Leonard Pitt, "The Beginnings of Nativism in California," *Pacific Historical Review*, 1 (February, 1961), pp. 23-28.

On the Chinese Six Companies and organization within the Chinese community see, for example, William Hoy, *The Chinese Six Companies* (San Francisco, 1942) and Sanford M. Lyman, *Chinatown and Little Tokyo: Power, Conflict and Community Among Chinese and Japanese Immigrants in America* (Millwood, N.Y.,1986).

A useful case study of Chinese settlement is Ronald H. Limbaugh's, "The Chinese of Knight's Ferry, 1850-1920: A Preliminary Study," *California History*, LXII (Summer, 1993), pp. 107-127. Also see Ramon D. Chacon, "The Beginning of Racial Segregation: The Chinese in West Fresno and Chinatown's Role as Red Light District, 1870s-1920s," *Southern California Quarterly*, LXX (Winter, 1988), pp. 371-398.

For negative reactions to the Chinese by a contemporary traveler see, Erasmus Doolittle, *Sketches, by a Traveller* (Boston, 1830).

An attempt to identify the Chinese with African American slaves is in Dan Cauldwell's, "The Negroization of the Chinese Stereotype in California," *Southern California Quarterly*, 1 (June, 1971), pp. 123-130.

The Chinese and education are analyzed in Charles Wollenberg's, *All Deliberate Speed: Segregation and Exclusion in California Schools, 1855-1975*, (Berkeley, 1976) and Victor Low's, *A Century of Educational Struggle By The Chinese in San Francisco* (San Francisco, 1982).

9

Changing Patterns of Settlement and Work

Mexican, Native American and Japanese Labor, 1880-1910

White Californians were determined to rid California of the Chinese. They were not only a menace to local society, but they were economically independent. By 1880, pressure from the Workingmen's Party and other nativist groups made exclusion a foregone conclusion. But the large farmers and the urban businessman still needed inexpensive labor. If workers could be hired in masses, discouraged from joining the fledgling labor unions and forced to live in small and isolated neighborhoods, then Anglo employers could control the negative influences of the ethnic population. The Spanish speaking, the Native American and Japanese workers found themselves competing in an oppressive labor market, but they were a ready source of labor. The Exclusion Act of 1882 effectively ended Chinese competition in the California marketplace.

Once Chinese immigration was banned, there was again a need for cheap labor. Mexican and Japanese workers became the major source of migrant labor from 1880 to 1910. But racial tensions resulted from the presence of white European labor. The influx of European workers found the Italians, Germans and Portuguese among others competing with Mexican, Indian and Chinese labor. As a result of this ethnically diverse work force, a sophisticated racism emerged. The Mexican and Native American workers were a known commodity, but the Japanese were an unfamiliar people with no past history. At least that is how race conscious Americans viewed the newly arrived Asian population.

The popular attitude toward the Japanese was much like that directed at the Chinese. Anglo race consciousness viewed the Japanese as gangsters, cheap labor and an alien people. Unwittingly, Japanese diplomats reinforced these stereotypes and contributed to the growing attitude that the Japanese were simply "another example of the Yellow hordes taking over California."

The Unfamiliar Japanese: Violence and Stereotypes for Another Asian Immigrant Group

In the 1880s, the Japanese began immigrating to California. As the twentieth century dawned, there were nearly 25,000 Japanese living in the United States, and the vast majority settled in California. In June 1888, Munemitsu Mutsu, a Japanese Government official, landed in San Francisco on his way to a diplomatic mission in Washington and expressed concern over the undesirable Japanese who lived in San Francisco.

Mutsu unwittingly created negative stereotypes about the shosei or the false students, as they were known, and he also complained about Japanese criminal intent. A few years later, Sutemi Chinda, the Japanese consul, complained about the "wrong type of Japanese living in California." What is significant about Japanese Government officials is that they pandered to negative racial concepts.

In the last two decades of the nineteenth century, racial attitudes were not only hostile toward immigrants, but Americans suddenly preferred some ethnic groups to others. Consul Chinda echoed this notion when he remarked that some Japanese were not suited to the Golden State. In China's view, this was a class bias. But in the hands of race conscious Americans, it created another form of California racism.

The first official act, at least in police records, of violence against the Japanese took place in 1890 when Japanese shoemakers were attacked for charging excessively high repair prices. As Japanese workers were harassed and intimidated, they organized self-help political groups. The Japanese were not as easily intimidated as other casual laborers, and, as a result, they quickly moved into their own economic sphere.

What significance did the rise of Japanese labor have on other ethnic groups? The stiff competition from Japanese workers allowed the employer to pay the Spanish speaking a lower wage. It was the Mexican American and Mexican worker who faced the most important challenges in the late nineteenth century, because their labor was less of a valued commodity. The California agribusiness community complained about the haphazard work habits of Mexican labor.

This was a ploy to lower wages. Mexican workers were a valued and much sought after labor source. From 1870 to 1900, Anglo men working in California agriculture dropped by 50%. Spanish speaking farm employment rose to its highest level in California history. As agribusiness farms dominated the California countryside, labor abuses intensified. This was one way to control the demands of Spanish speaking workers.

There was an irony to agribusiness racism in the late nineteenth century because the organizations and farmers who pilloried farm workers relied on them for cheap labor. California's economic transformation from 1880 to 1900 would have been impossible without Mexican, Indian and Japanese workers. This contradiction was not lost on the ethnic workers who were paid a low wage, had inadequate housing and little hope for their children's education. In frustration, they organized labor unions, wrote letters to Spanish, Chinese and Japanese language newspapers and lobbied the Federal and California Governments for change. The Mexican American was in a strong position to challenge the budding racism in late nineteenth century California.

A long history of political activism, a sense of community and some economic successes prompted Mexican Americans to challenge the power structure. The Mexican American experience differed from other ethnic groups because American businessmen resented the economic successes of the Mexican ranchos. Anglo farmers seized control of Spanish speaking land and created a legacy of racial conflict. White immigrants believed that they held the key to California's economic future and criticized Mexican Americans for their economic activity. American businessmen created an economic system which debased the Spanish speaking and forced them into a position of second class citizenship.

The Native American was virtually ignored in the late nineteenth century. By

1880, the Indian population had moved to small villages and out of the way rural enclaves. They were still "addicted to independence" and gravitated to frontier areas. As a result, the majority of Indians lived amongst the Spanish speaking. The city of San Juan Capistrano was an exception as a number of small Indian villages continued to prosper around this bucolic Southern California settlement. Although the San Juan Capistrano Indians lost their land and identity, because of laws and customs brought in by Americans, they remained independently minded. The Indian, Mexican American and Japanese all had problems due to the land question.

Mexican Americans in Southern California: From the Ranchos to the Fields

The large land grants in Spanish and Mexican California were placed in a precarious position by 1880. The Spanish speaking ranchers were unable to hire cheap labor, and this caused their profits to decline. The extensive litigation due to the Land Law of 1851 and the combination of drought and rain made agriculture a precarious occupation. Uneven taxation and hostile sheriffs added to these problems.

Don Julio Verdugo's Rancho San Rafael is the best example of a Southern California rancho in decline. Verdugo's land extended from the San Fernando Valley to northeast Los Angeles. In 1861, he borrowed $3,445.37 at a 36% yearly interest. In just seven years he owed almost $60,000. When he was unable to pay the debt, the sheriff threatened to hold a public auction to pay off Verdugo's bank loans. Humiliated, Verdugo asked for more time, but the bank refused his request.

To satisfy his debt, Verdugo sold part of his Rancho San Rafael. This sale didn't provide enough to pay his debts. So he sold his Rancho La Canada. He still owed the bank interest, and he was forced to subdivide land parcels to pay lawyer fees. In 1871, Verdugo estate had only 200 acres left for his children. He died a broken hearted man bilked by lawyers, unable to meet bank interest payments and hostile to American style taxes and laws. Verdugo's story was typical of the experiences of Southern California rancheros.

Andres Pico, a leading Los Angeles ranchero, protested the treatment of the Verdugo family. He called it a tragedy because the land had been granted to Verdugo's father, Don Jose Maria Verdugo, by the Spanish King in the 1790s. Pico charged that the sheriff, the banks and the law conspired to destroy the influence of Spanish speaking aristocrats.

The Lynching of Francisco Torres and Images of Hispanic Crime

The changes taking place in Southern California were reflected in Santa Ana. For more than two decades Anglo settlers complained about Mexican crime. This allowed the sheriff to control the farm workers who were essential to local fields. As the Spanish speaking formed labor unions, resisted the police and complained about racism, there was a growing concern among Anglos over the attitude of Spanish speaking workers.

The newly arrived Anglo settler needed to establish a segregated society and maintain controls over the independently minded Spanish speaking population. Francisco Torres was a field worker who protested the indiscriminate withholding of wages for an alleged road poll tax. The field boss collected $2.50 to pay the county tax collector for using local roads. Torres refused to pay the tax. He also committed the ultimate sin-he called the tax "a trick to rob the workers."

When the foreman made a point to humiliate Torres in front of his co-workers there was a violent confrontation. The following day the foreman, known simply as McKelvey, was found dead. Torres was accused of the killing. There was no evidence that Torres was the killer. It was a circumstantial case but one that the sheriff and newspapers blamed on "the Mexican penchant for criminal behavior." Someone had to make an example of Torres. The vigilante mentality was so pervasive that newspapers speculated on Torres's future.

The newspapers editorialized on Hispanic criminal intent. The *San Francisco Chronicle* reported that "a lynching was probable." "Torres would pay for his crime," the *Chronicle* argued, "and this would serve as a warning to other Spanish speaking workers." The *Santa Ana Standard* employed even stronger racial language when it editorialized that Torres was "a low type of the Mexican race." The *Santa Ana Weekly Blade* fell in line and suggested that Torres might try to escape. *The Weekly Blade* reported that Mexicans were "hard characters."

Because Torres fled to San Diego shortly after the killing, the sheriff believed that he was guilty. When he was captured in San Diego, local newspapers proclaimed his guilt despite the lack of evidence. Racial tensions were high, and most Anglos believed that Torres should be an example of what would happen to the lawless Mexican. But the Mexican American community was angry over the racial implications in the Torres case.

After Torres was arrested, he was held in the Santa Ana jail. Californios and Mexicans paraded in front of the jail to protest unfair treatment. The Santa Ana population was predominantly Spanish speaking and Indian. Every indication was that a local jury could acquit Torres. So he was lynched in his jail cell in the early morning hours of August 20, 1892. As his dead body dangled from a rope in his cell, a sign attached to his body read: *CHANGE OF VENUE.* The message was clear; the Anglo power structure would not tolerate protests from the Spanish speaking workers.

The small Spanish newspapers, notably *Las dos Republicas*, argued that Torres was guilty solely because he was Mexican. In the newspaper battle to cover the Torres trial, the meaning of "white," "Mexican" and "Indian" was apparent. The white power structure provided the laws, backed the sheriff and decided who was hired in the fields and in marginal business positions. *Las dos Republicas*, a tough critic of lawlessness, believed that Torres was innocent. To protest the Torres lynching, *Las dos Republicas* called attention to the number of Spanish speaking workers who were killed by the police. When a Mexican farm worker was murdered by a deputy constable, *Las dos Republicas* criticized the law for its insensitivity toward the Spanish speaking. "It is becoming a very common custom to murder or insult the Mexicano...." *Las dos Republicas* editorialized. The hostility toward Mexican and Californio workers reflected the population revolution.

The rise of an Anglo Santa Ana began a series of major shifts in land settlement. In the three decades after statehood, Southern California was a sleepy and seemingly backward part of the Golden States. This changed when the railroad was completed and the boom in American and European land holdings generated an American dominated civilization.

During the 1860s, a small group of German, Polish and Russian settlers moved into what is now Orange County. A German vineyard society found the area, and soon 25% of local land was owned by foreign investors.

Americans also envisioned opportunity in Southern California. In the 1870s, John

G. Downey, a major land developer, moved into Los Angeles and established a series of new cities. He purchased a large parcel of land from the San Pedro based Dominguez Family and founded Wilmington. He inspired other land pioneers. Charles Maclay bought the vast Rancho San Fernando and sold hundreds of lots to recently arrived American settlers. Pio Pico, one of the wealthiest local ranchers, sold much of his land in the 1870s because of bank debts and business deals gone sour. Soon the Spanish speaking population found itself migrating to east Los Angeles.

A barrio or local ethnic neighborhood arose that was virtually self-sufficient, but it was also economically, socially and educationally isolated from mainstream Los Angeles life. Local citizens who celebrated the Mexican character of Southern California were not concerned about the changes. The Spanish speaking population complained about declining job opportunities, inadequate housing, a double standard in police services and education and a lack of concern from city government. The descent into second class citizenship was quick and virtually unnoticeable.

Since the rancho era survived into the late nineteenth century, there was an immediate influx of Spanish speaking workers into East Los Angeles. As they left the ranchos, the Californios and Mexicans found themselves in neighborhoods with little opportunity. To outsiders, Los Angeles was a "sleepy town with little energy." This stereotype was largely the result of slow growth and little industry.

Despite the Anglo influx, the Spanish speaking population was determined to preserve the old ways. In November 1869, when the railroad began building into Southern California, Los Angeles was a sleepy pueblo that had more in common with Mexico than with American cities. Large ranchos still dominated the Southern California countryside. The quiet, pastoral nature of Los Angeles, as well as inexpen-

FIGURE 9-1. Late Nineteenth Century Mexican-American Fiesta.

sive land prices, soon attracted real estate speculators. But it was still a changing civilization dependent upon the railroad.

The arrival of the Santa Fe Railroad in the fall of 1876 prepared the way for a rush of tourists, businessmen, farmers, artists, writers and businessmen. For some time writers had praised Southern California's beautiful climate and prosperous business atmosphere. In the late 1860s, Charles Nordhoff's book, *California: For Health, Pleasure and Profit*, created new interest in Southern California real estate. A railroad publicist, Nordhoff wrote with unbridled optimism about California's future. A vision of orange fields prompted Los Angeles' real estate prices to increase 500 percent in 1868-1869. When the price of ranch land reached ten dollars an acre, there was a burst of cotton, corn tobacco and even silk farms. By 1873, the national depression and the problems of shipping goods east temporarily ended this agricultural boom, but it established the first wave of Anglo settlement.

When the Southern Pacific Railroad completed its Los Angeles connection in 1876, the real estate boomed renewed itself. Soon agricultural shipments to Arizona and throughout the Southwest created a new breed of ranching Anglo millionaires. The end result of this speculation was to decrease the power of the remnants of the Spanish speaking aristocracy.

From 1865 to 1900, second generation Californios came to maturity. As they watched Southern California grow, there was a feeling of powerlessness. The Spanish speaking were not part of the new economic change. As the large ranches fluctuated economically, so did Mexican American economic and political influences.

There were also some quirky political movements anticipating some of Los Angeles's later problems. In the San Fernando Valley, a Basque settler, Miguel Leonis, formed an army of one hundred Basque cowboys whose stated purpose was to eliminate the Spanish speaking population. Law and order frequently was a problem because of this vigilante mentality. Leonis in a nostalgic recreation of a California he never knew, predicted that new laws would force the Mexican "to respect American rights." Leonis had a vision of history influenced by his own self-interest and assisted by American law.

American laws were suddenly a threat to the old ways. To the north in Stockton, Major Jose Pico was arrested for purported land fraud. He tried to sell a parcel of land under California law that was located in Baja California. In a classic example of not understanding American law, Pico couldn't figure out why he was prohibited from selling his land.

The end of the Mexican American population as an independent economic force was due to the railroad. As a railroad war between the Southern Pacific and the newly completed Santa Fe line erupted in the 1880s, the Spanish speaking lost control of the land. It was inexpensive to settle in Southern California and land was sold at low prices. In March 1887 the cost of riding the railroad to Los Angeles from the Missouri Valley was a dollar bill. That year the Southern Pacific transported 120,000 people into Los Angeles. The Santa Fe unloaded three or four passenger trains a day, and the settlers fanned out throughout Southern California. The sleepy Mexican nature of Southern California ended. The pastoral era gave way to a bustling Anglo population.

Not everyone could accept the changes. Modesta Avila was a young woman in her mid-twenties living in San Juan Capistrano. Her father and other members of her family lived on the property in nearby houses, four hundred yards from a proposed Sante Fe Railroad track site.

Modesta owned a small plot that she farmed, and the family with eight children eked out a modest living. By 1880, Modesta had been educated in local schools and could read and write English. She was an avid history student who was aware of California's Spanish and Mexican heritage. As a result, she demanded that the railroad pay her $10,000 for the right to build on her land. In her dealings with the railroad, Modesta talked about Father Junipero Serra and the Spanish tradition and used her own Mexican heritage to suggest that she had a birthright obligation on the land.

No one took her seriously. She was simply a young Mexican girl who could read and write English. But the Santa Fe Railroad misjudged her ability to raise a public protest. She rallied local citizens against the railroad and created a nasty public relations problem.

Eventually, her father sold the land. Modesta's eldest brother, Vicente, married into the Jimenez Family who purchased the land that Modesta claimed was hers, and this began a long legal battle. She refused to leave her birthplace and the farm that she had known all her life.

Taking advantage of the cloudy legal issue, the Santa Fe Railroad built its track fifteen feet from her home. Avila complained that her residence was a Mexican pueblo which had been blessed by the missionaries. In protest, she laid a large log across the railroad tracks. On it she stuck a sign: "This Land Belongs To Me."

Modesta told family and friends that land ownership was important to her, and she believed that her family's lengthy residency was more important than Anglo law. She believed that the railroad must pay her for use of her land. The Santa Fe Railroad recognized its public relations problem. The area was predominantly Spanish speaking, and they couldn't afford to anger potential customers.

The Sante Fe Railroad urged its local agent to reason with Modesta. He was only too happy to intimidate her. The railroad agent, Max Mendelson, warned her that she was breaking the law. She would be jailed, tried and sentenced to prison if she didn't stop her barbarous attacks on the railroad. Mendelson told her that the sheriff was concerned about "her unladylike behavior." Avila laughed at him and warned that her lawyer would be in touch.

Not only did Modesta have clear title to the land that the railroad built on, but she also took the railroad to court. The Santa Fe line was forced to pay $10,000 for the use of her land. The *Santa Ana Weekly Blade* headlined: "Modesta Again," and the newspaper reported that she was not only hostile to the railroad but was also not acting like a typical woman. She scoffed at reports that the sheriff would make an example of her behavior. Then Avila rented a large hall in Santa Ana to hold a victory dance. The sheriff arrived and arrested her for disturbing the peace.

At her trial, Avila cursed the railroad, criticized the new power structure and complained about the second class citizenship forced on the Spanish speaking. The judge told her to accept American institutions; he warned Modesta that this was a minor crime, and she could face more serious charges. Then the judge asked for her opinion on the matter. Was she really a threat to the local community? This spirted young woman not only challenged the Judge to dispense real justice, but she also complained about the oppressive Anglo power structure. The judge responded by sentencing Avila to three years in California's maximum security prison, San Quentin. She died there after suffering personal abuses and failed to respond to minimal medical care. The feeling in San Juan Capistrano was that the sheriff and the prison system had killed Modesta Avila. It was a lesson not lost on other Mexican protesters.

Modesta Avila challenged the Anglo power structure and paid with her life. The lesson was not lost on subsequent generations of Spanish speaking settlers. The tension between the new European American society and Californio Mexican settlers intensified as land values increased and new businesses created unbridled prosperity.

But Southern California's minority population included more than the Spanish speaking. There was a large Native American work force which supplied labor and lived in and around Los Angeles. They quickly became a displaced people in the midst of the Anglo commercial and cultural onslaught.

The Indian in Southern California: A Displaced Native Population

The Indians in and around Los Angeles suffered greatly from the American invasion. White settlers filed disputed claims to seize Indian land. Local authorities quickly recognized the new American landowners. The Bureau of Indian Affairs ignored this outright seizure of Indian property, and this inspired Helen Hunt Jackson's *Ramona: A Story* which highlighted the problems of Indian land loss. Tales of land abuses explain the difficulties the Indian experienced in Southern California and analyzes how and why the dominant Anglo culture emerged.

There were many tales of abusing the Native Californians. Helen Hunt Jackson wrote about Jim Angel who put Chrysanto, a Native American, off his land with a Homestead certificate from the Los Angeles Land Office. Antonio Douro was another Indian evicted from his farm with a lawyer's land certificate. Douro's house was a local historical landmark, and the white man took it without a fight. Times were changing in Southern California and the Native Californians were crushed by the white man's onslaught.

Indian labor was forced to migrate to the ranchos. But since fewer Californio and Mexican rancheros produced goods for local markets, wages were low and working conditions substandard. As Spanish speaking land and agricultural production declined, so did the Mexican American influence. "The Indians are all gone—some to other villages, some living nearby...in the hills," a local historian remarked.

In San Diego, Juan Bautista Bandini remembered that he employed Indian labor from the hills. In an 1880 diary entry, Bandini wrote that a young boy, Jose, would help him plant and then wander off to spend five days in the hills. The Indians, Bandini observed, were caught between two cultures. One culture had a Mexican and American direction, but there was still a culture with some remnants of traditional Indian life. The Indian was unwilling to adapt to Southern California agricultural needs, and this resistance brought in new labor sources.

By the early 1880s, Chinese labor was working the fields in and around the San Gabriel Valley. The Chinese, wearing their trademark basket hats for protection from the sun, picked fruit, and the *Pacific Rural Press* reported that the Chinese were better workers than the Mexicans. The *Pacific Rural Press* editorialized that the need for farm labor made the Chinese highly employable. The *Pacific Rural Press* reflected the racism inherent in agribusiness newspapers. Ethnic workers had to refrain from criticizing the special taxes, the unscrupulous activity of the labor broker and the blatant racism of the large Anglo farmers. But after criticizing Spanish speaking labor, the *Pacific Rural Press* began praising the seasonal Mexican worker. This worker was paid a lower wage, and, as a result this led to an oppressive system of low wages and poor working conditions.

Mexican labor was encouraged to be co-operative and docile. William H. Hollister, a well known rancher near Santa Barbara, was a cattle rancher and horse breeder who became a millionaire and had lived in Santa Barbara since 1852. He was a typical Anglo who periodically called the Mexican population "half civilized" and suited for "controlled work." He criticized local rancheros who were not paying attention to the profit margins. One local newspaper, the *Ventura Signal*, on June 22, 187, described the Spanish speaking ranchero as "educated, wealthy" but lacking "the get up of the Anglo Saxon." This type of thought placed the Spanish speaking into a second class status that allowed racist ideas to control their employment, education, housing and status in local society. It was a class based exclusion which evolved into permanent poverty and personal degradation.

From 1877 to 1910, partially due to internal difficulties in Mexico, a steady stream of workers immigrated to California. While the adjustment to Southern California was difficult, Mexican labor earned wages that were 50% higher than in Mexico. Soon Los Angeles was filled with workers from Mexico.

As Mexican labor replaced Indians and Chinese workers, the nature and structure of Southern California society changed. Once Mexican labor began to dominate the fields, the development of a Los Angeles barrio took shape. Soon there was a dominant Mexican character to Los Angeles and Southern California.

One of the byproducts of Mexican labor was the creation of a pseudo Mexican culture. Americans recreated their own version of Mexican culture. The rich and famous in and about Los Angeles began a California ritual known as the "rancheros visitardores." This was where a visiting Mexican cowboy, known as a caballero, would ride into a city as part of a Mexican parade filled with pomp and circumstance. Historian Carey McWilliams labelled the rancheros visitadores a "desperate effort to escape from the bonds of a culture that neither satisfiesnor pleases."

During the 1880s and 1890s, the Spanish fiesta was a popular form of entertainment. The *Los Angeles Times* reported that the 1894 fiesta had "genuine Indians" in the parade. Increasingly, Spanish surnames graced streets, housing tracts, parks, business centers and newly founded cities. When the first signs of suburban life took place, there were new towns with Spanish names like Mission Viejo, Santa Ana, Dominguez Hills and Santa Clarita.

When Helen Hunt Jackson's novel, *Ramona*, was published in 1884, it brought attention to the plight of the California Indian and romanticized Spanish-Mexican influences. Jackson's novel was a staunch defense of Indian land rights. Ramona is a young, but illegitimate, Indian girl adopted by a Californio family headed by the cruel matriarch Senora Moreno who hates her adopted daughter. The trials and tribulations of the mixed marriage between a Scotsman and her Indian mother is a central theme in the book. When Ramona falls in love with the Indian, Allesandor, who is a spokesperson for his people, the central theme of the story emerges-the rape of Indian civilization, economically and culturally, by white influences. The worst stereotypes in the *Ramona* novel are the mission Franciscans who appear as wise and benevolent leaders helping the Indian achieve civilization. *Ramona* created a storm of protest because it charged that Americans had taken the last of the good Indian land. White squatters who settled on the land are portrayed as vicious but Mexican civilization is also described as "semi-civilized," and Jackson's novel reiterates popular stereotypes regarding the Spanish speaking.

The decline of Mexican Southern California was evident in the 1880s when the Spanish speaking barrio cut the Mexican American population off from its Anglo counterpart. It was the lack of political influence, not economic considerations, that initially placed the Spanish speaking on the road to second class citizenship. There were enough white Anglo Democratic voters in Southern California to persuade the Los Angeles party caucus to ignore the demands of Spanish speaking Democrats. Mexicans in Los Angeles now joined their northern brethren in exclusion from meaningful political participation.

Economic Decline: From the Land Law to 1851 to the Hispanic Tourist Boom

Economic decline quickly followed the loss of political influence. As the Land Law of 1851 continued to plague the Spanish speaking, the prosperous Spanish speaking ranchers hired lawyers to protect their land claims. This proved disastrous. Most American lawyers wound up owning Mexican land grants. The Dominguez Family of Santa Barbara County lost 75,000 acres to an unscrupulous lawyer simply because they had faith in him. In San Luis Obispo County, Parker H. French, a member of the California Legislature, preyed upon local Spanish speaking families and wound up owning huge chunks of original Mexican land grants. Parker was a lawyer who understood how to manipulate federal land law.

In San Diego County, lawyers were so ruthless in tricking the Spanish speaking out of their property that there were frequent public meetings and dozens of articles in Spanish language publications protesting the misuse of American land law. In 1860, more than 30% of all San Diego ranchers and casual farmers were Spanish speaking, but by 1880, they owned less than 2% of the working ranches. "This was the beginning

of poverty for many old California families," ranchero Dario Orena of Santa Barbara observed.

As rancho life broke down in Southern California there were numerous changes. The most obvious one was unemployment for the skilled Mexican vaquero cowboy. Suddenly many vaqueros were unemployed and living in the Los Angeles barrio. The leather craftsmen, the cooks and the casual workers left large ranchos, like Don Julio Verdugo's Rancho Camulos north of Los Angeles, and drifted into the Spanish speaking barrio.

Indian villages were also seized under American preemption law. In 1873, John G. Ames, a federal Indian agent, remarked that the village of San Pasqual was taken over by settlers using federal land law. But Ames approved of this seizure and remarked, "the Indian had no right to public land." Protests from Indian leaders went unheeded. In San Juan Capistrano the claims of local Indians were voided, and in 1873, Ames remarked that Indians often lived on Mexican land grants. Thus, Indian land settlement declined dramatically by the 1880s due to American land law.

Americans seized upon the dismemberment of Mexican lands to create a new economic system. Suddenly, small American farms sprung up. A number of new cities, all bearing Spanish surnames, were created to serve the new Anglo farms. As Americans developed their own economic and political institutions, the Spanish speaking population was placed in a position of second class citizenship. By 1900, the arrival of new California settlers sealed the fate of Spanish speaking Californians. From 1870 to 1900, California grew from 620,000 to almost a million and a half settlers. Nowhere was the surge of Americans more noticeable than in Southern California. Suddenly, the Mexican character declined. Hispanic influences were more often used to sell

FIGURE 9-2. Southern California, 1880.

homes in suburbs or to merchandise products with a California character. Not surprisingly, Anglos sold these goods, and the influence of the Spanish speaking ended a half century after statehood.

Some viewed east Los Angeles as a foreign country. Race conscious Anglos suggested that the barrio had a separate culture that made it impossible for Mexicans to assimilate. Mexican Americans were described as "foreign," "difficult" and "backward." The *Los Angeles Times* continually referred to the Spanish speaking as a "proud but vanquished people."

A Southern California tourist boom from 1873 to 1875 and again from 1887 to 1888 continued the decline of Spanish influences in Los Angeles. As railroad promoters set up cheap fares and negotiated land sales, the Spanish speaking population was all but forgotten. Anglos repeatedly sold newly arrived settlers on the "Spanish character" of California. Unfortunately, no Spanish speaking salesmen, businessmen or politicians greeted the new arrivals.

Spanish speaking Californians did not accept these changes easily. Mexican culture persisted. The large Mexican weddings, the cock fights, the barbecues, the fandangos

and the rodeos remained an integral part of local custom. Close family ties persisted, and soon the barrio was a shelter from the hostile Anglo world. Much of early Spanish and Mexican culture was preserved, but it was not until the 1880s that it was common for the Los Angeles' Spanish speaking population to observe Mexican Independence Day. The Juarez Patriotic Club in Los Angeles and the Los Junta Patriotica Mexicana in Santa Barbara staged elaborate celebrations. In San Francisco, the Spanish American Independent Political Club went further by nominating Spanish speaking candidates to run for public office. Because of their voting prowess, San Francisco Republican and Democratic leaders quietly incorporated the Spanish speaking into local politics.

Blind Chris Buckley, the San Francisco boss in the 1880s, instructed Mayor Washington Bartlett to pay lip service to Mexican political needs. In the 1890s, San Francisco Mayor Adolph Sutro campaigned heavily in Mexican American neighborhoods, promising better jobs and education for the Spanish speaking. In 1901, the San Francisco based Union Labor Party elected Eugene Schmitz as Mayor, and he proudly told a *San Francisco Chronicle* reporter that his ex-wife was of "Mexican descent." After the election, these promises were forgotten. Soon Spanish language newspapers complained about political deception. Mexican Americans charged that the Spanish speaking vote was used and abused by politicians with "American interests."

By the 1890s, Spanish speaking Californians were employed in the lowest paying jobs in the Golden State. The vast majority of Mexican Americans were confined to menial or unskilled positions, and this increased subsistence barrio living. Abject poverty and subsistence housing were the norm. There were few Mexican Americans in skilled trades and even fewer in white collar positions. A number of Catholic priests protested this slide into second class citizenship. Father Juan Caballeria remarked that: "the old settlers have passed away." Years later Caballeria pointed out that it was a mistake for the Los Angeles and Santa Barbara Mexican communities not to have taken a more vigorous stand against the drift toward second class citizenship.

What is ironic about Father Caballeria is that he was chastised for persisting to speak to his parishioners in Spanish. He was also warned for being "too political" and counseled not to talk about poverty.

As California's Spanish speaking population began the twentieth century, there was a loss of economic and political influence. After 1900, the bearers of Spanish-American culture were more critical of the economic and social system. When tens of thousands of Mexican braceros were imported to work in the fields of the Imperial and San Joaquin Valleys, there was immediate protest. But it was already too late. The decline of the large ranchos, the segregation of the Spanish speaking in the schools, the lack of adequate job opportunities and the rise of a Spanish speaking barrio cut off Mexican Americans from mainstream California life.

The Japanese and California: The Early Years and the Carry-over of Vicious Racial Stereotypes

Once the concern with Chinese immigration died down and Federal Law prohibited easy access to America, there appeared no need to be concerned about Far Eastern settlers. But once the Japanese settled in Hawaii in 1868, the next step was California. In the 1880s, an inflationary economy in Japan caused small rice farmers to lose their land and more than 300,000 small farmers were out of work.

By the 1890s, Japanese workers landed in California in large numbers. The Japanese migrants had to receive government approval to migrate, and women as well as men were allowed into California. Many had trouble finding suitable employment, and this created a self-contained economy. Edna Bonacich studied emerging Japanese business and concluded that they created "ethnic antagonism."

Much like the Chinese, the Japanese quickly experienced racial discrimination. They inherited the negative stereotypes that prevailed against the Chinese. The first generation Japanese, the Issei, were often called "chinks" in school, and newspaper editorials compared the Japanese to the Chinese. As a young child, Minoru Iino remembers that other school children sang: "Ching Ching Chinaman chopped off his tail." Iino cried and didn't understand the taunting. This scenario was relived by young Japanese students all over California. When and why did the Japanese first come to California?

The first Japanese settled in Alameda in 1868 when it was still not legal for the Japanese to immigrate to the United States. Alameda is a small town next to Oakland across the bay from San Francisco. Farm labor contractors would come into Alameda and hire the Japanese to work in the Hayward DeCoto pea fields and in the agricultural areas around Stockton.

In 1886, the United States legalized Japanese immigration, and this alerted California nativism to the new Asian menace. The Issei or Japanese born workers began immigrating to California in large numbers in the mid-1880s. By 1908, when the Gentlemen's Agreement was signed between the United States and Japan to restrict immigration, there were more than 40,000 Japanese living on the Pacific Coast; most of them residing in California. The need for inexpensive farm labor brought the Japanese into the San Joaquin Valley in large numbers. Soon they were independent truck farmers. The early Issei workers were welcomed because they worked for low wages and had a reputation for hard work.

George Shima was a typical Japanese immigrant. Born in 1863 in pre-Meiji Japan, he arrived in California in 1889 with less than a thousand dollars. After securing a job as a common laborer, he quickly became a labor contractor. He went into business with a number of other Issei and leased 15 acres of reclaimed land.

With advanced agricultural knowledge, Shima quickly developed a farm empire in the San Joaquin Delta. He took flooded or excessively wet lands and raised potatoes. By 1909, the *San Francisco Examiner* called Shima "California's potato king." By 1918, Shima's empire was approaching twenty million dollars.

Although he was a millionaire, Shima was ineligible for citizenship. When he purchased a home in Berkeley in 1909, there were immediate protests. Furious over the racial attitudes, Shima erected a high fence around his house. He told a University of California Professor that he would not allow his children to play with others in the neighborhood. Although he was a millionaire, an acknowledged expert in scientific agriculture and a shrewd promoter of the potato, Shima was not accepted in the conservative, middle class community of Berkeley, California. When Shima died in 1926, his pallbearers included Stanford University President, David Starr Jordan and San Francisco Mayor James Rolph, Jr. But Shima was not a typical Japanese settler. Although he was accepted into the white power structure, Shima never forgot the insults or derogatory remarks.

George Shima was a case study in the contradictions facing Japanese settlers. He was the subject of insults, racism and a double standard early in his business career. However, after becoming a millionaire,

Shima was accepted into the higher echelon of California society. It was a strange contradiction, because he never forgot that color made it more difficult to succeed in the business world. Shima wasn't the average Japanese businessman, he was an exception with enormous talent who succeeded despite the barriers.

The average Japanese immigrant settled in the "Little Tokyos" that grew up in San Francisco, Los Angeles, Sacramento and Stockton. Yet, despite the hostile racial climate, the Issei were successful businessmen. By 1909, a survey of the United States Immigration Commission indicated that California had 1,380 Japanese businesses, and they were generally prosperous and served a community need.

Japanese Labor at the Turn of the Twentieth Century: Preparing the Way for the Progressive Onslaught

By 1900, there was a noticeable anti-Japanese campaign in the Golden State. San Francisco Mayor James D. Phelan uttered racist remarks about the health hazard the Japanese posed, and he attempted to resurrect the old anti-Chinese hatreds in a new and more sophisticated form.

Labor unions worried about cheap Japanese labor. So in May 1900 the first large scale protest against Japanese labor took place. The Sailor's Union organized a group of labor unions who urged Mayor Phelan to support a ban on Japanese immigration. A coterie of speakers assembled outside San Francisco's City Hall and Professor E.A. Ross of Stanford University warned Californians that Japanese labor was too competitive. Denying any racial feelings, Ross suggested that his opposition to the Japanese was purely economic. As a respected member of the academic community, Professor Ross preached a scientific racism.

FIGURE 9-3. Anti-Japanese Sign.

Throughout California there was little organized racism directed toward the Japanese. This was because the majority of Japanese lived in San Francisco. However, soon California newspapers picked up anti-Japanese issues. Chester Rowell's *Fresno Republican* ran a series of articles on the dangers of Japanese labor, and in 1905, the *San Francisco Chronicle* headlined " The Japanese Invasion: The Problem of the Hour." The *Chronicle* suggested that there were at least 100,000 Japanese in California and called them "no more assimilable than the Chinese." The notion that they undercut white labor was the central theme of the story. In large headlines, the *Chronicle* noted that "Crime and Poverty Go Hand In Hand With Asiatic Labor."

The *San Francisco Chronicle*, owned by M.H. de Young, was conservative, Republican and California's most influential newspaper. William Randolph Hearst's rival paper, the *San Francisco Examiner*, quickly picked up anti-Japanese themes as well as a result of newspaper pressure, the California Legislature introduced an anti-Japanese bill in every biennial session for the next forty years. Anti-Japanese bills became an integral part of California politics.

San Francisco was the focal point of anti-Japanese activity. On May 14, 1905 the Asiatic Exclusion league was organized and campaigned until the end of World War II for state laws limiting the rights of the Japanese. The Asiatic Exclusion League objected to the Japanese for both economic and racial reasons. A statement of the League's position outlined its objections:

1. We cannot assimilate them without injury to ourselves.
2. No large community of foreigners, so cocky, with such distinct racial, social and religious prejudices, can abide long in this country without serious friction.
3. We cannot compete with a people who have a low standard of civilization, living and wages.
4. It should be against public policy to permit our women to intermarry with Asiatics.

The League's statements on the Japanese proved to be popular ones for politicians. As a result of this rhetoric, the anti-Japanese movement blossomed outside California. Soon Republican President Theodore Roosevelt wrote to leading California politicians suggesting the need to control Japanese immigration.

President Roosevelt faced a problem with the Japanese Government because he recognized that the Japanese had just defeated two Russian fleets and crushed the Russian armies. Japan was now a world power. Roosevelt recognized that he had to move slowly in limiting the Japanese's prerogative to move to the United States. Fortunately, President Roosevelt could depend upon Californians to raise the spectre of anti-Japanese sentiment. While Roosevelt didn't publicly support limiting the rights of the Japanese, he did agree with the California position on limiting Asian immigrants.

In January 1907, the California Legislature was surprised to hear outgoing Governor George C. Pardee criticized Roosevelt for not understanding the complex Japanese question. What Pardee suggested was that California had the right to segregate Orientals until the courts ruled in favor of laws

that allowed legal discrimination. President Roosevelt quickly called the entire California Congressional Delegation to the White House and asked the Golden State representatives to postpone anti-Japanese legislation. In a highly political move, President Roosevelt waited to see if the anti-Japanese movement was as strong a political force as public opinion indicated. Roosevelt quietly manipulated California into a position where state politicians would not appear publicly racist.

The newly elected governor, James N. Gillet, a conservative Republican, bowed to President Roosevelt's wishes, and California allowed pending anti-Japanese measures to die out. What Roosevelt was doing behind the scenes was working with the Japanese Government on a measure known as the Gentlemen's Agreement. After a year and a half of negotiations the Japanese Government agreed not to issue passports to the continental United States for both skilled or unskilled workers. The only passports issued under the Gentleman's Agreement would to be the parents, wives and children of laborers already in the United States.

President Roosevelt announced to California politicians that the Gentlemen's Agreement was exclusion. Californians didn't agree. Rather than end California's anti-Japanese tirade, the Gentlemen's Agreement intensified it. The Exclusion League, the *San Francisco Chronicle* and the *San Francisco Examiner* began suggesting that the influx of Japanese women, who were joining their husbands, was an indication that the Japanese population would increase dramatically.

In 1910,when the Republican Progressive Hiram Johnson was elected California's governor, the Progressives drew a color line. No longer could President Roosevelt or his successor William Howard Taft negotiate a political truce with California politicians. Johnson used the long standing anti-Asian focus of California politics to make the Japanese a major political issue. This began the first steps in influencing the Federal Government to pass immigration laws limiting Japanese entry into the United States. Much like the Chinese question, Californians were in the forefront of shaping national attitudes against Japanese immigration.

Bilbliographical Essay

Douglas Monroy, *Thrown Among Strangers: The Making of Mexican Culture in Frontier California* (Berkeley and Los Angeles, 1990) is the major source on Mexican labor, settlement and culture in the late nineteenth century. An excellent interpretive view of Mexican Americans is Albert Camarillo, *Chicanos In California: A History of Mexican Americans in California* (San Francisco, 1984, rev. ed. 1990).

On Southern California see Carey McWilliams, *Southern California Country: An Island on the Land* (New York, 1946); Leonard Pitt, *The Decline of the Californios: A Social History of the Spanish Speaking Californians, 1846-1890* (Berkeley and Los Angeles, 1966): Richard Griswold del Castillo, *The Los Angeles Barrio, 1850-1890* (Cambridge, 1979) and Ricardo Romo, *East Los Angeles: History of a Barrio* (Austin, 1983).

See Earl S. Pomeroy, *The Pacific Slope: A History of California, Oregon, Washington, Idaho, Utah and Nevada* (New York, 1965) for an excellent analysis of the change in land settlement. Also see Glenn S. Dumke, *The Boom of the Eighties In Southern California* (San Marino, 1955).

The problem of law and order and banditry is analyzed in an excellent monograph by Pedro Castillo and Albert Camarillo, eds., *Furia y Muerte: Los Bandidos Chicanos* (Los Angeles, 1973). This publication is from the Azatlan Publications Monograph series and represents the first serious attempt to place Spanish speaking bandits into a sophisticated historical context.

For the early Japanese immigration see, for example, Kazuo Ito, *Issei: A History of Japanese Immigrants In North America* (Seattle, 1973); Bill Hosokawa, *Nisei: The Quiet Americans* (New York, 1969); Ronald Takaki, *Strangers From a Different Shore: A History of Asian Americans* (New York, 1990); Yuji Ichioka, *The Issei: The World of the First Generation Japanese Immigrants, 1885-1924* (New York, 1988) and Yamato Ichihashi, *Japanese in the United States* (New York, 1969, reprint of 1932 work).

The Japanese contribution to the California labor market is examined in Edna Bonacich and John Modell's, *The Economic Aspects of Ethnic Solidarity: Small Business in the Japanese American Community* (Berkeley and Los Angeles, 1980) and also see Lucie Cheng and Edna Bonacich, *Labor Immigration Under Capitalism: Asian Workers In The United States Before World War II* (Berkeley, 1984).

Lisbeth Haas, *Conquests and Historical Identities In California, 1769-1936* (Berkeley, 1995) was a major influence on this chapter. Haas studied San Juan Capistrano and Santa Ana in what is now Orange County and recreated the racial tensions that shaped social economic change. For the Francisco Torres story see, Jean Riss, "The Lynching of Francisco Torres," *Journal of Mexican American History*, 1 (Spring 1971), pp. 90-112. For political economic change in Orange County see, for example, Gilbert G. Gonzalez, "Mexican Communities in Orange County," *Journal of Orange County Studies*, 3-4 (Fall 1989/Spring 1990), pp. 19-27.

See Helen Hunt Jackson, *Ramona: A Story* (New York, 1884, 1988 reprint) for many popular attitudes about the Spanish speaking and the Indian. Also see, George H. Phillips, "Indians in Los Angeles, 1781-1875," *Pacific Historical Review*, 49 (August 1980), pp. 427-445 and Florence Connolly Shipek, *Pushed into the Rocks: Southern California Indian Land Tenure, 1769-1986* (Lincoln, 1987).

10

Progressivism

The African American and Japanese in the Golden State

The Progressive Era celebrated white Anglo Saxon California values. When Governor Hiram Johnson was inaugurated in January 1911, he announced the triumph of middle class ideals and the end of the heinous railroad monopoly. The issue of monopoly had brought Progressives to power on a platform of equal opportunity and an emphasis upon morality in government. These concerns prompted ethnic Californians to speak out about their plight. What Johnson and other Progressives failed to recognize was the growing force of multicultural influences.

One of the tragic ironies of Progressivism is that it emphasized equality, opportunity, fairness and a sense of moral justice. Unfortunately, none of these ideals were applied to the ethnic population. Despite this liberal flaw, the Progressive Era was a period of ethnic recognition as employment, housing and educational advances took place.

The belief in progress prompted euphoria about the future. This optimism was due to San Francisco's position as the commercial and financial center of a diverse labor force. The rise of labor unions extolling a classless and colorless society was another characteristic of Progressive optimism. Eventually, the labor movement would include ethnic minorities. However, in 1900, the majority of skilled trades excluded minority groups, and because traditional unions narrowed their membership, ethnic unions took to the fields and factories to combat the lack of recognition.

San Francisco's Progressive leaders argued that opportunity was available to all ethnic groups. While racial patterns were never as restrictive in California, there was still a resistance to African and Asian American cultures. By 1900, California blacks had established a strong presence in the Golden State. The impact of the earthquake and fire of 1906 slowed the growth of African American migrants who remained at one percent of the state's total. This relatively small African American population made them an almost invisible minority. In 1900, stable families were the rule in black homes with 81.9 percent of all households headed by men. The African American community dominated the service industry in such positions as waiters, shoe shine stand attendants, beauticians and hotel porters. The income from these jobs created a black middle class population who challenged Progressive racism.

The Progressive politicians view of Americanization was one which led to second class citizenship. Governor Hiram W. Johnson's California provided opportunity for the white, middle class and ethnic workers found it more difficult to find employment. There was also rampant segregation. Ethnic neighborhoods expanded so rapidly during the Progressive Era that politicians simply left them alone. As a result, these neighborhoods developed newspapers, businesses and political influence. In particular, the African American and Japanese populations faced the hostility from the Anglo power structure and this was one of the reasons for their political, social and economic activity in the Progressive Era.

African Americans Challenge Progressive Racism

In a 1907 editorial a black newspaper, the *San Francisco Spokesman*, complained that segregation was "as real in California as in Mississippi..." African Americans challenged the Progressive picture of racial harmony. They publicized the inequities in housing, employment and public facilities. Urbanization and industrialization created stark contrasts in California society, and suddenly race was a deterrent to employment. As jobs became more plentiful, the African American population found itself unable to break out of the unskilled labor market.

The liberal tone of Progressivism obscured California's racial inequities. As the Golden State grew into an urban and industrial colossus, San Francisco and Los Angeles began to influence the American political system. When Hiram Johnson was elected the Progressive Republican Governor of California in 1910, President William H. Taft wrote a memo telling Johnson to "keep an eye on California political attitudes."

During the Progressive Era, African and Japanese Americans were active in combat-

ing Progressive racism. They organized ethnic labor unions, achieved some limited professional success and formed effective political action groups to protest the double standard in housing, employment and education. The rise of ethnic political and economic organizations destroyed the stereotype that California's minority population was happy. White America hardly noticed these changes, but during the Progressive Era, the seeds of rebellion and discontent were clear. California's multi-cultural population would no longer settle for a smaller share of the American dream.

African Americans in the Progressive Era: The NAACP and Newspaper Pressure for Equality

Although it was small in numbers, California's African American population challenged the Progressive Era pronouncement of equal opportunity. The rise of black political pressure groups, newspapers and unions created self-sufficiency and economic independence. In 1909 the National Association for the Advancement of Colored People (NAACP) organized to challenge black exclusion from the mainstream of American political economic life.

Initially, housing, not employment, was the initial battlefield. The NAACP and black newspapers protested the lack of affordable housing for African Americans and continually campaigned against landlords. There was a subtle racism practiced by local landlords. The forms was not filled out correctly, the deposit was late or the place was rented. This practice continued for years.

After the 1906 San Francisco earthquake, the *Oakland Sunshine* editorialized: "real estate agents do not care to rent to blacks in San Francisco." There was a practice, known as block busting, in which real estate agents informed prospective sellers that a particular neighborhood was about to be invaded by black property owners, thus scaring off potential buyers. This tactic allowed unscrupulous Realtors to purchase property at a reduced price. This real estate tactic accelerated racial tensions while creating a strong backlash against African Americans.

Despite the problems facing black Californians, the myth persisted that economic opportunity and political freedom existed in the Golden State. One example Progressives used to support this fallacious notion was labor unions. Progressive politicians proudly announced that they were granting new labor rights while providing a comprehensive welfare system and expanding direct popular democracy. The labor movement, Progressives argued, extended its vision to ethnic workers.

In 1910, when Governor Hiram Johnson was elected governor, he informed the nation that the initiative, referendum and recall placed the voter in charge of California politics. What Johnson failed to mention was that it benefited only the white, male voter. There was a nasty, though subtle, racism to Progressive politics.

The ethnic influx into California was substantial during the Progressive Era. African Americans doubled in population from 1910 to 1920. William E.B. DuBois, the African American writer and editor of the *Crisis* magazine traveled into California to counter negative racial attitudes. After spending some time in Los Angeles, DuBois wrote: "Los Angeles is not Paradise....The color line there is sharply drawn." In San Francisco and Oakland, DuBois described a free living and easy flowing atmosphere. The black population in northern California was suspicious of outsiders and easterners, DuBois reported, and they still had trouble being accepted in stores, hotels and restaurants.

There were nine black newspapers in California, the six located in southern California, complained about racist attitudes. The southern, redneck political mentality in

and around Los Angeles created segregated housing, inferior education and a restricted social life. In Oakland, there were two black newspapers critical of the Progressive Movement's double standard. San Francisco no longer had a black newspaper and the NAACP suggested that this was due to the acceptance of "Negro life."

Despite these problems, California was an attractive place to settle because of employment opportunities and affordable housing. It was often easier for African Americans to purchase homes than to rent. By 1917, there were five thousand blacks in Oakland, and a *Colored Directory* was published. This directory included hundreds of pictures of attractive homes and featured prominent black churches. The directory reflected African American business success and soon grew from 76 pages in 1915 to 140 by 1917. But there was concern with city services.

Racial complaints and NAACP pressure prompted the Los Angeles Police Department to hire its first black officers. But the complaints continued against the Los Angeles Police Department. The NAACP alleged that throughout southern California the white police demanded segregated bars and restaurants. A Los Angeles African American businessman remarked: "I feel like I'm in Mississippi." Black neighborhoods were patrolled by officers who continually insulted the local population. By 1915, the NAACP had filed hundreds of formal grievances alleging political brutality. The police learned very little from these complaints in southern California, but the liberal tradition to the north created a more equitable society.

The charge of excessive police brutality in Los Angeles was a catalyst to more sympathetic law enforcement in northern California. In San Francisco, the NAACP was able to provide guidelines to the mayor in order to maintain "proper racial relations."

In San Francisco it was easier to obtain a college education, and while jobs and houses were often the left over ones, they were still better than any available in Los Angeles. San Francisco's African American community quickly banded together and organized to maintain its few and hard earned rights.

One of the byproducts of the Progressive Era was the rise of political organizations. African Americans and other ethnic groups formed political pressure groups, labor unions and service clubs in order to extend their opportunities. There were also small groups of professionals, doctors, lawyers, nurses and business people who created a strong educational and economic contribution.

Progressivism: The Rise of Ethnic Organizations and Professionals to Combat California Racism

On August 1, 1907, the Lincoln-Roosevelt League formed and began campaigning for middle class political equality. This pressure group was organized by Progressive Republicans who hoped to establish a form of popular democracy which included the initiative, referendum and recall as devices for the common person to express political ideas. The Lincoln-Roosevelt League pitch for equality, however, didn't include ethnic minorities. While the Progressives were generally subtle enough to hide their negative racial attitudes, some African American groups noticed the racial disparity in Progressive thought.

In 1902, the National Negro Business League opened a branch in San Francisco, and five years later this organization approached the Lincoln-Roosevelt League hoping to play an active role in Progressive politics. They were rebuffed, thereby highlighting the racism in twentieth century California. Racism was so entrenched that it forced some black owned businesses to hire white workers.

The National Negro Business League complained that the African American owned Dry Dock Company of San Francisco employed white carpenters. When the NNBL met with company owners, they were informed that business contracts depended upon using white carpenters. It was impossible to acquire business with black carpenters, so the black owned Dry Dock Company of San Francisco dispatched white carpenter to selected jobs.

In Los Angeles, a well known black newspaper, the *California Eagle*, hired white typesetters. There was a widely held perception that African Americans couldn't master some skilled trades. Despite these attitudes, many African American businesses were successful and created a wide variety of new products. Inventive African American business people found lucrative areas for their talents.

Race products helped to develop a black business community. Allan Moorestone, a San Jose businessman, prospered as a mortician, and in San Francisco, Madame C.J. Walker and Mrs. A. E. Malone made fortunes manufacturing skin and hair products.

There was a small, but successful, African American professional class. The success of William L. Patterson, a law student at Hastings College in San Francisco, typifies the struggle of black attorneys. After graduation, Patterson was assigned as a clerk to future United States Senator Samuel Shortridge who refused to accept him because he was "a Negro." As a result, Patterson went to work for a black lawyer, McCants Steward, and did business with an all African American clientele. It was virtually impossible for African American attorneys to find clients. By 1920, there were only two black attorneys in San Francisco as the legal establishment continued to set up roadblocks to success. As Patterson suggested: "The Progressive dream was for whites only."

Black doctors and nurses were small in number and encountered discrimination as well. Not only did black nurses have trouble being accepted into nursing schools, but once they graduated, jobs and housing were difficult to find. San Francisco General Hospital allowed black physicians to admit patients but not to treat them. However, not all black doctors were thwarted by these attitudes. Dr. Earl T. Leaner founded the California College of Chiropodists and enjoyed a half-century of successful practice. He also earned a sold reputation for research and was awarded numerous professional honors.

The success of African American business and professional people was ignored by the press and general public. Racial attitudes made it difficult to recognize black men and women who made fortunes and supplied new products. Anglo attitudes suggested that the only legitimate black businesses were bars, dance halls, card parlors and restaurants. In this way, it was easier for Anglos to keep alive the negative stereotypes which doomed the black Californian to permanent second class citizenship.

There was a contribution in the social side of African American culture which set the tone for generations of musical, literary and art students to follow.

The Social Side of African Americans in the Progressive Era: Another Way to Make a Living

The social side of African American life was alive in the blacks bars, clubs and restaurant. There was no distinct or popular style of black music and dance prior to 1900. However, the prosperity of the Progressive Era and the rise of black business interests created new social freedom and, consequently, an African American culture. Soon black music and dance evolved into a distinctive part of California social life. But the black church and press cautioned against an excess of personal freedom. They believed that African Americans had to "live a model social life" to combat negative perceptions. Morality wasn't the sole domain of Anglo civilization, as the First African Methodist Episcopal Church demonstrated when it criticized white excesses in the black clubs.

The black owned newspaper, the *Oakland Western Outlook*, remarked on January 2, 1915, that young men looked "tough" and "danced suggestively" in local clubs. This was a casual reference to the growth of a rough and tough area where young people congregated to dance, drink and test the bounds of police authority.

The Tenderloin, a block from Market Street, was home to a number of San Francisco clubs which catered exclusively to African Americans. The city became so wide open with illegal liquor, drugs and prostitution that soon a reputation emerged for liberal attitudes which was rivaled only by New Orleans, New York, London and Paris.

There were a number of black clubs that catered to San Franciscans. Louis V. Purcell's Elite Cafe was the premier black night club on the west coast, and a well known dance, the Turkey Trot, became popular at the Elite Cafe. Lester Mapp, a West Indian, took over the Elite Cafe after Purcell's death in 1915 and maintained its reputation. The resorts which catered to whites, as well as affluent African Americans, were known as black and tan clubs, and their musical groups were instantly popular. Soon Lester Mapp's Jazz Dogs and Sid Le Protti's Crescent Orchestra made black musicians important cultural figures.

The Oakland newspaper, the *Western Outlook*, editorialized in 1914 that whites prefer "colored manipulators of the ragtime muse." There was no denying the popularity of black entertainment. As a result of the demand for black music, the Colored Entertainers Club opened in 1915 at 107 Columbus Avenue near Jackson and Kearny in the center of the Barbary Coast. This two floored club was an extravagantly decorated spot with beautiful art work and elaborate furnishings. It was a private club which required a key, making it a profitable venture.

As ragtime emerged by 1909 and jazz became a musical phenomena, the black church continued to express concern about excessive drinking, open vice and casual violence. One Oakland newspaper, the *Western Outlook*, was frightened by the changes: "Our young men and women have no other thought but dancing."

In 1913, the passage of the Red Light Abatement Act attempted to control houses of prostitution which were declared a public nuisance. Vice became a major political issue as well. A drive to control prostitution coincided with the passage of alcohol and drug reform laws. The *Oakland Sunshine* reported that the San Francisco Police Department demonstrated a belief that "Negroes were prone to vice and crime." At least that was the view of one policeman and his date during an interview at Sanguinetti's.

Sanguinetti's was a black restaurant which catered to a white clientele. This nicely furnished establishment complete with red velvet curtains and furnishings imported from Paris, was a restaurant on the waterfront which had the reputation as an exclusive, but rough, place to eat and drink. As a large breasted black woman danced to Stephen Foster songs, two black musicians played banjo and guitar while singing racially offensive tunes known as coon songs. This bar reinforced the negative attitudes which many whites had toward black Californians.

The entertainment business was a two edged sword. It allowed black performers economic independence but denied them real acceptance as performers. The *San Francisco Examiner* noted in a series of articles in September, 1913 and again in January, 1917 that there was a public movement to control the excesses of the cafes and resorts where alcohol flowed and the music played until the wee hours of the morning.

From 1917 to 1921 the premier African American night clubs Purcell's, the Jupiter and the Olympia were harassed by the police, because these black and tan clubs catered to a mixed population. The San Francisco Examiner wrote that "fashionably dressed white women...dancing with Negroes and...white men...waltzing on the floor with colored girls" was the norm.

When Lester Mapp's night clubs challenged white controls he was charged with violation of California liquor laws. In a lengthy and well publicized hearing in 1917, Mapp beat the charges. Four years later Mapp was once again acquitted of a federal charge of violating liquor laws. The Federal Alcohol Tax Unit spent four years investigating Mapp but his reputation as a businessman made it difficult to garner a conviction impossible.

The voters, however, were happy with the selective prosecution of black businesses and with elections around the corner, politicians acted to cater to the morality vote. Drinking, dancing and African American clubs suddenly became a political issue.

The San Francisco District Attorney's office, in an act of monumental stupidity, convinced the SF Board of Supervisors to ban dancing on Christmas eve for religious reasons. A Christmas eve raid at Mapp's Club led to numerous arrests and Lester Mapp finally gave up and moved his business to Chicago.

San Francisco's entertainment reputation made the city a popular migration point for

African Americans. The quality of life in San Francisco was preferable to other areas of the American West. By 1920 a recognizable black settlement grew up on Fillmore street and there was a feeling of cultural and social kinship among California's black population.

Allensworth: California's African American Town

Although California was liberal by western standards, African Americans felt the pain of segregation, the loss of economic opportunity and the insult of second class schools. As a result, a group of black Californians explored the possibility of establishing an African American city. Eventually, a plan was proposed, and it was named after its founder, Allen Allensworth. This small community, Allensworth, quickly became an independent business and cultural mecca for California's African American settlers. The plan for Allensworth, its success and eventual decline provides a microcosmic history of the problems black Californians faced.

On June 13, 1908 the *Delano Holograph* noted that a "race colony" was being built in the San Joaquin Valley. This black city, the *Delano Holograph* noted, was the dream of Allen Allensworth. Californians were intrigued with Allensworth who was born a slave in Louisville, Kentucky in April 1842 and entered the United States Navy in April, 1863. Two years later he achieved the rank of first class petty officer and served with valor on the gunboats the Queen City and the Pittsburgh. When the Civil War ended Allensworth took advantage of the new educational opportunities for African Americans.

He attended Roger Williams University in Nashville and studied Theology. Eventually, Allensworth became a chaplain in the 24th Infantry attaining the rank of Captain. For twenty years Allensworth ministered to

the black cavalrymen at Fort Apache in Arizona.

Lieutenant-Colonel Allensworth retired in 1906 and settled in Los Angeles. As he observed southern California ways, Allensworth realized that Mexican Americans also had problems with race conscious Anglos.

Allensworth observed that the celebration of Hispanic values by Anglos smacked of racism. Frustrated with Los Angeles life, Allensworth embarked upon a national lecture tour. His speeches to African American organizations suggested that blacks "do for themselves." He promised to set up an African American city with "a distinct Negro culture."

The black owned and operated *California Eagle* covered Allensworth's tour, and alerted other black leaders to Allensworth's message. "The Battle of Life and How To Fight It" and "Character and How To Read It" were popular speeches which caught William Payne's attention. He was a well known teacher and graduate of Dennison University who lived in Pasadena. Payne had been an assistant principal at the Rendsville School and later a professor at the West Virginia Colored Institute. In California, Payne was unable to find work because he was simply too well educated and independent.

When Payne and Allensworth met they planned an African American town. Initially, Allensworth believed than an important reason for establishing an all black community, other than to demonstrate that blacks were capable to managing their own affairs, was to provide a home for retired African American soldiers.

On June 30, 1908 Allensworth and Payne opened two Los Angeles offices to sell land in the California Colony and Home Promoting Association. Initially, the colony was to be located in Los Angles, but expensive land prices and southern California's dense population ended this dream. The *Los Angeles Times* reported that the proposed town would never be built. This negative publicity which attracted interest in Allensworth.

The Pacific Farming Company heard of the experiment and agreed to donate a parcel of land in rural Tulare County about thirty miles north of Bakersfield. It was an excellent site for a town, because there was a railroad spur line and depot nearby on the Sante Fe railroad line connecting Los Angeles to San Francisco. The soil was alluvial and water was available. Yet, there was no rush to settle Allensworth. It was a remote and isolated city. This changed when David Benjamin, an African American scientist, called Allensworth "a rare opportunity." A skilled agriculturist, Benjamin planted a new variety of cotton, Acala, helping to increase California's cotton production in and around the Imperial Valley, Riverside county and in selected parts of the San Joaquin Valley. The farmers who settled in Allensworth were inspired by Benjamin's pioneering agricultural experiments and followed his suggestions for cotton production. By 1909, despite Benjamin's influence, only thirty five families settled in Allensworth, Then the first successful cotton crops were sold and by 1912 there were 100 permanent residents. A combination of available land, excellent transportation and superior agricultural prices caused Allensworth to boom.

From 1912 to 1915, Allensworth prospered and the *California Eagle* observed: "There is not a single white person having anything to do with the affairs of the colony." The *Los Angeles Times* boasted that Allensworth was "an ideal Negro settlement." The *Oakland Sunshine*, a leading black newspaper, noted that businessmen generated $5000 a month and fashionable homes were being built.

In 1914, the Allensworth dream began to fade when the Santa Fe railroad built a spur line to neighboring Alpaugh. This forced rail traffic to bypass Allensworth and deprived the town of its lucrative carrying trade. One reason for this sudden public reversal was Colonel Allensworth's request to the California legislature to build an agricultural and technical college for African Americans. The railroad and other business interests opposed the proposed Allensworth College and a bill to establish the college failed to pass the California legislature.

The end for Allensworth was due to long standing water problems. When the land was purchased from the Pacific Farming Company, they agreed to supply sufficient water for irrigation. By 1910 the water problem was serious and in a nasty court battle the Allensworth Water Company won the right to supply its own water. This turned out to be a mistake, because the water system was old and desperately in need of repair. It wasn't until 1918 that pumping machinery was purchased and by then it was too late to provide local farmers with water.

In 1914, Allen Allensworth was killed by a speeding motorist, after delivering a fiery speech at a church in Monrovia. Soon a leadership crisis arose. Colonel Allensworth's death was a not only a blow to the city but occurred as the population was stagnant and the economy declining. During World War I, Allensworth supplied neither the agricultural goods nor the business enterprise to maintain itself.

The two leading citizens, William Payne and Josephine Allensworth, left the city. Payne signed a contract to teach in El Centro and Mrs. Allensworth moved in with her daughter in Los Angeles. From 1920 to 1945 Allensworth struggled to maintain itself. The Great Depression and World War II made it difficult.

In 1966, arsenic was found in Allensworth's water supply and this spelled the town's end. For the next decade

Allensworth was evacuated and in May, 1976 the California Department of Parks and Recreation approved plans to make it a state park. The formal dedication on October 6, 1976 remains a legacy to Colonel Allensworth's African American dream.

What were the realities of the Allensworth experiment? Colonel Allensworth's greatest contribution was to break down the stereotype that African Americans couldn't educate themselves, operate businesses, live in middle class surroundings or promote a strong cultural life. Allensworth proved all these notions fallacious.

Allensworth's success was modeled after Booker T. Washington's notion of racial self help. The upward mobility notion that blacks were taught in the South came into California was modest success. African American men and women controlled their own land and destiny, and they created businesses, established churches and a sense of community. White Californians had a positive example of the level of character and vision of black citizens.

Just as Allensworth appeared on the verge of success the transportation support of the Sante Fe railroad, the land sales to the Miller and Lux Company and the good sold to the Southern Pacific corporation vanished, thereby placing roadblocks to African American success. The inability to ship goods, have an adequate water and obtain financing brought an end to Allensworth. But these conditions also helped to create the World War I African American civil rights movement.

Black Californians: Civil Rights and World War I

Civil rights emerged in the Progressive Era. As black Californian's prospered and became middle class they demanded equal rights. For some time the National Associa-

tion For The Advancement of Colored People had been a force in California life. They challenged discriminatory hiring practices, the double standard in education and housing and held rallies to highlight problems of inequality.

As African American soldiers volunteered for service during World War I, there was also a demand for increased civil rights. Sacramento's American Negro Loyal Legion telegraphed President Woodrow Wilson that it had 3,000 volunteers ready to fight for their country. The message was clear, the ANLL believed that its members deserved more than to just fight for their country.

But entry into the service didn't change the nature of the African American's second-class citizenship. There were daily reminders of racial inequity. In San Francisco a group of black soldiers were prevented from boarding a street car reserved for whites. A fight broke out and two white civilians were found dead. The black soldiers were quickly tried and one was sentenced to death while two others received life terms.

The nastiest controversy during World War I occurred when the African American press, primarily the *Oakland Sunshine* and the *California Eagle*, criticized the military for its small number of black officers. There were fourteen training camps for white officers and none for African Americans. Despite the availability of African American college graduates, the number of black officers remained inconsequential. Eventually, pressure from these newspapers forced the military to set up a camp for black officers. In the first graduating class four Californians distinguished themselves.

During World War I African American's supported the war effort. A black bank, Mutual Savings of Tulare, raised more than nineteen times its quota in war bonds. Charlotte Boucher, an *Oakland Sunshine* editor, held a prestigious leadership position in the

California Council of National Defense which was an advisory body to the governor. The CCND publicized the patriotic role of African American's during wartime, and Boucher regularly publicized "the Negro's contribution to the war effort."

When World War I ended, black Californians had written their loyalty in blood while demanding greater civil, educational and economic freedoms. The black press, a group of excellent soldiers and an emerging business community made if difficult for Californians to continue the old racial stereotypes.

The Japanese American in California: The Creation of the Model Asian Stereotype

During the Progressive Era Japanese settlers continued to arrive in California. The first generation Japanese, the Issei, numbered more than 70,000 by 1910. By 1930 the Japanese were virtually evenly divided between first generation Issei and the second generation Nisei. Much like the Chinese, the Japanese experienced discrimination because of their skin color, culture and religion. They were the best educated immigrant group in California, but this failed to gain them acceptance.

In 1909 the Immigration Commission noted that almost 3,500 Japanese owned businesses operating in the western states. The majority of these were located in San Francisco, Los Angeles and Sacramento. Race conscious Americans complained about these businesses and nasty slogans were written over the walls of local houses and office buildings housing Japanese enterprises. The rise of racist graffiti was the first indication that the Japanese had made their permanent home in California. "Yellow Jap" and "Fire The Japs" were slogans painted on street corners near Sunset Boulevard in Los Angeles and on Van Ness Av-

enue in San Francisco. Choichi Nitta remembered that racial slurs abounded and "they threw things at us."

In Oakland, Los Angeles and Fresno the Japanese were forced to sit in the balcony of movie theaters. The predominantly male Japanese community had a difficult social adjustment. Gambling, drinking and loitering were the chief ways to kill time. There were forty one Japanese pool halls in San Francisco and thirty five in Los Angeles. There were Japanese bar restaurants who employed hostesses, known as Shafufu (barmaids), which perpetuated sexual stereotypes. Yet, these barmaids did little more than serve traditional Japanese foods and provide pleasant conversation.

Work was backbreaking. The Japanese laborer was up at four in the morning and off for the day. Tadashi Yamaguchi recalled that he had to serve breakfast in a club at six in the morning and usually finished his work after eight at night. He was typical of the casual, unskilled worker who lived in the Nihonmachi or Little Tokyo sections of Los Angeles and San Francisco.

They Came for Our Land: The Fear of Skilled Japanese Labor

Chester Rowell, the editor of the *Fresno Republican*, remarked to Hiram Johnson that "the Japanese came for our land." Johnson agreed that Japanese land ownership was a problem. But he would not be the governor until 1910. So Johnson urged the Lincoln Roosevelt League to make an Alien Land Law a legislative priority. The Progressives believed that there was a Japanese business conspiracy centered around land ownership.

The need to control alien land ownership was a central issue in California politics. In 1907, the California legislature debated a bill to deny land ownership to the Japanese. It would be another six years before the bill became law, but it helped Johnson to be elected governor.

When Johnson was inaugurated as governor in January, 1911, he brought in a Progressive-Republican administration which frustrated the Japanese. There was a scientific racism to California Progressivism. The use of social scientists and statistical models to suggest racial inferiority was one of the key parts of the Progressive strategy.

The California Department of Industrial Relations published elaborate statistics on Japanese business successes, and these government publications urged Californians not to frequent Japanese businesses. The result was the push the Japanese into the fields and the major cities.

Another racist state committee, the California Joint Immigration Committee, argue for exclusion. It was not until the 1920s that this committee began its dominant influence but the seeds of Anglo distrust were sown in the Progressive Era. In 1924 a federal immigration law was influenced by the Golden State.

In order to maintain land ownership, the Japanese leased, sharecropped and purchased land to meet the demand for fruits and vegetables. Japanese truck farmer sold their crops quickly and with great profit. By 1910 Japanese truck farmers produced 70% of California's strawberries. Soon they cornered the string bean, tomato, summer celery, onion and fresh green pea market. In 1900 there were only twenty nine Japanese farms, but by 1910 there were more than 500 Japanese truck farms supplying fresh fruits and vegetable to local stores. By 1920, Japanese truck farms were valued at $67 million and produced ten percent of California's total crops. This was one reason for race conscious Progressives to support the Alien Land Law of 1913.

The success of Japanese farmers led to the formation of a mutual aid societies known as Kenjinkai's. This organizations protected Japanese truck farmers from wandering mobs of Anglo reactionaries. They also organized Kobai Kumiai's, cooperatives which allowed the Japanese farmer to purchase bulk food to set up successful marketing programs. A credit organization, known as a Tanomoshi, was set up to provide funds for fledgling businesses.

The Movement to Exclude the Japanese: The Racist Side of California Progressivism

There was a decade long reaction to Japanese workers. Not only the small truck farmer but the casual field laborer faced California's Anti Asian prejudices. The reaction against the Japanese built slowly, but firmly, during the Progressive Era. In the farms and fields, there was constant conflict between Japanese workers and their white counterparts. There were a number of labor disputes which fanned the flames of Anglo discontent.

In 1902, Oxnard businessmen organized the Western Agricultural Contracting Company to end their dependence upon Japanese labor contractors. The presidents of the Bank of Oxnard and the Bank of A. Levy complained that Japanese labor, while efficient, commanded a higher wage than its Mexican competition. The manager of the American Sugar Beet Company complained that Japanese labor organized to take advantage of its strong position in the labor market. "They form labor unions like the white worker and then demand an exorbitant wage," he remarked. The Japanese were outraged and approached Mexican unions for an alliance against the WACC.

This led to the formation of the Japanese Mexican Labor Union. At the organizational meetings which set up the JMLU there was a sense of solidarity and mutual cooperation. For almost two decades the large growers were brutal in their treatment of farm labor and the result was that there was a militancy and spirit of cooperation among ethnic field workers.

In February 1903, the JMLU elected Kosaburo Baba as its President and began a series of meetings to solve local labor problems. This was the first time in California history that two minority unions worked together. By March, a strike was called and the Japanese Mexican Labor Union won it. But unwittingly, this began organized resistance to ethnic labor unions.

Although the Los Angeles County Council of Labor supported the new union, there was some disagreement among labor leaders about granting a full charter to ethnic unions. When the prestigious American Federation of Labor was approached for a charter by the Mexican Secretary of the JMLA, J. M. Lizarras, he was told that it was too soon to fully recognize ethnic unionization.

This rebuke by America's major labor union prompted exclusionists to attack Japanese economic gains. This attack began on October 11, 1906, when the San Francisco Board of Education instructed school principals to segregate Chinese, Japanese and Korean students. Although the Japanese government protested, it was to no avail. The movement had begun to systematically place the Japanese in a position of second class citizenship.

As attitudes became increasingly hostile to the Japanese, the California legislature worked to finalize the Alien Land Law. The Japanese were concerned and protested California's continuation of Anti Asian politics. When President Woodrow Wilson was inaugurated in March, 1913 Japanese Ambassador Sutemi Chinda called on the new Chief Executive during his second day in office to complain about California racism. Chinda complained about anti Japanese state laws and the President stated that he could not intervene. The message was clear; the California law would pass.

The Alien Land Law of 1913 was easily circumvented by Japanese businessmen, but the intent was clear. The Japanese landowner was not welcome, the Japanese businessman was considered a threat and various farm organizations made it clear that agriculture was a white man's world. The urban businessman was also imperiled but the Japanese did their best to ignore a volatile situation.

The hostility to the Japanese prompted many of them to acquire American partners. When Carl Lindsay purchased six city lots, it was discovered that he worked for the Tanji brothers. Guy Calden, a San Francisco lawyer, was a director for the Yamato Produce and Land Company, and he represented a wide variety of Japanese businesses. By using American lawyers and sophisticated business techniques, the Japanese evaded the Alien Land Law of 1913. Psychologically, however, it still hurt. The Japanese never felt a part of the California experience.

The California land law applied only to the immigrant Japanese who were ineligible to become naturalized citizens. Soon California Japanese language newspapers like the *Nichibei Shimbun* and the *Shin Sekai* complained that the native born Japanese, the Nisei, were also treated like unwelcome immigrants.

In 1921, Japanese immigration slowed when picture brides were banned. Kiichi Kanzaki ,of the Japanese Association of America, remarked that the Japanese were no longer interested in immigrating to California. "We have been insulted and treated like dirt," Kanzaki remarked.

But not all Japanese felt this way. Some hoped to became American citizens. The laws regulating naturalized citizenship were vague. Consequently, a group of Japanese businessmen mounted a challenge. Since the Japanese had made a strong economic and cultural contribution, it was assumed that the U.S. Supreme Court might hear a test case which would grant naturalized citizenship. Takao Ozawa provided the test case for Japanese naturalization.

In 1914, Ozawa applied for U.S. citizenship providing a history of accomplishment with his application. Landing in San Francisco in 1894, Ozawa graduated from high school in Berkeley and attended the University of California for three years. He took a job in Hawaii working for an American company and raised a family. When the U.S. District Court for the Territory of Hawaii denied Ozawa's request for citizenship, he took his case to the U.S. Supreme Court.

The Ozawa case reached the U.S. Supreme Court in 1922. V.S. McClatchy, the chairperson of the California Joint Immigration Commission, filed a brief with the Supreme Court opposing citizenship for the alien Japanese. Senator Hiram Johnson of California quietly lobbied behind closed doors and created a vision of Japanese economic contributions which threatened to place white workers in limbo. Governor William D. Stephens used the press and wrote a series of letters to members of Congress castigating the U.S. Supreme Court for considering the case.

The U.S. Supreme Court ruled that Ozawa was not entitled to naturalized citizenship. A Japanese newspaper, the *Shin Sekai*, echoed the frustration of the Japanese by noting that Europeans could be naturalized for no other reason than white skin.

In 1924, Congress passed a general immigration law which further excluded the Japanese from naturalized citizenship. Both the Japanese and Chinese were prevented from becoming citizens. The *Rafu Shimpo*, a Los Angeles newspaper, suggested that politicians were selling out American ideals because of the "cataclysmic racial strife" engulfing American politics.

The Japanese Nisei Generation: The Kakehasi Bridge

The Japanese American, known as the Nisei, had the advantage of an English language education. They were the best educated minority in California. Yet, despite their education, the only jobs available were in fruits stand or flower markets. The Nisei were called Kakehasi or the bridge to the mainstream of American society.

In the 1920s the Nisei grew from 27% of the Japanese population to 52%. They took American names. Yuriko became Lily, Sumire was Violet and Katsu was Victor. They were elected to high school and college student body offices. They played American sports. The Nisei worked in after school jobs. Yet, at the University of California only one of four Japanese American graduates found employment. The Oakland YWCA urged Japanese Americans to apply as domestic workers and an advertisement stated that a college degree would hurt their chances of employment.

Although the Nisei were economically successful and able to live in the suburbs, they still faced racism. In San Leandro, Fred Korematsu couldn't find a barber to cut his hair. When Togo Tanaka attempted to purchase a house in Los Angeles, he made almost 120 inquires before he found a willing seller. In Hayward, a sign on Main Street read: NO JAPS. This embarrassed city officials and it was quickly taken down.

The legacy of the Progressive Movement and Governor Hiram Johnson was to introduce the Alien Land Law forcing the Japanese into an ethnic community mold that they had tried to break. As John Modell has suggested: "the fruit stand was the bitterest of all symbols of Japanese frustrations." Despite their education, striving and pro American attitudes they were not accepted into the commercial, educational or social mainstream.

Bibliographical Essay

Lawrence B. de Graaf, "Recognition, Racism and Reflections on the Writing of Western Black History," *Pacific Historical Review* (volume 44, February, 1975) and Lawrence B. de Graaf, "The City of Black Angels: The Emergence of the Los Angeles, 1890-1930," *Pacific Historical Review* (volume 39, August 1970) and William Issel and Robert W. Cherny, *San Francisco, 1865-1932: Politics, Power , and Urban Development* (Berkeley, 1986) are the best starting points for the Progressive Era and ethnicity.

On Japanese Americans in the California labor market see, Edna Bonacich and John Modell, *The Economic Base of Ethnic Solidarity: Small Business In The Japanese American Community* (Berkeley, 1980). Also, see Gerald D. Nash, "Stages of California's Economic Growth, 1870-1970: An Interpretation," *California Historical Quarterly* (Winter, 1972).

For early Japanese labor activity see Tomas Almaguer, "Racial Domination and Class Conflict in Capitalist Agriculture: The Oxnard Sugar Beet Workers' Strike of 1903," *Labor History*, volume 25, no. 3 (Summer, 1984). Also see, Howard A. DeWitt, *Images of Ethnic And Alien Violence in California Politics, 1917-1930: A Survey* (San Francisco, 1975) for the reaction against ethnic in the latter part of the Progressive Era.

Roger Daniels, *The Politics of Prejudice: The Anti-Japanese Movement And The Struggle For Japanese Exclusion* (New York, 1968) is the standard work on the subject. Also see, Roger Daniels, *Asian America: Chinese and Japanese in the United States since 1850* (Seattle,1988). On the Alien Land Law also see, Spencer C. Olin, "European Immigrant and Oriental Alien: Acceptance and Rejection by the California Legislature of 1913," *Pacific Historical Review*, volume 25 (August, 1966).

The best recent example of analyzing Asian immigration is Bill Ong Hing, *Making And Remaking Asian America Through Immigration Policy, 1850-1990* (Stanford, 1993). For the Japanese in Los Angeles see, Brian Masatu Hayashi, *For The Sake of Our Japanese Brethren: Assimilation, Nationalism and Protestantism Among the Japanese of Los Angeles, 1895-1942* (Stanford, 1995), chapter 4, for the years from 1877 to 1918. The strength of the Japanese community is demonstrated in Stephen J. Fugita and David J. O'Brien, *Japanese American Ethnicity: The Persistence of Community* (Seattle, 1991).

The best recent history of Asian Americans is Suecheng Chan, *Asian Americans: An Interpretive History* (Boston, 1991). On the drive for Japanese citizenship see Yuji Ichioka, "The Early Japanese Immigrant Quest For Citizenship: The Background of the 1922 Ozawa Case," *Amerasia*, volume 4, no 2 (1977).

African Americans during the Progressive Era are analyzed in Albert S. Broussard, *Black San Francisco: The Struggle For Racial Equality In The West, 1900-1954* (Lawrence, 1993) and Douglas Henry Daniels, *Pioneer Urbanites: A Social and Cultural History of Black San Francisco* (Philadelphia, 1980). The Progressive Era is a misunderstood period due to some excellent early monographs. See, for example, George Mowry, *The California Progressives* (Berkeley, 1951); Spencer Olin, *California's Prodigal Sons: Hiram Johnson and The Progressives, 1911-1917* (Berkeley, 1968) and Walton Bean, *Boss Ruef's San Francisco* (Berkeley, 1952). These pioneering monographs remain stronger and more accurate than all subsequent study. The problem is that not one of these books dealt with ethnic questions. They are still the best starting point for the Progressive Era.

11

The Hidden Ethnic in California

Filipinos, Koreans, Asian Indians, Japanese and Chinese Experiences, 1920-1940

In 1924, V. S. McClatchy, editor of the *Sacramento Bee*, remarked: "the Japanese are the least likely to assimilate and the most dangerous group in this country..." This comment reflected a general California belief that the Japanese, Chinese, Filipino, Korean and Asian Indian immigrants were a danger to the Golden State. The rise of propaganda from racist organizations like the Ku Klux Klan, the rhetoric of super patriotic groups like the Better America Federation and the campaign promises from conservative Republican Party candidates made assimilation difficult.

"California is filled with hidden ethnic groups," Governor C.C. Young remarked in 1927. He was addressing an audience of businessmen who were concerned about the impact of the new Asian immigration. The reaction to these new settlers was much like the Chinese experienced in the nineteenth century as there was an almost hysterical concern with Asian immigrants. Laws restricted their rights, housing, jobs and education, and the sneers of local citizens made these immigrants wonder if the decision to relocate was a wise one. A repressive racism frustrated the newly arrived settlers.

Agriculture was the primary reason for Asians entering the California work place.

The need for field workers allowed Asian immigrants to secure employment in the San Joaquin and Imperial Valleys. Soon they introduced a wide variety of influences, among these were ethnic labor unions, gangs of workers who staged wildcat strikes for higher wages, ethnic boarding houses, community organizations to promote ethnic awareness and cultural groups featuring readings, poetry, plays and music of their country. This economic and cultural independence bothered race conscious Californians.

Interracial Marriage and California Nativism: Anti-Miscegenation Law as a Racist Device

The rise of numerous Asian groups revived the question of interracial marriage. Although the Japanese, Chinese, Asian Indian, Korean and Filipino workers were not inclined to marry outside their race, the California Legislature amended the 1880 anti-miscegenation law prohibiting: "intermarriage of white persons with Chinese, Negroes, mulattos or persons of mixed blood, descended from a Chinaman or Negro..." The law's insulting language brought criticism from a number of ethnic organi-

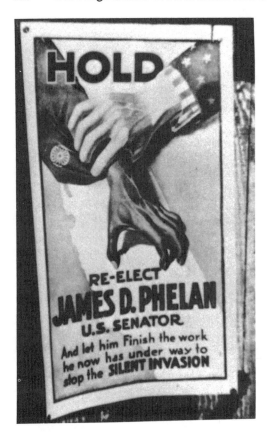

FIGURE 11-1. James D. Phelan, 1920 Election Campaign.

county clerk periodically enforced the anti-miscegenation law. Thus, if a good looking, blonde, white woman showed up to marry a Filipino, the clerk would not issue a marriage license. In 1930, this happened to Tony Moreno when he applied for a license to wed Ruby Robinson. The Los Angeles county clerk announced that he would enforce the anti-miscegenation law, and Moreno filed a law suit. Soon Filipino organizations challenged California law and contended that Filipinos were Americans, not Mongolians and, therefore, not subject to the law. In 1933, an appellate court ruled in the case of Salvador Roldan v. L.A. County that Filipinos could intermarry. This ended the question of Filipinos and the anti-miscegenation law, but it left bitter feelings in the Filipino community. "We never felt like we were fully accepted as citizens," Luis Agudo of the Filipino Labor Union remembered.

Fearing that restrictive legislation would resurface, the Filipino Federation of America took its fight to the California Legislature, and by 1948, the anti-miscegenation law was declared unconstitutional. Although Asian immigrants lacked a political base and had limited economic power, they were able to use the courts and lobby the government for their rights. From 1948 to 1967, a large number of Filipino groups petitioned the United States Congress for removal of these offensive laws. Finally, in 1967, all statues involving interracial marriage were rendered unconstitutional.

This is Still a White Man's California: The Ku Klux Klan and Resurgent Nativism

The rise of nativist groups like the Los Angeles based Better America Federation, the Ku Klux Klan, the Native Sons of the Golden West and the California Joint Immigration Committee forced ethnic organi-

zations. The NAACP charged that the law was "a way to socially and economically control the colored population."

The question of interracial marriage was one that had dominated California since 1850, and it was often an issue used to disenfranchise many ethnic groups. The Filipinos who viewed themselves as Americans and were classified as American nationals took exception to the slogan "Our Little Brown Brothers." However, they challenged state laws which restricted their right to intermarry.

In 1921, the Los Angeles City Council ruled that Filipinos were not subject to the anti miscegenation laws. However, the zations to become political and protest rising racism. Race was the key issue for the California Joint Immigration Committee. Committee director, V.S. McClatchy, remarked at meetings that: "this is still a white man's California." He created such hostility toward California's ethnic groups that some Republicans tried to approach McClatchy to run for public office.

The tradition of bigotry was carried on by his son, H.J. McClatchy, who was executive secretary of the California Joint Immigration Committee and later took over the committee. H.J. McClatchy reflected his father's influence when he wrote: "We have denied quota to those races which cannot be assimilated...who would always be a race apart." This letter was in reference to the Chinese, but McClatchy made it clear the Japanese and "our little brown brothers from the Philippines" deserved no better consideration. Eventually, he spoke out against Koreans, Mexican Americans and called African Americans "a blight in the city."

The McClatchys took their prejudices into the political arena. In 1929, they persuaded the California Joint Immigration Committee to advocate new immigrant restriction. The McClatchy's orchestrated testimony from the Commonwealth Club of California, the American Legion, the Native Sons of the Golden West and the California Federation of Labor which heightened public fears of "the immigrant invasion." For almost a decade the question of Americanization was a central theme in California.

The Americanization controversy began in 1921 when the Better America Federation announced that schools would teach "real Americanism," and the public libraries would respond to the interests of the "solid" citizen. The result was a form of intellectual terrorism which suggested that Asians were slow to learn and found it difficult to adapt to the American way of life.

When African Americans began migrating to California in the 1920s the Ku Klux Klan organized in Los Angeles, San Francisco, Sacramento, Fresno, Stockton, Oroville and Oakland, but they soon had an interest in other ethnic groups. The KKK criticized the Asian population for "race mixing."

FIGURE 11-2. KKK, 1921. Courtesy of the Santa Barbara Historical Society Library.

The center of KKK activity was in and around Los Angeles. What made the southern California KKK unique was its concern with the Japanese and Filipino farm workers. Encouraged by the Los Angeles Police Department's Red Squad, the KKK became an unofficial policeman in southern California who terrorized a wide variety of ethnic workers.

When the KKK took over the Anti-Saloon League in the 1920s, they published pseudo scientific studies concluding that African Americans were prone to excessive drinking. The KKK concluded that the Filipino used "dance and music to seduce white women." The Klan was on a mission to racially cleanse Los Angeles. "We just don't have Negroes to worry about," one Klan member remarked, "we have a whole bunch of foreign types." This comment is significant because it was made by a San Diego immigration inspector who was a Klan member. However, not all ethnic organizations were overtly racist.

The Native Sons of the Golden West was one of the most subtle groups in California. In theory, it is an organization dedicated to preserving and advancing history. As a civic minded group, it sponsored historical studies detrimental to Filipinos and Mexicans. V.S. McClatchy editor of the *Sacramento Bee* was a major figure in the Native Sons of the Golden West. It was the Japanese who McClatchy believed were the most detrimental to California's future. In a letter to his son, McClatchy vowed to rid the Golden State of "the Japanese menace."

He began his assault on the Japanese in 1920 when California voters approved a McClatchy sponsored initiative making it more difficult for the Japanese to lease or purchase real estate. For the next four years, McClatchy bombarded the Federal Government with statistics, observations and opinions on California's ethnic problem. In response to McClatchy and a growing national hysteria, the U.S. Congress passed the Immigration Act of 1924. This federal law created a quota system and California's farm labor population grew to 80% Mexican and about 20% Filipino. The Chinese and Japanese virtually vanished from the immigration rolls. The quota system favored European nations and discriminated against Asians. Since the Philippines were an American protectorate, Filipinos, theoretically, had the same rights as U.S. citizens. Although Filipinos were not granted citizenship, they were viewed as "American nationals." But theory and reality were quite different. California Filipinos faced racial insults and a segregated society.

The California Filipino Impulse: The Negative Reaction in the Golden State

Because they had the right to migrate to California, Filipinos had an immediate entry into the labor market. By 1930, the Pinoys, as the Filipinos called themselves, numbered 30,000. They landed in San Francisco and found taxi cabs with signs reading: "Mabuhay." This was a welcome from the labor brokers who had jobs for Filipinos in the California fields.

Because the Immigration Act of 1924 banned other ethnic groups from entering California, there was a demand for farm labor. Thus, Filipinos filled the need for agricultural and cannery labor. As Filipinos were brought into California, to fill the laboring jobs previously held by the Chinese and Japanese, they faced racial stereotypes. Such slurs as "Monkey" or "Goo-Goos" frustrated the young Filipino workers.

California Congressman Richard J. Welch and Senator Hiram W. Johnson were strong critics of Filipino labor. Politically, Welch and Johnson fanned the flames of racial hatred and continued the time tested, vote-getting anti-Asian sentiment which had

FIGURE 11-3. Carlos Bulosan, Filipino Writer. Courtesy of Visual Communication.

characterized California since the early days of Chinese immigration. This attitude perplexed Filipinos.

Carlos Bulosan, a Filipino writer who wrote the best selling memoir, *American Is In The Heart*, remarked: "Western people are brought up to regard Orientals...as inferior....I was completely disillusioned when I came to know this American attitude." Because of their dark skin and their accented English, Filipinos found themselves the victim of racial violence. But Filipinos had another surprise when they arrived from the long sea voyage from Honolulu.

When they landed in San Francisco, Filipino migrants were surprised that they were quarantined for disease at Angel Island. They were kept overnight, checked by doctors and then met by a throng of labor contractors near the Ferry Building. They were a ready source of farm labor and there was an immediate reaction to the Pinoy invasion.

In August 1926, there was a race riot in Dinuba and California newspapers expressed a general fear of Filipino farm labor. The *Dinuba Sentinel* headlined: "FILIPINO BOY CRISIS ALMOST STOPS DINUBA STREET DANCE." This headline expressed the fears of the Anglo population and suggests the difficulty that Dinuba citizens had adjusting to Filipino workers.

Dinuba, located in the San Joaquin Valley, was a natural migration point for the highly skilled Filipino workers. Once they excelled in local lettuce and asparagus fields, the Filipino's organized unions, and they were able to gain better wages, working conditions and standard of living. The *Dinuba Sentinel* took exception to the gains of Filipino workers and their general acceptance in the community. In a series of nasty editorials, they suggested that Filipinos could learn something from "Negroes (who) usually understood how to act..." The reaction in Dinuba was typical of the racism that Filipinos faced in other parts of the Golden State. Due to these attitudes, California's Filipino migration declined dramatically.

Another reason for the decline of the Filipino population was lack of economic opportunity. By 1930, one of four Filipinos was employed as a kitchen helper, bellboy, houseboy, elevatorboy, yardboy and chamberboy. The chamberboys referred to the toilets as "honey wagons." What this meant is that they had their first job which would lead them to their American fortune. In major California cities, Filipinos were called "the perfect servants." In Pasadena, the Huntington Hotel hired Filipinos because of their "manners and impeccable English." The urban Filipino was preferred because as San Francisco's Mayor James "Sunny Jim" Rolph remarked: "they know how to serve a drink."

There were only a small number of urban Filipinos in the Golden State. The majority of Filipino workers made their living in the fields, and it was here that the ugly signs of anti-Filipino activity emerged.

Violence in the Fields: California Filipino Farm Labor

The majority of Filipinos, however, worked in agriculture. There was a ready supply of skilled agricultural workers in Hawaii, thus the Filipinos quickly found their way to San Francisco and Los Angeles. A Filipino labor contractor, Hilario Camino Moncado, founded a boarding house for newly arrived Filipinos and made a fortune as a labor contractor. He provided much of the labor for the San Joaquin and Imperial Valleys. Soon large growers

streamed into Los Angeles to hire Mexican and Filipino farm labor. The exploitation of these farm workers created an explosion in ethnic farm labor unions.

Moncado exploited Filipinos. He controlled the Los Angeles newspaper, *Filipino Nation*, while meeting with Governor Rolph and President Franklin D. Roosevelt. Young Filipinos were pictured as good Americans in Moncado's elaborate publicity releases, and he used the phrase "my people were born under the Stars and Stripes."

Moncado founded the Filipino Federation of America which stressed Americanization and adherence to the law. Many FFA members joined because of the strict moral code. Moncado's followers didn't drink, smoke or frequent taxi dance halls. One

FIGURE 11-4. Filipino Labor Union, 1930s.

Moncadista remarked: "My mother taught me to smoke, drink and go to prostitutes; Mr. Moncado taught me morality." His followers had a religious zeal, and they were hired by large agribusiness companies at a minimal wage. This led discontent farm workers to form a union.

In 1934, when the Filipino Labor Union was organized to secure better wages and working conditions in the fields, Moncado urged his people to stay away from labor unions. The Associated Farmers of California, an agribusiness monopoly allied with Moncado, charged in sophisticated ad that Filipinos were un-American. The real issue was how poorly agribusiness companies treated their casual labor. Pay abuses, oppressive working conditions and unfair hiring practices were only a few of the issues which ethnic labor unions challenged. In order to understand the power of California agribusiness it is necessary to examine the growers economic power.

By the early 1930s 10.5% of all Imperial Valley farms produced 60% of the farm income. In the San Joaquin Valley large land

FIGURE 11-5. Filipino Pool Hall, 1934.

owning corporations, like Miller and Lux, dominated local agriculture. Because of oppressive working conditions, low wages and racial insults, Filipino workers unionized.

The Watsonville lettuce strike of 1930 was a brief strike in which Filipinos won major labor concessions. Shortly after this labor dispute ended, there was five days of anti Filipino rioting. The nearby Palm Beach tax dance club was the scene of numerous racial incidents and this began four years of intense anti Filipino feeling.

Race conscious Anglos charged that Filipino farm workers were prone to Communism and violence. When the Cannery and Agricultural Industrial Union organized and staged a series of stroke in the Imperial Valley in 1933-1934, Will J. French, the director of the California Department of Industrial Relations, concluded that they were the third wave of Asian immigrants. Hordes was the word that French used to describe the Filipino farm worker.

In 1934, the Filipino Labor Union won an important victory in the Salinas lettuce fields and again in 1936 they closed down Salinas Valley agriculture. The American Federation of Labor granted Filipinos a union charter and they became the Field Workers' Union Local 30326. Success in the fields brought Filipinos into San Francisco, Stockton, and Los Angeles and they became a part of the local community.

The success of the Filipino labor Union in the Salinas lettuce strike of 1934 was an indication of the power of ethnic labor unions. Filipino unionization was a reaction to the hostile economic social climate in the Golden State. In Sacramento, M.H. Iacaban, the editor of the *Bataan News*, urged Filipinos to develop a united front against racism. As Iacaban suggested this strategy, California's Filipino population was migrating from the fields to the cities.

The Rise of the Urban Filipino Between the Wars

In San Francisco, a "Little Manila" emerged on Kearny Street near Chinatown. It was a predominantly male enclave and soon signs of business, family and cultural life were evident. As Filipino life grew in San Francisco, a number of downtown hotels had signs that read: "NO FILIPINOS ALLOWED." When Roberto Vallangca walked into a Geary Street coffee shop, he was ignored by the waitress. "I realized then that I could not go anywhere because I was Filipino."

Social pressures were enormous because there were so few Filipino women. Many Filipino men married white women because there was no system of pictures brides used by the Japanese. Not only was the Filipino man well dressed, but he also had musical and dancing skills which were attractive to women. But key members of the Filipino community urged the young men to resist social integration. Hilario Camino Moncado complained about "race mixing" just before he went off to a private, white only, San Diego country club to play golf with a California politician.

However, integration happened and the rise of American born Filipinos created a new group of Americans. Liz Megino remembers in Oakland, just across the bay from San Francisco, with vivid memories of insults like: "go back were you came from" and "Monkey." She cried all through school and couldn't understand the reasons for the racial insults.

The social and sexual stereotypes suggested that taxi dance halls catered to the "oversexed young Filipino." The truth was that there were so few Filipino women, that clubs filled a legitimate social need. As an orchestra played, the young man paid ten cents a minute to dance with a statuesque blonde, white women. This created early sexual stereotypes about the Filipino male.However, the Filipinos prospered despite these attitudes. By 1940, Filipinos were an important part of the urban-rural employment market. They also organized a wide variety of groups to combat racial prejudice. When World War II broke out, they were among the first to volunteer and write their loyalty in blood.

Koreans in America: A Hidden Asian Minority

Koreans were a people who fled their homeland to escape the conflict with Japan. They arrived in Hawaii and had trouble fitting into the local economy. Under American law, Koreans could not legally enter California because the U.S. considered Korea a portion of the Japanese Empire. There was little incentive for Koreans to immigrate into California as the Alien Land Law of 1913 was extended to Koreans and the Asiatic Exclusion League labeled them "undesirable aliens." Despite these handicaps, from 1920 to 1940, 1711 Koreans entered the Golden State.

It was the Sacramento Valley that attracted the initial wave of Koreans because of its soil. Other Koreans settled in the San Joaquin Valley where they developed orchards, vineyards, nurseries and fruit packing plants. There were other employment opportunities in restaurants, hotels and domestic households for newly arrived Koreans. The typical Korean was a male in his early twenties with no education and little money for a business venture. The chong gak, as the bachelor was known, dominated the culture

The main problem for California Koreans was that they were often times confused with the Japanese. "During the first days of school life, children would call me a Jap," J. Lim remarked. Kwang-son Lee was agitated because her high school history teacher confused Far Eastern geography and used the term "Jap." These comments were made over and over by Korean students.

Housing was another problem. Living conditions were abysmal for Koreans. In the Mexican or predominantly black sections of San Francisco, a few Koreans rented homes. Outside of the major cities housing problems were even worse. Do-Yun Yoon remembers in Delano that "none of the nicer areas" had Korean rentals.

When Koreans were hired in the fields, they were often attacked by angry white mobs. In Upland, Bakersfield and Brawley, Korean workers were attacked by unruly mobs because they worked for low wages. There was also a sense of isolation, and the Korean workers generally kept to themselves.

Labor brokers brought them into the fields. They were moved in labor gangs from the fields, to the railroad yards and finally to the cities. The vast majority of Koreans were farm laborers. As they were organized into work gangs, a supervisor known as a sip-chang ("ten-head") led the men in highly supervised agricultural production. The Koreans were excellent farm workers who quickly developed a sense of their value. They would negotiate for higher wages, using one man who acted as the gang boss, and they would undercut other workers if there was a dearth of jobs.

In Dinuba, Korean farm laborers replaced Filipinos who organized unions. This created Filipino-Korean tensions, and the *Dinuba Sentinel* remarked that Asians were often hostile to each other. The *New Korea*, a newspaper published in San Francisco, wrote a series of articles on how Dinuba, California grape growers were becoming dependent upon Korean labor. Soon Korean work gangs were operating in Stockton's tomato fields and then in the Watsonville lettuce fields. Korean workers saved their wages and by the late 1930s established businesses.

There were few places for Koreans to spent their money. As a result, a small number of Korean farmers organized a Kae. This was a credit rotating system in which a group of Koreans would contribute money to be lent like a bank. The Korean workers who allowed this money to be loaned would make a profit. Soon money from the Kae was used to open new Korean business ventures. The Kae was the first step in a communal self-help organization for Koreans which made them an independent economic force in the Golden State. Despite their small numbers, a Korean economic aristocracy emerged.

Kim Chong-nim became so successful that he was dubbed the "Korean Rice King of the Sacramento Valley." From 1913 to 1921 he worked diligently in the fields and then formed a business partnership with Kim Ho of Reedley. This business marketed rice to all parts of the United States. They also formed the Kim Brothers fruit wholesalers. After some horticultural experiments, the Kim Brothers marketed a peach without fuzz that quickly became a staple of the American diet. Thus, after some years hard work, Kim became a millionaire.

Other farmers took his example, and by the late 1920s, there were almost 50,000 acres of rice in Willows that were cultivated by Koreans.

He also helped to establish Korean schools and generously contributed to four Korean newspapers. One Korean newspaper, the *Sinhan Minbo*, believed that discrimination would be minimal against Koreans because the Chinese came to "this country without abandoning their filthy habits and customs." Another Korean newspaper, the *Kongnip Sinmun*, suggested that Koreans were more westernized and not as traditionally Asian. The Korean community was building an American identity.

Korean language schools sprung up all over California in the 1920s. Korean churches and night history classes were part of a movement to establish Korean values in the Golden State. Korean nationalists became so strong that signs emerged in the Korean community which read: "DON'T BUY THE JAP'S RICE. OURS IS BETTER." Race conscious whites snickered at these signs.

As Japan militarily terrorized the Far East in the 1920s and 1930s, California Koreans vented their anger. Letters from California Koreans filled Korean and American newspapers with vehement protests concerning Japanese atrocities against the Koreans. The Japanese were described in these letters as savages who had ravaged the Korean homeland.

One newspaper, the *Sinhan Minbo*, boldly proclaimed that "we have no country to return to..." Korean cultural voices began receiving American attention. In 1931, Younghill Kang, a Korean who, at one time, washed dishes for restaurants, published an autobiographical novel, *The Grass Roof*. It was an immediate success, and two years later he was appointed a professor of comparative literature at New York University. After he was awarded a Guggenheim Fellowship, Kang worked diligently on a second novel.

In Kang's 1937 novel, *East Goes West*, he urged Koreans to support movements to destroy Japan. This book was more popular with Anglos than the Koreans and brought Kang fame and fortune. Yet, *East Goes West* was a best selling novel with another message for Koreans—assimilation and citizenship were the roads to acceptance.

While the hero in Kang's book hopes to become an American, he can never forget his homeland. His is caught between California and Korea and tortured by the prospect of never being fully Korean or American. This was a theme many Koreans experienced.

The Korean experience from 1920 to 1940 was one of isolation, racial taunts and second class citizenship. Racial boundaries were sharply drawn in California. Koreans lived in an isolated world. They were not on friendly terms with the Japanese. The Chinese ignored them, and the lack of a Korean town placed them in an immigrant limbo. They were an intelligent, worldly and well educated people who had a deep interest in international affairs but no one with whom they could share their passion.

Asian Indians in California: The Punjabis and the Myth of the Turbanned Stereotype

The Asian Indian immigrants who arrived in California between 1899 and 1914 were from India's Punjab province. The initial seven thousand who immigrated were the sons of landowning families. By 1920, the California State Board of Control concluded that: "the Hindu is the most undesirable immigrant in the state." This state report criticized the Asian Indian for lack of personal cleanliness, improper morals and a blind religious reasoning while, at the same time, ignoring the economic skills of the turbaned newcomers.

A national magazine, *The Independent*, published an article in 1922 lamenting the rise of the "Rag-Heads" in California. Rag-head was the racial slur used to describe the recently arrived Punjabi farm workers who were well trained to handle these attitudes. The Punjab, a frontier area near India's northwest border, was for centuries an area where the residents repelled invading conquerors. It was also a vast, flat geographical area watered by five rivers, and the name panj ab or five waters gave rise to Punjab.

Agricultural success was so vast that the British praised the Punjab as an area of "resourceful and intelligent people." The Jat cast was the dominant landowning group.

Punjabi farmers owned and controlled their land and marketed their own goods, and this history of agricultural productivity was transferred to California. In central Punjab, it was also common to work for wages, and this experience was important in the transition to the California fields.

California was an agricultural paradise for the Asian Indian. Wage earners in the Punjab brought in sixteen cents a day, whereas the California fields paid two dollars each day. Puna Singh remarked: "On arriving in the Sacramento Valley, one could not help but be reminded of the Punjab." This reaction was typical of Asian Indian immigrants. They saw a land of opportunity in California which lacked the negative influence of the British and had all the positive aspects of American democracy.

During their early years in California, the Punjabi immigrants worked on the railroad, in lumbering and in the fields. The vineyards, sugar beet fields and orchards in and around Marysville, Newcastle and Vaca Valley were early homes to these turbaned workers. Punjabi boardinghouses in Marysville grew up in the midst of Chinatown. In Brawley and El Centro, Punjabi hotels offered rooms, goods and access to jobs in the fields.

In 1920, the seven thousand Asian Indians living in the United States were predominantly California agricultural workers. Much like the Koreans, the Punjabis didn't immediately develop identifiable neighborhoods or a distinct ethnic community. Although they were referred to as "Hindus," the vast majority were not. About one third were Muslim, and the vast majority were Sikhs. The Sikhs believed in the five ks or kes which was the unshorn hair and beard, kaach or trousers to the knee, kara or iron bangle, kirpan or sword and khanga or hair comb. These were the symbols of Indian life which allowed this immigrant population to retain its ties to the homeland.

Hostility to early Asian Indians was predicated upon many reasons. They dressed differently. Their religious habits were not traditionally Christian. They consumed exotic foods. Their manner was courtly, but they didn't meet American health standards. The Indian didn't bathe and often used an oil that Americans described as having a repulsive air and they had little interest in explaining these cultural peccadilloes.

The Asian Indian was well educated, shrewd in business ventures and honest. As groups of middle class Asian Indians emerged, they mounted a campaign for citizenship. Since the federal law of 1790 reserved naturalized citizenship for "whites," the Asian Indians argued they in fact were white. Prior to 1920, there were two United States Supreme Court decisions which declared that Asian Indians were white. In California, a group of Marysville Sikhs hired a San Francisco lawyer to push for the right of naturalized citizenship. The educational level, the economic achievements and the ease with which the Asian Indian adjusted in California made it appear that there would be little trouble with naturalized citizenship.

V.S. McClatchy, head of the California Immigration Commission, alerted the Native Sons of the Golden West and the Commonwealth Club to the dangers of Asian Indian immigration. A subtle, but pervasive campaign began attacking Sikh culture. As the debate raged over Asian Indian citizenship, the Immigration and Naturalization Service arbitrarily denied some Asian Indians entry. Finally, in 1923, the United States Supreme Court in the U.S. v. Bhagat Singh Thind Case ruled that Asian Indians were ineligible for citizenship. The U.S. Supreme Court ruled that they were not white. As the Court suggested: the law uses the term "white persons" not Caucasian. Therefore, the U.S. Supreme Court concluded that

Asian Indians were Caucasian but not white. No one protested this twisted logic. The Founding Fathers, the court ruled, conferred citizenship upon "the class of persons known as white."

The flow of immigration from India slowed after the Thind decision. Puna Singh pointed out that he no longer had Indian citizen and now could not become an American citizen. "I am," he remarked, "a citizen of no country." When Vaisho Das Bagai committed suicide in 1928, he left a note lamenting his failure to become a naturalized citizen.

This led to an exodus of settlers, and from 1920 to 1940, more than 3,000 Asian Indians purchased one-way tickets home. But not all Asian Indians returned to the homeland. In San Francisco, a small group of intellectuals organized the Ghadr Party. This was an Asian Indian word for revolution. The high educational level and exceptional literacy of the Ghadr Party was demonstrated in its weekly newspaper, the *Ghadr*. This publication, in flowery but intelligent language, took Californians to task for their racial attitudes. Soon Sacramento, Fresno, Stockton and Marysville had active Asian Indian organizations.

The Ghadr Party leadership linked British Imperialism and American racism. In newspaper articles and speeches, members of the Ghadr Party complained about second class citizenship. Although the vast majority of Asian Indian immigrants were farmers or day laborers from the Punjab, they were literate in English and possessed a strong sense of history.

Throughout the 1920s, Indian labor was an important part of California agribusiness. In the San Joaquin and Imperial Valley agriculture, it was common to see groups of fifteen to twenty Asian Indian laborers working in the fields. Punjabi farm labor traveled with the harvest, and the turbans were a familiar sight. In the melon and cotton fields, local farmers preferred to hire the "tides of turbans" because of their reputation for hard work, honesty and non union activity. In cultivating and pruning, Asian Indian workers were precise and worked at a steady pace and, initially, abhorred unions.

Once they began working with Filipinos in the asparagus fields, however, Asian Indian laborers learned about unions. But unlike other ethnic groups, the Asian Indian workers did not form unions. A common religion, a similar language, a set of defined values and a strong sense of purpose influenced the Asian Indian worker to stand alone against California racism. Although they didn't form and join labor unions, they did organized for better wages.

It was common for a large rancher to work out wages with an Asian Indian boss or a gang leader. The boss would keep track of the book, and he often placed thirty or forty men on the payroll rather than the twenty to thirty who were actually working. This minor deception guaranteed an improved wage. This form of creative entrepreneurial activity was nominally a bonus and was rampant in the California fields.

There was a democratic sense to Asian Indian workers. Many Punjabi Indians remarked that the agricultural work gangs were much like a family. By the early 1920s, Asian Indian farm workers commanded wages equal to and often superior to Mexican, Filipino, Chinese, Japanese and white workers. Soon Asian Indians left the fields to open their own businesses.

In the Sacramento Valley and later in the Imperial Valley, Asian Indians leased and purchased land. They grew crops much like those they had raised in India and soon cotton and rice production boomed in the Golden State. In Holtville, Jawala and Bisaka Singh were so successful that they soon became the local "Potato Kings."

Babu Khan and his brother Naimat leased more than two thousand acres near Willows and used their attorney, Duard Gies, as the head of an agriculture corporation which evolved into a multi-million dollar business. This led hundreds of Asian Indians to set up false front partnerships. The directors of banks in Holtville, Marysville, El Centro and Willows granted loans to prosperous Sikh farmers in the area while looking the other way at the false front corporations.

Business success prompted Asian Indian men to settle permanently in California. It was common for them to marry Mexican women. In the 1920s and 1930s, half the wives married to Asian Indian men were Spanish speaking women. These marriages were seldom successful for cultural and social reasons. The divorce petitions filed in the Imperial Valley indicated that there was a three times higher divorce rate among Asian Indian men and Mexican women. A typical divorce complaint had the man complaining that his wife would not cook or clean for his Punjabi friends. Also, she refused to make foods he liked, shopped too much and spent an inordinate amount of time with her family. The petitions of Mexican women alleged that the Indian men drank excessively, beat them, were unfaithful and failed to provide money for household expenses. The problem was as much cultural as social and economic, and by the 1940s, Asian Indian men no longer married Mexican women.

Religion was the key element in Asian Indian survival. Muslim Asian Indians observed a period of fasting and demonstrated strong religious conviction. A priest known as a Hadji, because he had taken a "hadj" or pilgrimage to Mecca, was an important source of spiritual solace. In Stockton, bales of hay were placed almost ten feet high so a Hadji could read from the Koran. Soon Sikh temples, although small ones, sprung up when as few as twenty Sikhs were living in the area.

The Asian Indian in the Imperial Valley: The Rise of a Pujabi-Mexican Community

The Imperial Valley is located in California's southern border and is a hot, desolate, agriculturally rich area. Immigrants from the Punjab quickly became successful farmers as the Imperial Valley was transformed from a barren desert into a productive agricultural venue. They formed a small community through marriages to Hispanic women, and the *Holtville Tribune* frequently commented about the "strong sense of family in the Punjabi-Mexican community.

How and why did the Asian Indian worker arrive in the California fields? The establishment of the Punjabi-Mexican community in the Imperial Valley began in 1907 when water was diverted from the Colorado River for cotton production. About 500 Hindus were brought in to pick the cotton. The negative reaction was immediate, and the *Holtville Tribune* on September 26, 1910 wrote: "the Hindu...should be prohibited at once from landing in California." This remark was ignored because the Punjabi workers were needed in the fields, and had a strong work ethic.

By the early 1920s Punjabis leased more than 32,000 acres in the Imperial Valley, obtained bank ,loans and became respected farmers. In 1922, the Hindustani Farmers Company was formed to finance Punjabi farmers who were making inroads into the cotton industry.

Some discontented Anglo farmers demanded that the Alien Land Law of 1913 be applied to the Punjabis. However, the law was easily circumvented. Local judges could either enforce it or ignore the law. Most judges ignored it. In appreciation, the Punjabi's left sacks of money on the judge's doorstep. Special appreciation for local judges caused Punjabi families to give live

chickens at Christmas. One judge's daughter remarked: "Oh, how I hated to get up Christmas morning and see those gunny sacks filled with flopping, clucking chickens."

By the mid-1920s, prosperous Punjabi farmers with their Mexican wives and large families were an important part of the Imperial Valley. They established business connections with Anglo landowners, bankers and lawyers and became an integral part of the southern California agricultural community.

In Holtville, Punjabi men formed the Hindustani Welfare and Reform Society to assist Asian Indian farmers. Soon they formed a political lobbying group, the Pacific Coast Halsa Diwan Society, to fight for equal rights.

Despite marriages to Mexican women, the Punjabi men did not identify with or participate in Mexican American culture. Punjabi farmers employed Mexican workers and demonstrated a great deal of hostility toward them. They were also critical of Hispanic culture and had little use for Mexican American men. Women who married Punjabis were ostracized and subject to verbal insults by Mexican men.

Life in the Imperial Valley was far from idyllic for the Punjabi. Most schools were segregated by race. Punjabi students were placed in the non-white schools. These children soon became the focus of a politically motivated racism. The District Attorney of Imperial County, in an obvious bid for voter support, labeled Hindu Mexican students: "the meanest children our teachers have to deal with."

While the Punjabi-Mexican community carved out a small niche in the Imperial Valley, its families and children were never fully accepted. This made the Asian Indian more political, and beginning in the 1940s, with the second generation there was a new militancy. However, the Punjabi immigrants were an important force in establishing the first Asian Indian settlement in the Golden State.

Japanese Americans in the 1920s and 1930s: The Nisei and the Struggle for Equality

During the 1920s and 1930s, the American born Nisei created a strong presence in San Francisco, Los Angeles and the San Joaquin Valley. As Japanese businesses prospered, and their children received college degrees and trade ties with major farming companies emerged, there was a general sense of optimism. The beleaguered first generation Issei and the American born Nisei praised economic opportunity in the Golden State.

This euphoria ended in 1924, when a federal immigration law prohibited the entry of aliens ineligible for citizenship into the United states. This legislation was directed at the Japanese because the Chinese and Asian Indian had been excluded by previous laws. Karl Yoneda, a Japanese American longshoreman, remembered his parents crying over the law. "I was a little boy," Yoneda recalled, "and my dad felt like he had been slapped in the face."

The *Rafu Shimpo*, a Los Angeles based Japanese newspaper, accused politicians of fomenting "racial strife." The *Japanese Times and Mail* concluded that singling out the Japanese for exclusion was a way of negating their economic achievements. In San Francisco, a series of meetings in Japantown prompted angry Nisei to write letters to the *San Francisco Chronicle* about California racism. Much to the frustration of the Nisei, the *Chronicle* refused to print these letters.

Faced with such strong opposition to their presence in California, the Japanese Americans quickly made the 1924 immigration law a rallying point for more intense political activity. Governor Friend

Richardson, a Republican conservative from Berkeley, was the first politician to feel the wrath of the politically emerging Japanese. He ignored their letters and sided with United States Senator Hiram W. Johnson in demanding further exclusion.

The Japanese Americans were increasingly political because of economics. Invariably, they had degrees from the University of California; they opened successful businesses, and they were solid citizens. None of this mattered. When they ventured out to apply for jobs, they were hired in fruits stands, as gardeners and workers in the fields. The Issei returned home in larger numbers, and by 1940, 52% of the population were Japanese American.

But the Nisei were not a retiring lot. They voted, participated in politics when they could and continued to achieve despite the odds. During the Great Depression, a group of businessmen organized the Japanese American Democratic Club in San Francisco. They looked to Franklin D. Roosevelt's New Deal as a model for their own goals. Equal opportunity and an end to racial discrimination were two things the Japanese Democrats worked for during the 1930s.

When the Democratic Party met in Los Angles at their state conference and prepared to elect the first twentieth century Democratic governor, Culbert Olson, a group of Japanese American delegates arrived at the convention. Ruth Kurata presented some suggestions for federal legislation to make acts of racial discrimination punishable by law. She was listened to politely, but the Democrats ignored her and the rest of the delegation. Olson's New Deal for California was not for the Japanese.

Undaunted, the Japanese American Citizens League organized in 1929 to work for equal employment opportunities, improved housing and increased civil liberties. Generally, the organization was a voice in the wilderness. James Sakamoto, editor of the *Japanese American Courier*, was optimistic about the future. Speaking of the Nisei Sakamoto wrote: "The second generation are American citizens and through them will be reaped the harvests of tomorrow." The question of loyalty bothered Sakamoto and other Japanese professionals. World events cast Japan in a bad light in America, and the coming of World War II and the rise of fascism created strong fears over Japanese loyalty.

Patriotism became a cornerstone of the Japanese American community. These young men and women were born in America, spoke English exclusively, graduated from American schools and held jobs. To demonstrate their loyalty the Nisei organized the American Loyalty League in San Francisco and Fresno. In 1930, the Japanese American Citizens League held patriotic, pro-American celebrations to combat the images of fascism and communism which were being associated with the Japanese American.

By 1940, there were fifty chapters of the Japanese American Citizens League with six thousand members. The JACL attempted to educate Americans on issues of Japanese American loyalty, economic progress and cultural differences. The JACL newsletter, the *Nikki Shimin*, urged the Nisei to protest discrimination in the job market. By demonstrating a high level of patriotism the Japanese Americans believed that they would eventually be accepted into the mainstream of California life.

When World War II broke out, the issue of acceptance ended when the Japanese, whether Issei or Nisei, were placed in sand and cactus concentration camps throughout the United States. Assimilation, patriotism and model citizenship were excellent ideas, but they failed to garner the Japanese the American dream.

The Chinese Between the Wars: The Emergence of the Urban Chinese Californian

During the early 1920s, V.S. McClatchy of the California Joint Immigration Commission, discovered that one of four Chinese immigrants was a woman. More than 10,000 Chinese women arrived from 1907 to 1924, and McClatchy was relieved when the Immigration Law of 1924 temporarily halted the influx of Chinese women. This only reinforced the notion that San Francisco's Chinatown was a ghetto with unhealthy social vices, rampant prostitution and unsavory black market goods.

The image of California's Chinatowns led to an increase in Anglo tourists who were lured by tales of exotic adventures. Unwittingly, tourism was one of the reasons for increased Chinese acceptance. The stream of visitors, the tours of Chinatown and the presence of exotic goods paved the way for acceptance of Chinese culture.

By 1940, there were 77,504 Chinese on the mainland with more than 50% residing in California. Unlike the Japanese, the Chinese were urban, clustered in a large Chinatown and with seven years in California, they were able to manipulate the political system.

Small California towns like Sebastopol saw their Chinese population dwindle from a few hundred to almost nothing. Johnny Ginn suggested that "those old guys thought about...how they wanted to go back to China." Soon this migration either brought the Chinese to San Francisco or back to China.

Once the most numerous workers in California's fields, the Chinese fled to the city during the 1920s. Restaurant and laundry work were open to the Chinese, and 58% were employed in these areas. The Chinese worked in businesses owned by their countrymen. Peter Wong remembered: "I always worked for the Chinese, never for Americans."

Because of employment restrictions, the Chinese laundry man was a common sight in San Francisco ,and he contributed to one of the earliest and cruelest anti-Asian stereotypes. A common song of young San Francisco children was: "Chinkie, Chinkie, Chinaman, Sitting on the fence; Trying To Make A Dollar Out of fifteen cents." The Chinese resented the symbolism in this song. The popular notion was that Chinese labor worked too cheaply, too hard and solely in Chinatown. However, this was untrue as economic survival forced the Chinese to relocated in all parts of San Francisco.

The Chinese who remained in California were enterprising and able to make a living. Joe Shoong recognized the need for inexpensive goods and established Vallejo's China Toggery Dry Goods store. Nothing was sold for more than a dollar. Soon Shoong had a series of stores on the West Coast. He changed the name to the National Dollar Stores and became a multimillionaire. Unfortunately, Shoong exploited Chinese labor by establishing sweat shops that produced inexpensive goods with sweat shop labor.

The National Dollar Stores were so oppressive that disgruntled workers organized the Chinese Ladies Garment Workers Union and carried out a successful strike in 1937 which lasted for thirteen weeks. Shoong closed his factory rather than giving in to the workers, but race conscious white supporters praised Shoong and demanded an end to Chinese labor unions.

By the late 1930s, the Chinese expressed concern about Japanese aggression, and newspapers like San Francisco's *Chung Sai Yat Po* suggested that a new Chinese nationalism was engulfing California. Unfortunately, Americans didn't recognize how Chinese attitudes also reflected a strong California nationalism.

On the eve of World War II, the Chinese were an economic force in San Francisco and slowly gaining acceptance in the liberal city by the bay. The San Francisco Junior College welcomed Chinese students, and Jade Snow remembers her history class challenged the traditional role of the parent. As a new generation of Chinese Americans came of age in the 1940s, they increasingly were a bridge to the American way.

Bibliographical Essay

On Filipinos see, Howard A. DeWitt, *Anti-Filipino Movements in California: A History, Study Guide and Bibliography* (San Francisco, 1976); Howard A. DeWitt, *Violence In The Fields: California Filipino Farm Labor Unionization* (Saratoga, 1980) and Fred Cordova, *Filipinos: Forgotten Asian Americans, A Pictorial Essay* (Seattle, 1983). For the anti-radical feeling directed toward ethnic groups see, Howard A. DeWitt, *Images of Ethnic and Radical Violence in California Politics, 1917-1930: A Survey* (San Francisco, 1975).

Manual Buaken, *I Have Lived With The American People* (Caldwell, 1948) and Carlos Bulosan, *America Is In The Heart: A Personal History* (New York, 1946) are excellent memoirs by literate, historical minded, Filipino intellectuals.

Filipino labor activity is examined by Howard A. DeWitt, "The Filipino Labor Union: The Salinas Lettuce Strike of 1934," *Amerasia*, volume 5, no 2 (1978) Geoffrey Dunn and Mark Schwartz, *Dollar A Day, 10 Cents A Dance: An Historic Portrait of Filipino Farmworkers in America*, film and video (San Francisco, 1985) and H. Brett Melendy, *Asians in America: Filipinos, Koreans and East Indians* (Boston, 1977).

For materials on Japanese Americans see, for example, Ronald Takaki, *Strangers From A Different Shore: A History of Asian Americans* (New York, 1989), chapter 6; Yori Wada, "Growing Up In Central California," *Amerasia*, volume 13 no. 2 (1986-1987) and Jerold Takahaski, "Changing Responses to Racial Subordination: An Exploratory Study of Japanese American Political Styles," (unpublished doctoral dissertation, University of California, Berkeley, 1980).

For African American influences the classic study is B. Gordon Wheeler's, *Black California: The History of African Americans In The Golden State* (New York, 1993), chapter XIV covers the years between the wars. Also, see, Douglas Daniel, *Pioneer Urbanites* (New York, 1980).

On Koreans in California see H. Brett Melendy, *Asians in America: Filipinos, Koreans and East Indians* (Boston, 1977), chapters 8-13 and Ronald Takaki, *Strangers From a Different Shore: A History of Asian Americans* (New York, 1989), chapter 7. Also see, Sun Bin Yim, "The Social Structure of Korean Communities in California, 1903-1920," in Lucie Cheng and Edna Bonacich, eds., *Labor Immigration Under Capitalism: Asian Workers in the Untied States Before World War II* (Berkeley and Los Angeles, 1984); Sonia Sunoo, *Korea Kaleidoscope: Oral Histories* (Davis, Ca., 1982) and Younghill Kang, *East Goes West* (New York, 1937).

See Sucheng Chan, *Asian Americans: An Interpretive History* (Boston, 1991) and Roger Daniels, *Asian America: Chinese and Japanese in the United States since 1850* (Seattle, 1988)

for an excellent interpretive overview of the interwar years.

Howard A. DeWitt, "Communism and the Appeal to Ethnic Minorities: The Cannery and Agricultural Workers' Industrial Union in the Imperial Valley," *New Labor Review* (June 1980) examines the anti-Filipino attitudes which developed when they united with Mexican labor unions.

For Asian Indians see H. Brett Melendy, *Asians In America: Filipinos, Koreans and East Indians* (Boston, 1977), chapters 14-22 and Ronald Takaki, *Strangers From A Different Shore: A History of Asian Americans* (New York, 1989), chapter 8. Also see, California State Board of Control, *California And The Oriental* (Sacramento, 1922), pp. 115-116 for Asian Indian hostility.

Juan L. Gonzalez, Jr., "Asian Indian Immigration Patterns: The Origins of the Sikh Community in California," *International Migration Review*, volume 20, no. 1, pp. 40-54 for an important analysis of Asian Indian beginnings. For a typical contemporary racist view of the Punjabi see, Annette Thackwell Johnson, "The Rag-Heads-A Picture of America's East Indians," *The Independent*, volume 109, number 3828, October 28, 1922, pp. 234-235.

12

Community in Crisis

The Mexican and African Californian, 1920-1940

The Pacific Electric Interurban Railway created a transportation revolution in Los Angeles. This rapid transit system connected Santa Ana to Los Angeles, Santa Monica and Watts and began the initial suburbanization of the greater Los Angeles area. For more than two decades, suburban property values increased dramatically, and there was a slow, but steady, influx of middle class Anglo settlers to what had been previously considered remote areas of Los Angeles. Real estate speculators were rampant. By the mid-1920s, unscrupulous investors were looking for Spanish speaking communities that were unincorporated areas. The agents for large real estate firms could target these settlements for change by attempting to create a new city. Belvedere, a Spanish speaking, undeveloped and unincorporated area, was an early realtor's target. It was the perfect place for real estate interests to seize by creating a city. Although Belvedere was not connected to the Pacific Electric Interurban Railway, there was talk of rapid transit expansion to the area, and this exited the speculators. Residents of Belvedere, on the other hand, became alarmed and called a meeting.

On June 12, 1927, a community meeting in Belvedere protested plans to create a city. Belvedere, an isolated and inexpensive settlement area for Mexican immigrants, was invaded by Anglo real estate and business speculators who tried to force Mexican landowners to sell their homes. By creating a city government and levying a tax for police, fire and city service, the real estate interests could make it too expensive for homeowners to remain in Belvedere. This would force the Spanish speaking citizens to sell their property. It was projected that during Belvedere's first five years as a city, taxes would increase three times, and this would drive out most homeowners.

But the slick talking and nattily dressed real estate speculators spoke glowingly about Belvedere's future. Initially, they failed to warn homeowners about the new expenses of city government. The creation of a city in Belvedere, real estate brokers argued, allowed only for a minimal tax to be placed on residents for services. The reality was that these taxes would force the predominantly Mexican working class population to sell their homes.

Zeferino Ramirez: The New Californian, Mexican Style

A local Mexican businessman, Zeferino Ramirez, recognized the dangers of slick talking real estate agents. In June, 1927, he organized a community meeting to protest the creation of a city. Ramirez called this tactic an attempt to move the Spanish speaking out of Belvedere. Ramirez was furious about this attempt to seize Belvedere's prime real estate. So, he urged the development of "Mexican pride" in order to create a new Californian, Mexican style, who resisted Americanization, was not concerned about citizenship and celebrated Mexican holidays.

Although he was a respected community leader, few people in Belvedere were familiar with Ramirez's background. Ramirez immigrated to southern California from Mexico with little knowledge of English and no marketable employment skills. But he was bright, hard working and recognized economic opportunity. He worked in the mines and on the railroad and saved his money. When he was between jobs, Ramirez lived in an insect infested room and paid an exorbitant rent to an Anglo landlord. He resented the second class citizenship forced on Mexicans in Los Angeles and planned to do something about it. Ramirez realized that home ownership and business success were the keys to a stable future.

Ramirez had a strong personality and ignored the continuous racial insults in and around southern California. After securing a job as a highway laborer, Ramirez ate only one meal a day and saved his money in a tin can. He was not only suspicious of banks, but he was also critical of the interest Mexicans paid on loans. After working seven years on the highway, Ramirez saved enough money to purchase a Belvedere home. Then he decided to better himself professionally and looked for a new way to make a living.

Ramirez convinced a local undertaker to train him as an unpaid apprentice. A quick learner, Ramirez soon became an accomplished mortician and with help from Protestant missionaries, established the leading Belvedere mortuary. After opening his own mortuary, Ramirez quickly established himself as a community leader. He was a founder of the Mexican Chamber of Commerce, and at weekly meetings, he urged a sense of Hispanic pride. Ramirez argued for a Spanish speaking business community as a means of lifting the oppressive Anglo racism in and around Los Angeles.

He had a strong commitment to religious and social life. His friends were surprised when he converted to the Protestant faith, but Ramirez used his conversion to protest the barrio Catholic priests who refused to raise their voices against the institutionalized racism that kept the Spanish speaking from an acceptable standard of living. By serving as a lay preacher at a Methodist Church on Brooklyn Avenue, Ramirez encouraged the Los Angeles Spanish speaking population to become politically involved.

Ramirez's Anglo friends commented that he had "an old Mexican sense of morality." His daughters were well known and respected music teachers. But he insisted that they respect the Mexican social and cultural standards. They never went out unchaperoned, and they were carefully schooled in Mexican manners, morals and social customs. One of his daughters remarked that her father was caught between two cultures.

As the issue of Belvedere becoming a city dominated local politics, Ramirez was in the forefront of the fight to prevent it. He argued forcefully that it was simply another way of disenfranchising the Mexican. His critics pointed out that he was not a citizen. However, Ramirez responded that he refused to apply for naturalization. When he was asked why he was so politically active, even though he could not vote, Ramirez responded that it was to preserve Mexican culture. Anglo racism, Ramirez argued, was displacing the hard working Mexican who had diligently saved money for a home. Belvedere was the beginning of a real estate conspiracy, Ramirez told his followers, to force the Mexican into a small, uncomfortable and poverty ridden ghetto.

To many, Ramirez was a contradiction because he refused citizenship while promoting a Spanish speaking business culture presence. Time and time again, Ramirez suggested that he did not want to became an American citizen. He was a Mexican and proud of it. With support from the Mexican Chamber of Commerce, Ramirez founded a Spanish language school in Belvedere. He was also an active promoter of Mexican history. When a Mexican library opened in Belvedere in November 1926, Ramirez proudly announced that there was a new interest in Mexican culture. Soon the League of Mexican Culture organized, and Belvedere had a sense of social, economic and political growth.

On May 2, 1926, La Escuela Mexico, a barrio school in Belvedere, opened with desks that Ramirez purchased and donated for the school. Ramirez' interest in a Spanish school was so intense that he drove to downtown Los Angeles to purchase chalk, blackboards and maps.

What bothered Anglos was that La Escuela Mexico emphasized a curriculum with Hispanic ideas and culture. These cultural notions were then infused with Mexican history. Unlike Spanish speaking children in other parts of California, the Belvedere students understood their Spanish and Mexican roots. A trip to the Southwest Museum connected the Belvedere students with their Indian roots. Soon the Better American Federation and the Ku Klux Klan were openly talking about the dangers of La Escuela Mexico. But financial problems forced the school to close. However, the school's success goes a long way to demonstrate how fearful the Anglo majority was of Hispanic culture. It was fine to sell real estate with Hispanic names but not to educate the blue collar worker's children in a Spanish language school.

The Belvedere controversy suggests that the California dream was a difficult reality for southern California's Spanish speaking population. But they fought the Anglo notion of placing a Hispanic tag on real estate, streets, schools, auditoriums and parks. It was a tactic to sell real estate, create a myth of a happy multicultural state and induce the notion that the Spanish speaking were assimilated. Zeferino Ramirez fought this tendency and demonstrated that the Mexican immigrant was a force for change in the Golden State.

The Mexican in California: The Common Immigrant as a Force of Cultural Change

The Mexican who crossed the border into California in the early twentieth century is a forgotten pioneer. The massive movement of individuals and families who came over the border into California was due to employment opportunities. Mexican workers thought of California as a labor source. The Associated Farmers of California preferred Mexican labor to Filipino, Japanese, Chinese or Asian Indian workers. As V.S. McClatchy remarked: "the Mexican is generally not a troublemaker." The typical Mexican migrant was used to coming into southern California to work and then returning to Mexico to spend his money. There was prestige in being a California worker. Paul Taylor, a pioneering agricultural economist, concluded: "the agreeable...experience in the United States far overshadowed the disagreeable."

FIGURE 12-1. Chicana Secretary, 1920s.

When the U.S. Border Patrol was established in 1924, it did very little to slow the influx of legal or illegal Mexican workers. There was an arbitrary nature to Border Patrol enforcement which increased racial tension. In San Diego, Border Patrol agents often asked political questions and lectured incoming Mexican workers on Communism, political radicalism and what was expected of them morally in America. California's agribusiness interests had a subtle, but close, relationship to the Border Patrol, and this led to government intimidation upon migrating Mexican workers. The result was that the Mexican immigrant joined mutual aid associations which offered protection from government interference.

In the 1920s, California's fruit and vegetable farms were a logical destination for Mexican field workers. Not only did the Mexicans replace the Japanese in the California fields, but they also proved to be a hard working and dependable labor source. There were many Mexican nationals who became important contributors to California civilization.

Zeferino Valazquez: California is the Promised Land and Guadalupe Salazar's Magic of Los Angeles

Zeferino Velazquez arrived in Los Angeles in 1919 and wrote home that southern

California was "the promised land." The twenty-five year old Mexican had taken a circuitous route from El Paso, Texas, through Kansas City, Missouri and into Los Angeles to start a new life. His young wife had died shortly after giving birth to his son in Kansas City. Once he arrived in California, Velazquez settled in Los Angeles's Lincoln Heights barrio. He found a job as a laborer with the Los Angeles Paper Manufacturing Company and during layoffs worked in the Imperial Valley fields.

Like most Mexican immigrants, Velazquez had trouble maintaining a permanent job. In the 1920s, he was fired from a job because he was a Mexican. "If I was a citizen," Velazquez lamented, "I would have held down a regular job." Velazquez's nomadic work patterns from the Los Angeles barrio through the Imperial Valley were typical of Mexican immigrants.

Like most Mexicans, Velazquez settled in Los Angeles after living in a number of other cities and states, and he believed that southern California had excellent economic opportunities. It was an option for employment that offered a fair living standard. The large and growing Los Angeles Mexican community was attractive to the Spanish speaking as they established barrios in central and eastern Los Angeles. Initially, there was less of a sense of ghettoization with the Spanish speaking, but inadequate housing, second rate schools and unskilled jobs, combined with exploitive Anglo landlords, created a barrio. The Anglo attitude was "this is better than Mexico." But there was still opportunity.

When Guadalupe Salazar rode the train from Chicago to Los Angeles, she was filled with a sense of adventure and anticipation. She had just divorced her husband, Arcadio Yniguez, and she hoped to find a new life in California. When Guadalupe arrive in Los Angeles with her five year old son, it was 1931 and California was in the midst of a major depression.

But Guadalupe built a new life in Los Angeles as a single parent and an independent Mexican woman. She reunited with her father, found a job and married Tiburcio Rivera, a musician from Mexico. They had four daughters and in the midst of the Great Depression were solid, productive citizens. Both Guadalupe and Tiburcio worked to provide their children with a stable, middle class life. Eventually, Guadalupe received the "Mother of the Year" award from the Senior Citizens Clubs of East Los Angeles. She was featured in *La Opinion* and praised as a role model. Her story was typical of the men and women who survived in the rough and tumble years between the wars. For Guadalupe Salazar there was a magic to Los Angeles. "I had opportunity, and I took it," she remarked.

The Mexican who settled in Los Angeles was enchanted by the rising metropolis, the trolley cars, the automobiles and the growing skyline. It was a beautiful city that offered a future. But many Mexicans were upset that they could not retain their culture. By the 1920s, there were programs offering Americanization for the Mexican immigrant.

The Americanization process failed because it centered around altering traditional Mexican culture. The attempt to limit Spanish in the home, the pressure to change the traditional role of women through night school and jobs and the emphasis upon changing eating habits met with resistance. When the Great Depression of 1929 began, the Americanization movement ended and more than a half a million Mexicans were repatriated. The Mexican who was no longer welcome began questioning American intent.

The disenchantment with American values intensified in 1921 when the Los Angeles' Spanish speaking community celebrated the one hundredth anniversary of Mexico's independence from Spain. A month long celebration, ending on September 16, 1921, reminded the Hispanic community of its Mexican roots.

The editor of the Los Angeles based *El Heraldo de Mexico* suggested that Mexican heroes be given a place in California history. The newspaper also called for an end to slick real estate promoters using Hispanic themes to sell land, food and travel to California. Pressure from Mexican settlers prompted the founding of Spanish language libraries in southern California, and the League of Mexican Culture organized to promote "Spanish language civilization."

The Mexican immigrant who settled in Los Angeles survived by creatively adapting to American culture and retaining strong, although flexible, family ties. The Spanish speaking settler who refused citizenship and didn't adapt wholly to California culture was an indication of multicultural independence. On Sunday mornings, the Los Angeles Central Plaza came alive with the sights and sounds of Mexico. Visitors remarked that the Old Plaza seemed more like a part of Mexico than Los Angeles, and, unwittingly, they were recognizing the pursuit of the Mexican dream.

We Have Our Own Culture: The Rise of a Mexican Influenced Los Angeles

During the 19th century, the term Californio was used to describe the Spanish speaking population. By the twentieth century, the term Chicano evolved after Mexicans and Mexican Americans studied their Mexican Indian, Spanish and mestizo roots. The use of the term Chicano suggests a community spirit, as well as a political-cultural identification, and it was the warning sign that an ideological Mexican American history was on the rise. Chicano is a term which derives from many influences.

Chicano historians believed that there is a "trans-creation;" known as the process of blending Mexican and American cultures. In Los Angeles, these historians argue, there is a tendency to draw upon African American, Indian and other ethnic cultures to create a pure California culture, one which blends all the multicultural influences in the Golden State.

To some historians, notably Albert Camarillo, the term Chicano suggests an important tool in "understanding a people who have greatly influenced the formation of the region's society for two centuries." In the 1920s, there was a renaissance of Mexican culture in the movies, in music and in the publishing industry. There was a strong market for Spanish speaking movies and Hollywood brought in Ramon Navarro, Lupe Velez and Dolores del Rio to meet the demand. But these movies did little, if anything, to clarify the Spanish speaking presence in California history. But a separate Mexican culture quickly developed.

The Mexican music industry and more than thirty Chicano playwrights provided a rich cultural heritage in and around Los Angeles. When Los Hermanos Banuelos recorded "El Lavaplatos," they created a strong market for Mexican records. The theme behind "El Lavaplatos" (The Dishwasher) was that Mexican workers faced obstacles, but with humor, dignity and hard work they were able to win the battle with American life. "We have our own culture," a member of Los Hermanos Banuelos remarked. Soon American race record labels such as Okeh, a subsidiary of Columbia and Bluebird, a subsidiary of RCA, were producing records for the Spanish speaking market. These were known as race records, and the major record labels used this designation to maintain a separate culture.

Soon Spanish language radio was broadcast from KELW in Burbank and by the mid-1920s, ethnic radio was a visible part of Los

Angeles culture. Mexican radio was 88% music, 4% news and 8% community service announcements. *La Opinion*, Los Angeles' major Spanish newspaper, praised the newly emerging Mexican culture and suggested that a vibrant Hispanic influence had grown up in and around Los Angeles. But cultural growth didn't equal economic success.

The Mexican California Character: Cultural Advances and Economic Decline

In southern California, from Santa Barbara to Los Angeles, the Mexican American population occupied a lower economic status. The typical Californian saw no distinction between the native born and the Mexican immigrant. So racism was universal toward Mexicans, whether foreign born or of native stock.

During the 1920s, the predominant Mexican American character of towns like Santa Barbara changed into an American retirement community. As expensive homes were built along the Pacific Ocean and suburbs with Hispanic names cropped up, the Mexican American population slid into economic oblivion.

To counter the business and residential invasion of Anglos the Mexican American population formed self-help groups. In Santa Barbara, the Foresters Junipero Serra Court NO. 147 emerged to celebrate Mexican holidays and protest the pollution of the environment. The Eagles Club included native born Mexicans and was a social group that sponsored picnics and other functions to celebrate the Hispanic heritage.

The most startling change in Santa Barbara during the 1920s when the decline of Spanish surnamed voters fell from almost 16% in 1910 to 3.2% in 1930. The migration and settlement of large numbers of foreign born Mexicans created a growing hostility to Mexicans. The result of this hostility forced the Spanish speaking into the barrio.

The continual need for inexpensive contract labor was another reason for the rise of barrios. A readily available supply of labor in the barrio helped to create the illusion of success. In reality, the barrio labor system was akin to slavery. As Pedro Castillo remarked that the barrio was located near commercial areas which used cheap labor in transportation, construction and service industry jobs.

By 1930, Los Angeles had the largest concentration of urban Spanish speaking workers in the United States. The reason was a simple one. Mexican labor was inexpensive, productive and employers believed that the workers were not prone to labor radicalism. But the Mexican and Chicano worker soon found that the barrio was uprooted for the construction of city commercial buildings, government offices and entertainment facilities. The final insult was that barrio land was a valuable commodity.

In East Los Angeles, Chicanos were prevented from living in key areas of town due to racial restrictions which prohibited the sale or rental of real estate to Mexicans. This process of institutionalized racism spread to other parts of California including San Bernardino's Westside barrio, San Francisco's Mission District, Sacramento's J and K streets and 35th Street in east Oakland. The creation of the San Diego barrio took place in the area just southeast of downtown. By 1920, about 30% of the Mexican population lived in shacks in this area of San Diego in a neighborhood which was also black. But in the 1920s, a housing boom brought in more than 20,000 Mexican workers who began living in Logan Heights. Suddenly, there were two distinct Mexican sections of town-one for middle class Mexican Americans and the other for the recently arrived immigrant.

By 1930, Governor C.C. Young's Mexican Fact Finding Committee reported that Mexicans were laborers in the construction, transportation workers and farm industries. This report also indicated that Spanish speaking employees had a wide range of skills but were predominantly semi or unskilled workers. However, the stock market crash brought an end to the California dream for the Spanish speaking.

The Great Depression and the Rise of Repatriation

The Great Depression was a watershed in the California Mexican experience. The economic decline, the rise of hostility toward legal and illegal Mexican immigrants and the increasing demand from Mexican Government officials for repatriation led to an exodus back to Mexico. What is the significance of the repatriation program to California's Spanish speaking population? One aspect of the repatriation controversy was that it politicized the Spanish speaking. Traditionally, though, historians have concentrated upon the programs which returned Mexicans to their native country. However, there has been very little study regarding the social change and psychological trauma resulting from repatriation.

Few Americans blamed the Great Depression for California's economic problems. Charles P. Visel, head of a Los Angeles relief committee, warned that "aliens and illegals" were helping the economy plummet to new lows. Colonel Arthur Woods, President Herbert Hoover's director for the Emergence Committee for Employment, was an intellectual terrorist who sent out frightening memos to Spanish newspapers urging them to "expose deportable aliens."

These attitudes encouraged federal immigration officials to round up suspected aliens. The results were often embarrassing. After a well publicized sweep through the predominantly Spanish speaking Plaza District on February 26, 1931, the *Los Angeles Times* reported that only seventeen aliens were taken into custody-eleven Mexicans, five Chinese and one Japanese. There was no mention that only four were illegals.

Whether intentional or not, repatriation created fear and suspicion in California government. Maria Olazabal of Belvedere remembered Mexican men leaving home each morning in search of work and returning at night with empty pocketbooks and stomachs. She was a middle class Chicana whose husband made a living in his grocery store, and so she decided to open a food bank. She gathered a group of women and sold tamales at cost. When asked why she didn't give them away, Mrs. Olazabal responded: "We don't want to hurt their pride." The Cooperative Society of Unemployed Mexican Ladies, as Mrs. Olazabal's group was known, criticized state and federal officials for their lack of understanding and compassion toward the Spanish speaking during the Great Depression. "There is a double standard," Mrs. Olazabal remarked, "and we must fight it."

The rise of Spanish speaking Californians who organized mutual aid societies during the Great Depression created a strong community economically, politically and socially, and intensified hostile feelings toward Americans.

When Los Angeles County officials announced that they would pay the train fare of all Mexicans on relief to the border, there was strong criticism from *La Opinion*. Undeterred, a county official pompously announced that a one way fare was cheaper than welfare. On March 23, 1931, the first trainload of repatriates left Los Angeles. The Mexican consul, Rafael de la Colina, criticized this action, calling it an act of terrorism.

The vast majority of California's Spanish speaking population did not want to be repatriated. Mexico's economy was stagnant; most immigrants had adopted California ways, and established family, friends and a social life. In Los Angeles, the vibrant Hispanic culture convinced most Mexicans to wait out the Great Depression. By the mid 1930s a large number of repatriated Mexicans planned to or had returned to Los Angeles. Clearly, repatriation was a failure, but its success was in politicizing the Spanish speaking community.

The seizure of Mexicans by immigration officials and the rough and often brutal deportation to Mexico led to organized protests. The end result of the repatriation/ deportation movement led to a Chicano political solidarity which emerged during World War II.

Black Californians: The 1920s and 1930s

Black Californians faced many of the same pressures that Mexicans faced. Racism, lack of educational opportunity, job discrimination, inadequate housing and governmental indifference plagued the African American community. But a black middle class, albeit a small one, had grown up in the Golden State. By 1920, the African American vote was predominantly Republican and, therefore they voted for Warren Harding. Like most Californians, the black population was conservative, and African American leaders believed that the post World War I economic upturn would bring greater equality.

Because labor unions generally refused black membership, there were only a few African Americans in the skilled trades. In the early 1920s, San Francisco's union movement faced the rise of the open shop which allowed non-union workers to replace their union counterparts. Since the 1880s, Los Angeles city officials had perpetuated a booster myth. Charles Fletcher Lummis, the

editor of the *Los Angeles Times*, and its owner, Harrison Gray Otis, fostered the notion of a colorful, multi cultural, prejudice free city of happy Mexicans and laid back Anglos. Just the opposite was true in Los Angeles as the police and Otis' *Los Angeles Times* created class warfare to rid the City of the Angels of labor unions and political radicals.

What Los Angeles found attractive in the 1920s were religious sideshows like Aimee Semple McPherson, eccentrics like pandering holyman Ottoman Bar-Azosht Ra'nish or drug induced Hollywood types like Roscoe "Fatty" Arbuckle. However, black workers were simply not welcome in Los Angeles. Thus, in the midst of the 1920's Jazz Age, African Americans moved into Watts or fled for the liberal San Francisco climate.

The black urbanites who arrived in California in the early 1920s were unskilled and competed with the Mexican and other minorities for lower paying jobs. Black Californians were often the last hired and the first fired. The National Urban League, founded in 1910 by a white, wealthy woman, Ruth Standish Baldwin, lobbied for better jobs. She organized branches in California and pressured state government agencies for improved housing and employment. A multi-racial coalition that hoped to promote integration, the National Urban League created a civil rights impulse.

In Los Angeles, Ed Cornelius Pope published a monthly newsletter, the *Golden Opportunity*, and the National Urban League sponsored publication that presented hypothetical solutions to employment problems. One of Pope's tactics was to publicize employment-housing opportunities in the cities. This helped to create new jobs in Los Angeles, Fresno, Stockton, Sacramento and San Francisco. The rest of California had a dismal record in employing and housing black Californians. Yet, there were those who believed that African American opportunity was on the rise. Professor Charles S. Johnson, an African American college professor, was a strong believer in racial progress. He was a brilliant and respected academic who envisioned a new future for black Californians. After a lengthy study of Los Angeles and San Francisco employment patterns, Professor Johnson published his findings, and they suggested some opportunity for black Californians.

Charles S. Johnson: An African American College Professor and Negro Opportunity

In Los Angeles and San Francisco, there were some who believed that economic opportunity was improving. Professor Charles S. Johnson was an African American sociologist who studied employment patterns in Los Angeles and San Francisco. Not only was Johnson a recognized authority on "Negro employment," but the Fisk University scholar was also a widely published and praised scholar.

In 1926, Johnson published a lengthy study on black employment patterns. He concluded that 50 out of 456 major manufacturing plants hired black workers. The report highlighted a number of workers who had risen to supervisory positions. Johnson noted that major department stores preferred black elevator operators because they were more efficient and polite. The white male elevator operator, one department store manager remarked to Johnson, "flirted with the girls." This strange conclusion suggested that some employers maintained strict view on race when hiring. Gump's Department Store in San Francisco, for example, hired African American workers only for maintenance. There were no sales people and none in the business or accounting ends either. Johnson ignored these examples.

The role of the African American worker intrigued Johnson who wrote a scholarly book, *The Negro War Worker in San Francisco: A Local Self-Survey*, in which he surveyed almost three hundred black families. Johnson's study, published in 1944, examined the war years, but the book also contained a wealth of information concerning the problems of ethnic employment. Johnson concluded that it was easier for black Californians to secure jobs in the 1930s and early 1940s because of the rise of war industries. The black families who had lived in San Francisco for more than a decade found it easier to secure employment.

Professor Johnson's report documented the large number of southern blacks who migrated to the Golden State for the well publicized employment opportunities. However, these positions were more often for employment in the unskilled, menial or service sector. Yet, as Johnson suggested, there was a rush for these positions. Johnson's findings are not surprising because the small number of African American professionals worked in a white environment and had little contact with the working class.

Because of racial restrictions, it was difficult for black Californians to enter the professional working sector. The number of African American lawyers and doctors was minuscule, but black insurance agents, small store owners, morticians, laundry clerks, restaurant workers and night club proprietors were numerous, and they created a black economic aristocracy. Eventually, these businesses attained a degree of political influence.

African American Politics: The Slow Progress Between the Wars

In politics, San Francisco minister Francis J. Grimke was a continual thorn in the side of local politicians. He attacked the saloons, the gambling dens, the prize fights and the open prostitution as examples of moral corruption. Not only was Grimke a moral voice but he also helped to sway the black vote to reform corrupt politicians. Grimke urged African Americans to unite politically.

During the 1924 election, the two premier black newspapers the *Oakland Sunshine* and the *California Eagle* urged voters to support the Republican Party. As a result of Reverend Grimke's politics and the black newspapers editorials, the Democratic Party began courting the African American vote. The reasons for Democratic interest were more political than altruistic. With only about thirty percent of the California vote, the Democratic Party was counting on the emerging African American vote to bolster its electoral standing. So Democratic candidates talked at length about better jobs, improved housing and solving the legal problems of black Californians. These promises had a hollow ring as the Democrats had little political influence. As a result, during the 1920s, California's African American population remained overwhelmingly Republican.

When the Great Depression struck in October 1929, there was no sign of a shift in black California votes. Jobs weren't plentiful for Californians, but loyalty to the Republican Party continued. From 1930 to 1938, the insensitivity of Governors James Rolph and Frank Merriam caused a slow, but steady, shift to the Democratic Party. By May, 1935, black Californians represented seventeen percent of people on public relief, and there was sharp criticism toward the Republican Party. President Franklin D. Roosevelt's National Recovery Act set up guidelines for jobs and wages, and black Californians were employed in large numbers in these make-work government jobs. The New Deal began to align African American voters with not only the Democratic Party but with labor unions and liberal civil rights organizations as well.

When a black Californian, Robert C. Weaver, was appointed to a management position in President Roosevelt's Department of the Interior, there was applause from African American newspapers. As the *California Eagle* suggested, there was a window of recognition for the African American. A disproportionately high number of black workers found jobs through New Deal relief agencies, and soon 17.3% of San Francisco's black laborers were classified as emergency workers. These statistics were among the highest of any city in the United States.

The Great Depression and the Changing Nature of African American California and Rising Business

Generally, the Great Depression was not a pleasant time for the average black Californian. The 1930s were difficult economic years. Because of trouble finding skilled jobs, there was little growth in the black population. California's Governor James "Sunny Jim" Rolph, Jr. was perplexed when asked about race. Rolph's only comment was: "the Negro has a place in my heart." This obvious vote getting quote demonstrated that Governor Rolph had no programs for the African American community. He was a hand shaker who rode a white horse in parades and talked continuously about finding "something for the Negro population to do." The black working class suffered under Rolph and his Republican successor, Frank Merriam, and the result placed the black worker into limbo.

Yet, despite the Great Depression, there were a number of African American businesses prospering. The Butler Funeral Home at Sutter and Fillmore in San Francisco was the most profitable black enterprise. John Howard Butler, a local businessman, owned the funeral home and quickly became a millionaire. Butler was also involved in real estate investments. Other black real estate moguls included Philip A. Payton and Hannibal T. Sheppard who later served as president of the San Francisco chapter of the NAACP. Sheppard owned the Inter-city Finance Company and helped many African Americans purchase their first home.

Although California's black community was barely visible from 1920 to 1940, it organized the first large scale protests against discrimination. The black migrant, with the aid of organizations like the NAACP, pressured white employers to hire them. While there was only minimal success in the employment market, a politically sensitive African American community continued to emerge to challenge traditional racism.

Many black Californians lived in a middle class environment, and this helped to erase stereotypes that had dominated white thinking. In education, health care and housing, black Californians made steady progress between the wars. Due to racism, they still lagged far behind whites, but Black Californians had proven their willingness to work, pursue education and be devoted to family life. Moreover, the black church remained a staunch supporter of urban morality and the presence of African American ministers at city council meetings attested to the black political presence. Although the old stereotypes about blacks being lazy and not wanting a share of the American pie were challenged during the 1920s and 1930s, there was still a need for progress.

In San Francisco, black ministers, social workers, editors and community activists were recognized as leaders. The posh dinner parties, the lavish teas and the stylish bridge parties set the black elite apart from the rest of San Francisco's African American population. The Sojourner Truth Club held dances to celebrate black pride in the 1920s, and there were numerous professional groups that pursued economic and educational change. San Francisco's black elite celebrated its history, but there was strong opposition to a Colored American Day because no black Californians envisioned themselves as Americans, and they complained about needlessly defining color lines.

There were other events that the black elite attended. For example, San Francisco's most important social event was the annual formal dance given by the Cosmos Club. This organization, founded in 1919 by William Henry Lashly, was an interracial social club. The monthly meetings at San Francisco's International Institute featured music, fashion shows, poetry, literature and historical lectures. African American blues, folk and jazz music was featured with dancing usually rounding out the evening.

Joe Foreman, a popular doorman at the exclusive Shreven's jewelry store, was an important African American social figure. A young San Francisco columnist, Herb Caen, remembered Foreman as an elegantly dressed gentleman who attended all the right social functions. Foreman often served as a hired doorman at white events and was the Cosmos Club's master of ceremonies. He brought out the biggest names to the annual Cosmos Club ball and regularly supplied newspapers with interviews on black culture.

The clubs in and around San Francisco created a social intimacy between black and white Californians creating a new sense of understanding. The opportunity to eat, drink and dance together brought a racial harmony in San Francisco which was unknown in the American West. It also led African American associations to strive for great acceptance.

African American Protest Organizations and the Embryo Seeds of Civil Rights

San Francisco's black community struggled for civil rights gains. Dignity and respect were important goals of California black organizations. The National Association For The Advancement of Colored People (NAACP) was the earliest challenger to attitudes of white supremacy and racism. Since San Francisco had a long tradition of Irish-Catholic and labor union activism, it was not long before black Californians reached sympathetic ears.

Not surprisingly, the first serious protest was over a vicious racist movie. In February 1915, *The Birth Of A Nation* opened in San Francisco and soon thereafter opened in Oakland. The Negro Equity League, the Negro Welfare League and the Equal Rights League joined with the NAACP to protest the movie. *The Birth Of A Nation* viciously stereotyped black Californians as lazy, intellectually incompetent and in need of culture. The Southern way of life and slavery were lionized in the film as the perfect civilization. The NAACP suggested that this hateful movie did nothing to advance racial harmony.

A San Francisco businessman, Walter A. Butler, urged Mayor James "Sunny Jim" Rolph and Governor Hiram W. Johnson to boycott the movie. Neither responded to Butler's request. As one of the chief officers of the NAACP, Butler's opinions were important. Eventually, City Attorney Percy Long announced that he favored shutting down the movie.

What made the protest against *The Birth Of A Nation* significant is that it united black leaders throughout northern California. Eventually, the film was banned by the San Francisco Board of Supervisors, prompting other western cities to follow suit. It would take more than fifty years for these stereotypes to fade, but the NAACP was determined to protest the negative image of African Americans in film.

The drive to eliminate racial discrimination in San Francisco often brought black leaders into white organizations. The Bay Area Urban League, for example, included many prominent black leaders, and there was a multiracial drive for harmony. The Bay Area Urban League was in the forefront of the drive to bring black Californians into the economic mainstream. The small number of African Americans living in the San Francisco Bay Area, about 10,000, fought for a precarious equality. In Los Angeles, there were almost 40,000 black settlers, but this only made it more difficult to achieve equality. Harrison Gray Otis, editor of the *Los Angeles Times*, was typical of white Californians who remarked: "the Negro has to earn his place."

In Los Angeles, A.M.E. churches were at the center of political protest, and they encouraged the Afro-American Congress to meet in southern California. But political protest was also an integral part of the northern California experience. San Francisco's Booker T. Washington Community Center was a busy meeting place for black Californians. The nightly meetings served a wide variety of needs in the black community and created a sense of destiny and brotherhood. The end result was that San Francisco's black community was well organized politically, economically influential and increasingly prone to middle class demands. The main problem for black Californians was lack of political access.

There weren't many African American officeholders or political appointments, and few black Californians were selected to run for political office. In 1934, however, a Los Angeles African American, Augustus Hawkins, was elected to the United States House of Representatives. He succeeded another Los Angeles black politician,

Frederick M. Roberts, who held a House seat from 1919 to 1934. But generally black candidates were not encouraged to run for political office. Chester Rowell, the *San Francisco Chronicle* editor, summed up the attitudes of local Californians when he suggested that a gradual approach to integrating blacks into California life should take place. Rowell did recognize a race problem, but he believed that Californians were making progress toward solving it. Rowell erroneously wrote: "there is nothing to do about the problem but wait for time to cure it." This would remain one of the prevalent myths of white liberals that stayed intact up until the violent civil rights protests of the 1960s.

The gains made by African Americans were interrupted when the Japanese bombed Pearl Harbor on December 7, 1941 and when the United States entered World War II. The result was that California's black population suddenly had new opportunities and challenges.

Bibliographical Essay

For African American influences the classic study is B. Gorton Wheeler, *Black California: The History of African-Americans in The Golden State* (New York, 1993); chapter IV covers the years between the wars. Also, see, Douglas Daniel, *Pioneer Urbanites: A Social and Cultural History of San Francisco* (New York, 1980) for a detailed examination of the problems during the interwar years.

Albert S. Broussard, *Black San Francisco: The Struggle for Racial Equality in the West, 1900-1954* (Lawrence, 1993) is a major reinterpretive study of the San Francisco black experience. Also, see, Arthur E. Hippler, *Hunter's Point: A Black Ghetto* (New York, 1974) and Albert S. Broussard, "Organizing The Black Community in the San Francisco Bay Area, 1915-1930," *Arizona and The West*, XXI (Winter 1981).

See Charles S. Johnson, *The Negro Worker in San Francisco: A Local Self-Study* (San Francisco, 1944) for an intriguing look into the changes in the African American employment market.

Richard Romo's *East Los Angeles: History Of A Barrio* (Austin, 1983) is a model study of ethnic problems from 1900 to 1940, and the section on the interwar period is exceptional. Camille Guerin-Gonzales, *Mexican Workers and American Dreams: Immigration, Repatriation and California Farm Labor, 1900-1939* (New Brunswick, 1994) is an excellent analysis of the problem. Also see Juan Gomez-Quinones, *Roots of Chicano Politics, 1600-1940* (Albuquerque, 1994) for a broad view of Mexican Americans in California. Also important is Juan Gomez-Quinones, *Mexican American Labor, 1790-1990* (Albuquerque, 1994).

A pioneer study of labor problems in southern California is Gilbert G. Gonzalez, *Labor and Community: Mexican Citrus Worker Villages in a Southern California County, 1900-1950* (Urbana, 1994). Also see, Howard A. DeWitt, "Communism and the Appeal to Ethnic Minorities: The Cannery and Agricultural Workers' Industrial Union in the Imperial Valley," *New Labor Review* (June 1980).

The tendency to equate radicalism with ethnic groups is the central thesis in Howard A. DeWitt's, *Images of Ethnic and Radical Violence in California Politics, 1917-1930: A Survey* (San Francisco, 1975).

The best study of ethnicity, culture and political identity is George J. Sanchez, *Becoming Mexican American: Ethnicity, Culture and Identity in Chicano Los Angeles, 1900-1945* (New York, 1993). On Mexican education see, Mary Kay Vaughan, *The State, Education and Social Class in Mexico, 1880-1928* (DeKalb, 1982), pp. 215-238, for the Los Angeles impact of Mexican education.

The theory of "trans creation" is seen in Juan Flores and George Yudice, "Living Borders/ Buscando America: Languages of Latin Self-Formation," *Social Text*, volume 8, number 2 (1990).

For early attempts at restricting Mexican immigrants see Mark Reisler, *By The Sweat of Their Brow: Mexican Immigrant Labor in the United States, 1900-1940* (Westwood, 1976). For material on the Mexican family see

Mario T. Garcia, "La Familia: The Mexican Immigrant Family, 1900-1930," in Mario Barrera, Alberto Camarillo and Francisco Hernandez, editors, *Work, Family, Sex Roles and Language* (Berkeley, 1980).

An important source on the barrio is Pedro G. Castillo, "The Making of a Mexican Barrio: Los Angeles, 1890-1920" (Ph.D. dissertation, University of California, Santa Barbara, 1979). This work deserves mainstream publication and is an important source in analyzing Mexican blue collar labor.

On repatriation see Abraham Hoffman, *Unwanted Mexican Americans in the Great Depression, 1929-1939* (Tucson, 1974). Also see, Francisco Balderrama, *In Defense of La Raza: the Los Angeles Mexican Consulate and the Mexican Community, 1929 to 1936* (Tucson, 1982). An interesting analysis of relief for the Spanish speaking in the Great Depression is Donald L. Zelman, "Mexican Migrants and Relief in Depression California: Grower Reaction to Public Relief Policies as They Affected Mexican Migration," *Journal of Mexican-American History*, volume 5 (1975), pp. 1-23.

Historians differ on the immigrant experience. The seminal work on immigration, Oscar Handlin, *The Uprooted: The Epic Story of the Great Migrations That Made the American People* (2nd edition enlarged, Boston, 1973) has a new chapter which includes non-whites. The California experience is contrary to Handlin's argument that the Spanish speaking fit into American culture. For contrary views see Juan Gomez-Quinones, *Chicano Politics: Reality and Promise, 1940-1990* (Albuquerque, 1990); Octavio Romano, "The Anthropology and Sociology of the Mexican-Americans: The distortion of Mexican-American History, *El Grito*, volume 2, number 1 (Fall 1968), pp. 13-26 and Alex M. Saragoza, "Recent Chicano Historiography: An Interpretive Essay," *Aztlan*, volume 19, number 1 (Spring 1988-1990), pp. 112-113.

The Mexican farm worker's adjustment in the United States and then the readjustment upon the return to Mexico is brilliantly examined by Paul S. Taylor, *A Spanish-Mexican Peasant Community: Arandas in Jalisco, Mexico* (Berkeley, 1933).

Southern California's eccentricities are examined by Carey McWiliams, *Southern California Country: An Island on the Land* (New York, 1946) and Kevin Starr, *Material Dreams: Southern California through the 1920s* (Oxford, 1990).

A brilliant analysis of many of the problems faced by African Americans in Arizona which paralleled California conditions is found in Bradford Luckingham, *Minorities in Phoenix: A Profile of Mexican American, Chinese and African American Communities, 1860-1992* (Tucson, 1995), chapter 8.

13

World War II

Prisoners without Trial, Japanese Americans

The Japanese bombed Pearl Harbor shortly after sunrise on Sunday, December 7, 1941. Most Americans were shocked by the attack. The *San Francisco Chronicle* asked: "Who was the enemy?" The *Los Angeles Times* countered: "Was it the Germans or the Japanese?" In California, the answer was the Japanese. In San Francisco, there was concern regarding the Presidio's security. The hysterical outburst of super patriotism created a wartime "Yellow Peril" which placed the Japanese and their rights in limbo while making them prisoners, without trials, during World War II. Surprisingly, there was little hostility toward the Germans.

To many Americans, the 40,000 Germans who supported a pro-Nazi German-American Bund were simply people using their legitimate political rights. While the Japanese Americans were quiet and patriotic, the Germans were holding boisterous meetings to protest American Government plans that were going to limit alien rights. When the Alien Registration Act was passed and required that all resident aliens register and be fingerprinted, the German-American Bund protested. One Japanese American Citizens League official called the measure "a responsible restriction during wartime." Because Germans were white, successful in

a mainstream educational-career manner and prone to assimilation, the fear of German infiltration subsided. But to Californians, Japanese American loyalty was a paramount issue.

On December 8, 1941, the Department of Justice issued an order to close all land borders to the Japanese. At the San Francisco Presidio, Western Defense Command leader, General John L. DeWitt, applauded the Department of Justice's decision and issued an order excluding his men from fraternizing with Japanese Americans.

General DeWitt began making speeches to civic groups emphasizing the dangers of Japanese American sabotage. J. Edgar Hoover, the FBI chief, dispatched special agents to California in order to investigate the loyalty of the American born Japanese-the Nisei. The patriotic frenzy surrounding the bombing of Pearl Harbor made it necessary to find a scapegoat; it would be the Japanese. The Navy had already admitted its errors by ordering the dismissal of Admiral Husband E. Kimmel, the Pearl Harbor commander, and restructuring naval security in the Hawaiian Islands.

Lieutenant General John L. DeWitt was responsible for American security on the West Coast and was considered an authority on Japanese subversion. But DeWitt was not competent and had a nasty racial personality. A sixty-one-year-old career officer who had accomplished very little, DeWitt was bigoted and indecisive.

From late December 1941 until mid-February 1942, General DeWitt created extraordinary public pressure to intern the Japanese. He did this with fiery speeches and racist diatribes against Japanese Americans. Even the usually liberal Earl Warren, the Attorney General of California, was caught up in the hysteria. There was no link between General DeWitt and Warren until the bombing of Pearl Harbor and then, in the midst of patriotic fervor, they both crusaded to intern the Japanese.

In February 1942, Warren testified before a Congressional committee and spoke of "the Japanese menace." As he walked to the podium in Washington D. C., Warren looked nervous as he spoke he spoke about his fears of "fifth column activities." The Japanese were a hidden menace, Warren insisted, who could sabotage without being seen. When pressed for proof of Japanese American sabotage, Warren offered none. Incredulously, he stated that he believed Japanese Americans appeared patriotic in order to

lull Americans into "a false sense of security."

Executive Order 9066 and Japanese Relocation: Milton S. Eisenhower's Concentration Camp Nightmare

Shortly after Warren's testimony, President Franklin D. Roosevelt signed Executive Order 9066 interning the Japanese in a series of makeshift concentration camps. There was little regard for property rights, civil rights or loyalty in day-to-day citizenship. The 112,000 Japanese internees included 71,000 Nisei or American born citizens and 41,000 Issei or Japanese born.

The Japanese were herded like cattle into assembly camps at the Santa Anita Race Track near Los Angeles and the Tanforan Race Track near San Francisco. At first, they were indignant with the chow line atmosphere and the armed guards. At heart, however, the Japanese were American, and they proved it in the camps. The internment notice required the Japanese to report with only what they could carry. The remainder of their goods would be stored "at the sole risk of the owner." Their bank accounts were seized and other financial assets frozen. As a small number of Japanese fled in their cars to the mid-West, armed posses formed at the Nevada border. Signs reading: "No Japs Wanted" were everywhere. Hysterical patriotism had taken over.

In California, a relocation camp at Tule Lake and an assembly camp in the desert at Manzanar placed the Japanese in isolated geographical areas. Milton S. Eisenhower, the director of the War Relocation Authority, had grave misgivings about the relocation camps, but he never expressed his concern directly to President Franklin D. Roosevelt. However, on June 18, 1942, Eisenhower wrote to Roosevelt and resigned. Clearly, Eisenhower viewed the in-

FIGURE 13-1. Japanese in World War II.

FIGURE 13-2. Japanese American WACS in World War II.

ternment centers as concentration camps. With World War II raging in Europe, he couldn't express his indignation over the abuse of Japanese American rights. In his memoirs, Eisenhower relates how he attempted to educate President Roosevelt on the "high degree of Japanese loyalty" and the problems of "avoidable injustices."

It took only a few months to place Japanese Americans into relocation camps, but it was nearly four years before they were freed. The prevalent belief was that the Japanese American was quickly released from the sand and cactus concentration camps. This myth was fostered largely by the success of the 442nd Regimental Combat Team. This Nisei brigade distinguished itself in Europe, and the "Go For Broke" motto of the 442nd Regimental Combat Team

prompted it to become one of the most decorated military units in American history.

Few Americans realized that as late as December 1, 1945 every camp still had Japanese American detainees. At Tule Lake, there were 12,543 Japanese Americans held as a threat to the war effort. This is strange considering that the war with Japan ended earlier in 1945. An internal Army memo reported that as late as March 1, 1946 there were still 2,806 detainees at Tule Lake. This outrageous violation of civil rights was never addressed by the U.S. Government nor was compensation provided for the detainees. In a series of U.S. Supreme Court cases, the Japanese American Citizens League and the American Civil Liberties Union challenged the Government's right to intern the Japanese.

The U.S. Supreme Court Defends Japanese Relocation

Despite the harsh treatment Japanese Americans still remained California residents, and soon began to file law suits. In 1942, Gordon K. Hirabayashi was a senior at the University of Washington. He was a Quaker whose parents had raised him in a fundamental Christian home. Although ethnically Japanese, he had grown up like any other American. Indignantly, Hirabayashi refused to obey General DeWitt's curfew order, and he failed to report for evacuation. He also sued the U.S. Government and challenged its right to intern him. In May 1943, the U.S. Supreme Court heard the Hirabayashi Case and his attorney argued that he was raised as a fundamentalist Christian with little knowledge or understanding of "things Japanese." Hirabayashi, his attorney contended, was like any other American and should not be interned. This argument fell on deaf ears as the Supreme Court ruled 9 to 0 that he had to report for internment. Chief Justice Harlan Fiske Stone ruled that a temporary cessation of civil rights would not endanger future Japanese rights. But the American Civil Liberties Union found another case which questioned internment's legality.

On December 18, 1944, Fred Korematsu's case was decided by the U.S. Supreme Court. Korematsu, a California born graduate of an Oakland high school, also challenged the right of the Government to intern him. Justice Hugo Black wrote the majority decision which once again supported internment. The wartime threat of internal subversion, the Court maintained, was more important than civil liberties. "In wartime," Justice Hugh Black wrote, "citizenship carries heavier burdens than in peacetime." This justification angered Japanese Americans, especially those willing to fight for America.

The constitutional nightmare for Japanese Americans continued once again on December 18, 1944, when the U.S. Supreme Court, in the Mitsuye Endo Case, ruled that a Japanese American woman could not return to California because she refused to sign a loyalty oath. A clumsily handled and insultingly worded loyalty oath led many Japanese Americans to refuse it. Endo was outraged over the document. She challenged the right of the War Relocation Authority. Justice Felix Frankfurter was outraged over her refusal to sign the loyalty oath. Her public criticism of relocation prompted the Supreme Court to lecture her on loyalty, and by not supplying the WRA officials with the right answers on questionnaires and refusing their loyalty oath, Endo spent thirty months in jail while her fellow camp mates were sent home. She was treated like a war criminal for no other crime than disagreeing with the Government. The wartime emergency was justification, Justice William O. Douglas maintained, to provide a temporary cessation of all Japanese rights.

Japanese relocation decimated the Issei who lost their property, dignity and willingness to live in the Golden State. The California born Nisei moved to the forefront, and a model minority image was developed during the next two decades. When William Peters praised Japanese Americans in a 1966 article in the *New York Times Magazine*, the public rehabilitation of the Japanese American was complete. Although the Japanese were quiet about their plight, they continued to resent relocation. The anger of older Japanese Americans was a clear indication of the psychological scars of internment. In 1981, President Jimmy Carter's Commission on the Wartime Relocation and Internment of Civilians held hearings all over the United States and the Government was met with accusations of unfair treatment.

FIGURE 13-3. President Ford Signing Proclamation 4417, "An American Promise," Rescinding Executive Order 9066 on February 19, 1976. Courtesy of National Archives.

The tragedy of Japanese American relocation helped to change public attitudes. In 1948, when a group of anti-Japanese zealots introduced a ballot initiative to make it difficult for the Japanese to own land, there were strong protests from American and Japanese organizations. This proposal was much like the Alien Land Law of 1913 which restricted the Japanese truck farmers. After a vigorous campaign, financed largely by the California Real Estate Association, voters overwhelmingly defeated this proposal. The mandate was clear as a 59 percent no vote ended the last vestiges of hostility toward Japanese Americans. There was little sentiment to limit Japanese American economic rights, and there was an apologetic public air over internment.

World War II and the Mexican American: The Rise of Community Activism

When the Japanese bombed Pearl Harbor there was a burst of patriotism in east Los Angeles. As the United Stated entered World War II, local draft boards were besieged with recruits who hoped to enter the military. On Monday, December 8, 1941, Pedro Aguilar was the first Los Angeles resident to volunteer for the service. His induction was a cause for celebration in the barrio. Aguilar was a Mexican American who was eager to "kick the hell out of the Japanese." Mexican Americans were, like most citizens, patriotic and eager to aid the war effort. Surprisingly, during World War II, the notion developed that the Spanish speaking were prone to draft dodging. This idea grew up because race conscious Anglos could not tell the difference between Mexicans and Mexican Americans. Mexican Americans joined the army and fought proudly for their country. But there was a tendency to identify non draft age Mexican Americans as slackers or draft dodgers.

The Mexican worker was a temporary resident who took up the job slack. Yet, this casual, temporary worker was looked upon as an able bodied man who should be in the service. When the United States Government decreed that Mexicans could become citizens by enlisting in a branch of the armed services, there was enormous pressure for them to join the Army

The young Spanish speaking population in and around Los Angeles became a large and readily identifiable subculture. Their clothing was different; their language was unique; their music was upbeat and their swagger was so strong that it indicated an arrogance and independence which bothered middle class Californians. A nation at war expected conformity in dress, manners and morals, and war weary Americans were unwilling to accept nontraditional behavior.

As Americans flooded into draft board offices to join the Army, young Mexican-Americans had more freedom. The fifteen to seventeen-year-old worked, bought cars and a new wardrobes and cut a wide social path. With teenagers having a disposable income, the result was the emergence of a youth culture where loyalty, personal freedom and the code of the neighborhood replaced family, religious and school ties.

Some writers used the term "pachuco" to describe these young men. Octavio Paz's controversial book *The Labyrinth of Solitude: Life and Thoughts in Mexico* is an attempt to explain how Mexicans felt when they arrived in Los Angeles. A Mexican writer, Paz spent two years in Los Angeles during the mid-1940s and, with the keen eye of a soci-

ologist, traced the rise of the Mexican youth culture. Paz wrote of the Los Angeles gangs:

"The pachucos are youths, for the most part of Mexican origin, who form gangs in Southern cities; they can be identified by their language and behavior as well as by the clothing they affect. They are instinctive rebels....but the pachucos do not attempt to vindicate their race....Their attitudes reveals an obstinate, almost fanatical will..."

Paz was struck by the abrupt, often hostile, nature of these young men. He recognized them as Mexicans, but, as Paz wrote of the pachuco: "He does not want to become Mexican again, at the same time he does not want to blend into the life of North America." The young Mexican was caught between two cultures.

This description of the pachuco has prompted Chicano historians to suggest that the youth broke with past tradition. What is significant about the pachuco is that they were young males who defied authority and developed a sense of racial pride. Chicano culture is a concept which recently has emphasized "trans-creation." This is a term which describes how culture develops as Mexican and American values merge with African American, Asian and other ethnic influences to form a separate and unique identity. The pachuco in Los Angeles was the heir to a culture which moved from rural Mexican areas to urban centers, like Los Angeles. The pachuco was fluent in both Spanish and English, and he was an instinctive rebel who disliked rules and regulations. As historian Carey McWilliams has suggested: "The pachuco stereotype was born in Los Angeles." In his newspaper columns and books, McWilliams described the tensions surrounding Mexican Americans in Los Angeles and predicted that the problem would escalate.

The rise of youth gangs, the increase in urban crime and the frequent editorials from the *Los Angeles Times* urging controls on delinquent behavior created public pressures against the youth culture. When a young boy was found beaten to death in an east Los Angeles swimming pool, the media had a field day, and the event led to a public lynching of the pachuco.

The Sleepy Lagoon Incident of August 1942

On August 2, 1942, a young man, Jose Diaz, was found dead on a dirt road near the popular swimming spot known as the Sleepy Lagoon Pool. The yellowish water in the pool and the presence of large weeds was an indication that the city of Los Angeles paid little attention to maintenance. The pool was a place where gangs congregated. Surprisingly, the Sleepy Lagoon Pool was segregated and not open to Mexican Americans.

The night before the killing a party at the nearby Williams Ranch led to a number of fist fights. Diaz was at the party and fought with members of the 38th Street Gang. When he turned up dead, the police announced that this was an outgrowth of problems between the 38th Street Gang and the Downey Boys. The 38th Street Gang's turf was the Sleepy Lagoon Pool and police, after a brief investigation, which included the round up of six hundred pachuco youths, the police arrested twenty-two gang members for Diaz's murder.

A lawyer in the Los Angeles District Attorney's Office, Clyde Shoemaker, announced that the young man had a criminal appearance. The police case against the twenty-two gang members centered around the charge that they had participated in a criminal conspiracy by crashing a party at the Williams Ranch. George Shibley, a lawyer who represented eight of the defendants, was shocked that the police could turn a case of trespassing into a murder case.

The trial of the Sleepy Lagoon defendants was a spectacular and tension filled incident. As the case prepared to go to trial, there was a feeling in east Los Angeles that racism was the cause of the indictments. To counter these feelings the Los Angeles Sheriff's Department sent Lieutenant Ed Duran Ayres to testify to the Grand Jury and to hold press conferences.

Not only was Ayres insulting but he also lacked basic skills in public relations. Surprisingly, Ayres headed the Foreign Relations Bureau of the LA County Sheriff's Office. He described the Spanish speaking as those who "generally preferred to kill, or at least get blood." There was universal disbelief among east Los Angeles citizens, and community meetings were called to protest this vicious stereotyping.

The *Los Angeles Times* published a series of front page stories congratulating the police for fine work. But the police didn't have any physical evidence and no eye witnesses to the murder. They announced that the killing was due to pachuco gang violence. A shoddy police investigation with fabricated evidence led a number of people to challenge the wholesale arrests of the 38th Street Gang.

On January 12, 1943, three of the defendants were convicted of first degree murder, nine of second degree murder, five of lesser charges and the remainder went free. But the conduct of the Los Angeles District Attorney was reprehensible. When the gang members appeared before the Los Angeles County Grand Jury, they were dirty, poorly dressed and looked tired. The Judge, Charles W. Fricke, denied their request to get haircuts, take baths and be provided with suits to make a proper court impression. Clyde C. Shoemaker, the Los Angeles Assistant District Attorney, remarked that the defendants were not allowed haircuts or a change of clothing because witnesses might not be able to identify them. Shoemaker held numerous press conferences and was trying the case in the newspaper long before it went to court.

A liberal Los Angeles writer and political activist, Carey McWilliams, began writing articles and delivering speeches challenging the police version of the Sleepy Lagoon incident. One of McWilliams's charges was that more than 300 young Mexican Americans were arrested in a search for evidence, because the police were groping in the dark for evidence and found none. Many of the police reports were filled with innuendo and generalizations.

Shortly after the trial, the Sleepy Lagoon Defense Committee was established, and lawyers were hired to appeal the convictions. Carey McWilliams, the Defense Committee head, was instrumental in rallying liberal opinion. In the **Nation**, a liberal left wing magazine, McWilliams described the "lynch mob" attitude of the Los Angeles Police Department. This prompted Lt. Ayres to give out a series of interviews defending the police. Ayres' pseudo-biological and sociological information made the LAPD look like racist jackals.

Perhaps the most significant result of the Sleepy Lagoon incident was to make the police appear not only bigoted but also less than professional in handling criminal matters. The appeals handled by American Civil Liberties Union attorneys went well, and on October 4, 1944, the defendants who still were in jail were freed. The guilty verdicts were reversed and the east Los Angeles barrio was united in its resolve to protest and combat police indifference. This was a beginning of a sense of community and a cohesive political organization in east Los Angeles.

The Sleepy Lagoon incident wasn't the first sign of police harassment, but it galvanized the community to protest police investigations, attitudes and hiring. It also allowed the community to have a greater

FIGURE 13-4. Leaflet Handed Out for Sleepy Lagoon Defense Fund Concert July 2, 1944. Handout and Ad Courtesy of Howard A. DeWitt.

say in police services. Hollywood liberals helped to establish the defense fund. Orson Welles helped to write a pamphlet defending Mexican American youth, and a benefit jazz concert was held by Norman Granz on Sunday Afternoon July 2, 1944 at Los Angeles's Philharmonic Auditorium. This "Jazz At The Philharmonic" concert featured Nat King Cole, Les Paul and Illinois Jacquet among others. The seventy-five cents to a dollar-and-a-half admission benefited the "Sleepy Lagoon Defense Fund." There was no longer a willingness for the Hispanic community to turn its back on city and police indifference.

The Zoot Suit Riot of 1943: Chicanos and the Military Doing Battle

At the height of World War II, in the summer of 1943, young Mexican Americans wandered around Los Angeles in flashy zoot suits. This was the classic garb of the Mexican American hipster with a long suit coat, pegged trousers and a key chain which swung out from the coat. A menacing hat and a sneer made the zoot suiters appear formidable foes. There was no need for them to be the enemy, but they were viewed as rough Mexicans who refused to adjust to American society.

The image of the zoot suiter was apparent when Municipal Judge Arthur S. Guerin of Venice, a small beach community south of Los Angeles, lectured Alfred Barela and a group of his Chicano friends for being loud and obnoxious. When Barela pointed out that he and his friends were innocent, the Judge believed him and let them go. But Barela was still upset. He complained to Judge Guerin that the officers made fun of his clothes, used racial slurs and threatened to cut his long hair. After he left court, Barela returned home and wrote the judge a lengthy letter complaining about "Anglo justice" and the "second class citizenship forced on the Spanish speaking." Barela's sense of outrage was typical of the Spanish speaking. Unwittingly, Barela's discontent spoke to a larger problem. The City of the Angels was about to wage a race war. Historians labeled it the Zoot Suit Riot of 1943, but it had deeper roots and a larger consequence.

The Zoot Suit Riots took place in Los Angeles from June 3 to 13, 1943 but no one was killed. There were no massive injuries. Property damage was minimal. There were few convictions for disturbing the peace. In sum, this so-called riot was little more than a confrontation between Anglo servicemen and Mexican zoot suiters.

But the conflict had lengthy roots. Throughout 1942 and 1943, sailors and marines often fought with zoot suiters. In April 1943 some marines beat up two hundred Mexican and African American zoot suiters in Oakland. In Venice in May 1943, there were fights which led to the arrest of anyone wearing a zoot suit. A San Jose store had a collection of zoot suits taken from the local Mexican community. In Stockton, signs read: "No Zoot Suiters Allowed." For months hostility toward the zoot suiter smoldered. However, police harassment, military insults and years of second class citizenship prompted the zoot suiters to fight back. This incensed the military, and they vowed to "clean up east Los Angeles."

The actual Zoot Suit Riot began on Thursday, June 3, 1943, when a group of sailors left the Chavez Ravine Armory carrying sticks, clubs and palm saps. The sailors began cruising the streets for Zoot Suiters, and a week of rioting began. On June 7, the *Los Angeles Herald Express* headlined the details of the riot and blamed it on draft dodging Mexican Americans.

The *Los Angeles Times'* sensational coverage of the rioting helped to further intensify anti-pachuco feeling. The real problem was confrontation between servicemen and zoot suiters. Since Los Angeles was a temporary home to a large concentration of military personnel, there were continuous fights. After Mexican American political activists complained to Mayor Fletcher Bowron and Police Chief C.B. Horall, an investigation took place which resulted in the arrests of nine sailors. They were charged with disturbing the peace. Then a group of zoot suiters were arrested and taken in chains to jail. Spanish speaking political activists charged that the police treated the zoot suiters like criminals. By the weekend, the rioting was over and southern Californians, as well as the rest of the nation, read headlines from the *Los Angeles Herald Express*: ZOOT GIRLS STAB WOMAN or the *Los Angeles Times*: ZOOT CYCLISTS SNATCH PURSES. In an editorial, the *Los Angeles Herald Express* wrote: "It was a sad day when zoot suiters began to molest some United States Navy men and some members of their families....They (the zoot suiters) have added a very serious side to juvenile delinquency problems."

The Los Angeles Grand Jury concluded that Mexicans practiced "criminal behavior." The findings of the LA Grand Jury so incensed the east Los Angeles citizenry that they organized the CSO, or the Community Service Organization, to promote better education, housing and job opportunities. The United Latin American Citizens was another group which concentrated upon the inequities of public education. They both criticized the Grand Jury's unwillingness to recognize the oppressive conditions of east Los Angeles citizens.

The significance of the Zoot Suit Riot is that it intensified the already troubled racial atmosphere in and around Los Angeles. The hostility of the east Los Angeles barrio was reflected in the behavior of the young pachucos who not only rejected American values, but also established an independent culture. There was a sense of cultural and political liberation which spread to labor markets, especially the agricultural labor market.

Mexican Americans and Farm Fascism: The Abuse of Bracero Labor

The farm labor abuses which had plagued California since the late nineteenth century led to the growth of a strong Mexican American agricultural labor movement. From 1890 to 1940, Spanish speaking labor unions organized in the fields, despite repressive laws and brutal police action. Although these unions were only marginally successful, they did provide a precedent for Cesar Chavez when he emerged as a labor leader. Chavez eventually became successful because large ranchers abused ethnic workers.

When ethnic labor unions organized in the 1930s, the Associated Farmers of California labeled them as Communists and in cooperation with county sheriffs shut down many of the unions. In the Hayward-DeCoto pea fields, armed sheriff's deputies stood guard on key ranches to prevent labor organizers from talking to the workers.

This intensified ethnic labor organization and caused the unions to take an increasingly militant stance. There were a number of successful strikes during the Great Depression. Filipino led unions won strikes in Salinas in 1934 and 1936 which led to AFL-CIO charters. When Democratic Governor Culbert Olson took office in January 1939, there was a great deal of evidence of farm fascism. The workers had to pay for their picking sacks and rides to the field. Ten to twenty percent of their pay was held back for food in a company owned store; there were few toilets; housing was inadequate and children had no schools. After a half century of these conditions and abuse from the ranchers, the migrant worker was ready to join a union. Soon an articulate voice emerged to describe the horrible conditions that surrounded California agribusiness. The first voice was a novelist who was a farm worker with a story.

This novelist was a highly literate farm worker, Ernesto Galazara, who wrote an autobiographical tome, *Barrio Boy*, which traced his experiences with agribusiness in the Southwest. Galazara hit a nerve not only with Chicanos but with everyone interested in farm labor abuses. His second book, *Merchants of Labor*, analyzed the bracero program and concluded that transporting temporary Mexican contract workers on loan was a basic violation of labor rights and offered little permanent value to the Mexican worker. His emotional tales of the indignities suffered by farm workers touched a new generation that began to work for reform in the fields.

During World War II, there was a labor shortage in the California fields. In 1942, Congress and the Mexican Government signed an agreement allowing Mexican workers to temporarily work in agribusiness. This began the bracero program. In Spanish, bracero means "the strong armed ones." The Associated Farmers of California praised the agreement because they believed that "Mexicans appreciate the work." This condescending attitude made it clear that the farmers looked upon the braceros with an unsympathetic view.

Soon the bracero program came under public scrutiny. From 1942 to 1947, more than a quarter of a million braceros worked in the fields, and a large number remained in the Golden State. Some unions were critical of the bracero program and contended that braceros took jobs away from union workers. Critics argued that California's powerful Farm Bureau hired cheap labor without the social responsibility of providing adequate housing, education for the children and medical care.

California braceros were excellent workers in the strawberry, asparagus, lettuce, sugar beet, grape, vegetable and cotton fields. Soon Mexican labor dominated the fields as the Filipino, Japanese and Oakie-Arkie laborers moved to the city.

In the small town of Arvin, in the San Joaquin Valley, the DiGiorgio Corporation employed almost a thousand minority workers. Working conditions were abysmal; pay was low and the corporate attitude was arbitrary and repressive. As a result, on October 1, 1947, workers began picketing the DiGiorgio Farm near Arvin. The only workers to report were braceros. This intensified the Mexican American resolution to expose the malevolent business practices of California agribusiness. The DiGiorgios became an early symbol of repression, and their patriarch acted as though labor unions had no rights.

Joseph DiGiorgio, the founder of the DiGiorgio Fruit Corporation, would not meet the American Federation of Labor's demand for a 10 cent an hour wage and some minor fringe benefits. He was an arrogant, insensitive scion to an agricultural empire which had brutalized workers for decades.

Despite these problems, the DiGiorgio strike of 1947 experienced some minor successes and marked the beginning of militant farm labor strikes. Local 218, known as the National Farm Workers Union (NFWU), was made up primarily of ethnic workers. They charged that the DiGiorgio Corporation failed to meet the basic needs of the farm worker and began publicizing agribusiness abuses. Increasingly, television was used as a vehicle to complain about working conditions.

The DiGiorgio Corporation responded by accusing the unions of being radical or Communist fronts. In an attempt to destroy the unions, the DiGiorgios enlisted California politicians into a campaign to discredit ethnic labor unions. But an investigation by state Senators Hugh M. Burns and Jack Tenney, who co-chaired the California Senate Committee on Un-American Activities, failed to turn up any evidence of radical activity. This angered the DiGiogrios and they vowed never to unionize.

The charges of ethnic radicalism continued as Congressman Alfred J. Elliot demanded a federal investigation into the California rural labor unions. In November 1949, federal hearings in Bakersfield brought southern California Congressman Richard M. Nixon back into the state, and he used the investigation to flog ethnic labor unions. Once again, however, no evidence of radicalism was found in California's rural labor unions, and Elliot and Nixon were only demagogues who delivered emotional speeches on the dangers of farm labor. The result was to intensify agricultural unions and bring a new sense of urgency and solidarity to the union rank and file membership.

For fifteen years the National Farm Labor Union with the financial resources of the American Federation of Labor and a skilled leadership fought the battle for better working conditions. But to casual observers the NFLU was ineffective and its membership declined each year. Soon the NFLU was declared inoperative and in February 1959, the AFL-CIO formed the Agricultural Workers Organizing Committee to begin a new phase of Chicano labor activity.

Black Californians: World War II and its Aftermath: The New Civil Rights Impulse

When World War II broke out, black Californians flocked to recruiting offices to join the armed forces. The national racial climate was more liberal and African Americans were ready to be integrated into the armed forces as a result of World War II. San Francisco's black population grew by more than 600% between 1940 and 1945 due to wartime employment opportunities and the troops stationed at the Presidio.

California offered employment in a wide variety of occupations and African Americans arrived to secure these new jobs. The Richmond Shipyard and Marinship in Sausalito offered skilled and unskilled positions for recently arrived black workers. White and black pipe fitters, steam fitters, dock workers, casual labor and engineers worked side by side, thus, establishing a sense of social, political and racial equality.

Black Californians: Social and Business Change in California During World War II

During World War II a restaurant-music industry flourished on San Francisco's Fillmore Street, and this led to the rise of black nightclubs like Jimbo's Bop City. This Fillmore street club served as many white patrons as black ones. However, soon social problems occurred, but the police and the press kept these fights out of the news. Music, good food and a wide open social atmosphere made these clubs popular. In west Oakland, Slim Jenkins' club on Seventh Street catered to a mixed crowd which greatly increased white and black music, good food and top entertainment acts like Slim Gaillard and Count Basie played for huge crowds. Jenkins was a black entrepreneur who catered to the expanding market of African American culture. Soon he opened a place in San Francisco and used the combination of good food and top entertainment to expand his fortune. When a patron drove in Jenkins' parking lot, a tuxedoed attendant-bodyguard opened the door and made the patron feel at home.

But job discrimination remained a problem. The black newspapers pointed out that early in the war when African American labor was needed there were plenty of jobs. However, once the war effort slowed, the old strains of racism and second class citizenship emerged. A number of black labor leaders attacked the decline in African American employment. A. Philip Randolph, President of the Brotherhood of Sleeping Car Porters, the nations preeminent black union, announced a march on Washington to protest job discrimination. This was a shrewd move on Randolph's part as it forced President Roosevelt to offer new employment venues. Because America was fighting for world freedom, President Roosevelt quickly assigned new defense industry jobs for African Americans. Thus, a series of hasty press conferences were called and President Roosevelt's Executive Order 8802 reaffirmed the Federal Government's policy of nondiscrimination against black workers.

The Port Chicago Explosion and the Mare Island Mutiny: The Modern African American Civil Rights Movement Is Born

As World War II progressed ,black unions worked for wage increases and improved working conditions for African Americans. There were also a large number of enlisted black sailors and soldiers living in the San Francisco Bay area. While President Roosevelt talked about racial harmony, black sailors and soldiers remembered tension.

Joe Small, a Navy enlisted man, recalled constant friction with the white officers. "They didn't seem to be able to accept us," Small remarked. But Small also appreciated the opportunity to earn a living free of excessive racial strife. California might not be perfect, Small told his family, but it was better than the South.

The Port Chicago naval ammunition base was where Small worked. It was located on the Sacramento River near San Francisco Bay about thirty miles from the city. A naval ammunition storage center, the Port Chicago facility was largely staffed with black sailors but the commissioned officers were white.

Seaman First Class Joe Small woke up on July 17, 1944, and looked forward to another day's work. Although he was twenty-three, Small was older than most other sailors. He was also wiser. The attitudes of the white officers brought quiet condemnation from Small,and he blanched when the white officers referred to African Americans as "sons of Satan." They considered this a humorous reference, Small reasoned, but it hid a blatant prejudice. Generally, he kept quiet and counseled the younger sailors to ignore such remarks.

The ammunition depot at Port Chicago supplied the Pacific Fleet and was essential to the war effort. Small and his fellow workers took pride in swiftly loading ammunition for deployment to the Far East. At breakfast the men of the Fourth Division talked about the war. After finishing their food they drove to the pier and began loading ammunition at precisely 8:00 A. M. They were a punctual and highly skilled group of ammunition loading specialists who loved their work. "The war made us work together," Small recalled: "We became a team."

As they loaded ammunition, bombs and other high explosives from the railroad boxcars, there was a constant fear of explosion. By Monday night, July 17, 1944, the moon had vanished and a slight breeze blew off the Bay. It was necessary to unload explosives at night to keep up with the war demands. For four days the E.A. Bryan was docked in Port Chicago taking on explosives. Another ship, the Quinalt Victory, was also moored in Port Chicago and this brand new vessel glimmered next to the Bryan.

Lieutenant Commander Alexander Holman noticed that the Quinalt Victory was turning its engine over. He told the watch commander to monitor the situation so that an explosion would not occur. But at 10:18 P.M., a mammoth blast rocked Port Chicago. Cyril Sheppard, an enlisted man in the Fourth Division, was sitting on the toilet and suddenly found himself on the floor. Sheppard thought that the Japanese had bombed San Francisco.

Soon a second blast went off. The University of California at Berkeley's seismograph recorded two jolts with the ferocity of a minor earthquake. At the nearby Roe Island lighthouse, Erven Scott and his wife, Bernice, finished a cup of coffee as the explosion shook their lighthouse to its foundation. As he ran to the top of the lighthouse, Scott saw a huge column of smoke and flame rising above Port Chicago.

When the smoke lifted, little was left of the ships in the harbor. The E.A. Bryan was blown into small pieces, and the Quinalt Victory was lifted by the blast out of the water and the stern smashed into the water upside down more than five hundred feet from its moorage. The people standing nearby on the pier and those aboard the two ships died instantly. The death toll was 320, and 202 were black enlisted men.

Port Chicago was also heavily damaged by the explosion. As reporters streamed into Port Chicago, the naval base was reduced to rubble and three hundred homes were heavily damaged.

The Port Chicago explosion was the worst disaster on the American home front, and it was a tragedy that focused upon inept naval leadership. Safety had never been a concern and the explosion embarrassed the Navy. The Navy had only one choice: find out who was responsible for the Port Chicago disaster. This began an investigation which led to the black sailors becoming the scapegoat for naval misconduct.

Just four days after the Port Chicago explosion, a Naval Court of Inquiry convened. The three senior naval officers who made up the Court were Captains Albert G. Cook, Jr., John S. Crenshaw and William B. Holden. They began investigating and as the inquiry continued on for months, it was obvious that the Navy was looking for someone to blame.

The Judge Advocate Lieutenant Commander Keith Ferguson indicated the direction of the Navy's findings when he concluded: "Colored enlisted personnel are neither temperamentally nor intellectually capable of handling high explosives." Commander Ferguson's statement further intensified racial attitudes. Black sailors talked of a work stoppage. They were insulted, but Joe Small spoke for the men and defended their fine work record. It was Small who began asking if another explosion was possible. The Navy did not want to answer this question. Obviously, safety conditions had not improved.

Naval technology could not guarantee that there would not be another explosion. The African American sailors realized that they were in great danger. As one black sailor remembered: "We didn't want no more loading ammunition because of what happened at Port Chicago." Joe Small believed that poor working conditions led to the explosion; however, the lack of safety procedures and inept commanders accelerated the safety problems.

Soon Small became the informal leader of a group of black sailors who were determined to avoid another explosion. As a sailor, Small was a quick learner, and he quickly mastered the mechanics of ship loading. Because of his ability and leadership qualities, the men looked to Small for a solution to the safety question. Small urged a work boycott. The Navy attempted to solve the problem through an investigation and concluded that only black sailors would now load ammunition. This caused an uproar. The white sailors would not be put into jeopardy.

To protest the Navy's policy, Small suggested a work stoppage. Just three weeks after the explosion, as only black sailors loaded the ships, a large number of the men refused to report for work. They were scared to death. This work stoppage was unacceptable to the Navy.

Lieutenant Ernest Delucchi reported the action to the base commander. A group of officers met and attempted to shame the men into returning to work. They ordered the base chaplain, Lieutenant Commander Jefferson Flowers, to talk to the men about their patriotic duty. The sailors who failed to report to work were imprisoned, and the 328 men who were ordered to work, 258 were imprisoned on a barge. Civilian contract stevedores had to be hired to load and unload the ships.

Quickly, Small called a meeting on the barge. There was a great deal of resentment and a sense of discord. Small urged the men to "knock off their horseplay." They met and came up with a plan.

On August 11, 1944, the men were marched from the barge to a baseball diamond. They were assembled under heavy guard. Admiral Carleton H. Wright addressed the men: "I have handled ammunition for approximately thirty years, and I'm still here." Wright glared at the men and announced that anyone not going back to work faced "the hazards of a firing squad." The men stood in stunned silence. A death threat made by an admiral was not something to take lightly.

After this meeting, fifty men refused to return to work. The remainder continued to load ammunition in an atmosphere of fear and recrimination. The black sailors believed all decisions were racial ones and that white sailors were not placed in the same peril. The fifty mutineers, as the Navy labeled them, were taken to the brig at Camp Shoemaker. The Navy announced that they would be tried for mutiny. Joe Small was placed in solitary confinement because he was considered the ringleader.

The stage was set for the Navy to try the fifty black sailors for mutiny. The Navy was determined to punish the remaining 208 men who refused to load the ships with various court martials. The fifty who continued "to override authority" would be prosecuted on mutiny charges. President Franklin D. Roosevelt urged the Navy to go cautiously, and he suggested minimal sentences. After all, President Roosevelt wrote Secretary of the Navy James V. Forrestal: "it was dangerous." Forrestal ignored the President's advice.

With reckless abandon, the Navy pursued a course determined to make the workers pay for defying authority. When the mutiny trial opened on Thursday, September 14, 1944, there was national media attention which centered around racial equal-

ity. Judge Advocate James F. Coakley was ruthless in his prosecution. Coakley would not recognize the difference between a strike and a mutiny. When pressured on the issue, Coakley called the Port Chicago incident "an unintentional mutiny." As the trial progressed, a number of people complained about the Judge Advocate's behavior. One African American attorney, Thurgood Marshall, held a press conference to condemn Coakley.

Before the trial opened the defense suffered a major defeat. In the pretrial brief, Lieutenant Gerald E. Veltmann, the defense attorney, sought to have the mutiny charge dismissed. Veltmann pointed out that the men had disobeyed an order, and they had not conspired to mutiny. The military court disagreed. Veltmann was stunned. Mutiny was a planned conspiracy, and the Navy had no proof. The Navy was going to make an example of the black sailors, and Veltmann's defense had no impact upon the case.

When the trial began the men pled not guilty. The prosecution presented evidence of the work stoppage and its impact. In cross examination, the defense pointed out that fifty men were on trial for refusing to load the dangerous munitions; however, there were 258 who still refused to work.

The key witness during the trial was Lieutenant Ernest Delucchi, commanding officer of the Fourth Division. Delucchi identified 25 of the accused mutineers and provided testimony which convicted them. The key evidence was Delucci's statement that he ordered the men to fall into two groups-one which was willing to obey orders and another which was not; the military court ruled that a mutiny had occurred.

The mutiny trial defense was a simple one. The loading of ammunition was not safe. Even naval officials conceded this point. The defense attorneys argued that the men were afraid and had not conspired against anyone. Court room observers were horrified by trial procedures. The judge and naval jury openly showed their contempt for the defendants. As Thurgood Marshall observed the trial, he became increasingly angry with the Navy. After watching prosecutor Coakley continue a vigorous line of questioning which bordered on racism, Marshall held a press conference. He accused Coakley of racial prejudice and vowed to personally handle the appeals.

As Marshall watched from the gallery, a trio of African American workers testified that they were "terrified" to load the ammunition. A Navy psychiatrist, Richard H. Pembroke, testified for the defense and pointed out that this was a legitimate fear. When the trial ended, it had lasted thirty-three days, and the transcript was more than 1400 pages.

Despite the complexity of the Mare Island Mutiny Trial, the trial board deliberated just eighty minutes and found all the defendants guilty. When word got out that the trial board had enjoyed a leisurely lunch during the deliberations, Joe Small remarked: "I felt like I had been lynched."

The trial board's decision was only a part of the process. Final sentencing would take place after Admiral Wright reviewed the case. After a great deal of negative public pressure, the NAACP and its magazine, *The Crisis*, urged the Navy move to liberalize its racial policies. To save face, the Navy formed a review board and pronounced its proceedings fair but announced that mitigating circumstances would be considered. This allowed the Navy to ease the considerable racial tension which resulted from the Mare Island Mutiny Trial and eventually, forty-seven of the fifty Mare Island mutineers were returned to active duty and given honorable discharges.

The significance of the Mare Island Trial is that it began a civil rights movement in San Francisco which spread throughout the Golden State and impacted the civil rights atmosphere of the next decade. World War II was a major turning point for African Americans and the Mare Island controversy demonstrated a willingness for black Californians to stand up for their rights.

Black Californians: The 1950s Onward: Prosperity, Jobs and Another Civil Rights Impulse

By the early 1950s, black Californians were moving into blue collar jobs. Schools were opening themselves to accommodate black children, and the general prosperity of the Golden State boded well for African Americans. The Richmond Shipyards continued to employ black workers and there were jobs in hotels, restaurants and state and local government offices. In the professions, however, black Californians continued to find resistance. Doctors, lawyers, CPAs and corporate positions remained generally unreachable.

But there were some positive changes. In Richmond and Oakland, small middle class communities of African Americans emerged. The increase in California's African American population was dramatic. By 1950, there were 462,172 black Californians compared to only 124,306 in 1940. However, most new black Californians settled in southern California.

The Central District in Los Angeles was home to a growing middle class black population, and there was also an increase in African American settlers in the San Joaquin Valley. The California economy was like a roller coaster in the 1950s with jobs plentiful at one time and hard to find at other times.

Black ghettos, like Los Angeles's Central District and San Francisco's Hunters Point created a closed society. While there was a small professional and business class, the majority of black Californians were unskilled or semi-skilled workers. The dream of a middle class life for black Californians in the 1950s was a fragmented fantasy that existed for only a small number of African Americans.

As housing prices soared in California, owners refused to sell to prospective black buyers. The National Association For the Advancement of Colored People challenged this concept but was unable to prevent discrimination in the selling and renting of homes. In Los Angeles, the NAACP filed and won a number of housing suits, but the practice of selective selling continued. The California courts seldom awarded damages to African Americans whose rights were violated, and there was a right to sell mentality that continued to dominate real estate transactions.

Black attorneys were also in a second class position. It was not until 1950 that the Los Angeles Bar Association granted black attorneys membership. Country clubs, most suburbs and many apartment buildings refused to rent to blacks, even professional blacks, or allow them to buy homes or memberships. It was a quiet, hidden and almost unseen segregation. Yet, on the surface, Californians maintained their belief in equality, equal opportunity and an end to racism. Actions, however, were not in line with deeds.

When the United States Supreme Court in 1954 in the Brown v. Topeka Board of Education decision ruled that segregation violated the law, the civil rights movement took shape. Black civil rights advocates and organizations began to challenge the discrimination that had increased after the American Civil War. The result was the birth of a civil rights movement which changed the direction of California history.

By 1954, San Francisco's African American community was more than a century old and a respected part of the city power structure. But looking back upon the mid-1950s, a decade later, Herb Caen the *San Francisco Chronicle* columnist wrote: "The Negro 'problem' is very much with the city..." What Caen suggested was that San Francisco's liberal image was largely fabricated and hid serious racial tensions. In the 1960s, these forces would explode into open rioting and facilitate changes in California society.

Larry Itliong and the Agricultural Workers Organizing Committee

In 1959, Larry Itliong's Filipino Farm Labor Union founded the Agricultural Workers Organizing Committee in order to pressure the landowners for higher wages, better working conditions and union recognition. The AWOC was an American Federation of Labor-Congress of Industrial Organization (AFL-CIO) sponsored union providing Filipino farm workers legitimacy in the fields.

Few people knew Itliong. He was a menacing figure to the DiGiorgios who described him as a "radical and troublemaker." He had arrived in Seattle from the Philippines in 1929, and although he was only fifteen years old, he joined a farm workers strike in Monroe, Washington. Eventually, Itliong moved to California where he became a respected labor organizer. In the fields with his black crew cut, thick glasses and three fingers missing from his right hand, Itliong was an imposing figure. He often sported a small beard and wore dark jackets and jeans filled with political buttons. To Filipinos, Itliong was the first labor organizer to speak out against the stereotyping of Filipino workers. Itliong complained that they resented being called "short, squat pickers who were built close to the ground." Not only did Itliong take growers to task for these racial descriptions but he also continually spoke out for ethnic labor solidarity.

Soon Itliong became friendly with Cesar Chavez. They talked at length about common goals. For half a decade Itliong urged Chavez to bring his union into a common organization with Filipinos in order to pressure local ranchers. Chavez resisted. However, they continued to talk about ethnic solidarity and the farm workers union.

When Chavez emerged as a major labor leader, it was due to Itliong's wise and patient counsel. Among Itliong's contributions was the suggestion that the AFL-CIO grant charters to farm workers. The AWOC believed that union success was impossible without a major union charter. As Itliong suggested, the dock workers would refuse to unload produce if ethnic workers were affiliated with the AFL-CIO. It would also be easier to picket businesses and set up boycotts against non-union products. Itliong's lessons to Chavez were important ones. But the chief message from Itliong to Chavez was to organize a union that would catch public attention and interest the media.

The impact of the AWOC was an important one, and it continued apart from Chavez' organization to be a catalyst to ethnic labor growth. It helped to organize Filipinos. By 1969, the Filipino American Political Association was formed and held its first convention in Delano. Itliong was elected President and Chavez was the first featured speaker. Filipinos were in the forefront of the movement for ethnic labor unity, and they preached the importance of ethnic labor solidarity. The AWOC continued to represent Filipino workers, and in 1970, two major growers, Bianco Vineyards and Bruno Dispoto agreed to union contracts with the AWOC. For a decade and a half, Itliong was in the center of the farm labor movement and was a witness to the June 26, 1970 agreement in which 26 Delano grape growers signed union contracts. Much of the success of this agreement was

attributable to the Filipino-led AWOC. As a result, Itliong remains one of the most important labor leaders in California ethnic history.

The AWOC was not the only organization Chevez participated in for in 1962, Cesar Chavez and Dolores Huerta co-founded the United Farmworkers Union. The thirty-five-year-old Chavez was the heart and soul of the UFW. He had spent ten years organizing Mexican labor with minimal success. But in March 1962, he moved his family to Delano, a city of some 14,000 inhabitants in the San Joaquin Valley.

FIGURE 13-5. Cesar Chavez. Courtesy of National Archives.

Chavez was an official with a Mexican American community service organization, and he was the product of the California fields. He was born on a small farm near Yuma, Arizona and worked as a migrant farm laborer. After attending forty schools, Chavez had achieved only eight years of education. His difficulties were ones he didn't want his children to have to face.. He experienced poverty, yearly changes in schools and the indignities of second class citizenship. He was determined to end this cycle, and Chavez believed that it was rooted in the exploitation of farm workers.

When he moved his family to Delano, Chavez realized that it was the perfect choice for a field workers union. Wages were low; working conditions were brutal and local attitudes were condescending. Chavez finally teamed up with Larry Itliong, and James Drake of the California Migrant Ministry to begin the establishment of the UFW.

After establishing monthly dues of $3.50, the UFW began providing services to its members. It arranged for a group insurance policy to cover burial. A credit union was set up because banks and financial institutions would not lend money to farm workers. A cooperative to purchase auto parts, tires and gas was established. There was a counseling staff who helped with immigration, welfare, Social Security, health services and workingmens' compensation. Most significantly there was a feeling of unity and pride.

In 1964, the organization changed its name to the National Farm Workers Association. After three years of establishing rural unionization, the farm workers carried out their first strikes. Almost 90% of table grapes consumed in the United States were grown in the San Joaquin Valley, and the NFWA began to concentrate upon Delano.

Filipinos provided much of the labor in and around Delano. So, Chavez came to-gether with the Agricultural Workers Organizing Committee and its forty year old leader, Larry Itliong. In the Coachella Valley, south of Delano, in the spring of 1965, Filipino grape pickers walked off the fields when they were paid less than the braceros. Many of the discontent Filipinos moved north to Delano and joined with Chavez's union.

The Delano Strike and Ethnic Labor Solidarity in the California Fields

After the Filipino based AWOC agreed to cooperate with Chavez, a lengthy strike against the DiGiorgio Corporation ensued. On September 16, 1965 which was Mexican Independence Day, Chavez called for the vote to unite with Itliong's AWOC. The strike began with less than $100 in the treasury as the unions joined together to shut down 33 grape growers in Delano. The pickets urged workers to leave the fields. How many actually joined the strikers is unknown, but few believed that the strike had a chance to succeed.

Robert DiGiorgio's office in San Francisco became a meeting point for discussions between the union and the DiGiorgio Corporation. Even though DiGiorgio refused to see union leaders, they continued to show up at his office. Nothing had changed over the years as DiGiorgio remarked that he would not allow union elections. He defied the new union to strike. When union leaders called on DiGiorgio in his San Francisco office one time too many, he had them arrested. There was no choice but to strike and for a long period. The DiGiorgio interests made it clear that they would not settle. But college students, sympathetic liberals and outraged unions joined to protest this seemingly small and insignificant labor strike. Safeway, Albertsons and Luckys quickly found that selling DiGiorgio's S and W canned goods or Gallo wine brought out pickets and hurt business.

By 1966, the Delano Strike was nine months old and Californians were boycotting Gallo wine and other products. In the San Francisco Bay area union dock workers refused to unload grapes from struck vineyards. There was a national boycott against DiGiorgio's S & W canned goods and against stores that sold them. Safeway lost almost a third of its business and urged settlement of the strike. This forced the Schenley Industries and the DiGiorgio Corporation to settle with Chavez.

On April 6, 1966, Schenley Industries announced that it was negotiating a settlement to recognize the National Farm Workers Association as the bargaining agent for farm workers. The following day the DiGiorgio Corporation issued a statement allowing its workers to vote for a union. Larry Itliong and Cesar Chavez united ethnic labor front won the support of DiGiorgio employees. What Chavez and Itliong had accomplished was extraordinary because California had a long history of unresolved farm labor abuses. Not only did the strike win recognition for Mexican and Filipino workers, but the successes of the Delano Strike also created better pay, improved working conditions and gave the ethnic field worker a voice. Clearly, by the mid-1960s the fragmented dream was becoming the California dream.

When Cesar Chavez looked upon the Delano Strike he recalled that Larry Itliong and Philip Vera Cruz were the main reason for ethnic labor solidarity. Vera Cruz, like Itliong, was a primary force in the ethnic farm labor revolution. "It's really more to their credit than our." Chavez wrote of his Filipino labor allies "that we're together."

Bibliographical Essay

On Japanese American relocation see, Roger Daniels, *Prisoners Without Trial: Japanese Americans in World War II* (New York, 1993); Roger Daniels, *Concentration Camps, USA* (New York, 1972); H.L. Kitano, *Japanese Americans: From Relocation To Redress* (Seattle, 1991); Peter Irons, *Justice At War: The Story of the Japanese American Internment Cases* (Berkeley, 1983) and Yasuko I. Tekezawa, *Breaking The Silence: Redress and Japanese American Ethnicity* (Ithaca, 1995). The most critical account of Japanese American relocation is Richard Drinnon's, *Keeper of Concentration Camps: Dillon S. Myer and American Racism* (Berkeley, 1987). Milton S. Eisenhower, *The President Is Calling* (New York, 1974) provides important insights into the War Relocation Authority Chief. See Page Smith, *Democracy on Trial: The Japanese American Evacuation And Relocation in World War II* (New York, 1995) for a study which argues that the War Relocation Authority was necessary to protect Japanese American citizens.

For an early mass media expression of the model Japanese minority stereotype see, William Peterson, "Success Story, Japanese American Style," *New York Times Magazine*, January 6, 1966.

B. Gordon Wheeler, *Black California: The History of African-Americans in the Golden State* (New York, 1993), chapters 16-17 is an important source. Albert S. Broussard, *Black San Francisco: The Struggle For Racial Equality In The West, 1900-1954* (Lawrence, 1993) is an important study of political and economic changes. Also, see Charles S. Johnson, *The Negro War Worker In San Francisco* (San Francisco, 1944).

Albert Camarillo, *Chicanos In California: A History of Mexican Americans in California* (Sparks, 1984) is a good introduction to the period. Also, see Rudolfo Acuna, *Occupied America: A History of Chicanos* (New York, 1988, revised 3rd. edition). Juan Gomez-Quinones, *Roots of Chicano Politics, 1600-1940* (Albuquerque, 1994), chapter 4, provides some excellent insights into World War II and the Sleepy Lagoon incident. Also see Carey McWilliams, *North From Mexico* (New York, 1975, revised edition).

For Mexican culture see Octavio Paz, *The Labyrinth of Solitude: Life and Thought in Mexico* (New York, 1961).

On the Zoot Suiters see Mauricio Mazon, *The Zoot Suit Riots: The Psychology of Symbolic Annihilation* (Austin, 1984) and Stuart Cosgrove, "The Zoot Suit and Style Warfare," *History Workshop Journal*, 18 (1984), pp. 77-91.

For Cesar Chavez see, Richard Griswold Castillo and Richard A. Garica, *Cesar Chavez: A Triumph of Spirit* (Norman, 1995, Jacque Levy, *Cesar Chavez: Autobiography of La Causa* (New York, 1975) and Peter Matthiessen, *Sal Si Puedes: Cesar Chavez and the New American Revolution* (New York, 1969). Also important is Richard A. Garcia, "Dolores Huerta: Woman, Organizer, Symbol," *California History*, volume LXXII (Spring 1993). pp. 56-71.

For the Larry Itliong and the Agricultural Workers Organizing Committee see, Howard A. DeWitt, "Agricultural Workers Organizing Committee," in Franklin Ng, editor, *The Asian American Encyclopedia* (North Bellmore, NY, 1995), pp. 5-8.

The role of the labor union in combating racism is analyzed with vision and clarity in Harvey Schwartz, "A Union Combats Racism: The ILWU's Japanese-American 'Stockton Incident' of 1945," *Southern California Quarterly*, volume LXII (Summer, 1980), pp. 161-176. A useful general history of labor in California is David F. Selvin, *A Place in the Sun: A History of California Labor* (San Francisco, 1981).

14

California's Ethnic Garden of Eden Explodes

The Watts Riot and Racial Tensions

FIGURE 14-1. David Ray Kennedy: California Vietnam Paratrooper.

The 1960s was a period of dramatic change. Demonstrations on college campuses against the Vietnam War, the drive for civil rights and the emergence of ethnic studies programs at major universities, the rise of feminist politics and the conservative reaction against these changes culminated during Governor Ronald Reagan's election in 1966. The notion that California was a state unburdened by racial differences was a myth built to epic proportions by the media.

California's problems were reflected in racial tensions throughout Los Angeles. The sizable African American, Latino, Native American and Asian American population obscured the virulent racism of the Los Angeles Police Department, the double standard in hiring practiced by downtown businesses and the lack of adequate schools. Los Angeles had a mystique that hid its faults. One African American intellectual, Langston Hughes, called Los Angeles "more a miracle than a city, a place where oranges sold for one cent a dozen; ordinary black folks," Hughes wrote, "lived in large houses with miles of yards and prosperity seemed to reign..." What Hughes missed was the subtle bigotry which made it difficult to confront racism and forced many African Americans into second class citizenship.

Before the Watts Riot of 1965 erupted, California's government, major universities and corporations prided themselves as models of fairness. The Golden State considered itself a laboratory of racial equality. However, beneath the surface there were serious problems. The explosive racial tensions, which few Californians recognized, caused many to question the Golden State's "Ethnic Garden of Eden."

The Birth of Racial Tensions: The Decade Prior to the Watts Riot and African American Politics

"The birth of racial tensions is a product of the white man's refusal to recognize our progress," Don Barksdale, an Oakland businessman who was an Olympic gold medalist in basketball and the first African American to play in the National Basketball Association, remarked in 1958 to a Rotary Club. This statement suggests the bitterness of African American businessmen and the importance of civil rights legislation. Barksdale's comments did no go unnoticed.

Shortly after he took office in 1959, Governor Edmund G. (Pat) Brown supported a civil rights bill. The Democratic Party leader in the California Legislator, Jesse "Big Daddy" Unruh, guided a comprehensive civil rights bill through the legislature. The Unruh Civil Rights Act and the California Fair Employment Act hoped to combat racial discrimination. These laws also inaugurated a period of political liberalism

FIGURE 14-2. Dr. Alan Kirshner Speaks at a Teach-In Combating California Racism.

FIGURE 14-3. Professor Walt Halland: "I think the 1960s brought a new freedom to California except in racial matters."

which intensified conflict between conservative and reform-minded citizens.

When Jesse Unruh sponsored the Fair Employment Practices Act of 1959, he guaranteed the right of employment without regard to "race, creed, color, national origin or ancestry." The resistance to Unruh's legislation was immediate. Few employers took the law seriously. By 1964, the chief offenders were the large supermarkets, Safeway and Lucky. The Lucky chain was targeted because it had only 50 black employees; Safeway refused to release statistics on African American workers.

Many employers refused to hire African American workers for sales positions. The auto dealerships on San Francisco's Van Ness Avenue and members of the California Real Estate Association refused to hire black janitors. The Congress of Racial Equality (CORE) and the National Association for the Advancement of Colored People (NAACP) used sit ins, picketing and boycotts to force these businesses into fair employment practices.

In San Francisco, Mayor John F. Shelley negotiated a series of hiring agreements between CORE and the Lucky supermar-

ket chain. Shortly after this pact was signed, demonstrators began picketing the Cadillac dealership on Van Ness Avenue. Dr. Thomas Burbridge, president of the SF branch of the NAACP, orchestrated a highly publicized campaign that accused he auto dealers of having racist hiring policies. Then the NAACP picketed San Francisco's Sheraton Palace Hotel as well and negotiated a minority hiring policy with hotel management. Housing was the next political target for black Californians.

The road to housing reform began in 1948 when W. Byron Rumford became the first African American assemblyman elected to the California Legislature. Representing the Oakland-Berkeley District, Rumford was critical of housing, education and employment practices. Using his considerable clout in the Democratic Party, he lobbied for civil rights and housing legislation. In 1963, the Rumford Fair Housing Act passed the California Legislature and required real estate agents to sell to anyone regardless of race. The California Real Estate Association responded by organizing a voter initiative in support of a "right to sell" law. Proposition 14 was approved by a wide margin in 1964, and white landlords refused to rent, sell or lease to African Americans.

The Rumford Fair Housing Act and the passage of Proposition 14 created a civil rights debate. The NAACP complained that the scarcity of jobs, inadequate education, rampant racism and general political indifference to the African American community was scandalous. A coalition of liberal student activists, black ministers and Democratic politicians joined hands to protest California's indifference to racial problems.

The racial climate in California during the early 1960s had many warning signs. At the University of California, Davis, a predominantly white student body continued to preserve past traditions. Hazing in fraternities was encouraged and Chancellor Emil Mrak did little to prevent racial slurs toward Mexican Americans. Eventually, UCD fraternities were exposed for calling Spanish speaking pledges "wetbacks," "beans" and "taco eaters." Only after an extensive letter writing campaign to the California Legislature, did UCD ban racial hazing policies. However, in Fremont, California, a twenty-minute ride from Oakland, there wasn't a single African American homeowner.

In the early 1960's, San Mateo County announced that it would not allow the Bay Area Rapid Transit system to build its line into the peninsula area south of San Francisco because property values would decline. The *San Mateo Times* was typical of local newspapers who printed letters from homeowners expressing a fear of "low income renters." In the exclusive San Mateo County suburb of Hillsborough, the local police routinely stopped anyone who was African American, and this backfired one day when a group of African businessmen were prevented from attending a party at Shirley Temple Black's house in their honor.

The civil rights atmosphere of the time prompted many complaints about patriotic groups. The NAACP and CORE suggested that there was a conspiracy to keep African American homeowners in San Francisco. In 1963, the FBI investigated complaints of intimidating prospective homeowners but found no evidence to prosecute the John Birch Society, the Ku Klux Klan or the American Nazi Party. While these organizations were active, the FBI reported, they were not part of the racial terror in and around Oroville. The KKK, however, was prominent in northern California, San Leandro and Santa Rosa, but once again the FBI found no violation of federal law.

These isolated incidents ranging from college campuses to upper-class suburbs were warning signs. The roots of the Watts Riot of 1965 were embedded in the unpleasant racial controversies which led African Americans to march into the streets frustrated and unhappy about their lack of civil rights.

The Marquette Frye Incident and the Birth of the Los Angeles Riot of 1965

At six in the evening on August 11, 1965, California Highway Patrolman Lee W. Minikus stopped an African American, Marquette Frye, and asked him to take a sobriety test. Fry had consumed a number of screwdrivers to celebrate his brother's discharge from the Air Force. As Frye was taking and failing the sobriety test, a crowd surrounding Frye and Minikus grew to three hundred people.

What began as a minor confrontation at 166th Street and Avalon Boulevard, just two blocks from Frye's house, turned into an ugly incident. When Frye volunteered to walk home, the officer refused his request. Officer Minikus announced, in a loud voice, that Frye had failed the sobriety test and informed the young man that he was under arrest.

Suddenly Marquette Frye's mother, Rena, started hollering at her son and berated him for drinking. Marquette who was cooperating with the officers began cursing his mother and hollering at the officers. Then Rena Frye became offended by Officer Minikus's attitude and jumped on his back. She was only five feet tall but she weighed about 147 pounds. It took the officer some time to get her off his back.

The crowd became hostile as three California Highway Patrol officers arrived. Afraid of the crowd, Minikus drew a shotgun and put it to Frye's head. Later, Mrs. Frye claimed that she was slapped on the face and hit on the knee with a blackjack. She was also arrested, and, finally, a little after 7:30 in the evening the Frye brothers and their mother arrived at the police station.

As the remaining officers nervously prepared to leave, someone in the crowd spit on two of them. They ran into the crowd and arrested Joyce Gaines, a twenty-one-year-old who was 5 foot 7 inches tall and weighed 132 pounds. She was restrained with what the crowd believed was excessive force. Gaines was wearing a smock which made her look pregnant and onlookers booed and hooted at the police. As the crowd continued to build, the officers left the scene. From a little past eight in the evening until midnight, a mob formed, stoning automobiles, pulling white people from their cars and destroying property. By one in the morning, order had been restored, and twenty people were arrested. But this began six days of looting and the Watts Riot of 1965 ended California's so called racial harmony.

The earliest looting took place at 8:00 A.M. on a hot August 12th morning as a supermarket at 116th and Avalon was emptied of its goods. With Watts rioting, politicians and civic leaders moved in to mediate the differences. Congressman Augustus Hawkins and NAACP leader H. Claude Hudson arrived for a meeting in the Athens Park Auditorium, eleven blocks from the incident. The hostile audience complained about police procedures. To listen to community grievances, the LAPD and other law enforcement agencies sent their top brass to Watts. Community leaders pointed out that one of four complaints against the LAPD was for police brutality, and more than 80% of these complaints originated in Watts. When asked about these statistics, members of the Los Angeles Police Department, the Sheriff's Office and the District Attorney's Office, who were in attendance at the meeting, declined to comment. They maintained that the South Central Los Angeles area had a high crime rate. This infuriated the NAACP, and city officials were castigated for suggesting that African Americans were prone to crime.

The community responded with charges of police brutality, inbred racism and a general lack of interest in the welfare of the black community. During the meeting, black ministers suggested that white police officers be withdrawn from the neighborhood, but this request failed to wake up Los Angeles politicians.

By Friday, August 13th, the police had lost control of south L. A. As violence escalated, prominent black citizens requested a meeting with Deputy Chief of Police Roger Murdock at the 77th Street station. The African American community presented a detailed plan for an increase in minority police, but they met with resistance and were thrown out of the station. Murdock not only handled the problem poorly, but he also had little interest in community relations. Murdock told the group that he was "a law and order man."

In the meeting with Deputy Chief Murdock, black ministers, businessmen and homeowners presented a list of grievances. They pointed out that the community was in a state of chaos and disorder. This frightened Murdock, and he called Police Chief William H. Parker. After discussing the incident, Murdock and Parker had no idea how to deal with these grievances. They agreed that law and order was a problem in South Central Los Angeles, but they had no plan to guarantee public safety. As the LAPD continued to act indecisively, the violence and looting continued.

The Watts Riot of August 1965 led to looting all over the Central District resulting in 34 deaths, over a thousand people injured and nearly four thousand arrested. More than a thousand buildings were damaged and estimated property losses exceeded two hundred million dollars. The riot involved 35,000 people with another 72,000 spectators. The National Guard sent in 16,000 troops and the Los Angeles Police Department, California Highway Patrol and other law enforcement agencies had their forces on hand as well.

The Watts Riot took place in a twenty square mile district of Watts-Willowbrook and destroyed the South Central District of Los Angeles. The question of what caused the riot disturbed city officials. Police Chief William Parker announced that "outside agitators" instigated the riot, but he was personally ill equipped to handle the riot.

Like a military general, Parker stood in front of a L. A. map and pointed out war zones in the city. He treated the black sections of the city as if they were populated by aliens ready for an invasion. Parker made one insulting statement after another for fifteen years about African Americans. "You cannot ignore the genes in the behavior pattern of people," Parker often remarked. Thurgood Marshall, an NAACP attorney and the first African American appointed to the U.S. Supreme Court, remembered that Los Angeles police "refused to allow Negroes freedom outside Watts."

The Causes of the Watts Riot and the Politicians Respond

There were three primary causes of the Watts Riot of August 1965. First, Watts was a racially isolated area. The blocks of inadequate housing, the lack of employment opportunities and the absence of city services built up long standing community resentment. As television beamed a picture of middle class America, this dissatisfaction intensified.

A second cause of the Watts Riot was long standing grievances against Chinese, Jewish, Italian, Korean and Anglo merchants who charged high prices in small grocery stores, bottle shops and retail stores.

The final reason was the emergence of an educated, politically sophisticated and economically independent African American community. This new generation of black political activists and business people came of age during the civil rights era.

The day after the Marquette Frye incident, Chief Parker stated that the LAPD would control the rioting. He held a press conference and announced that the African American community was in a state of rebellion. The Chief then admitted that he could not control Watts. The Los Angeles Mayor Sam Yorty decided to call in the National Guard. The lines of communication were so blurred between the Mayor and the Police Chief that it was impossible to tell who was in charge.

Then Chief Parker tried to blame the California Highway Patrol for the riot. Finally, Mayor Yorty stepped in and silenced Parker. When help was requested from Governor Edmund G. (Pat) Brown's office, his press secretary informed Mayor Yorty that the Governor was on vacation. The Lt. Governor, Glenn Anderson, was in Santa Barbara, and he ordered troops into the Watts area.

On the evening of August 12, 1965, Lt. Governor Anderson arrived in Los Angeles. He realized that the LAPD couldn't control the rioting. However, he couldn't do much about it, so he announced that he would quickly move the National Guard into South Central Los Angeles.

The Los Angeles Police Department had to give final authority for the National Guard to take up its position. In a moment of monumental stupidity, Chief Parker delayed deploying troops until another three hours of rioting had taken place. Parker told Mayor Yorty that his department could handle the problem. But Mayor Yorty wisely overruled the chief and called in the National Guard. They quickly ended the riot and hastened Chief Parker's retirement.

When Governor Pat Brown was located on vacation in Athens, Greece, he agreed that the National Guard should be called on "to protect life and property." By Friday evening there were 1,336 National Guard troops assembled to protect Los Angeles. By seven o'clock in the evening, the day Governor Brown was informed of the situation, the National Guard unit was in place in the Central District. An African American minister remarked: "If we had those kinds of services, there would be no riot."

The LAPD officially lobbied Chief Parker, and he refused to recognize the Lt. Governor's authority. The Los Angeles County Sheriff Peter Pitchess was respected in the black community, and he urged Parker to use National Guard troops. Parker did, but the *Los Angeles Times* asked: "Did the Los Angeles Police Department's conduct cause the riot?"

The Los Angeles Police Department and the Watts Riots: A Question of Conduct

In the aftermath of the Watts Riot, the Los Angeles Police Department came under heavy attack when a Governor's Commission was set up to investigate police behavior during the Los Angeles riot. John A. McCone, a well-known businessman and former director of the CIA, was placed in charge of the McCone Commission which had two African Americans, Judge Early Broady and the Reverend James Jones, among the eight commissioners. The subsequent hearings created more controversy.

With a $250,000 budget, the McCone Commission hired seventy-one people and began hearing testimony. After seventy-nine witnesses testified, the commission interviewed more than two hundred people, including more than ninety arrested during the Watts Riot. A questionnaire was distributed to more than 10,000 Los Angeles citizens. The results of this questionnaire demanded better police service, respect for the African American community and a willingness by city officials to clean up the LAPD.

On December 2, 1965, the eighty-six page McCone report used the term "Violence In The City-An End or a Beginning?" as a title to its controversial report. This theatrical title caught people's attention. However, the report was filled with suspect conclusions. The rioters were referred to as "marginal people" and "not representative of the Negro population." The report ignored police harassment, lack of jobs, poor housing, inadequate city services and political isolation. Not only did the McCone Commission misunderstand the depth of African American feeling, but the committee also ignored the cultural differences threatening to tear the Golden State apart.

In harsh language, the McCone report blamed African American ministers and political activists for the Watts Riot. However, compared to Oakland and San Francisco, there was little evidence of black radicalism in Los Angeles. Surprisingly, the report did recognize that there were "legitimate Negro grievances." In 1966, an African American, Marvin Watson, who was a political aide to President Lyndon B. Johnson, remarked: "the basic condition of the Negro in that part of Los Angeles (Watts)...is fundamentally unchanged since the riots." Soon a new form of African American protest arose with Huey P. Newton and the Oakland based Black Panthers.

The Black Panther Party: Huey P. Newton, Oakland's Ethnic Robin Hood and Black Power

In the mid-1960s, a new sense of African American pride and nationalism surfaced. Such nationally prominent black leaders as Stokley Carmichael and his successor as Chairman of the Student Non-Violent Coordinating Committee (SNCC), H. Rap Brown, spoke out against "a racist and white dominated America." One of the most significant young civil rights groups, SNCC, combined white radicals and black activists to advance civil rights.

SNCC influenced a young junior college student, Huey P. Newton, who was reading, writing and thinking by day and smoking dope and robbing people by night. Strangely, this young black man who lived in two different worlds became the Robin Hood of the African American political experience before he was assassinated by a drug dealer.

For black nationalists at Merritt College, there were a number of political clubs which extolled the virtues of African American students. They argued that white dominated economic and educational systems were destroying African American pride. Huey P. Newton was recognized as the most intelligent observer on the Merritt campus.

In Berkeley and Oakland, the increasingly militant African American community was the focal point of a new political consciousness. In the fall of 1966, the paramilitary and highly militant Black Panther Party surfaced in Oakland's Fruitvale section. The party was organized by Huey P. Newton and Bobby G. Seale. They met at Merritt College, a two year junior college in the Oakland hills, and began studying the writings of Malcolm X and Frantz Fanon.

Newton and Seale wrote a Black Panther platform which included demands for political concessions, full employment and an end to police brutality. In public debate, Newton and Seale were informed, intelligent, articulate and aware of their rights. They carried law books and lectured the police on violations of civil rights. Not surprisingly, a literal war broke out between the Oakland Police Department and the Black Panthers.

The Black Panthers dressed in stylish black leather, wore black berets and marched in a military style. To many white Californians, they were a strange and unfathomable group. To African Americans,

however, they represented the first direct challenge to a white dominated society. On October 15, 1966, the Black Panther Party was officially founded with Bobby Seale as the Party Chairperson and Huey P. Newton as the Minister of Defense. The Black Panther symbol came from a ballot emblem for an African American civil rights party in Alabama.

Eldridge Cleaver became the intellectual voice of the Black Panthers. His career as a political strategist was launched by *Ramparts* magazine writer, Bob Scheer. A goateed, bespeckled white radical, Scheer ran for Congress in the Oakland area with the help of Newton and Seale. He lost, but won a large segment of the black vote. Cleaver was the brains behind Scheer's campaign in the black community, and his writing caught *Rampart's* attention. Cleaver was an intelligent, highly articulate Oakland resident who had served two prison terms. He was convicted of selling marijuana at age 18, and after his release, he wrote the best selling book *Soul On Ice*. Although Cleaver's book was ghost written by his attorney, Beverly Axelrod, he articulated the rage and contempt of young black men. His writing was an example of the popularity of watered down revolutionary thought and the liberal need to embrace black intellectuals. But Cleaver could not escape his criminal ways. He violated probation and returned to prison.

At first, authorities ignored the young men who marched around Oakland in black leather jackets with black berets tilted to the side of their heads. However, as the Black Panthers carried their law books, tape recorders and cameras on patrols, they drove the police crazy.

In May 1967, Huey P. Newton, the founder of the Black Panther Party, led a group of twenty-six armed black troopers into the state capitol building in Sacramento. They marched in military formation carrying unloaded guns. Amidst a frenzy of news reporters, the Black Panthers pushed their way past the sergeants-at-arms in order to protest proposed restrictions on guns. Newton found an obscure state law which allowed carrying unloaded guns in public and used this statute to push the boundaries of individual freedom.

Suddenly, Newton was a hero. A poster of Huey P. Newton sitting in a wicker chair with a shotgun sold all over California, and the image of Black Panther radicalism was a major news topic. Newton proclaimed black pride while acting like a thug. After being fitted for a suit from his tailor, Newton beat the man because the cuffs on his pants were too short. Soon newspaper tales surfaced of beatings, intimidation and threats against Black Panther critics.

The Black Panthers were popular in the Oakland ghetto because of their breakfast program for children and for the establishment of a special school which taught black pride. Such Panther phrases as "Black is Beautiful" became a trademark of its influence. The party also persuaded San Francisco State and other colleges to inaugurate black studies programs. One African American intellectual, Nathan Hare, produced a serious magazine, *The Black Scholar*, which put into a moderate perspective into some of the Black Panthers' arguments on racism. He was refused tenure at San Francisco State University because his publications "lacked serious scholarly intent."

From 1966 to 1969, the Black Panthers were a source of inspiration to young African Americans. Then in December 1969, federal agents conducted simultaneous raids on Black Panther headquarters in Los Angeles, Vallejo, Chicago, Philadelphia and a number of other cities. These raids revealed caches of guns, explosive materials and politically sensitive materials. These findings created a media field day.

When African American California State Senator Mervyn Dymally arrived at Black Panther headquarters in Los Angeles, in an attempt to mediate problems between the Panthers and the Los Angeles police, he was beaten viciously by the LAPD. The LAPD didn't recognize Senator Dymally, and their reaction was a reflection of police racism.

Soon Black Panthers were demanding a movement to "Free Los Angeles." An African American led organization, the United Civil Rights Council, intensified criticism of Los Angeles police tactics. They predicted more race riots. Respected black voices like Dr. Ralph Bunche, undersecretary of the United Nations, and Carlotta Bass, editor of the *Los Angeles Eagle*, echoed the same complaints.

The shame of Los Angeles was evident to everyone. The National Association for the Advancement of Colored People and the American Civil Liberties Union criticized Los Angeles officials for refusing to integrate schools, police and fire departments and city government. In 1963, a law suit, Crawford vs. Board of Education of Los Angeles, was brought before the court, alleging racial discrimination in the schools. The case finally reached the trial phase in 1968-1969. After a lengthy trial, Judge Alfred Gitelson found the Los Angeles School Board guilty of various and prolonged acts of bad faith. The result was to change school financing, thus allowing for some equity in funding the public school system. Gitelson's decision helped to equalize funding for inner city schools and began some minimal educational reforms as well.

Oakland Racism and the Black Panthers

The Black Panther Party leader argued that they organized in response to Oakland racism. In 1966, there were only sixteen black officers on the 600 plus member police department and the city council had one black elected representative from west Oakland. However, he rarely spoke at city council meetings, and African Americans were outraged at their lack of political influence.

Black separatism was the Panther cry. The radicalism and militancy of the Black Panthers was the perfect foil for Governor Ronald Reagan who argued that black radicalism had to be met with strong police powers. Since his inauguration in January 1967, Reagan warned of Panther violence. An incident soon took place which changed the direction of the Black Panther Party, and validated Governor Reagan's arguments.

On the morning of October 28, 1967, Oakland police officer John Frey pulled over Newton. After a night of celebrating his release from probation, for stabbing Odell Lee, Newton was in a boisterous mood. When he stopped Newton, Officer Frey was a rookie policeman. He realized that he had stopped the most prominent Black Panther and quickly called for backup. Officer Herbert Heanes, a twenty-four-year-old just beyond his rookie training, responded to the call.

The insulting and manipulative Newton and the inexperienced Frey became involved in an argument. When Huey opened a lawbook and informed Frey that he had no reason to arrest him, a scuffle ensued and Frey was shot to death. Newton was also shot. He then forced a passing motorist, Dell Ross, to take him to the home of David Hilliard. The fellow Black Panther took Newton to the Kaiser Hospital. It was there that Newton was arrested.

The Oakland Police Department moved quickly and indicted Newton for murder. An Alameda County grand jury returned a three-count murder indictment. After a series of legal maneuvers, Newton was convicted of voluntary manslaughter. He was sent to the Men's Colony in San Luis Obispo while radical attorney Fay Stender worked on an appeal. There was an immediate outcry that Newton had been framed. Years later, however, he would brag to friends that he shot Frey.

With Newton in jail, the Black Panthers raged against the Oakland police. One night, Eldridge Cleaver organized four carloads of Panthers to, as Cleaver remarked, "do some shooting." While moving guns from Cleaver's house to west Oakland, the police stopped Cleaver and a gun fight took place. Cleaver escaped and fled to a nearby house. One Panther, Bobby Hutton, was shot to death.

Rather than focusing upon Cleaver's use of guns, the media made a hero of young Bobby Hutton. After the Oakland police captured Cleaver and Hutton, they marched them to a paddy wagon. Hutton stumbled and dropped his arms. The police believed that he had a gun and shot him to death.

Hutton became a Black Panther martyr. Cleaver charged that the Oakland police murdered him. The Hutton killing brought in celebrity supporter Marlon Brando who became a fund raiser for the Panthers. He appeared in the San Francisco area to create a defense fund and was joined by Norman Mailer, Susan Sontag, Ossie Davis, LeRoi Jones and James Baldwin.

Soon the list of Black Panther supporters included almost 100 white students at the University of California, Boalt Hall Law School. Then 400 white doctors and health care workers founded the Medical Committee For Human Rights to support the black power movement.

With Newton and Cleaver in jail, the Black Panther leadership was decimated. As Bobby Seale and Kathleen Cleaver raised money for the Black Panthers' defense fund, problems with the Oakland police escalated. By the summer of 1968 the Black Panthers were America's media circus as they fended off the FBI, the Oakland police and critical comments made by Governor Ronald Reagan. The Panthers were on the downside of their power.

The changes in California's African American community were ones that resulted in better education, improved job opportunities, adequate housing and more political influence. A sizable number of well to do African American businessmen were featured in newspapers and magazines. Clearly, a black middle class emerged, and the old days of second class civilization were not over, but they were seriously challenged.

Suddenly, black Californians were not as supportive of the Black Panthers. Most paid lip service to a fair trial for Huey P. Newton and many supported Eldridge Cleaver. However, money for the defense fund came primarily from white liberals. Although, there was no need for a defense fund because when the judge revoked Cleaver's parole, he fled to Cuba and eventually to Algeria. With Newton in jail, there were no important Black Panther leaders on the Oakland streets.

The void in Panther leadership ranks ended on August 5, 1970 when Huey P. Newton was released after spending nearly two years in prison. Fay Stender's brilliant 170 page appeal argued that the Alameda County Grand Jury systematically excluded poor people, black people and denied Newton the right of pretrial confrontation of his accusers. This argument was enough to win his release. The appeals court found that the trial judge failed to instruct the jury that it could rule that Newton had committed either voluntary or involuntary manslaughter. So, Newton went free.

In the midst of the appeal, a free Huey Newton movement created public sympathy for the Black Panther's release. On August 5, 1970, Newton walked out of the Alameda County Prison and was greeted by a battery of news people. Newton's release was the beginning of another round of Black Panther and police confrontations.

Newton began a personal descent into drugs and alcohol and found it increasingly difficult to remain an effective leader. But the Black Panthers weren't through. In 1973, Bobby Seale ran for Mayor of Oakland and Elaine Brown for the city council. Brown lost her bid for the city council seat, but Seale forced incumbent Republican Mayor John Reading into a runoff. Tom Nash, the editor of the black owned *Oakland Post* remarked: "The thing that kept Bobby from winning that election was his affiliation with the Black Panther Party."

Soon, the Black Panthers began to make fools of themselves. They hired Ike and Tina Turner for a fund raising concert and Ike stormed off the stage of the Oakland Auditorium when the Panthers could not come up with the $7,500 advance. In retaliation, one of Turner's guitar players was beaten by a Newton bodyguard.

Throughout the 1970s, Newton attempted to revive the Black Panther Party without success. With a massive cocaine habit, an unstable personality and delusions of grandeur, Newton drove the old leadership from the party. White radicals continued to blindly follow him. However, none was blinder than David Horowitz who kept the Black Panther school in the Oakland Community Learning Center open to disadvantaged children. A rich kid playing at radicalism, Horowitz was a leftist intellectual with an elite education and a family fortune. He played at the game of equality as a journalist and community fund raider. Horowitz was also the editor of the ultra radical *Ramparts* magazine which portrayed Huey P. Newton as "Robin Hood" and the Black Panthers as cultural icons standing up to white oppression. Horowitz symbolized much of what was wrong with the Black Panther Party. He held fund raisers with $100 bottles of Mumms champagne and brie while Hollywood starlets snorted cocaine and bedded Newton.

Horowitz's heart was in the right place. He raised more than $100,000 for the Black

Panther school, but he had no idea that Newton maintained an elite hit squad. Eventually, an event took place that made Horowitz begin to question the Black Panther organization.

When Horowitz asked Betty Van Patter, an employee of *Ramparts,* to do the books for the Black Panther Party, she agreed. Horowitz urged her to ignore questionable activity and not to verify Black Panther sources of funds. Spending was another concern, and Van Patter was horrified to discover that Federal Government grants were spent on drugs. She was a consummate professional and soon uncovered outright fraud. When Van Patter confronted Newton, he told her to leave him alone.

Then on a cold Friday night in December 1974, Van Patter vanished from Berkeley Square, a rock music bar she frequented. She was found five weeks later when her body washed up on the western shore of San Francisco Bay. Newton and the Panthers had killed her, but there was no evidence.

With local support declining, Huey P. Newton announced that he was returning to school. He enrolled at the University of California, Santa Cruz to pursue a Ph.D. The first week in school he was arrested with his bodyguard, Bob Heard, for fighting in a Santa Cruz bar.

The University of California, Santa Cruz is an experimental college. Grades are not considered important and the faculty is leftist, elitist, eastern educated and prone to trendy intellectual fads. Historian Page Smith was chairperson of the admissions committee, and he was unhappy with the graduate education system. Smith admitted Newton partially out of disdain for graduate education. Newton had no trouble earning his doctorate and completed the degree despite prodigious drug intake and partying.

In the midst of Newton's UC, Santa Cruz education in 1978, a journalist, Kate Coleman, wrote an article "The Party's Over" for *New Times*, a small free weekly newspaper, which exposed the Black Panther legacy of hatred and foul deeds. Not surprisingly, David Horowitz was a major source for Coleman's article, but he demanded anonymity. Horowitz was afraid of the Black Panthers but succeeded in exposing the violent nature of Newton and the Black Panthers. Horowitz believed that he was responsible for Van Patter's death, and he attacked the Panthers in print with a vengeance.

But the publicity made Newton even more of a campus celebrity at UC, Santa Cruz, and students registered for classes they believed he was taking. A blind student who was sitting next to Newton in class, without realizing it, blurted out: "When is Huey Newton coming? I enrolled in this class because Newton is supposed to be here."

One of his professors, Bob Trivors, a Harvard educated sociobiologist, remarked that Newton "was one of the four or five real geniuses I've met in my lifetime." A majority of faculty members interviewed requested anonymity, and they were critical of Newton's graduate education program. His Ph.D. thesis was 175 pages and entitled: "War Against the Panthers: A Study of Repression in America." This dissertation violated the concept of a graduate education which was to provide a paper with in depth, original research that had academic objectivity and a dispassionate writing style. Despite this flagrant abuse of the educational system, Newton was awarded a doctoral degree in the History of Consciousness.

By the 1980s the Black Panther Party had faded into obscurity. Newton was a crack addict, and the Black Guerrilla Family regularly provided him with free drugs.

Then in July 1988, Newton was sentenced to six weeks in San Quentin for failing to report to his parole officer. In San Quentin, Newton angered members of California's leading black drug gang, the Black Guerrilla Family. The leadership of the BGF made it known that a reward would be given for "taking care of Huey."

On a hot August 22, 1989 morning, Huey P. Newton was smoking crack cocaine in an apartment at 10th and Cypress when someone burst in with the news that people were looking for him. But he was a sickly, mentally inept and a dirty former hero who walked the mean streets of Oakland in a fog.

The madness that invaded Newton's life frightened everyone and as he left the crack house death was inevitable. Newton met Tyrone Robinson, known as Double R, and one of his friends, Brian Walton. There was an argument over crack cocaine and Double R shot Newton to death. "I'll make rank! I'll make rank!" Double R shouted. The Black Guerrilla Family offered a high level position in the family for Newton's death. But Robinson was arrested, and two years later a jury convicted him of second degree murder.

The Black Panthers: The Historical Legacy and the African American Middle Class Emerges

What was the significance of black power and the Black Panthers? The term Black Panther was as much of a media creation as a reality. Economic success, education, a decline in racism and the rise of a middle class African American consciousness made the Panthers appear increasingly out of step.

In the aftermath of Newton's death, there was effusive praise for his leadership. National NAACP spokesperson Benjamin Hooks called Newton a voice for "disillusioned and often bitter youths in the 1960s." Biko Lumumba of Uhuru house, a militant black organization, remarked: "America

wants us to have heroes like Bill Cosby and Eddie Murphy." Lumumba bitterly charged that heroes like Newton meet early deaths.

The defenders and detractors of Huey P. Newton engaged in journalistic fisticuffs after his death. Ken Kelly, a journalist writing for the *East Bay Express*, praised Newton, using a quote from an elderly black woman who called Newton the Moses of black Californians. But Kelley also charged that Newton was a bully, gun totter, drug addict and had violent tendencies toward women.

David Horowitz, now a well-known conservative media critic, entered the battle with an article in the national magazine *Smart*. In this article, he described Newton as a "crazy nigger." This racial slur angered people and Elaine Brown, a former Panther leader, criticized Horowitz for his racist writing. In December 1989, the People's Organized Response (POR) was formed to continue the Black Panther Party and a newspaper, *The Commentator*, was launched to pay tribute to Newton. Both quickly faded from sight, and the Black Panthers became a historical curiosity.

By the late 1960s, black Californians were a major part of California life. Since 1965, when Operation Bootstrap was organized as a business self-help coalition in Los Angeles, African American blue collar workers increased dramatically. This group hoped to develop job skills for the hard-core unemployed and the resulting increase in blue collar jobs was dramatic. In San Francisco, the National Economic Growth and Reconstruction Organization, known as NEGRO, operated a clothing factory and a construction business. In August 1966, an African American managed a subsidiary of Aerojet-General and set up its operation as the Watts Manufacturing Company. It secured a $2.5 million contract to produce tents for the Defense Department.

The Black Panthers were all but forgotten as African Americans entered the mainstream of California life. But they were important in creating a black cultural nationalism which brought pride to the community and forced the white establishment to guarantee employment.

The Post 1965 Asian Impulse in the Golden State: Once Again a Case of Strangers

In 1965, a new immigration law went into effect. This act ended quotas and restrictions on Asian immigrants. By removing the term "national origins" from immigration law, the Government could no longer restrict Asian immigrants.

In 1965, there were one million Asians living in the United States but by 1985 five million resided permanently in the country. This led to a resurgence of anti-Asian feeling. These newcomers were better educated, often had sizable economic resources and were more often professionally trained. They were equipped to challenge the racial insults and resist any government attempts to limit their rights.

A more sophisticated hostility toward the Vietnamese, Korean, Laotian and Cambodian immigrants introduced a new chapter in anti-Asian politics. As Asian Americans became California's fastest growing ethnic census group, the reaction against their successes and influences mounted.

The vast majority of Asians settled in major California cities. In 1960, there were only 877,934 Asians in America, representing one-half of one percent of the population. By 1985, more than five million Asians made up 2.1% of the population. By 1990, San Francisco County was approximately 25% Asian, and this prompted two University of California faculty members to urge a state initiative to restrict Far Eastern immigrants.

To many Californians an Asian was either Chinese or Japanese. After 1965, however, Koreans, Filipinos, Southeast Asians

and Asian Indians settled in California in large numbers. The number of Japanese permanently residing in California declined dramatically, but this was hardly noticed in the renewed anti-Asian hysteria.

The reason for the resurgence of anti Asian feeling was the change in immigration patterns. With one of every two immigrants arriving in California from Asia, there was a resurgence of past history. The anti-Asian impulse resurfaced and from 1965 to 1995 the number of racial incidents involving Asians increased by 500%. This is surprising since the majority of Asian immigrants were skilled workers, but the Golden State still viewed them as undesirable aliens.

Suddenly, there was a new stereotype, one which feared the skilled Asian worker. These new stereotype led to changes in immigration law. In 1976, Congress restricted a wide range of professional workers from entering America because they caused Americans to lose their jobs. The following year the Eilberg Act continued to target Asian professionals as the United States Department of Labor required employers to file a certification of employment. Finally, in 1986, another federal law restricted children of U.S. citizens from entering the country. This was an obvious attempt to stifle immigration of the children of American soldiers from the Vietnam War. The main reason for these laws was economic as a new stereotype emerged; the educated immigrant was no longer welcome because he or she worked too hard, had too much money and was too successful. Carey McWilliams, noted California journalist and historian, had mentioned this stereotype during the 1930s and suggested that it was an enduring myth. The myth grew as hostility to the minority population escalated. By 1996 this stereotype was so widely held that there was a statewide feeling to end the right of immigrants to be educated.

Entering the high tech and service economy Asians quickly became a wealthy California subculture. Southeast Asians, Indian Asians and the Chinese make up the majority of the California immigrant population. Recent Chinese arrivals are called San Yi Man (new immigrants), and they are the third largest immigrant group after Mexicans and Filipinos. But the new Chinese bear no resemblance to their ancestors.

Chinese Immigrants Since 1965

The post 1965 Chinese immigrant came from large urban areas and was often a refugee from the People's Republican of China. After a brief stay in Hong Kong, he or she immigrated to San Francisco. The new arrivals were different from past Chinese immigrants. They were more often women (49%), had managerial, professional or technical training, and they were increasingly college educated. They didn't live in Chinatown. Instead, they purchased homes in the Sunset and Richmond Districts of San Francisco. They moved into the peninsula south of San Francisco and purchased homes in the suburbs of Walnut Creek, Antioch and Orinda.

Most Chinese immigrants were shocked at the poverty and poor living conditions in San Francisco's Chinatown. There were many Chinese who lived on the edge of society because language and culture had a near poverty existence. Not only were wages lower for the Chinese in California but unemployment was double that of other states. Despite these problems, the Chinese population prospered, and the first suburban Chinatown, Monterey Park, emerged in Los Angeles.

Monterey Park is a striking contrast to San Francisco's Chinatown. In 1960, this area was 85% white, 12% Hispanic and 3% Asian. By 1990, the Chinese population made up 55% of Monterey Park's population. In the early 1980s, Lilly Chen was elected Mayor of Monterey Park, and, as a result, the city experienced racial tension. A few years later, a sign on a gas station read:

> WILL THE LAST AMERICAN TO LEAVE MONTEREY PARK PLEASE BRING THE FLAG.

Despite this sign of racism, Monterey Park quickly grew into one of California's wealthiest suburbs. A great deal of Monterey Park's money came from Hong Kong and a local realtor, Frederic Hshieh, labeled the city the "new Chinese Beverly Hills." By 1990, almost 80% of Monterey Park's property was owned by Chinese investors.

The notion that all Asians are educated, wealthy and successful continues to dominate California thought. The truth is that poverty continues to exist alongside wealth. In San Francisco and Los Angeles, sweatshops continue to employ Chinese who don't speak English and work for less than the minimum wage. Women dominate the garment industry in San Francisco's Chinatown and are abused in this labor market. Those who do not work in the clothing industry are restaurant workers who find better jobs because of language barriers.

Some Asian workers learn the American way and take their cases to the courts. Kim Wah Lee, a factory owner, was sued by Jennie Lew over piecework wages. When the case went to court, Lew's attorney proved that she made $1.65 an hour. The 1971 settlement of Lew's case led to the court awarding her five years of back wages. But this case was not typical. Increasingly, Chinese workers find themselves stuck in low paying jobs with no chances of advancement. More than twenty-five years after the Lew Case, abuses in the garment industry and Chinatown employment in general continue to haunt California.

Filipinos Since 1965: No Longer Strangers at the Gate

Since 1965, the Filipino immigrant has been a professional who assimilates easily into the general population. Unlike the Chinese, the Filipinos no longer head for the little Manila Towns, and San Francisco's Kearny Street Filipino community has vanished. From 1965 to 1996, Filipino immigrants represented the largest Asian group to enter California.

The connection between the Philippines and California is a long and tenuous one. After almost a half-century of American colonial rule, the Philippines became independent and since the mid-1920s, Filipinos settled in California. The Clark Air Base and the Subic Bay Naval Base are two American facilities that employed Filipinos in the Philippines. As a result of this employment, many Filipinos migrated to California because of their pleasant experiences working for the U.S. Government.

Recent Filipino immigrants are often women who are trained as nurses as well as teachers, accountants and business people. Only one of ten Filipino immigrants is a laborer and almost 70% are professional and technical workers. The Filipino has a strong business, cultural, educational and political presence in the Golden State.

Education and politics are the main reason for Filipino immigration. From 1965 to 1985, the oppressive policies of Philippine President Ferdinand Marcos led to an exodus by the middle class. When Corazon Aquino replaced Marcos in the mid-1980s, there was little change in the internal corruption of the Philippine Government, but there was a sense of democracy and oppor-

tunity previously unknown in the Philippines. However, immigration to California continued, and the Filipino became an integral part of the Golden State.

The rise of educated Filipinos created a backlash. The *Los Angeles Times*, in a 1972 article, described an employment market glutted with skilled Filipino workers. In the Philippines, where the number of college graduates was second only to the United States, Filipinos found it difficult to secure employment. So immigration to California was a natural choice.

As Filipino nurses and doctors dominated the newly formed medical organizations, there was organized protest against them. The 50,000 Filipino nurses working in the United States earned twenty times their Philippine wage. The Teamsters Union complained about the large number of Filipino nurses who were nonunion workers. This forced the Kaiser Permanente Medical Organization to defend its use of skilled Filipino nurses and the resulting publicity confirmed their excellent medical training. Few Californians realized that even more Filipino doctors migrated to California. The University of Santo Tomas Medical School had more doctors employed in California than any other foreign medical school. By the 1990s, nearly one of four foreign doctors came from the Philippines.

Koreans: The Post 1965 Second Wave

Prior to the Immigration Act of 1965, Koreans were a hidden minority. They were small in numbers and integrated into the general population. Then the Immigration Law of 1965 helped to create a Koreatown on Olympic Boulevard in Los Angeles. The almost 200,000 Koreans who live in this Los Angeles neighborhood feel at home with churches, nightclubs, retail stores and even Korean Rotary and Kiwanis clubs.

The California Korean is typically college educated, a technical worker or a professional still retaining strong loyalty to the homeland. The vast majority of Koreans are married and apply for citizenship after the mandatory five year wait. There is a business side to the Korean character and a strong belief in technology. These values are nurtured in Korea and find ready acceptance in the Golden State. So Koreans who settle in California easily find work in the Silicon Valley near San Jose or in Los Angeles's Koreatown.

Much like Filipinos, the Koreans include medical professionals with doctors, dentists, nurses and pharmacists in abundance. In California the first wave of discrimination was against Korean doctors. Because they specialized in anesthesiology and radiology, they were shunned by surgeons and internal medicine specialists. The medical professionals believe that these areas of medicine require less skill, and the American Medical Association has done nothing to erase this racist stereotype.

There were some outright examples of racism in recognizing Korean professionals. For example, California law excluded Korean pharmacists from taking the licensing exam, and, in Los Angeles, there were more than 300 experienced pharmacists working in a garment factory.

As a result of discriminating laws, many professionally trained Koreans have become small business people. By the mid-1980s, Koreans had made inroads into Californian's lucrative fruit and vegetable markets. With a strong work ethic, Koreans have also prospered in small restaurants, donut shops and service businesses.

Swap meets are one of the most lucrative Korean businesses. The swap meets are indoor flea markets that operate every day of the week with discount prices on clothing, electronic goods and a wide range of other consumer items. In Los Angeles, there are 905 Korean owned swap meets. The hostility toward Koreans was evident when African American and Latino customers complained that they were rude. The Los Angeles Police Department pointed out that there were four times the number of robberies at Korean businesses than any other ethnic group.

The primary reason for hostility to Korean businesses is their unrestricted use of rotating credit associations known as kyes. They have used these self-help credit facilities to raise funds to purchase many of the liquor stores in the predominantly black South Central Los Angeles district. Part of the blame for the rise of Korean liquor stores is due to African American businessmen selling these stores at an inflated price of about $300,000 when the stores were worth half that amount. The Korean immigrants could not find work, thus they raised money from kyes to purchase these businesses. The deregulation of liquor prices created enormous profits, but this also opened up the question of the Koreans exploiting the African American community. As the Reverend Jesse Jackson suggested, the Koreans looked to the easiest way of making a living. Jackson's criticism was unfair and intensified racial differences.

The rap artist Ice Cube warned Korean businessmen in his song "Black Korea" to respect African American heritage or, as Ice Cube sang, "we'll burn your store right down to a crisp." Ice Cube's CD *Death Certificate* was so popular that even conservative black ministers held it up in church to address the problem of Korean businesses in the South Central District of Los Angeles.

Republican Governor Pete Wilson never addressed the growing hostility between Korean businessmen and the African American community. As he entered his second term, Governor Wilson did little, if anything, to ease the racial tensions engulfing California. Then, as the 1996 Presidential preferential primaries approached, Wilson used racial problems as a main point in his bid for the Republican presidential nomination. By doing so, Wilson followed a long line of right wing, demagogic politicians who preyed on white fears to further a political career built on innuendo and misrepresentation of the ethnic population. The problems in Los Angeles were ignored by Governor Wilson and most politicians. Los Angeles Police Chief Willie Williams seldom mention black-Korean differences. Once again, these racial problems were due to ineffective LAPD leadership.

Much of the blame for not handling these racial problems was due to the ineffective leadership of Deputy Chief Matthew Hunt. Not only did Hunt fail to recognize the serious problems between Korean Americans and African Americans, but he praised the Koreans while suggesting that blacks were prone to crime. Throughout the 1980s, there were serious confrontations, and soon Korean merchants began arming themselves. Finally, on March 16, 1991, an incident took place that almost caused a riot. Korean shopkeeper Soon Ja Du shot a fifteen year old African American girl, Latasha Harlims, to death over a dispute involving a bottle of orange juice. Had the police recognized and dealt with the problem, this tragedy might have been averted. Deputy Chief Hunt, who commanded the South Central District LAPD facility, did little to inspire confidence or respect from the community.

The roots of Korean American and African American differences go back to the 1970s when the largely middle class, college educated Koreans had no other place to work than in low income Los Angeles areas. The Korean businessmen who came into Los Angeles had sums of money ranging from $60,000 to $250,000 to invest in small businesses. As a result, Koreans became an integral part of the L. A. small business community.

The average income of Koreans in Los Angeles in the 1980s was more than $40,000 while the African American population made just over $20,000. This was another reason for viewing Koreans as exploiters. By the 1980s, Korean owned businesses numbered more than half of all investments in the South Central Los Angeles area.

Annie Cho, a former executive director of the Korean American Grocers Associations, known as KAGRO, suggested that hostility toward Korean merchants was due to the collapse of the local economy. She complained that "the economy has been very bad, people are losing their jobs." Cho also stereotyped the black population. She labeled African Americans as the least likely to succeed because they watch an inordinate amount of television and are influenced by crime shows. The average Korean businessmen in the black community often describe his customers as "criminals, welfare recipients and drug addicts." This attitude outraged the African American community and resulted in numerous boycotts.

A Korean radio station, KBLA, announced that the boycotts might lead to violence. The LAPD seemed disinterested in protecting Korean businesses, and Radio Korea, as KBLA was known, intensified the hostility by urging Koreans to arms themselves against the black invasion. Someone needed to step in, but the politicians wouldn't intervene, and the LAPD acted as though everything was fine.

When the boycotts began in the 1980s, Danny Bakewell who was representing KAGRO announced that Korean businesses would submit to a good business practices code. Price gouging, rudeness and lack of services were issues that incensed the African American community. Bakewell vowed to bring in good business practices and a fair price. KAGRO also announced that it would provide 100 jobs for South Central Los Angeles residents. This was not enough as the Central District was once again preparing to explode.

The rise of Korean businesses in the South Central District and the growing feeling that Korean merchants were exploiting African Americans, created a hostile environment. Black ministers complained that the Korean grocers and liquor store owners charged exhorbitant prices to build their fortunes.

By the late 1980s, Korean Americans owned more than 425 million dollars worth of businesses and property in the South Central Los Angeles District. Despite their successes, Koreans still used the word "han" to describe their experiences in the Golden State. Han means sorrow or anger, and some Koreans suggest that they suffer from hwabyong, a sense of frustration and rage following misfortune.

Southeast Asian Immigrants and the New California

The passage of the Indochina Migration and Refugee Assistance Act of 1975, Refugee Act of 1980 and the Amerasian Homecoming Act of 1987 began the flow of Southeast Asian immigrants into California. Politicians recognized that they could lure voters to the polls with anti-Asian statements. Governor Pete Wilson was in the forefront of this rhetoric, and by 1990, he built a political career on warning Californians about "foreign influences."

Then the U.S. Congress restricted the number of Asian professionals and other workers allowed to immigrate and demanded employment verification for the newly arrived Southeast Asian worker. As a result, the number of nurses, doctors and other professionals was reduced. Despite these restrictions, large numbers of Southeast Asian immigrants settled in California and the Federal Government reimbursed the state for cash assistance, medical treatment and social services.

Because of strong family tradition, Southeast Asian families who were separated by the war were reunited in California. More than 40% of all refugees from Vietnam, Laos and Cambodia settled in California. Generally, they were less educated, poorer and found it difficult to adapt to city life. Gravitating toward small businesses, the Cambodians and Laotians opened donut shops, 7-11 franchises, small convenience stores and liquor emporiums. With a large family unit, it was easy to make a decent living.

Asian Americans in the Work Force: The Recent Experiences

Larry Alcantara is a Filipino American who is a middle manager for a Californian city government office. One day, his boss called him into the office and directed Alcantara to discipline an incompetent employee. The disciplined worker was African American and Alcantara wondered if he was selected for his supervisory position because he was an Asian American. "I think we are being used as pawns in corporate and government jobs." Many other Asians echoed Alcantara's complaint that Asians were a model minority.

By the late 1980s, a "racial bourgeoisie" of Asian American bosses had surfaced in California government. Some years ago, Carey McWilliams complained about the "model Asian" stereotype. As McWilliams suggested, the African American population worked too slow and the Asians too fast. Both views, McWilliams argued, were unfair ones. In 1995 House Speaker Newt Gingrich reinforced this stereotype by complaining that Asian Americans were the victims of race based preferences. Gingrich's agenda was to dismantle affirmative action, and he erroneously pointed to Asian American workers as examples of a minority group that was successful without quotas or affirmative action.

In the work place, Asian American bosses are often a buffer between white executives and African American and Mexican American employees. "If white, historically, is the top of the racial hierarchy...and black...is the bottom, will yellow assume the place of the racial middle?" Professor Mari Matsuda of Georgetown University Law School asked in a San Francisco speech. The fear is that Asian Americans are becoming a racial wedge, and this is leading to a growing hostility from other ethnic group.

Lillian Galledo, executive director of Filipinos for Affirmative Action, suggests that Filipinos have not benefited from civil rights legislation. "We don't have a collective history of how to get those benefits," Galledo remarked in reference to protection under Civil Rights Acts. But many Filipinos disagree with Galledo's beliefs. Diosdado Banatao, a forty-nine-year-old Filipino American executive in the Silicon Valley argued that "merit not race" is the way to judge people.

By the mid-1990s the controversy over Asians in the work place created some nasty repercussions. Although the status of Asians in California has dramatically improved there are still tensions that need solutions. If the Golden State is to develop a harmonious civilization, it will need to create greater ethnic cooperation and a sense of Anglo understanding which has not been apparent in the twentieth century.

Bibliographical Essay

Robert Fogelson, editor, *The Los Angeles Riots* (New York, 1969) is an important contemporary document analyzing the problems of the McCone Commission. Mark Baldassare, ed., *The Los Angeles Riots: Lessons for the Urban Future* (Boulder, 1994) is an excellent collection of essays comparing the Watts Riot of 1965 with the Los Angeles Riots of 1992. Also see, Armando Navarro, "The South Central Los Angeles Eruption: A Latino Perspective," *Amerasia Journal*, 19, no 2 (1993), pp. 69-85.

The best study of the Watts Riot is Gerald Horne, *Fire This Time: The Watts Uprising and the 1960s* (Charlottesville, 1995). Also see, Thomas Muller, *Immigrants and the American City* (New York, 1993).

For Los Angeles, see Spencer Crump, *Black Riots in Los Angeles* (Los Angeles, 1966), Mike Davis, *City of Quartz: Excavating the Future of Los Angeles* (New York, 1993), Raphael J. Sonenshein, *Politics in Black and White: Race and Power in Los Angeles* (Princeton, 1993) and David Rieff, *Los Angeles: Capital of the Third World* (New York, 1991). A contemporary journalistic account of the Watts riot with a scholarly perspective is Jerry Cohen and William S. Murphy, *Burn, Baby, Burn!: The Los Angeles Race Riot, August, 1965* (New York, 1966).

B. Gordon Wheeler, *Black California: The History of African-Americans in the Golden State* (New York, 1993) is an excellent source. On Huey P. Newton and the Black Panthers, see Hugh Pearson, *The Shadow of the Panther: Huey Newton and the Price of Black Power in America* (New York, 1994) and Reginald Major's, *A Panther Is a Black Cat* (New York,1971). For the memoirs of a participant, see Bobby Seale, *Seize the Time* (New York, 1970, reprinted 1991). Also see Elaine Brown's thoughtful memoir, *A Taste of Power: A Black Woman's Story* (New York, 1992) and Maulana Karenga, *The Roots of the U.S. / Panther Conflict: The Perverse and Deadly Games People Play* (San Diego, 1976).

Ronald Takaki, *Strangers From A Different Shore: A History of Asian Americans* (New York, 1990), Sucheng Chan, *Asian Americans: An Interpretive History* (Boston, 1991) and H. Brett Melendy, *Asians In America: Filipinos, Koreans and East Indians* (Boston, 1977) are the best studies of the California Asian population.

For Koreans, see Regina Freer, "Black Korean Conflict," Mark Baldassare, editor, *The Los Angeles Riots: Lessons for the Urban Future* (San Francisco, 1994), pp. 175-203, Ivan Light and Edna Bonacich, *Immigrant Entrepreneurs: Koreans in Los Angeles, 1965-1982* (Berkeley, 1988), Sumi K. Cho, "Korean Americans vs. African Americans: Conflict and Construction," Robert Gooding-Williams, *Reading Rodney King, Reading Urban Uprisings* (New

York, 1993) and Eui-Young Yu, et al., eds., *Koreans in Los Angeles* (Los Angeles, 1982).

A brilliant reinterpretation of ethnic problems in California is contained in the last section of Philip L. Fradkin's book, *The Seven States of California: A Human and Natural History* (New York, 1995). This part of Fradkin's book entitled "The Profligate Province" is an important inquiry into the racial strife that has dominated recent California history.

To understand violence in recent California history see Robert M. Fogelson, *Violence as Protest* (Garden City, N.Y., 1971) and the

essays in Spencer C. Olin, *Racism in California* (New York, 1972).

For issues of race, class and change in recent California, see, for example, Roger Lotchin, *Fortress California, 1910-1961: From Warfare to Welfare* (New York, 1992).

Recent Filipino reflections on the Golden State are offered in Yen Le Espiritu, *Filipino American Lives* (Philadelphia, 1995). On Monterey Park, California see, Timothy P. Fong, *The First Suburban Chinatown: The Remaking of Monterey Park, California* (Philadelphia, 1994).

15

Los Angeles Racism

From Rodney King to O.J. Simpson, Race and Class in Southern California

Los Angeles is a city beset by historical problems. Labor violence, urban riots and controversy over immigrants have made the City of the Angels a volatile town. As the 1990s dawned, Los Angeles's first African American Mayor, Tom Bradley, announced that black/Korean problems were improving and a new spirit of cooperation was dawning. This was wishful thinking in the midst of Bradley's fifth term, and the Mayor's comments suggested that Los Angeles was ignoring its problems.

By 1992, Los Angeles was a cauldron of racial discontent as African American, Asian and Latino activists challenged Mayor Bradley to produce jobs, provide adequate housing and put an end to violence and gang warfare. The Mayor responded by stating that California's economy provided new jobs and that the tensions which had been going on for four decades, between the black dominated Central District and the L. A. Police Department had ended.

Mayor Bradley's politics no longer inspired confidence, and the Los Angeles Times urged him to clean up the problems tearing the city apart. The honeymoon was over; Bradley was losing his power. But, in many ways, Bradley's political career mirrored the opportunity and pitfalls in California.

When Bradley was hired as a Los Angeles police officer, he went to school at night and became a lawyer. He also rose through the ranks to become police chief. Eventually, he entered politics and in the mid-1960s, Bradley was a key Los Angeles city council member. The city was in a state of turmoil and more than 2,000 members of local law enforcement agencies belonged to the ultra right-wing John Birch Society. The more conservative officers and firefighters formed the Fire and Police Research Association and published a magazine, Fi-Po News, which criticized local ethnic groups. Council member Bradley never uttered a critical word as police and fire department employees pushed a right-wing, often racist, political agenda.

In 1972, despite the volatile nature of Los Angeles politics, Bradley won the first of five races for mayor, and in 1982, he was almost elected as California's Democratic governor. Bradley's political career appeared to be on the verge of state or national office. But he never broke out of local politics because he was shortsighted. Power corrupted Mayor Bradley, and he accepted too many positions on bank boards and corporations. These financial arrangements led to charges of political intrigue and pork barrel politics.

Finally, in 1989, a scandal erupted linking Bradley to a Chinatown bank where he served on the board of directors. The Mayor had made a phone call to the Los Angeles treasurer which resulted in the bank receiving preferential treatment. The *Los Angeles Times* reported that Bradley was serving on a number of boards and had business interests that were far ranging. Soon, the *Los Angeles Times* charged that Mayor Bradley made dubious financial transactions, and this fueled the hostility toward his policies.

There was also a long history of Los Angeles police brutality. The African American and Mexican American communities were hit hardest by institutionalized racism. Gangs, drugs and a sense of despair provided a different focus for young people. The street corner man, the drug dealer, the pimp and the hoodlum dominated in the ghetto. Rap musicians created a multi-million dollar industry with gangster rap songs glorifying inner city values. These new heroes presented city police with a host of problems.

Los Angeles was the California city most troubled by the last quarter century of growth. Economic rewards were uneven and tended to ignore Latinos and blacks while allowing the Koreans, Vietnamese, Cambodians, Laotians, Asian Indians, Japanese and Chinese to prosper.

The number of new Korean businesses proliferating in black neighborhoods led to conflict. Complaints over police conduct, an exclusion of some minorities in the employment market and second rate schools produced a sense of hopelessness which periodically exploded into riots. The Rodney King incident soon brought these issues into the public forum.

The Rodney King Incident and Los Angeles Police Brutality: A Case Study in Ethnic Problems

At approximately 12:40 p.m. on March 3, 1991, an amateur photographer, George Holliday, videotaped a group of Los Angeles police officers beating an unarmed, non-resistant black man. When this vicious attack ended, twenty-five-year-old Rodney King, an unemployed construction worker, suffered eleven skull fractures, a crushed cheekbone, a broken ankle, a burn on his wrist and internal damages. He stood before the video camera beaten to a pulp by laughing policemen. Holliday, a white plumbing company manager, realized that he had a hot commercial product. The eighty-one second video captured the sense of police violence and brutality in Los Angeles.

The controversy began when King's speeding car was chased on Highway 210 by CHP officers Melanie Singer and her husband Timothy. King was driving a white Hyundai at high speeds of 110 to 115 m.p.h. Worried that they could not catch King, the CHP officers called a Los Angeles Police dispatcher and requested assistance.

A Los Angeles Police Department car assigned to Officers Laurence Powell and Timothy Wind joined the pursuit. After Rodney King was stopped, more than twenty Los Angeles police officers were at the scene. The officers informed the CHP that they would handle the incident. However, no one at the scene realized that George Holliday's apartment afforded a perfect view of this episode.

The Sunday, March 3, 1991, incident took place a few minutes after midnight. But it was a couple of days before a local television station broadcasted King's beating. At first, Holliday offered the tape to a commander in one of the police substations. The police refused the tape and Holliday sold it to a TV station. After a local television station purchased Holliday's tape, the confrontation became national news. Sergeant Stacey Koon was shown ordering his men to hit Rodney King in the elbows, knees and wrists to make him submit to police procedures. A tazer gun used by Sergeant Koon to subdue King prompted some police officers to laugh at the spectacle. After King was subdued, Officer Thomas Briseno stepped on King's neck because he saw his leg lift. Later, Officer Briseno testified that he feared King's hand was headed for his waistband, so stepping on his neck, Briseno remarked, was reasonable force.

The King beating was an unspeakable horror that angered African Americans and shamed their white counterparts. There was no question that the police were out of control. When a Los Angeles television station, KTLA, bought the tape and broadcasted it, there was an immediate controversy. Then, Cable News Network (CNN) broadcasted the tape, and it resulted in an immediate investigation. By March 6, the Federal Bureau of Investigation, the Los Angeles District Attorney's Office and the Los Angeles Police Department's Internal Affairs Division had investigators collecting evidence.

Rodney King wasn't the entire issue. The real controversy was Los Angeles's police brutality, inept leadership by a wide variety of police chiefs, including the present one, Daryl Gates, and the condescending politicians who assured the voters that everything was all right. The Grand Jury investigation was swift, complete and professionally handled. The evidence of police misconduct was overwhelming.

Consequently, Officers Laurence Powell, Timothy Wind, Ted Briseno and Sergeant Stacey Koon were indicted for the King beating and also charged with filing a false police report. On March 14, the officers pleaded not guilty. Soon thereafter Mayor Tom Bradley appointed former Deputy Secretary of State Warren Christopher to head a commission to investigate brutality in the LAPD. Then Chief Daryl Gates was suspended for a variety of leadership failures, and he eventually announced his retirement.

The Christopher Commission issued its report on July 9, 1991 and included the recommendation that Chief Gates retire. The commission also listed a series of procedural and structural reforms necessary to restore confidence in the LAPD. The commission suggested that the LAPD eliminate racism by establishing "community policing." This meant that Los Angeles needed to focus on crime prevention. The presence of more neighborhood police substations, increased drug education in the schools, a minority hiring program and police living in the community were some suggestions for "community policing." One LAPD officer remarked: "Now we are supposed to be social workers; Chief Gates wanted us to be Marines." Not surprisingly, there was some confusion among officers about their role.

Although the Christopher Commission concluded that police behavior bordered on outright hostility toward Los Angeles's multiethnic population, there was no immediate movement for reform. The professional organization representing the police officers was hostile to change and made it clear that the LAPD would not implement any reforms. As late as 1994, there were no civilians on the Los Angeles citizens review board and the police officers were in charge of monitoring their conduct.

Initially, the Grand Jury refused to indict any of the police officers who were bystanders. The *Los Angeles Times* praised the Grand Jury, but the African American press had another view. The *Los Angeles Sentinel*, a moderate black newspaper that began publishing in 1932, questioned the Grand Jury's decision. The level of corruption and police malfeasance, the *Los Angeles Sentinel* reported, was a time bomb ready to explode.

When the Grand Jury did issue its recommendation, Officers Koon, Briseno, Wind and Powell were indicted for the King beating. Immediately, the question of a fair trial for the four accused policemen was raised. The attorneys for the four white Los Angeles police officers pointed out that they could not obtain a fair trial in Los Angeles, and the case was moved to Simi Valley where a large contingent of LAPD officers lived. Ironically, more Los Angeles police officers lived in this sleepy suburb north of Los Angeles than in any other city.

The police officers also benefited from the Second District Court of Appeals' decision to remove a black Judge, Bernard Kamins, from the King case. The court ruled that there had been improper communication between the judge and the prosecutors. The new Los Angeles Superior Court Judge Stanley M. Weisberg was white and had an excellent reputation. He selected Ventura County and the city of Simi Valley for the trial, and the scales of justice tipped in favor of the police officers. Whether intentional or not, this decision led to an acquittal for the four officers. It was the nature of Simi Valley's suburban mentality that lent itself to the acquittal.

A small and remote suburb, Simi Valley was two percent black and, according to the LAPD attorneys, not subject to Los Angeles media pressure. The town housed the Ronald Reagan Presidential Library, and a city pamphlet boasted "affordable housing for everyone." The majority was white, middle class, well-educated and conservative Republican. Brian Arkin, a Simi Valley resident, observed: "We like living in a place with educated people....I don't believe skin color is a criteria." Yet, few African Americans lived in Simi Valley. Local residents described their suburb as "safe." The truth is that Simi Valley's white, middle class

population was prone to join political organizations like the John Birch Society and the National Rifle Association.

On April 29, 1992, the white police officers were cleared of assault charges by the Simi Valley jury which was composed of six white men, four white women, one Hispanic and one Asian. They had many reasons for their decision. The Holliday tape was a key piece of evidence in the acquittal as the defense attorneys did a marvelous job suggesting the tape proved that King was resisting and acting crazy.

The jury was a conservative group who had little understanding about people in low income neighborhoods or how they were treated differently by the police. But behind closed door, the jurors were faced with four dissidents who refused to consider the evidence. They were pro-police and demanded an acquittal. The rest of the jury went along. The Hispanic juror had some minor reservation, and one female juror who appeared on Larry King's CNN show made it clear that the men on the jury were pro-police.

The Simi Valley case was prosecuted by an African American lawyer, Terry L. White, who tried the case with little enthusiasm. White was frustrated by the jury and did his best to present a moderate, reasoned prosecution. The result, unfortunately, was to make his case appear weak and some jurors believed that White's arguments lacked conviction. A more plausible answer is that Los Angeles District Attorney Ira Reiner showed little interest in the prosecution.

Within hours of the verdict, two black neighborhoods in the South Central Los Angeles District erupted into a three day riot. Property in an area of almost 60 square miles was damaged. The riots began on Wednesday afternoon at 3:43 p.m. when the police received a report that a young man in Hyde Park threw a brick at a passing pickup truck. A mob moved in and attacked and beat a white pedestrian and threw him into a dumpster. As the crowd assembled and drifted toward shops and markets, systematic looting began. Much of this violence targeted Korean shopkeepers. As police made arrests for vandalism more than half of those taken into custody were Hispanic, not African American.

A second wave of violence began at 4:17 p.m. at Normandie and Florence when a group of young blacks began throwing rocks at motorists. At 6:30 p.m., an 18 wheel truck hauling 27 tons of sand mistakenly drove into the intersection. The white driver, Reginald Denny, was pulled from the cab and beaten viciously while TV cameras recorded the scene. Denny was rescued by an African American man and woman who took him to Freeman Memorial Hospital.

Soon the police headquarters, Parker Center, was picketed by the radical Progressive Labor Party and the Revolutionary Community Party. They charged the LAPD with police brutality and demanded Chief Daryl Gates's resignation. Mayor Bradley requested the National Guard to maintain order. Governor Pete Wilson agreed that Los Angeles was in a state of seize. These events shouldn't have surprised anyone. They were simply part of the larger racial history of southern California.

Federal Punishment for the LAPD: The Federal Civil Rights Trial of King's Assailants

The demonstrations over the Simi Valley trial pointed to the Los Angeles Police Department as the catalyst to insurrection in the black community. Lou Cannon, a national columnist for the *Washington Post*, labeled L. A. "a police state." Joe Walker, a black L. A. police officer, recalled that his first partner stopped any black motorist who drove a better car than the officer. Mike Rothmiller, a white LAPD officer who left the force, described "Negrophobia" as a

part of the police mentality. These attitudes and their resulting policies prompted President George Bush to direct the Justice Department to prosecute the officers who beat Rodney King for violating his federal civil rights.

The Federal Government entered the King case when the Justice Department sent Barry F. Kowlaski, Deputy Chief from the Justice Department's Civil Rights Bureau, and Steven D. Clymer, from the Los Angeles Bureau of the U.S. Attorney's Office, to investigate the King case. They concluded his civil rights had been violated and the stage was set for a federal trial.

In February 1993, a second trial for civil rights violations began in the Central Federal District Court in Los Angeles. The trial also called into question LAPD procedures and exposed the brutal racist philosophies in the department. Officer Powell was convicted of beating King during the arrest, and Sergeant Koon was found guilty of allowing the beating to take place. Both men went to prison in October 1993 and Koon's lawyer, Theodore Olson, began an appeal. Officers Wind and Briseno didn't file appeals and simply served their sentences.

There was a controversy over lenient sentencing and the Court of Appeals in San Francisco upheld its convictions in 1994 but ordered new sentencing after ruling that the original jail terms were too lenient.

Chief Willie Williams, an African American, defended the LAPD and suggested that the Rodney King case was an aberration and that the police didn't mistreat the black community. But a racially mixed jury convicted the officers, and they were sent to prison. Almost a year and a half later the O.J. Simpson murder case would once again raise the specter of LAPD racism.

The O.J. Simpson Case and the Question of Los Angeles Racism

On June 13, 1994 the body of Nicole Brown Simpson, the former wife of professional football legend O.J. Simpson, was found brutally murdered alongside a casual acquaintance, Ronald Goldman. When police contacted Simpson, who was in Chicago on a business trip, he expressed concern and remorse.

Under the glare of TV cameras, Simpson returned from Chicago, and cooperated with the police. As detectives searched through Nicole Brown Simpson's home and later O.J.'s Rockingham estate, they found evidence which seemed to link Simpson to the murders. One of the key pieces of evidence discovered at O.J.'s home was a bloodstained glove that matched one found at the murder scene. After an exhaustive search of Simpson's estate and the murder scene, the LAPD believed that it had the evidence to prosecute the former football legend.

When Los Angeles District Attorney, Gil Garcetti, held a press conference to announce an arrest warrant naming O.J. Simpson as the alleged killer, he looked more like a candidate for governor than a law enforcement officer. Garcetti lectured the press on domestic violence, praised the LAPD's diligent investigation and concluded that justice would be quick and swift. In his stylish suit and razor cut hair, there was a smugness and arrogance to Garcetti. However, he failed to control the investigative mistakes of the LAPD, and he was never able to answer the media's questions about alleged racism within the department. Eventually, tainted evidence, sloppy police work, racial hostility and a second rate prosecution made the LAPD and the District Attorney's Office appear like a group of amateurs. Garcetti was more interested in appealing to the voters than in reforming the police department or helping his staff prosecute Simpson effectively.

For half a century there were charges of racial abuses made against the Los Angeles Police Department and each internal investigation reported that there was no racism. Historically, rather than reform the police, the Mayor and District Attorney, the various investigations into city malfeasance had been handled by hand picked commissions. The Christopher Commission was no exception and while it had the illusion of independence, it was much like past investigative panels. It found that problems could be solved internally by the LAPD. Then, the Simpson case exposed the ugly racism rampant in the LAPD. No one could deny that these problems existed for a century. Although police racism was confined only to a small number of officers and didn't extend to the majority of police employees, the racism which did exist survived due to a code of silence among the officers.

After Garcetti's press conference, no one could find O.J. Simpson. Much of the nation was watching the Houston Rockets on television as they were on their way to winning the NBA title. Suddenly, television news crews interrupted regular programming and showed O.J. Simpson's Chevrolet Bronco driving slowly on the San Diego 405 freeway with thirty CHP officers chasing him. Al (A.C.) Cowling, O.J.'s friend since the San Francisco Hunters Point Project days, was driving and urging Simpson to let the police serve the warrant.

As southern California motorists stopped and waited for Simpson, signs went up reading: "Go O.J." and "We're Behind You Juice." The event took on a tragic, yet comic opera, tone as Simpson finally drove into his Rockingham residence. Speculation that he was leaving the country was rampant. It turned out that O.J. was confused and unsure of his feelings, a natural reaction, whether guilty or innocent, to the events surrounding his wife's death.

Four days after his wife's death, Simpson was arrested, arraigned, denied bail and placed in jail to await a murder trial. The nation was stunned when Simpson was charged with murder, and the case quickly became a media event. Unwittingly, racial issues surfaced from the first day and provided a glimpse of much of what was wrong with California's ethnic climate.

Lance Ito: A Japanese American in Charge of the Simpson Legal Circus

Once he was taken into custody, O.J.'s impending murder trial became a case study in race relations. Even the selection of the judge, Lance Ito, was dictated by questions of fairness and ethnicity. In private discussions among the judiciary, the appointment of a white judge was rejected. The selection of Lance Ito, a Japanese American, was an excellent choice as both the prosecution and defense respected this young, but experienced and fair, judge. Most Californians knew very little about Lance Ito. He was a Japanese American whose parents were interned during World War II in the Heart Mountain, Wyoming camp. When they were released, the Itos resumed their careers as teachers. On August 2, 1950, Lance was born in the Silver Lake section of Los Angeles. It was a multicultural neighborhood, one decidedly blue collar. Aimee Semple McPherson's Four Square Gospel Temple was nearby, and ethnic restaurants, synagogues, Japanese schools and German and Yugoslavian cultural centers existed side by side in this polyglot section of Los Angeles. Young Lance revealed an early capacity for education. At age three, he entered elementary school and demonstrated academic skills. Lance's parents sent him to Japanese school on Saturday to maintain his culture when the other children were playing. Ito

told a Los Angeles television reporter that he resented Japanese school but learned lessons that helped him to handle the multiracial California civilization.

Growing up, young Ito became a cub scout. Soon Lance met Delbert E. Wong, a scoutmaster, who was also California's first Asian judge. They became close friends and Wong encouraged Ito to study law. Eventually, Lance became an Eagle Scout, and with new found confidence, self esteem and character he prepared for college.

Early in his life, when Lance decided to study law, he spent an inordinate amount of time reading. Judge Wong encouraged him and provided reading materials and advice. At John Marshall High School, Lance was president of the student body and remembered as an excellent student, though something of a prankster. In 1968, he entered the University of California, Los Angeles. Robert D. Rose, a college friend, remarked that Ito arrived on campus with "a new Mustang automobile, a girlfriend and a stereo system."

To support himself at UCLA, Ito found a job as director of the parking division. He was a history major and an A student.

"A few beers, some good music and heavy studying" is how one of Ito's friends described him. The prankster side of his personality surfaced at times. A good example of this occurred on December 7, 1968, when Ito streaked down the hall of his dorm naked while chanting "Bonsai, Bonsai" to call attention to the bombing of Pearl Harbor. In four years, Ito graduated with honors and was accepted to the prestigious University of California, Berkeley law school.

In 1972, Ito entered Boalt Law School and graduated in three years. He was hired by a well-known Los Angeles law firm but quit in 1977 to join the Los Angeles District Attorney's Office. Ito hoped to become a trial lawyer. Soon, he was prosecuting organized crime and hard core street gangs. Peter S. Berman, a member of the gang task force, spoke highly of Ito's ability to handle complex cases. While working as an assistant DA, Ito met and married Margaret York.

Ito's reputation as a prosecutor reached its pinnacle in 1986 when he tried a serial killer, Brandon Tholmer and obtained a conviction. Consequently, California Governor George Deukmejian appointed him as a municipal court judge, and in 1989, Ito was elevated to the California Superior Court. He was quickly linked to some of the Golden State's highest profile cases.

In 1991, Ito was the judge in the Charles Keeting fraud trial. The subsequent savings and loan scandal turned into a media event. But Judge Ito prevented the press from turning it into a circus. He was strict, but fair, with the press and the case went to the jury four and a half months early. After Keeting's conviction, the verdict was upheld by an appeals court. The *Los Angeles Times* editorialized that Judge Ito was an outstanding judge with a reputation for fairness.

Ito also presided over the pretrial proceedings of Erik and Lyle Menendez. The Los Angeles Grand Jury indicted the Menendez bothers and later Judge Ito sealed the trial transcripts. He reasoned that there was too much media attention and the conflict between the press' first amendment rights and the defendants' sixth amendment right to a fair trial could only be protected by limiting media access.

Then, Ito presided over Hollywood Madam Heidi Fleiss's arraignment which was followed by the murder indictment of rap star Snoop Doggy Dog. In each of these cases, Ito handled the pretrial proceedings fairly and controlled the press. He was not only a respected judge but also one who was rapidly gaining a reputation for knowledgeable rulings. He appeared to be the perfect judge for the Simpson trial.

The Simpson Trial and Problems of Celebrity Jurisprudence

During the Simpson proceedings, the evidence against the legendary football star was circumstantial. There was no murder weapon, no witnesses, no evidence of conspiracy to commit murder and the prosecution's evidence was largely based on circumstantial evidence, conjecture and DNA testing.

The Simpson dream team of Robert Shapiro, Johnnie Cochran and F. Lee Bailey soon turned into an ever expanding roster of high-priced, skilled attorneys who questioned every step of the prosecution's case. The prosecution hoped that DNA tests would erase any question of Simpson's guilt. But defense lawyers Barry Scheck and Peter Neufeld were brilliant and made the LAPD crime lab look like the three stooges were running the show. Charges that evidence was contaminated appeared credible as Scheck pointed out that DNA tests were not as foolproof as fingerprints. The defense motions become so nasty during the trial that Ron Goldman's father called a number of press conferences to complain about the lawyer's tactics.

As the case progressed, lawyers from all over were asked how to handle the Simpson case. Every day newspapers were filled with quotations from defense attorneys. On CNN, the Larry King Live show had a permanent panel of judges and lawyers who analyzed the trial each night.

The trial created pressure for Simpson news. Not surprisingly, Judge Ito warned the jury not to discuss the case among themselves and he frequently admonished the defense team for its media statements. Finally, Ito attempted to clear the air about the trial by submitting to a number of personal interviews. These forays into the media backfired as he was accused of seeking the spotlight. Ito's interviews suggested that he was shy and uncomfortable with the media.

Judge Ito was interviewed by the *Los Angeles Times* and remarked that "a judge would be crazy to handle the case." When Ito was assigned the case his marriage to the highest ranking woman on the LAPD force was mentioned by the judge who assigned the case. When the defense and prosecution accepted Ito as the judge, they stated that his wife's position in the police department would have no bearing on the case. Later, when the Mark Fuhrman tapes were discovered, Ito's wife became a point of contention because she was mentioned in derogatory terms by Detective Fuhrman.

It was the controversy over his wife that demonstrated Ito's strength of character and high level of integrity. He talked about how "he was pained, as any husband would be" when nasty references were made about his wife. As Ito complained over national television about the unwarranted attack on his wife, a new level of public sympathy and support emerged for the embattled judge, but his problems in the courtroom persisted.

The extensive media coverage concerned It, and he did his best to thwart publicity conscious witnesses who hoped to profit from the trial. The most blatant publicity hound was Faye D. Resnick who wrote a book which claimed that Simpson conspired to kill his wife. In purple prose, Resnick wove lurid tales about taking drugs with O.J., and she ridiculed the defense notion that a Colombian drug cartel murdered Nicole Brown Simpson. Celebrity journalist Dominick Dunne got into the act and defended Resnick in the pages of *Vanity Fair*. Prosecutor Marcia Clark was the only sane voice and she complained that Simpson's guilt became a low priority because of the publicity.

The unwarranted intrusion of celebrity observers was a problem. When the producer of Laugh-In and Real People, George Schlatter, wrote Judge Ito a letter complaining about how the lawyers played to the TV camera, Ito responded by writing a number of news organizations urging them not to print interviews with Resnick for fear of polluting the jury. Although Judge Ito couldn't stop the attorneys from giving out interviews, he vented his displeasure to Johnnie Cochran as the defense team used the media to argue Simpson's innocence.

The media was everywhere during the Simpson trial, and Judge Ito agreed to a personal TV profile that he later regretted. Ito was trying to demystify the legal system through a five part series with a Los Angeles television station. When he was through, the press castigated Ito for these insights into his personal life.

When Tritia Toyota on Channel 2 in Los Angeles conducted the five part interview with Ito, the judge gave out some interesting personal insights. He talked at length about a judge's role in the legal process and was relaxed and entertaining. The fallout from this television appearance was immediate, and he was criticized for being too media conscious. This incident convinced Ito to try to keep the media under control. He also hoped to maintain a low-key-style, and this caused many to misinterpret Ito's abilities.

The Progress of the Simpson Trial: The Media Circus and O.J. Becomes a Spectator

Once the trial began to weave its way through thirty-five weeks of in-depth testimony, Simpson was a minor figure sitting in the shadow of his famous dream team. Robert Shapiro and Johnny Cochran took turns lecturing the army of reporters who waited outside the courtroom. In Cambridge, Massachusetts, Alan Dershowitz watched the case on television and faxed suggestions to his colleagues. Johnnie

Cochran talked about racial problems, conspiracy and botched investigations. Depending on the day of the trail, Cochran argued that the LAPD was stupid, inept and bungling. On days when he discussed conspiracies, Cochran wove tales of police planting evidence.

These outbursts by the defense caused critics to complain that Judge Ito had lost control. He allowed too many witnesses to be called and let them take too long. Among the early prosecution witnesses was Detective Mark Fuhrman. His testimony was quick, decisive and short. It was also perjured and, later in the trial, Fuhrman took the fifth amendment. He refused to incriminate himself. The general consensus was that he had lied on the witness stand.

Fuhrman was the first witness that one of Simpson's defense attorneys, F. Lee Bailey, called a racist. This became the theme of the trial. The Simpson defense team tried the LAPD and the history of the City of the Angels. Suddenly, the O.J. Simpson case mirrored the past half century of California's racial turmoil.

The specter of O.J. Simpson jurors fighting with one another over real and imagined racial slights further added to the Los Angeles mystique. As jurors were systematically eliminated for misconduct, they held press conferences to announce their new books. By examining the Simpson jury, it was obvious that race was the key issue.

The O.J. Simpson Jury and California's Racial Problems

When the jury was being selected for the O.J. Simpson case, Roy Innis, the Chairperson of the Congress of Racial Equality (CORE), visited Los Angeles to talk with the judges and attorneys. Innis hoped to minimize race, and he reminded both sides of Los Angeles's acrimonious racial history.

Although the Simpson jury was predominantly African American, decidedly female, educated in comparison to other Los Angeles jury pools and selected after an exhaustive questionnaire and a great deal of legal wrangling, the members immediately began to fight with one another.

The issue of juror misconduct also reared its ugly head. On April 5, 1995, a thirty-eight-year-old African American juror, Jeanette Harris, was removed from the panel by Judge Lance Ito. Harris's dismissal was due to a police report in 1988 in which she failed to disclose that she accused her husband of domestic violence.

Angry over Judge Ito's abrupt termination of her spot on the jury, Harris arranged an exclusive television interview. On Los Angeles's channel 9, the news anchorwoman interviewed Harris who expressed her scorn and contempt for Prosecutor Marcia Clark and Detective Mark Fuhrman. She then accused Nicole Brown Simpson's sister, Denise, of attempting to gain fame. Harris, the dismissed juror, made it clear that she would have voted for Simpson's acquittal. Suddenly, Judge Ito had a public relations problem as well as an unhappy jury. Harris made it clear that she believed racial tensions were dividing the jury. Johnnie Cochran, Simpson's lead defense attorney, was dismayed and suggested that Harris was "a sympathetic ear." Her attorney, Milton Grimes, used his spot on Larry King's CNN show to strike back at Harris's critics, and he suggested that she was simply a good citizen.

Another Juror Michael Knox was released for failing to report that he had attacked a former girlfriend. Knox was surprised and angry over his dismissal. When his hostility cooled, he teamed up with a professional writer and turned out a quickie book, *The Private Diary of an O.J. Juror*, published by Dove books on July 3, 1995. Knox's insights into race and class problems suggested reasons as to why the Simpson jury was fighting. He also provided some key insights into how African Americans viewed the LAPD double standard and alleged that black Californians had a different view of city government. Clearly, Los Angeles was a city divided by race.

Knox's description of the four African American women who sat in the jury indicated a wide divergence in attitude and opinion about the Simpson case. The commonly held perception that black jurors would not convict an African American defendant were laid to rest in Knox's book and defense attorney Milton Grimes echoed this sentiment on the Larry King Show. There was one problem with the jury: many of them didn't like one of the white jurors.

The white juror, Tracy Kennedy, a fifty-six-year old Amtrak engineer, was described by Knox as "intelligent....Yet T.K. was totally obnoxious." Kennedy was hostile to African Americans, Knox wrote. When he was removed from the jury, Kennedy had copious notes for a proposed book and made a deal with a deputy to hide his notes.

On September 6, 1995, Kennedy appeared on the NBC Dateline television show and remarked that he had considered suicide. Kennedy complained about the embarrassment of being excused from the jury. Ito released Kennedy from jury duty for writing a book. Initially, he denied it. Then, as he appeared on Dateline, Kennedy announced that he had a book ready for release.

There were many problems among the jurors. The most significant hostility was between a Latina woman, Farron Chavarria, and an African American post office manager, Willie Cravin. They glared at each other in an elevator, Judge Ito was told, and after an investigation, they were removed from the jury. Personal animosity was the reason for their dismissal.

Then, as the jury problems relaxed, and the trial seemed to be moving toward a con-

clusion, a bomb shell broke. Detective Mark Fuhrman, one of the earliest prosecution witnesses, became the center of a racial controversy.

Detective Mark Fuhrman: The Grinch Who Stole the O.J. Case and Strange Justice

After more than five months of trial, attorneys Johnnie Cochran and F. Lee Bailey announced that they had evidence to impeach Detective Mark Fuhrman's earlier testimony. It was Fuhrman who had found key evidence, a glove, that linked Simpson to the murders. Cochran and Bailey argued that the Los Angeles Police Department planted evidence. Police Chief Willie Williams denied defense allegations and District Attorney Gil Garcetti called the charges "nonsense." Initially, the allegations against Fuhrman appeared to be little more than a defense plan to continue to argue the conspiracy theory. They needed proof and soon a series of tapes with Fuhrman uttering racial slurs emerged. The Fuhrman tapes were a major turning point in the trial.

During the first five months of the Simpson trial, Cochran and his colleagues attacked the evidence with ferocity, and the Fuhrman tapes seemed to vindicate their charge of tainted evidence. Defense attorneys Cochran, Bailey and Shapiro alleged that the police planted a bloody glove that would link Simpson to the double homicide. Cochran and Bailey suggested that Detective Fuhrman planted the evidence, but the LAPD denied the charges. Then Laura Hart McKinny, a part-time college professor and unpublished screenwriter, was subpoenaed.

In 1985, Fuhrman met McKinny at a restaurant near the UCLA campus. For ten years, McKinny and Fuhrman taped interviews for a collaborative movie. Critics suggested that the amateur screenplay had little appeal, but it was written from a series of interviews with Detective Fuhrman about the LAPD. The evidence in these tapes, the defense suggested, was strong enough to imply racism, planted evidence and sloppy police work.

When Cochran and Simpson's defense team listened to the tapes, they revealed that Fuhrman had used the word "nigger" forty-one times. He had previously testified that he had not used a racial slur during the last ten years. The tapes were viewed by Simpson's defense team as a key piece of evidence to impeach Fuhrman's earlier testimony.

Then, controversy arose once more when the defense requested that Judge Lance Ito allow the tapes to be introduced as evidence. As Ito listened to some of the tapes, a conflict arose because his wife, Margaret York, is a high ranking officer in internal affairs. If Fuhrman violated department policy, she could be assigned to investigate, and then it was revealed that Fuhrman had made abusive statements about the judge's wife.

The McKinny tapes created public hostility toward Fuhrman and the LAPD. But only two small segments were allowed into trial testimony. Johnnie Cochran called it the "most devastating" blow to the defense during the trial. He accused Judge Ito of not being fair and suggested the tapes would impeach much of the LAPD's circumstantial evidence. An angry Ito responded by pointing out that the defense attorneys had failed to prove that Fuhrman planted the glove.

Another devastating part of the McKinny tapes was Fuhrman's statement that the police covered up crimes. Prosecutor Christopher Darden unwittingly elicited this information from McKinny in a vicious cross examination. However, when McKinny finally left the stand, she had seriously damaged the prosecution's case with her allegations of "police cover-ups."

On September 6, 1995, Detective Mark Fuhrman, now retired and living in Idaho, returned to Judge Ito's court and took the fifth amendment when asked if he had lied or planted evidence. Fuhrman visibly nervous, looked tired and continually turned to his attorney for advice. Once a star witness, Fuhrman was reduced to an object of hatred and contempt. He became the grinch who stole the O.J. Simpson trial.

By September 1995, the defense attempted to bring Fuhrman back in front of the jury to take the fifth amendment. Judge Ito prevented this by ruling that Detective Fuhrman would not be allowed to testify. He also stated that the jury would be told "that Fuhrman was unavailable as a witness and the jury could consider that in determining his credibility." Prosecutor Clark, in a fit of rage, appealed Ito's decision and publicly admonished him for a faulty decision. The Appeals Court agreed and reversed Judge Ito's ruling.

The endless appeals continued when Johnnie Cochran filed another motion to bring Fuhrman to the stand. The Appeals Court ruled that the defense could not recall Detective Fuhrman or have his testimony stricken from the record. This set the stage for the final summation of the case.

These events also set off a flurry of charges and counter charges that prolonged the trial. District Attorney Garcetti held a press conference, after the appellate court ruling, and suggested that overturning Judge Ito's ruling was unprecedented. In a monumental act of poor taste, Garcetti attacked Ito and suggested that he was mishandling the case. Johnnie Cochran reacted angrily, and the defense team decided to extend its closing arguments.

Throughout the trial, Judge Ito's attitude was one of fairness and impartiality, but he became visibly angry during the last month of the trial. He spent hours listening to specious arguments as Prosecutor Marcia Clark and Defense Attorney Johnnie Cochran went beyond the bounds of good taste and professional ethics, and through all of it, Judge Ito presided fairly.

In the final summation, the defense spent its time discrediting the gloves which didn't fit O.J. and concentrated upon a DNA scientist who argued that the government lab was unreliable. Earlier the defense brought Dr. Henry Lee, a world renowned scientist, to testify about the contaminated evidence. A man of great integrity and scientific precision, Lee's testimony hurt the prosecution. The prosecution responded with a vicious attack upon Dr. Lee that had subtle racial overtones and featured testimony from FBI agents that Lee had made look foolish in previous cases.

Outraged at the attack on his credibility, Dr. Lee held a press conference and stood behind his scientific observations. He stuck with his finding that there was more than one shoeprint at the murder scene. When an FBI agent suggested that Dr. Lee was wrong and hurled aspersions on his scientific character, it was the first time that he was attacked in court. Dr. Lee, the number one forensic scientist in the nation, vigorously defended his findings. The FBI agent was equally confident, and it was up to the jury to decide who was right.

One of the most bizarre days in the trial occurred when two Mafia informants who had entered the witness protection program, Craig "Tony the Animal" Flato and his brother, testified but weren't seen on television. Judge Ito blacked out their testimony because they were in the witness protection program. They were called by the defense to suggest that lead investigator Philip Vannatter considered Simpson a suspect before analyzing the evidence. The Flattos were arrogant, nasty and threatening on the stand and didn't give the answers that Johnnie Cochran hoped for and their testimony embarrassed everyone.

During the last two weeks of the trial, Judge Ito was visibly angry with the petty, vicious attitudes on both sides. The trial degenerated into an attack upon the LAPD, and the public verdict was guilty. The city needed to reform its police practices. This was a historical problem, and few people understood how to correct it.

Finally, on September 22, 1995, the prosecution and defense rested, and O. J. Simpson was allowed to address the court with the jury absent. Simpson's remarks were as controversial as the trial. Standing in court in an Armani suit, he waived his right to testify and made an emotional speech proclaiming his innocence. It was a brilliant move on Simpson's part as he appealed to the public to accept his innocence. He took a verbal shot at Prosecutor Marcia Clark when he remarked: "I have confidence, a lot more it seems than Miss Clark has, of their integrity..." After Simpson's emotional plea and self-righteous declaration of his innocence, an angry Clark wondered if the words would get back to the jury.

Simpson's emotional speech prompted Fred Goldman, the father of murder victim Ronald Goldman, to hold an impromptu press conference, and in choking, sobbing tones he criticized Simpson for his public grandstanding. Like many observers, Goldman suggested that the "court of public opinion" was where O.J. was trying his case.

After thirty-five weeks of courtroom argument, the Simpson trial was closing in on a verdict. In late September 1995, as the closing arguments in the Simpson case raged, Los Angles, once again was put on trial.

The prosecution in the Simpson case concluded its arguments with Marcia Clark methodically building a mountain of evidence against the former football star. Clark also explained in uneasy and at times defensive language that Detective Fuhrman was not a credible witness and that the crime lab had made mistakes, then she pulled the evidence together against Simpson. Her colleague, Christopher Darden, was stronger and more convincing as he pointed his finger at Simpson and called him a murderer. Darden was effective in using photographs of Nicole Simpson's bruised face and he called these photos and her phone calls about the beatings "a road map to the killer."

As Johnnie Cochran arose to address the jury he began by calling detective Mark Fuhrman a "lying genocidal racist." Then Cochran systematically tore apart the officers who investigated the case. "They are setting up this man," Cochran raged. The glove found at Simpson's estate had a Caucasian hair on it, Cochran screamed. The implication was clear that Fuhrman planted it.

Cochran's performance was a spellbinding one which cast doubt upon the prosecution and reiterated charges of official racism. Calling lead detective Philip Vannatter "a liar," Cochran urged the jury to acquit. It was a sad moment for Los Angeles and suggested why the city had such a long legacy of racial problems.

The O.J. Simpson Verdict and the Fragmented Dream

When the Simpson jury returned with a no guilty verdict after only three and a half hours of deliberation, there was shock. Harold Fijman, an immigrant from Honduras who owns Aaron's Body Shop in Hayward, California was sitting in his office smoking a cigarette and watching television. "I was shocked with the quick acquittal," Fijman remarked. "Come to think of it, I wasn't shocked, I was mad as hell. The bastard bought his freedom. Justice is how much money you have and how much freedom you can buy with it." Fijman's remarks were echoed by many Californians. There was also dissent to this view.

Black Californians viewed the Simpson acquittal as justice.

Looking Back Upon Los Angeles History: The Forces Shaping the Southern California Racial Character

The controversies over the Rodney King beating and O.J. Simpson murder trial suggest that racial insensitivity, tourist boosterism, Hollywood myth making and repressive, conservative politics dominated in Los Angeles. The line between personal fantasy and social reality was difficult for the average Los Angeles citizen to perceive and there was a Disneyland mentality amongst its citizens. As the twentieth century progressed Orange County became the prime example of what Los Angeles citizens val-

FIGURE 15-1. Don Stewart: "The O.J. Simpson Trial was a tragedy because it divided Californians racially."

ued. White racism, middle class values excluding Africans Americans and Hispanics led to the rise of the Ku Klux Klan and made Los Angeles the center of a right wing political mentality. Novelists and historians have found little to praise in Southern California.

Thomas Pynchon's book *The Crying of Lot 49* searches through Southern California for a historical past. He finds none. Oedipa Mass, the novel's heroine, sees the trash cans of the state as its only legitimate historical artifact. This exaggerated view is an important one, because it suggests the contemporary wasteland that Los Angeles exemplifies. So it is not surprising that Rodney King's beating is viewed as just another accident of history. But hostile racial attitudes were also directed toward the ethnic middle class.

Glenn Spencer, head of Voices of Citizens United, remarked: "In L.A., the situation is approaching civil war." Spencer who was pro-Proposition 187, headed a group determined to prevent illegal immigration. Proposition 187 was designed to punish schools, employers, landlords or virtually anyone who provided services to illegal aliens. "We are being invaded by Mexico," Spencer concluded. "We have to get these people out of Southern California." This is a feeling that the majority of California voters expressed in public opinion polls and in a recent vote on immigration restriction. It doesn't bode well for a multicultural future as three of four illegal Mexican immigrants who entered the United States settled in California.

In Los Angeles Wei Ming Wong, a forty one year old immigrant from Hong Kong, remarked that she helped to bring twelve of her relatives to Southern California. "No one in my family is left in Hong Kong," a smiling Wong remarked. Peter Brimlow's controversial book, *Alien Nation*, argues that the wrong type of immigrants are streaming into California. Brimlow believes that they are unskilled, prone to welfare and not willing to adopt to American culture. Cali-

fornians agree with Brimlow, at least if Proposition 187 to ban illegal immigrants is an indicator. The popularity of Brimlow's racist assumptions influenced politicians and Governor Pete Wilson spoke fondly of the book.

In California where do legal immigrants settle and why? From 1991 to 1993 more than 2.2 million legal immigrants settled in the United States. Of these, more than a 250,000 resided in California. The vast majority, 32,163, settled in Los Angeles while 13,139 resided in San Francisco and 10,933 lived in San Jose. Los Angeles residents were 44% from Mexico, El Salvador and Guatemala. In San Francisco the Chinese were 26.1% of the new population followed by 12.1% Filipinos and 8.2% Vietnamese. In San Jose, the Vietnamese were 36.1% of the new population followed by 13% Mexicans. California has a multi cultural dispersion which has made Los Angeles predominantly Spanish speaking, San Francisco a Chinese center for settlement and San Jose a Vietnamese enclave.

In 1996 ethnic change in California is dramatic. In Fremont and Hayward, California there is a large population of Afghanistan business people who have filled a strong need in the service industry. Afghanistan restaurants, auto repair shops and small convenience stores abound in these suburbs. In Fremont, a suburb south of Oakland, W. Reed Severson, President of Insured Benefits Brokers, recognized the need to serve the local Asian community. He brought Jessica Ngyun-Hum, a Vietnamese businesswomen married to a successful Chinese businessman, and this expanded Insured Benefits Brokers business by a third. The Asian and Indian community in Fremont prefer to do business with Severson's firm, because Insured Benefits Brokers is sensitive to multi cultural needs.

In Fresno, a third of the Laotians who arrived in the United States settled in this San

Joaquin Valley town and opened donut shops and small businesses. Many work in the fields and a Laotian church is filled every Sunday. Thailand immigrants have settled in large numbers in Fresno, Sacramento and Visilia. A small number of these settlers are on welfare but the vast majority work or own small businesses.

Healdsburg, California is a sleepy, rural town in Sonoma County north of San Francisco. In 1980, Healdsburg was more than 90% Anglo and had few foreigner settlers. It appeared to be one of the last Anglo bastions in California, but in 1996 more than a 30% Spanish speaking population had settled into this small wine country village. These new settlers were increasingly middle class and reflected ethnic movement from the city to the bucolic countryside. The significant and relatively easy integration of a large Latino population suggests that cultural diversity is often accomplished with little controversy.

California in the late 1990s is a multi cultural state with an uncertain future. The tensions resulting from the Rodney King and O.J. Simpson trials resulted in further racial division but also made the Golden State more sensitive to its racial problems. California's ethnic future is uncertain but there is no doubt that ethnicity is a concern and the state represents the fragmented dream.

Jimmy McCracklin: An Oakland Blues Legend and the Fragmented Dream

In a luxurious home, complete with a private recording studio, on a grassy hill in

FIGURE 15-2. Jimmy McCracklin: Oakland Blues Legend.

Richmond, California, blues singer-songwriter Jimmy McCracklin puts the finishing touches on his latest CD. He is scheduled to drive to Los Angeles with his band to perform at the House of Blues. Looking on the wall of his den, McCracklin smiles as he views the thirty seven albums which have made him a household name as a blues artist. He recalls the hard times and the days of segregation in the Golden State.

When McCracklin came to Oakland it was shortly after World War II. The Do Drop Inn, Esther's Orbit Room, the Brown Derby, the Tappers Inn, the Club Savoy , the Devil's Inn and the Long Island Club were African American night spots that helped McCracklin hone his craft. "The black clubs created my sound and gave my songwriting a direction," McCracklin remembered. As a result of playing in these clubs, McCracklin began to closer attention to the business side of the industry. He formed his own songwriting company in the mid-1960s, Budget Music, and began to copyright the almost nine hundred songs that make up his publishing empire.

"The old days in Richmond and Oakland were wonderful," McCracklin remarked. "We played our music and made a little money. Then the 1960s came along and the black man got a chance." As McCracklin reminisced he remembered playing in all black clubs, he recalled the images of Oakland's Continental Club, the Rum Boogie and Ruthie's Inn. These clubs catered to an African American audience but the music helped to integrate California socially and economically. "Suddenly in the 1970s, my audience began to become broader based. The whites discovered my music." When this happened McCracklin's songs were recorded by a wide variety of artists and he earned a nice living from songwriting.

Prince, L.L. Cool J., Redhead Kingpin Smith and Salt and Pepa recorded McCracklin's classic blues tune "Tramp." They added new words to it but kept the music and song structure intact. The result was to increase McCracklin's already formidable reputation as a songwriter. "I have been lucky, California gave me the chance to show my talent," McCracklin remarked. From his first major pop hit "The Walk" in 1959 through subsequent rhythm and blues hits like "Just Got To Know," "Every Night, Every Day," "Think," "My Answer" "Come On Home," "Shame, Shame, Shame" and "The Georgia Slop," McCracklin's reputation grew each year. Not only did other artists want to record his songs, but he became a guru to a new generation of musical acts.

One example of McCracklin's influence occurred in the early 1990s when McCracklin and his manager went backstage to met Los Lobos. It was a rare night of musical camaraderie as McCracklin and David Hidalgo sang a medley of Jimmy's hits. Then Los Lobos asked Jimmy what songs the shysters in the music business stole from him.

"I am mad as hell that 'The Thrill Is Gone' was never credited to me," McCracklin remarked. In 1949, McCracklin recorded Roy Hawkins performing "The Thrill Is Gone" at Sierra Studios in Berkeley. Nothing came of the tune and Hawkins left for Los Angeles. When Modern Records issued "The Thrill Is Gone" (Modern 826), the Bihari brothers, who owned the label, failed to copyright it. Everyone forgot about the song.

Then, in 1957 a two small time Seattle jazz musicians, Art Benson and Dale Petite, produced an album for Corky Corcoran, "Sounds of Jazz, Volume 1," which included a jazz version of "The Thrill Is Gone." When Benson sent his copyright form into ASCAP, he found that there was no copyright on the tune. Immediately, Benson sent in the forms and it was his song. Benson's Grosvenor House Publishing Company administered the tune. But, once again, "The Thrill Is Gone" failed to chart as a jazz tune.

Then, in 1971, B.B. King cut a monster hit version of "The Thrill Is Gone" and Benson collected the royalties. "B.B. cut that song just the way I had Roy Hawkins do it," McCracklin remarked. He looked exasperated as he remembered the pain of losing "The Thrill Is Gone." Jimmy McCracklin was left out in the cold. "I gave that song to Bob Geddins (a song plugger) and he sold it for $50, I didn't know how to protect myself in those days," McCracklin concluded.

A long court battle began, which is still ongoing, and McCracklin's publishing company presented affidavits and other information on where Jimmy wrote the tune and recorded it. Relaxing in his Richmond home,

McCracklin remarked: "B.B. knows its my song, he never denied it. But I've survived and B.B. and I are still close friends." What McCracklin remembers is that he had the copyright blues. "It was a learning experience and it brought me into the mainstream of the business part of the music industry," McCracklin concluded. What had been a fragmented dream became a reality for McCracklin as his earnings increased in proportion to his willingness to challenge those who had stolen his songs in court.

As he sat backstage at the King Biscuit Festival in Helena, Arkansas, where he headlined in 1995, McCracklin remarked: "California has been good to me. I have earned a nice living, but it hasn't always been easy." As he recounts the early and lean

FIGURE 15-3. Jimmy McCracklin, Oakland Blues Legend, with Los Lobos.

years in California, McCracklin talked at length about racial progress. "The black man finally has a chance, race is still an issue, but we all have a dream that we can pursue." McCracklin's remarks suggest the importance of economic progress. "The black family can live anywhere in California," McCracklin concluded, "and this allows them to pursue their dreams."

John Wong, the CEO of the Mission Peak Company, echoed McCracklin's sentiments when he suggested that as a home builder he tried to make dreams come true. "Quality, honesty and integrity, those are my watchwords," Wong remarked. California is the place where anyone can become anything they desire, Wong suggested in conversation. The dream is a reality for many Californians. Watching Wong direct the

building of custom homes in Fremont, California, it is obvious that he felt no restrictions due to ethnicity. What McCracklin and Wong have in common is that they have shared the California dream. For them it has not been a fragmented dream.

Bibliographical Essay

For the Rodney King incident see Hiroshi Fukurai, Richard Krooth and Edgard W. Butler, "The Rodney King Beating Verdicts," in Mark Baldassare, ed., *The Los Angeles Riots: Lessons For the Urban Future* (Boulder, 1994), pp. 73-102; Robert Gooding-Williams, *Reading Rodney King, Reading Urban Uprising* (New York, 1993) and Tom Owens with Rod Browning, *Lying Eyes: The Truth behind the Corruption and Brutality of the LAPD and the Beating of Rodney King* (New York, 1994). For a history of the LAPD which emphasizes its

FIGURE 15-4. Blues Legend Jimmy McCracklin with Troyce Key, Eli's Mile High Club. Courtesy of Howard A. DeWitt.

racial problems see, Joe Domanick, *To Protect and Serve: The LAPD's Century of War in the City of Dreams* (New York, 1994). Also see, Jan Golab, *The Dark Side of the Force: A True Story of Corruption and Murder in the LAPD* (New York, 1993) for an investigation which revealed that LAPD officers were found to be running a prostitution ring, selling automatic weapons and engaging in insurance fraud, a small number of officers committed armed robbery and a police officer was indicted in a murder for hire case.

Dan Hazen, *Inside the L.A. Riots* (New York, 1992) provides an excellent perspective on the 1992 riots. For racial conflict set within the structure of city politics see, Raphael Sonenshein, *Politics in Black and White: Race and Power in Los Angeles* (Princeton, N.J., 1993)

The material on the O.J. Simpson case is shallow, filled with personal views and tends toward sensationalism. Michael Knox with Mike Walker, *The Private Diary of an O.J. Juror* (New York, 1995) is a mass market paperback with some useful insights.

For two excellent, interpretive views of recent Los Angeles see, Peter Theroux, *Translating L.A.: A Tour of the Rainbow City* (New York, 1994) and Bill Barich, *Big Dreams: Inside the Heart of California* (New York, 1994).

The controversy over Asian merchants in Los Angeles is given an academic interpretation in Paul Ong, Edna Bonacich and Lucie Cheng, *The New Asian Immigration in Los Angeles and Global Restructuring* (Philadelphia, 1994).

Korean merchants and Mayor Tom Bradley's insensitivity to their problems is examined in Mike Davis, *City of Quartz: Excavating the Future in Los Angeles* (London, 1990).

16

The Color Bind in Proposition 209

Race and Affirmative Action in California

> **"**As an anthropologist, I know that when you've got diversity, you've got a problem, which means that you've got to come up with ways to deal with it in the most realistic way possible.**"**
> —Professor Glynn Custred, California State University, Hayward

Race and class have always been an integral part of California history. Since the 1850s when anti-Chinese zealots, nativists and those with xenophobic fears created the politics of reaction, California has been a hotbed of racial controversy. By the turn of the century, the Golden State began to discriminate against the Japanese, turned its attention to radical labor and berated the contribution of Filipinos who migrated in the 1920s to work in the fields. V.S. McClatchy, a member of the illustrious *Sacramento Bee* newspaper family, began to argue that the ethnic impulse was an unsavory one. For the next seventy years Californians debated issues of race. It became a permanent part of the political culture.

In the 1990s this atmosphere persists and continues to influence the direction of the Golden State. The continuous fears of illegal aliens reached its apex when California faced a voter initiative to place restraints upon financial aid to illegal aliens. It was this move to organize anti-immigrant sentiment which provided the catalyst to a voter initiative to ban the use of affirmative action.

California suddenly experienced a "color bind" attached to race and affirmative action. The political atmosphere became so heated that outgoing Republican Governor Pete Wilson sued the California Community College system to make sure that it enforced Proposition 209, which banned affirmative action. Governor Wilson's lawsuit was mean spirited because he sued as a private citizen. This allowed his lawyers to appeal any state court decisions involving affirmative action which was not to the former governor's liking. The roots of anti-affirmative action feeling began sowing their seeds in the late 1970s. The issue of reverse discrimination gave birth to the movement to ban affirmative action.

Since the 1978 Bakke case, Californians have debated affirmative action, special admissions and the general question of ethnicity. In the process, the arguments for and against affirmative action have been often obscured by other issues. The force of feminism, the demands of right and left wing extremists and the continuing fear of illegal immigrants are issues that created a contentious atmosphere. This led to a debate which produced Proposition 187, denying federal and state aid to illegal or undocumented aliens.

Proposition 187: The Politics of the Illegal Alien

In November, 1994, California voters approved Proposition 187, an initiative that forbade funds being allocated for public education or medial care for undocumented or illegal workers and their families. Under the state initiative process, citizens can suggest new laws or changes in the state constitution. By simply collecting signatures and placing a measure on the ballot, the average voter can influence the direction of California government. But to write a ballot measure approved by the voters takes a great deal of skill.

When Proposition 187 was drafted by Ron Prince, an accountant living in Orange County, he represented the conservative force of Southern California politics. He was joined in the process by Harold Ezell, a regional director of I.N.S. and Alan C. Nelson, director of I.N.S. during the Reagan Administration. They believed that the flood of illegal Mexican workers created insoluble problems. Apparently, many Californians had the same feeling. The initiative was so popular with voters that Governor Pete Wilson declared it would pass with little debate.

No one was fooled by Governor Wilson's comments. From the day that he entered Golden State politics, Wilson was a foe of the immigrant. The governor helped to raise more than two million dollars for television ads urging Proposition 187's passage. In television interviews, Wilson made the Mexican immigrant appear to be a insidious menace. He also solicited millions of dollars to help Proposition 187 run television ads.

One of the campaign commercials showed night vision video clips of immigrants sneaking across the border from Mexico into San Diego. Governor Wilson pointed out that California spent $2.5 billion in tax dollars to support illegal aliens. His conclusion was that this was bankrupting the Golden State.

Proposition 187 was popular with California voters, so the governor supported the initiative in his bid for reelection. Wilson was in political trouble during the early period of the 1994 gubernatorial election. Proposition 187 helped to bail him out. When he won the November election, receiving 55.2% of the popular vote, he rode in on the coattails of Proposition 187 which received a 58.9% voter plurality. It was Governor Wilson's stand on immigration which not only won him a second term as governor but brought his name up as a potential Republican presidential nominee. So the governor jumped on the Proposition 209 bandwagon.

A political opportunist with a penchant for attacking the ethnic community, Wilson wasn't a racist. He was simply a consummate politician who would use any means possible to secure a political victory. But not even Governor Wilson realized the potential political force of Proposition 209. When he did, Wilson became its staunchest supporter. The background of Proposition 209 explains a great deal about ethnic tensions and social-economic-educational-political differences in the Golden State.

FIGURE 16-1. California's unsettled ethnic atmosphere.

The Origins of the California Civil Rights Initiative

In 1992 Professor Glynn Custred faced his California State University, Hayward, anthropology students. He had noticed for more than two decades the changes in the student body. In 1976 Custred had a freshman class which was 63% white, 20% African-American, 8% Asian or Filipino and 5% Latino, but by 1992 demographic change had resulted in 34% of the students identified as Asian, 18% African-American, 16% Latino and 24% white. The majority of the other CSU campuses experienced a similar make up.

No one knew what drove Custred, but he had a feeling that ethnic diversity was becoming a problem. He worried about reverse discrimination. One of his graduate students in the 1970s remarked: "We were all on a first name basis and he was a fine teacher, but there was something about the changes taking place at California State University, Hayward, and these changes unsettled him." Custred began looking for a means to end what he viewed as the unfairness of affirmative action. This was surprising because the California State University system wasn't an exclusive admissions enclave.

The California State University system accepts the top third of the Golden State's high school graduates, and thus partially the working class, ethnic diversity. As Custred taught this new class of students, he found that there was little difference between them and previous classes. Student performance didn't vary from the 1970s to the 1990s.

What had changed was the faculty. They tended to be more diverse and include more women. They tended to change the standard reading lists. They tended to organize forums, exploring new topics such as feminism and diversity.

The university granted African-American students the right to hold their own graduation. There is no record if any of this bothered Custred, but he began planning what would become Proposition 209.

The changes in university policy had a great deal to do with Custred's emerging conservative political radicalism. In the spring of 1979, Robert Portillo, the assistant to the president of California State, Hayward, sent a memo to the faculty on the impending retirement of many of the faculty: "It is vital to recognize this and to begin taking steps to insure appropriate minority representation in our faculty." When new faculty members were hired they were shown Portillo's memo. A fair minded man and a good administrator, Portillo didn't realize that he had threatened white faculty members, and his clumsy explanations did little to alloy their feelings.

Soon the faculty was in turmoil over the future. Barbara Paige, an African-American woman with a Ph.D. in philosophy from UC, Berkeley, began a cross cultural educational program to bring multicultural courses into the mainstream of the college curriculum. Black writers like Toni Morrison and Alice Walker were on her course reading lists. These writers became an integral part of course study in a number of departments. This wasn't surprising: It was a trend that was taking place all over the country. Another new Hayward faculty member, Gayle Young, who had a degree in communications from UCLA, joined in the multicultural course push. Soon Glynn Custred joined in the debate over the direction of course content. This led to fierce partisan debate and Custred found himself isolated and at odds with his colleagues during these sessions.

Custred became uneasy in the presence of the multicultural scholars who seemed

intent on attacking the system rather than understanding it. These scholars defended themselves by suggesting that Custred was antagonistic and not open to new ideas. He responded that the ethnic scholars weren't interested in broad academic debates.

The issues of multicultural differences quickly escalated. The Center for the Study of Intercultural Relations was established at CSU, Hayward. A conference was held in the late 1980s but once again Custred was uncomfortable over those invited. The number of white scholars in ethnic or multicultural studies was limited. There appeared to be an academic racism. Even senior white scholars who had authored pathbreaking books were not invited. A member of the CSU, Hayward faculty defended this practice, suggesting that the white scholars had their forum. It was now time for the ethnic professors to have their day. Custred argued that it wasn't an academic conference with open debate, but a group of young scholars who were uncomfortable with their own university positions. The level of tension and name calling created a nasty atmosphere.

The California State University, Hayward administration raised tensions with an announcement that seemed to exclude white scholars from being considered for university positions. During the 1990 budget crunch, the university announced that there would be job cuts. Terry Jones, an African-American tenured professor, urged the administration to fire white instructors to maintain a balanced faculty. It was this action which spurred Custred to begin thinking about an ballot initiative to outlaw affirmative action. Jones defended what he called "affirmative hiring" and this further split the faculty.

The California State University, Hayward in-fighting received no media attention. But it served as a microcosm for battles over affirmative action in more prestigious universities. At Stanford, the University of California, Berkeley and the University of Michigan, there was a revolt against requiring the History of Western Civilization. The course was viewed by the minority faculty as European centered, heavily male oriented and employing a reading list of dead white scholars and authors. At the University of California, Davis, the faculty was reticent to hire ethnic scholars. As a result, UC, Davis had little, if any, cultural diversity courses and its Ph.D.'s were generally unemployable. But there were many who believed that the UC, Davis faculty had the right idea. The U.S. Secretary of Education, William Bennett, attacked the shift to nontraditional history courses with a third world or Asian centered course of study as being ridiculous. The *Wall Street Journal* complained that Stanford was bending to "noisy" minority faculty.

Enter Thomas Wood: The Second Piece in the Anti-Affirmative Action Puzzle

While Glynn Custred was arguing with his colleagues at California State University, Hayward over the direction of multicultural courses, he met Thomas Wood, a University of California, Berkeley, Ph.D. in philosophy. Out of work and looking for a tenure track professor slot, Wood was convinced that as a white male he had no chance to break into the academic mainstream. He had interviewed in a number of situations but his speciality was comparative religion. There were academic positions in this area. His frustration boiled as one school after another rejected him.

Then in 1990, two key events brought Wood into the anti-affirmative action

puzzle. Proposition 140 passed in California; this initiative limited the number of terms a state legislator could serve. The term limits law gave Wood an idea. He realized that as many people were unhappy with affirmative action as they were with politicians who remained in office for years. So wasn't it possible there was the same frustration with affirmative action? Then Wood read the *Newsweek* issue featuring the debate over politically correct history courses. The academic battles over Western Civilization brought a backlash against political correctness. It was at this point that Wood met Custred. They were two white males who felt like they were on the outside of the system. No one listened to them.

Both Custred and Wood were bothered by the partisan, left wing nature of the university system. When they were denounced for questioning affirmative action, they felt frustrated and isolated. The academic dean in charge of the CSU, Hayward anthropology department urged Custred to keep his opinions to himself. When Custred met Wood, they had similar feelings about their positions. So they began crafting the language which would make up Proposition 209.

The Crafting and Early Problems of the California Civil Rights Initiative

From 1992 to 1995, Custred and Wood experimented with the language of the California Civil Rights Initiative. They were amateurs in a nasty political arena. They had no money, few contacts and didn't possess a great deal of knowledge about the initiative process. They did have one strength. Both were skilled academics. Their research skills were excellent and they began burrowing into the library stacks for information supporting their initiative. It was in the University of California, Berkeley Law Library that they found the center point to their argument against affirmative action.

They discovered a 1974 U.S. Supreme Court decision in which Brian Weber, a white Louisiana steel worker, was denied a place in a job training program at a Kaiser steel plant in Gramercy, LA. In this case, the United Steelworkers of America set up a series of minority training sessions and denied whites some places in these classes. With the training classes divided in half between whites and blacks, no one expected a problem. But Weber sued alleging reverse discrimination. Justice William Brennan ruled in favor of the United Steelworkers of America and concluded that private employers operated in "an area of discretion" and denied Weber a place in the training program. What intrigued Wood and Custred was that scholars labeled the Weber decision a major departure from the intent of the Civil Rights Act of 1964. It was Wood, an assiduous researcher, who discovered public opinion polls which indicated that voters were hostile to quotas and preferences. As a result, Wood and Custred were determined to publicize how affirmative action led to unfairness in education, housing and job promotion.

It was the Weber case which convinced Wood and Custred to write their initiative and not focus solely on affirmative action. They wrote the California Civil Rights Initiative to outlaw preferential treatment. This was a shrewd move because it conveyed an air of fairness. In order to secure passage of the bill, the professors needed an ally in the state legislature.

A Republican assemblyman, Bernie Richter, a former high school government instructor elected to the assembly in 1992, had mixed feelings about affirmative action. The proposed Custred-Wood initiative appealed to his sense of fairness. In October, 1993, the California Civil Rights Initiative was filed with the state attorney general. Custred and Wood had no reason to believe there would be immediate interest in their proposal. They were wrong; there was a ground swell of support.

Proposition 209's wording was written to build on the strong public opposition to affirmative action. The text of this initiative read:

"prohibited state, local governments, districts, public universities, colleges and schools, and other government instrumentalities from discriminating against or giving preferential treatment to any individual or groups in public employment, public education or public contracting on the basis of race, sex, color, ethnicity or national origin."

Immediately after Proposition 209 was introduced, the arguments pro and con began flooding the media. Those in favor of the initiative called it the "right thing to do" and they concentrated upon reverse discrimination. The announced supporters of Proposition 209 included Governor Pete Wilson and Ward Connerly, a UC regent. Those who opposed affirmative action restrictions argued that Proposition 209 would prevent minorities from gaining jobs and educational admissions. It would return California to the days when Latinos and African-Americans were not represented at the University of California or in the job market. Proposition 209 quickly turned into a fight between liberals and conservatives.

William Rusher, the publisher of the arch conservative *National Review*, praised the initiative and recommended it to his constituents. The dour faced and combative fringe Republican candidate for president, Patrick Buchanan, took up the battle by equating the California Civil Rights Initiative with fairness. Then Assemblyman Richter introduced Assembly Bill 47 which prohibited the state from taking race or gender into account in hiring, letting out contracts and establishing educational admissions. There was no doubt that there was great interest in the initiative.

The most surprising support for the California Civil Rights Initiative came from University of California Regent, Ward Connerly. An African-American, Connerly condemned the use of affirmative action. Connerly's explanation was that he had never needed special help. After attending American River Junior College and graduating from Sacramento State, Connerly became a state employee. While working for the California Redevelopment Agency, he established a reputation for getting a problem solved. This led to a job with the Department of Housing and Community Development. After half a dozen years in state government, Connerly opened his own business.

Connerly and Associates was a consulting firm working with local governments who needed to implement changes in planning laws. Soon Connerly was a respected and well-to-do businessman. He also changed his voter registration from Democratic to Republican and began contributing large sums to Pete Wilson's campaign for governor. After Wilson was elected governor, Connerly was appointed to the University of California Board of Regents. His early actions as a regent saw Connerly oppose fee hikes, oversee financial decisions and frequently speak out for free speech. In January, 1994, he wrote a letter questioning the use of affirmative action. Connerly was the first person to raise the question of re-

verse discrimination. He believed that white Californians were suffering discrimination. He wasn't the only regent to feel this way.

In 1994, a new regent, Jerry Cook, was appointed and when his son didn't gain admission to any of the University of California Medical Schools, he took all the applications home and reviewed them. Cook was horrified that his son didn't gain admission. "I came to realize it wasn't about my son but about affirmative action." Soon Cook was allied with Connerly to oppose affirmative action.

Surprisingly, Governor Pete Wilson supported affirmative action. The governor's media advisers warned him it was a potentially volatile and explosive issue. Yet, Wilson believed that it had political value. He was after all a political animal, and would support Proposition 209 if it would help him get reelected. After Connerly and Cook talked with him and showed him University admission files, and exposed him to the rhetoric of the more radical University of California professors, Wilson became a staunch Proposition 209 advocate.

As Pete Wilson ran successfully for governor and was reelected in 1994, another phenomena hit the Golden State—the angry white male. This was a term the media projected, but the truth was that the angry white male was less than 25% of the California vote. Yet, the feeling engendered by males who felt powerless was a beginning point for Proposition 209 supporters.

The Angry White Males of 1994 and Affirmative Action

The birth of the angry white male as a political coalition occurred when they voted 63% in 1994 in favor of Proposition 187. Wilson was elected governor and he recognized the force of this new voting coalition. Governor Wilson envisioned a backlash to affirmative action, and he embraced the vote of the angry white male.

Larry Rutherford, a retired police captain, remarked that Proposition 209 looked like "an exercise in futility." In a lengthy interview, Rutherford, an athletic man with a full head of hair who retired at age fifty three, continued to lament the problems with Proposition 209. "If this thing passes, I have no doubt that the courts will not allow it to be implemented." Rutherford continued in a subdued rage, explaining the problems that affirmative action had caused the white male. In this interview, he proved to be a case study of the Angry White Male. When asked, "Will you vote for Proposition 209? Rutherford remarked: "I will vote for it. What does affirmative action do? It helps a few and is to the detriment of many," Rutherford concluded.

On December 27, 1994, the *Washington Post* featured a story on the California Civil Rights Initiative. The passage of Proposition 187, the *Post* concluded, was an indication that the California voters would entertain an initiative on affirmative action. That opened the way for Custred and Wood's California Civil Rights Initiative to become a part of the California political landscape.

During the first six months of 1995, the reaction against affirmative action continued. Public opinion polls suggested that voters wanted to ban "preferential treatment." It was also a fact that voters were hostile to quotas. Then in June, 1995 the U.S. Supreme Court intensified the debate by ruling that "all racial classifications" by federal agencies were "inherently suspect and presumptively invalid." This decision, Adarand vs. Pena, made it more difficult to award minority construction companies state contracts. After this U.S.

Supreme Court ruling, the California Civil Rights Initiative had no trouble raising funds to publicize it.

The vote of the angry white male began to form when Governor Pete Wilson spoke out against what he termed the unfair nature of affirmative action. "We cannot tolerate university policies or practices," Wilson remarked, "that violate fundamental fairness, trampling individual rights to create and give preference to group rights." When Governor Wilson's political popularity, which had been sagging badly, revived due to his strong stand against affirmative action, he began supporting the California Civil Rights Initiative even more intensely.

As 1995 drew to a conclusion, money was no longer a problem for the California Civil Rights Initiative. The deadline to officially place the measure on the ballot was February 21, 1996, and the million plus signatures guaranteed that the measures would appear on the November ballot. Governor Wilson and the Republican party deserved much of the credit for popularizing the CCRI in the Golden State. They also had a campaign fund that would create a large amount of effective media advertising.

The Coalition Opposing the California Civil Rights Initiative

The Democratic party made a number of mistakes in their battle against the California Civil Rights Initiative. When Kathleen Brown, the sister of former Governor Jerry Brown, decided to seek the 1994 Democratic gubernatorial nomination, she embraced the CCRI. Earlier, she had also supported Proposition 187 and suggested that undocumented workers be given special privileges. The floundering Republican party looked like it could be defeated. Brown was a classic liberal in the California tradition. Her father,

Edmund G. (Pat) Brown, had been a two-term governor and her brother, Jerry, was also a former two-term chief executive.

As the Democratic candidate for governor, Kathleen Brown was 15% points ahead of Governor Wilson some six months before the November, 1994 election. After she campaigned in support of affirmative action, her candidacy fell apart. She barely received 40% of the popular vote and lost to her Republican opponent in a landslide. It was Brown's gubernatorial defeat which convinced the Democrats to form a coalition to oppose the CCRI. They realized it had a very good chance to pass.

For political reasons, the Democratic party failed to take a strong stand against the CCRI. They believed they might continue to lose elections because of the popularity of the measure. There was only one group who emerged to do battle with the Custred-Wood initiative and this was the National Organization for Women. In many respects affirmative action benefited women more than ethnic minorities, but the NOW believed that it would set women back educationally and in employment opportunities. In Los Angeles, Katherine Spillar organized NOW to mobilize women against the CCRI. It was Spillar who approached civil rights leaders from the 1960s and suggested that the CCRI was another example of racial bias. Soon there was a tenuous political unity between Los Angeles and San Francisco civil rights advocates.

It was the women's groups and the civil rights advocates who began to picket, demonstrate and petition the press for a rethinking of the CCRI. It was women, the ethnic vote and those who were not in the Republican or Democratic political mainstream who were approached to defeat the CCRI. But lobbying by women and civil rights groups had little impact upon the initiative. The public said very little as these debates surged. One observer suggested that there was a "closet racism" in the Golden State.

In May, 1995, northern and southern Californians who opposed Proposition 209 met at the Marriott Hotel near Los Angeles International Airport. No one could decide on a strategy to defeat the initiative. The result was that the two groups split. David Oppenheimer, a San Francisco civil rights lawyer, believed that it was necessary to disavow the radical feminist approach of Los Angeles's Katherine Spillar. As a result, there were two separate groups who opposed the CCRI, and neither one was successful. President Bill Clinton further complicated the issue by talking out of both sides of his mouth. He privately informed Oppenheimer that he believed affirmative action was unfair. Then Clinton held a press conference and vowed to support the principals behind it while talking about guaranteeing that reverse discrimination would not occur. President Clinton was all things to all people and supported both sides of the Proposition 209 argument at one time or another.

The Republican Party and the Battle to Pass the CCRI

In May, 1996, the Republican party began its push to pass the CCRI. Plans were made to bring in some of America's best political speakers. Republican presidential candidate Bob Dole, conservative columnist and sometimes Republican presidential candidate, Pat Buchanan, and General Colin Powell all spoke out against affirmative action. These speakers used the time tested race baiting tactic of suggesting that the negative influence of affirmative action far outweighed its benefits.

The voters were confused. It was hard

to tell where these famous speakers stood on Proposition 209. But there were some nasty Republicans who made it very clear that the initiative must be passed.

Pat Buchanan was the strongest voice favoring the CCRI. When he began his career as a minor aide to President Richard Nixon, Buchanan demonstrated that he was a race baiter. Although he was not a racist, Buchanan thought and often talked like one. He informed his Republican colleagues that they could win votes not only in California but throughout the nation supporting the CCRI. Then Buchanan mounted a bid for the Republican presidency and won the Louisiana presidential preferential primary. His importance was to make California Republicans believe that opposing affirmative action was the means to power.

Then Paul Gigot of the *Wall Street Journal* labeled Buchanan a bigot, racist and anti-Semitic fringe politician. When Buchanan's representatives approached Ward Connerly about supporting the CCRI, he declined. After rejecting Buchanan's endorsement, Connerly began to try to control the Republican right. He realized that racism, or the charge of it, would doom the CCRI. Connerly was rescued when Republican presidential front runner, Bob Dole, announced that he no longer supported affirmative action.

In the year prior to his unsuccessful run for the presidency, Senator Dole supported federal legislation to end affirmative action. By the November, 1996 election Dole was identified so heavily with anti-affirmative action forces that he was the symbol of Republican opposition in the Golden State. Politics, not conscience, appeared to rule most politicians.

The Democratic Party: Feminists and the Ethnic Impulse to Defeat the California Civil Rights Initiative

After the split between northern and southern Californians who opposed the CCRI, Democrats met in San Francisco to push a program they called Equal Opportunity Without Quotas. They believed that they could defeat Proposition 209, as the CCRI was now known, with a cleverly written initiative which would allow for equal opportunity without quotas. Early polls indicated that this idea was more popular than the CCRI.

Then a bombshell burst. The California legislative analyst ruled that the alternative initiative would end educational programs designed for minorities. This was a program that had quotas and received enormous federal funding. David Oppenheimer, a law professor who had written the counter initiative, recognized that it was too late to write a new proposal.

On January 26, 1996, in a conference room at the American Civil Liberties Union office on Mission Street in San Francisco, forty anti-Proposition 209 advocates met to discuss their political strategy. Aleita Huguenin, a member of the California Teacher's Association, stood up and said that it would be difficult to defeat the CCRI. She pointed out that Governor Pete Wilson had helped to raise more than one million dollars to pass Proposition 209 and that the voters were heavily in favor of it.

Then Professor Jerome Karabel of the University of California, Berkeley, and David Salniker, a lawyer, suggested that they send out bigot busters. A group of people with expert knowledge on affirmative action would stand next to CCRI backers who were gathering signatures and educate the voters on the need for fairness. But cooler heads prevailed, and the idea of bigot busters was abandoned. Everyone believed that it would hurt the anti-Proposition 209 forces.

In Southern California when Katherine Spillar organized the NOW to defeat Proposition 209, she made a number of mistakes. From her plush office in Beverly Hills, Spillar began coordinating a five million dollar advertising campaign to sink the Custred-Wood initiative. The message was that women, labor unions, Mexican-American, African-Americans and immigrants would be placed into an educational and employment limbo if Proposition 209 passed. The mistake she made was ignoring key Latino and African-American organizers. They came to view her as part of a feminist elitist. As a result, the San Francisco-Oakland based opponents of Proposition 209 went their

own way. This effectively split the movement to defeat the Custred-Wood initiative. But Spillar persisted and talked of using statistics to strike down the proposal.

To defeat the California Civil Rights Initiative, Spillar reasoned, they would have to draw support from one of four white male voters while gaining 60% of the women's vote, 60% of the Latino vote and 60% of the African-American vote. By May, 1996, an organization known as "Women Won't Go Back: The Campaign To Save Women's Rights & Civil Rights" had raised substantial sums for advertising. Lorraine Sheinberg, whose husband Sidney was a former chairperson of MCA, was a catalyst for the fundraising. But the in-fighting among Los Angeles feminists and those in San Francisco prevented them from effectively attacking the CCRI.

FIGURE 16-2. Affirmative Action is not the only issue.

feat CCRI never got off the ground.

The only real success that anti-affirmative action forces had was when they took Attorney General Dan Lungren to court in July, 1996, and won a decision the following month from Sacramento County Superior Court Judge James T. Ford who ordered the attorney general to rewrite Proposition 209, because affirmative action was missing from the initiative ballot proposal. The judge said that this confused the voters.

Then disaster struck in the anti-Proposition 209 forces. The National Organization for Women decided to stop campaigning against Proposition 209. By September, 1996, the anti-affirmative action forces were in disarray. They had little money and were bickering. This prompted Mexican-American and African-American forces to intensify the move to defeat Proposition 209.

Mexican-American and African-American Opposition to Proposition 209

The white liberals from Beverly Hills and the activists from Berkeley and San Francisco had proven that they could not effectively oppose Proposition 209. This frustrated the minority community. As a result, Anthony Thigpen, a former member of Oakland's militant Black Panthers, and Jan Adams, a former organizer for Cesar Chavez' United Farm Workers of California, teamed up to create a grass roots ethnic opposition to the CCRI. They viewed both the Republican and Democratic party coalitions as ones which attempted to manipulate the minority community for political gain.

Thigpen and Adams began a campaign to turn out a strong ethnic anti-Proposition 209 vote. They knew that they faced an uphill road. Thigpen began canvassing

neighborhoods in South Los Angeles. For more than half a century, city neglect, police brutality, drugs, inadequate education and sporadic rioting had turned parts of Los Angeles into a festering urban sore.

As Thigpen approached African-American voters in and around Los Angeles, he made it clear that times were going to get worse. When Thigpen grew up not far from 103rd street in Watts, he had watched the 1965 riot that exploded and virtually destroyed the African-American community. He took his campaign to defeat Proposition 209 to St. Brigid's Catholic Church in South-Central Los Angeles where he assembled 250 volunteers who began spreading the word that eliminating affirmative action would take away African-American education and job opportunities.

The forty-three-year-old Thigpen became California's most effective anti-Proposition 209 spokesperson. His goal was to find 75 occasional voters in each of the 1000 Los Angeles-wide voting precincts who would vote against the CCRI. But Thigpen's volunteers found it difficult to convince African-American voters that they stood to lose from Proposition 209. The black middle class was disinterested in the issue and the poor weren't inclined to vote. This did not bode well for Thigpen's strategy of mobilizing an anti-Proposition 209 vote.

By October 19, just two weeks before the election, it was obvious that for all his skill, Thigpen had been unable to turn the tide against the CCRI. A small segment of the African-American community put up a strong, but losing fight to defeat Proposition 209.

The Mexican-American community organized behind Jan Adams. She was the only child of a bookkeeper and preschool teacher who had grown up in Buffalo, New York and moved west to attend the

New York and moved west to attend the University of California, Berkeley. During the 1960s, she witnessed the turmoil and general unfairness of the academic world. Despite the male oriented nature of the history department, she considered a graduate degree. After graduating from UC, Berkeley, she studied for a Ph.D. in modern European history at Harvard University. After finishing her M.A., Adams left Cambridge to work for the Catholic Workers newspaper, the United Farm Workers of California, and began consulting for anti-apartheid organizations in South Africa. By this time, she was a committed activist and was looking for a political position. She found one when Angie Fa hired her to guide her victorious 1992 campaign for the San Francisco school board. Then Adams went to work for the Applied Research Center in Oakland and met Emily Goldfarb, the executive director of the Coalition for Immigrant Rights.

This led Adams into a position where she organized San Francisco's minority community to challenge Proposition 187. She helped to turn out an 83% no vote in the predominantly Latino Mission district, a 70% no vote in Chinatown and a 70% no vote in the predominantly African-American Bayview and Hunters Point areas. She was heartened by the people who didn't traditionally vote who turned out for this election.

When Eva Paterson, the executive director of the San Francisco Lawyers' Committee For Civil Rights, organized a committee to defeat the California Civil Rights Initiative, Adams volunteered. The committee recognized that Adams' strength was in organizing grass roots opposition to Proposition 209. Adams proposed that she organize 6,000 of California's roughly 25,000 voting precincts. She identified the 6,000 as those

she could turn against Proposition 209. Soon she put together a group known as Californians for Justice and they began publicizing the negative implications behind Proposition 209.

Then Adams produced a 95 page campaign manifesto which detailed how to combat fears concerning affirmative action. This prompted her to inaugurate a campaign that eventually became known as the Million Voices For Justice. This idea resulted from a million signatures Adams collected against Proposition 209, but the Californians For Justice, or the CFJ as it was known, was still the primary anti-Proposition 209 vehicle. From mid-September until the November election the CFJ canvassed Latino, African-American, Asian and liberal democratic political neighborhoods. The results were not as strong as Adams had envisioned. The reason was that pro-Proposition 209 advocates were running a radio commercial which stated that the initiative didn't discriminate but provided fairness for everyone. "I heard the commercial," Adams remarked, "then I heard Ward Connerly's name." She was frustrated because most everyone equated Connerly's African-American heritage with fairness. At this point, Adams knew privately she would lose her battle to defeat Proposition 209.

Proposition 209: The Passage and the Reasons for It

Arnold Steinberg, the campaign manager for Proposition 209, realized that he had a winner in late August, 1996. The backlash against affirmative action was still strong. In the final two months before the November, 1996 general election the pro-Proposition 209 forces hauled out their trump card. He was Ward Connerly. Not only was Connerly an African-American, but he was a reasoned, articulate voice against affirmative action.

Suddenly, California was filled with posters bearing Connerly's likeness and a message of fairness. A series of sixty second radio commercials bearing Connerly's endorsement were sophisticated attacks on affirmative action. The radio spot began as a melodramatic reflection on a friend of Connerly's who had recently died. When the commercial ended, its heartfelt conclusion was that affirmative action was unconscionable. The radio went as follows, Connerly:

"Last year, one of my closest friends died. In eighteen years, we had never discussed race or color. It never came up that he was white and I'm black. That wasn't important. For me and millions of other minorities what is important is that we all have an equal chance to compete."

Another Connerly ad was equally devastating to opponents of Proposition 209. It went as follows, Connerly:

"I thought equal treatment is the law. But if equal treatment is the law, why is the government so involved in giving preferences to some people—just because of their race or sex? Goals, timetables, set-asides: everyone knows we're talking about quotas. Race and sex discrimination are wrong, regardless of who's favored. Proposition 209 would prohibit discrimination and preferential treatment."

This type of radio advertising worked. The polls demonstrated strong support for Proposition 209. The public mood was set to pass the Custred-Wood initiative.

The Final Drive to Pass Proposition 209: The Organizations Fight For and Against The Initiative

By the Fall of 1996, there were so many players in the Proposition 209 game it was hard to tell them without a score card. Alleged racists, feminists, rock stars, television and radio personalities, journalists, university regents, Republican and Democratic politicians all had their say in TV or radio ads, speeches, forums and special rallies. They all spoke, contributed money and proselytized one way or another for Proposition 209. It became a media event like no other in California history. But first and foremost, it was political.

Arnold Steinberg was the campaign manager for Proposition 209. In August, 1995, he made a number of phone calls to prominent politicians. They all had one question. "What is the California mood on affirmative action?" The answer was a simple one. Steinberg declared Proposition 209 a winner.

In August, 1996, the Republican party met in San Diego to nominate Bob Dole as their presidential candidate. But Steinberg was nervous over Dole's support of the initiative. If Dole continued to decline in the polls and suffered a defeat as expected at the hands of incumbent President Bill Clinton, perhaps the Republican party would take Proposition 209 down to defeat.

When Senator Dole and House Speaker Newt Gingrich spoke in California in favor of Proposition 209, public opinion polls showed a decline in support for the measure. This worried Steinberg and caused those who favored the initiative to distance themselves from the Republican party.

Patricia Ewing, the campaign manager for Defeat Proposition 209, saw an opportunity to undermine the initiative. She convinced San Francisco Mayor Willie Brown to begin making appearances opposing Proposition 209 and she also enlisted the NAACP and the ACLU to support the need to maintain affirmative action.

Students had shown little interest in Proposition 209. Then, California State University, Northridge Associated Student Body President Vladimir Cerna, an immigrant from El Salvador, organized a panel on affirmative action and invited the controversial Louisiana politician, David Duke, to campus. Cerna, a supporter of affirmative action, believed that the sensational arguments which Duke would make in favor of Proposition 209 would hurt the initiative with voters.

As an ex-member of the Ku Klux Klan, Duke could place supporters of Proposition 209 in the position of being called racists. The media turned out by the hundreds to quiz CSU President Belinda Wilson. An African-American, Wilson received a nasty phone call from Ward Connerly. He then tried to secure her phone records. When this failed to intimidate her, Connerly asked for an injunction. He didn't believe that Duke should speak on campus. The pressure upon President Wilson was enormous and she was cautioned that her job was in jeopardy.

When Duke arrived in California, he highlighted the fact that some supporters of Proposition 209 were racists but many more were not. Duke served to confuse the issues. Suddenly, affirmative action was no longer the question. Race was now in the forefront. When Duke spoke at CSU, Northridge, it was a small, largely disinterested, audience who greeted the Louisiana politician. The

crowd was polite and largely multi ethnic. Joe Hicks, the executive director of the Los Angeles based Multicultural Collaborative, provided strong counters to Duke's arguments. But the fallout over Duke's comments were minimal. Californians were still in support of Proposition 209.

As Californians debated Proposition 209, the incumbent Democratic president, Bill Clinton, was silent on the issue. While Clinton announced that he supported affirmative action, he had no interest in getting into the political arguments over the initiative. Sounding very much like a candidate, Clinton talked out of both sides of his mouth. He supported affirmative action but was against quotas. In effect, President Clinton was both for and against Proposition 209. It was the smart political thing to do.

Further intensifying the arguments over Proposition 209, California feminists enlisted the support of rock star Bruce Springsteen, actresses Candice Bergen and Ellen DeGeneres, the Rev. Jesse Jackson and farm labor organizer Dolores Huerta. They filmed a series of radio commercials opposing Proposition 209. These ads were largely gender ones. Since more than 50% of California's voters were women, the ads suggested that passage of Proposition 209 would end maternity leave, girls sports, tutoring and girls outreach. The message was clear, the young and upcoming feminists would suffer from Proposition 209's passage.

During the final week of the campaign, the National Organization for Women launched its only television ad. The ad was a controversial one. It showed a man stripping a woman of her college education, her stethoscope and medical lab coat, a police officer's cap and a hard hat. The ad stated that if a woman wanted to become a professional, forget it. If she wanted to break into a man's profession, it would be forbidden with the Custred-Wood initiative. The NOW made Proposition 209 a gender rather than an affirmative action issue. It was not a success. Polls showed that the ads had little effect upon the vote.

The voters appeared disinterested in the wide variety of ads. As President Clinton remarked of Proposition 209: "I knew it's maybe popular, maybe not. But, let me tell you what I know. I'm old enough to remember, in my home state, when I would go into county courthouses and the restrooms were divided between white and colored." President Clinton continued with a weak defense of affirmative action. He was clearly uncomfortable talking about the subject.

As California voters prepared to go to the polls, the Democratic party remained lukewarm in their commitment to Proposition 209. No one could really understand where the Democrats stood. Only Governor Pete Wilson was a strong supporter of the initiative. Most politicians believed that it was political suicide to take a strong stand on the measure.

Election Day: The Final Vote on Proposition 209 And Its Aftermath

On November 4, 1996, the day before California voters went to the polls, local television programs were flooded with lengthy features on the need for affirmative action programs. Dennis Richmond of Channel 2 KTVU News in Oakland summed up the media's viewpoint. "We have a responsibility to make the public aware of the backlash that might result from the passage of Proposition 209."

The image of racism was a strong one in the final day prior to the general election. David Duke's appearance in California continued to be a reminder of the unsavory force of race prejudice that supported Proposition 209. The Texaco Company was another that favored Proposition 209 and then word leaked out that Texaco had berated its African-American employees when a discrimination suit was filed. It was alleged that Texaco destroyed evidence to protect itself against discrimination cases. But none of these tales had an impact upon California voters.

The 9 million plus voters who went to the polls voted 54.6% for Proposition 209. What prompted the initiative to pass? No one was sure. There were a number of explanations but the overwhelming evidence was that it was a popular proposal. Jan Adams at the Oakland headquarters of Californians for Justice suggested that President Clinton's weak support cost her coalition the chance to defeat Proposition 209.

The *Los Angeles Times* exit poll reported that 74% of African-Americans, 76% of Latinos and 61% of Asians voted against Proposition 209. The white vote was 63% for the proposition and many voters complained that they didn't understand what the initiative intended to accomplish.

In Sacramento, the Proposition 209 campaign forces met at the Hyatt Regency for a victory celebration. Custred and Wood basked in the limelight and received the plaudits of their admirers. Ward Connerly gave a victory speech and everyone basked in the glow of victory.

What has changed due to the passage of Proposition 209? One obvious result is the end of affirmative action in the college admission process. For hiring purposes, affirmative action is still largely in place. Most college affirmative action officers use federal law as the primary hiring guideline. The issue is far from a dead one. Many corporations and educational institutions continue to employ affirmative action. "I think it is fair to be committed to minority hiring," a Laney College official remarked. "We try to be fair," a member of the Walnut Creek school board remarked, "but it is against the law to continue to use affirmative action."

When voters in Florida, Nevada and South Dakota approved initiative measures similar to California's Proposition 209, the issue moved beyond the Golden State. Governor Pete Wilson was the person responsible for the passage of the measure. He helped with its wording, quietly raised funds behind the scene and exploited racial tensions in his campaign for reelection.

What Proposition 209 demonstrated was that California remained a "fragmented dream," one that has a different meaning for everyone. The question of race and class remain an essential tenet of the Golden State's political, educational and economic culture.

Proposition 209: The Color Bind in the Golden State

One of the most heated issues in the November, 1996 California election was Proposition 209. When it passed with 54% of the vote, the state was set for a lengthy court debate over the measures constitutionality.

In early April, 1997 a group of Californians supporting affirmative action began planning an appeal to block the implementation of Proposition 209. Since this Golden State referendum made affirmative action illegal, its opponents theorized that the court might find it violated the 14th amendments' equal protection clause.

A series of judicial decisions took place which further added to the controversy. On November 28, 1996, Chief U. S. District Judge Thelton Henderson blocked enforcement of the anti-affirmative action referendum. Henderson, an African-American and former Justice Department lawyer, ruled that the proposition had a "strong probability" that it would be overturned by the U.S. Supreme Court. His decision was based on the premise that Proposition 209 violated the Civil Rights Act of 1964. Governor Pete Wilson and Attorney General Dan Lungren were prohibited form taking any action to enforce Proposition 209 until a hearing on the constitutionality of the measure. In his ruling, Judge Henderson called Proposition 209 an "iron cage" that would strangle the progress and lessen the opportunity of minorities. Judge Henderson's experience as a civil rights lawyer weighed heavily upon his decision.

The next legal interpretation of Proposition 209 came in April when the 9th U.S. Circuit Court of Appeals upheld the initiative. Attorney General Dan Lungren, a conservative Republican, moved quickly to dismantle affirmative action programs. He called them an example of reverse discrimination and unequal opportunity for the ethnic community. Angered over the court ruling and Lungren's insensitivity, those opposing the initiative organized. This led to a series of demonstrations against Proposition 209 which kept the controversial measure in the public eye. At the University of California, Riverside, twenty students were arrested in mid November in a demonstration that saw 200 people gather outside administration offices. University Chancellor Raymond Orbach met with protesters but could not convince them to leave the UC, Riverside administration building. The police were finally called in and arrested those who would not disperse.

Unlike many university system branches, UC, Riverside, maintained an excellent affirmative action program. They had a larger African-American student body than UCLA and their minority population had the highest acceptance into graduate school of any branch of the university. But affirmative action was on its last legs.

In late August, 1997, Proposition 209, banning affirmative action, went into effect after a bitter court battle. When the proposition was approved by 54% of the California voters in November, 1996, it faced an uphill court battle to become law. The thinking was that this proposition was illegal. So opponents of Proposition 209 challenged the state measure in a federal district court. The argument presented by an attorney for the American Civil Liberties Union was that the law's sole goal·was to end programs that attempt to counter discrimination against women and minorities.

When the final court hearing concluded, Proposition 209 was ruled as a valid ballot measure. The American Civil Liberties Union announced that the battle was far from over. Mark Rosenbaum, the A.C.L.U.'s Southern California legal director remarked: "Certainly this is a case the Supreme Court ought to have the final word on." The controversy over Proposition 209 escalated.

The University of California, Berkeley, dropped its special admissions program and in the last year of affirmative action it admitted twenty African-American students to the prestigious Boalt Law School The following year only one black student was admitted and the N.A.A.C.P cried foul. African-American students no longer felt at home at Boalt Law School and most opted for other universities.

By October, 1997, civil rights leader Jesse Jackson was marching on the California state Capitol in Sacramento in opposition to Proposition 209. One hundred people showed up at the steps of the state capitol to protest the inequities of not having an affirmative action program in place. The controversy over Proposition 209 suggests much of what is right and wrong with the Golden State. The liberal left and the radical rights have spent a century and a half battling over political prerogative and the fight over Proposition 209 was simply another skirmish in that long tiff.

Bibliographical Essay

Lydia Chavez, *The Color Bind: California's Battle To End Affirmative Action* (Berkeley, 1988) is the best study of Proposition 209. The Civil Rights Act of 1964 is important to Proposition 209. For this law, see, for example, Charles Whalen and Barbara Whalen, *The Longest Debate: A Legislative History of the 1964 Civil Rights Act* (Washington, 1985) and Hugh Davis Graham, *Civil Rights and the Presidency: Race and Gender in American Politics, 1960-1972* (New York, 1990).

The best defense of affirmative action is Barbara R. Bergmann, *In Defense of Affirmative Action* (New York, 1996). For a virulent defense of affirmative action, see, Richard Walker, "California Rages Against the Dying of the Light," *New Left Review*, Number 209, January/February, 1995, pp. 42-74.

Among the best critiques of affirmative action are Allan Bloom, *The Closing of the American Mind* (New York, 1987), Thomas Sowell, *Race and Culture: A World View* (New York, 1994); Thomas Sowell, *Inside American Education: The Decline, the Deception, the Dogmas* (New York, 1993) and Dinesh d'Souza, *The Illiberal Education: The Politics of Race and Sex on Campus* (New York, 1991).

For newspaper reaction to affirmative action and one of the authors of Proposition 209, see, for example, B. Drummond Ayres, "Fighting Affirmative Action, He Finds His Race An Issue," *New York Times*, April 18, 1966, A.1.

For state and federal government reports see, "Affirmative Action Lawsuit, Dismantling Race and Gender Based Preferences in California," *Report of the Office of Governor*, August 10, 1995; William J. Bennett, "A Report on the Humanities in Higher Education," *National Endowment For The Humanities*, Washington, D. C., 1984; California Department of Finance, Demographic Research Unit. *Population Projections by Race/Ethnicity for California and Its Counties, 1990-2040* (Sacramento, 1993); California State Legislature Report, "Discrimination and Affirmative Action," *Committee on the Judiciary, Report of the Hearing of May 5, 1995* and "The Furor Over Affirmative Action," *Documents on Affirmative Action complied by the California Senate Office of Research* (Sacramento, 1995).

For neutral academic readings on affirmative action, see, George E. Curry, ed., *The Affirmative Action Debate*, (Reading, Ma., 1996). The problems of affirmative action in Los Angeles can be analyzed in Mike Davis, *City of Quartz* (New York, 1992).

Criticism of changes in traditional history courses are included in "The Stanford Mind," *Wall Street Journal*, December 22, 1988, p. 14 and John Searle, "The Storm Over The University," *New York Review of Books*, December 6, 1990, p. 39.

For Governor Pete Wilson and the connection between Proposition 187 and the 1994 gubernatorial election, see, *Sacramento Bee*, November 16, 1994, B4: Los Angeles Times, October 29, 1994, p. A1, November 9, 1994, p. 1.

On the California initiative process, see, for example, Daniel H. Lowenstein, "California Initiatives and the Single Subject Rule," *UCLA Law Review*, volume 30, number 5, June, 1993; Eugene Lee, "Representative Government and the Initiative Process," *California Party Choices* (Los Angeles, 1990, volume 6) and Jim Shultz, *The Initiative Cookbook* (San Franciso, 1996). An interesting document that helps to explain the initiative process is "Blueprint For Our Future: Increasing Voter Participation and Reforming the Initiative Process," *Senate Office of Research*, Sacramento, January, 1991.

Paul Sniderman's, *The Scar of Race* (Cambridge, 1993) presented some evidence that whites were in favor of affirmative action but opposed to preferential treatment. It was this book which influenced the final wording of the California Civil Rights Initiative and made "preferential treatment" the key phrase in the initiative. For the first significant mention of the California Civil Rights Initiative outside the Golden State, see, *Washington Post*, December 27, 1994, p. 3.

An important U. S. Supreme Court decision which influenced the California Civil Rights Initiative is Adarand Constructors vs. Pena, 115 Sup. Ct. 2097, 2113 (Washington D. C., 1995). Also see the Gallup/CNN Poll for March, 1995 which indicated that 55% supported affirmative action while 63% opposed quotas. This helped Custred and Wood to write the document in such a way as to gain increased support for the California Civil Rights Initiative, *USA Today*, March 24, 1995, p. 3A.

On Kathleen Brown's problems with affirmative action in the 1994 gubernatorial campaign, see, Gerald C. Lubenow, ed., *The 1994 Governor's Race* (Berkeley, 1995). For Bob Dole's opinions on affirmative action, see, *Los Angeles Times*, November 19, 1995, p. M5. For the article in which Paul Gigot calls Pat Buchanan a racist and anti-Semitic, see, *Wall Street Journal*, April 12, 1996. For comment on Pat Buchanan, see, *San Francisco Examiner*, February 3, 1994.

A document demonstrating why Proposition 209 passed is "Campaign Plan, California Civil Rights Initiative for November, 1996," Arnold Steinbert and Associates, Inc., 1996). For those who tried to defeat the CCRI, see, "A Strategic Analysis of the Anti-CCRI Campaign," prepared by Lou Harris, July 1996. This is the result of a carefully and scientifically conducted survey by the Feldman Group in June, 1996. For help in understanding the reaction against affirmative action, see Stanley Greenberg, *Middle Class Dreams: The Politics and Power of the New American Majority* (New York, 1995).

For comments on David Duke in the Proposition 209 controversy, see, *Los Angeles Times*, September 11, 1996, p. A3; *San Francisco Chronicle*, September 5, 1996, p. A1; *Washington Post*, September 26, 1996, p. A3; *Sacramento Bee*, September 27, 1996, p. A3.

For voting in the 1994 election, see, Exit Field Polls, "A Summary of Voting In the 1994 Election," *Campaign Opinion Index*, January, 1995 and Stephen Green, ed., *California Political Almanac* (Sacramento, 1995).

To understand the force of multicultural history in the Golden State, see, for example, Howard A. DeWitt, *The Fragmented Dream: Multicultural California* (Dubuque, 1995) and Ronald Takaki, *Strangers From A Different Shore* (Boston, 1989).

About the Author

Howard A. DeWitt is a Professor of History at Ohlone College, Fremont, California. He received his B.A. from Western Washington State University, an M.A. from the University of Oregon and a Ph.D. from the University of Arizona. He has also studied at the University of California, Davis and the University of Paris.

For thirty years Professor DeWitt has been in the vanguard of ethnic history. He has published more than 100 scholarly papers, popular articles, reviews and books. His work has appeared in the *Journal of American History, Amerasia*, the *California Historical Quarterly*, the *Southern California Quarterly*, the *Pacific Historian* and the *Journal of the West* among others. He is the author of 13 books including three on Filipinos in California and two major textbooks *California: An Interpretive History* and *Readings in California Civilization: Interpretative Issues* both available from Kendall/Hunt.

Professor DeWitt has lectured on Filipinos in California at the University of California, Los Angeles, and taught at Cochise College, Chabot College, the University of Arizona and the University of California, Davis. His seven books on rock and roll music offer another side to his scholarly character. DeWitt's book *Sun Elvis: Elvis Presley in the 1950s*, published by Popular Culture Ink., was nominated as one of the best rock and roll books of the 1990s by the American Association of Recording Societies. Professor DeWitt publishes regularly in a wide variety of rock and roll magazines including *Blue Suede News, Discoveries and Juke Box Digest.*

As a scholar in the field of ethnic studies Professor DeWitt has spoken before the major historical conferences and in 1995 he was a featured speaker in Manila to commemorate 100 years of Philippine independence.

Other Books by Howard A. DeWitt

Images of Ethnic and Radical Violence in California Politics, 1917-1930: A Survey (San Francisco, 1975)

Anti-Filipino Movements in California: A History, Bibliography and Study Guide (San Francisco, 1976)

California Civilization: An Interpretation (Dubuque, 1979)

Violence in the Fields: California Filipino Farm Labor Unionization During the Great Depression (Saratoga, 1980)

Readings in California Civilization: Interpretative Issues (Dubuque, 1981)

Van Morrison: The Mystic's Music (Fremont, 1983)

Jailhouse Rock: The Bootleg Records of Elvis Presley (co-author with Lee Cotten) (Ann Arbor, 1983)

Chuck Berry: Rock and Roll Music (Ann Arbor, 1985)

The Beatles: Untold Tales (Fremont, 1985)

Beatle Poems (Fremont, 1987)

Paul McCartney: From Liverpool to Let It Be (Fremont, 1992)

Sun Elvis: Elvis Presley in the 1950s (Ann Arbor, 1993)

Index

Grimke, Francis J., 176-177
Guerin, Arthur S., 191
Guest, Francis F., 23
Gwin, William, 83-84, 98-100

H

Haight, Governor Henry H., 94
Halcyon Days (Mexican California), 50-51
Hall, George W., 109-111
Hall, William Henry, 79
Halland, Walt, 207
Hammond, Creed, 107
Harding, Warren, 175
Harlims, Latasha, 222
Hare, Nathan, 213
Harris, Jeanette, 236
Harte, Brett, 116
Hartnell, William, 53-55, 65
Hawkins, Augustus, 179-180
Heanes, Herbert, 214
Heard, Bob, 216
Hearst, William Randolph, 132
Hibernia Savings and Loan Society (and Irish Catholic politics), 89-90
Hilliard, David, 214-215
Hirabayashi, Gordon K., 186-187
Holden, William B., 196
Holland, Andrew, 83
Holliday, George, 228
Holliday, S.W., 83
Hollister, William H., 127
Holman, Alexander, 195-198
Home Rule, 47-48, 54-55
Ho, Kim, 158
Hooks, Benjamin, 217
Hoover, Herbert, 174
Horowitz, David, 215-218
Horrall, C.B., 191
Hotel Hackett, 91-93
Hsieh, Frederic, 219
Huerta, Delores, 200-201
Hughes, Langston, 206
Hunt, Matthew, 222
Huse, Charles E., 7
Hutton, Bobby, 214
Hyde, George (Alcalde), 68

I

Iacaban, M.H., 156
Ice Cube, 221
Ide, William, 64
Imperial Valley, Asian Indians in, 162-163
Indians,
    concept of god, 10
    progress in Mexican California, 52-53
    revolts in Mexican California, 53-54
    Southern California labor, 126-128
    Spanish definition of, 19-20
    Spanish stereotypes of, 7-8
    Topangana, end of the world, 11
    view from the Spanish world, 17
Indizuela, 26-27
Indochina Migration and Refugee Assistance Act of 1975, 223
Innis, Roy, 236
Insured Benefits Brokers, 241
Irish Catholics in 19th century California, 87-101
Isaacs, Issac, 82-83
Isle of Santa Cruz, 2
Itliong, Larry, 199-201
Ito, Lance, 233-240

J

Jackson, Andrew, 60-61
Jackson, Helen Hunt, 126-127
Jacquet, Illinois, 190
Japanese American Citizens League, 164-165
Japanese Americans,
    in the 1920s and 1930s, 163-164
    in World War II, 183-187
    model Asian stereotype, 144
Japanese labor, 1880-1910, 130-134
Japanese in the Progressive Era, 135-148
Japanese Mexican Labor Union (JMLU), 145-146
Japanese Relocations, 183-187
Jazz in the African American community, 139-141
Jenkins, Slim, 194-195
Jimenez, Fortun, 2
Johnson, Charles S., 176
Johnson, Hiram, 133-148, 152, 161, 193
Johnson, President Lyndon B., 211
Johnson, T.T., 74
Jones, Jarnes, 211
Jones, Leroi, 214
Jordan, David Starr, 131
Juarez Patriotic Club, 129

K

Kachinas (defined), 20
Kae (Korean self help bank), 158
Kakehasi bridge, 147-148
Kamines, Bernard, 230
Kang, Younghill, 158-159
Kelly, Ken, 217
KELW (Spanish broadcasting radio station), 172-173
Kanzaki, Kiichi, 146

Keeting, Charles, 234
Kennedy, David Ray, 205
Kennedy, Tracy, 237
Khan, Babu and Naimat, 161
Kimball, Jack, 82
Kimmel, Husband E., 183-187
King, B.B., 244
King, Larry, 230, 234
King, Rodney, 227-246
Knight's Ferry, Chinese settlement in, 106-107
Knight, William J., 106
Knox, Michael, 236-237
Koon, Stacey, 229-231
Koreans in California, 157-159
    since 1965, 220-223
Korematsu, Fred, 147, 186
Kowalski, Barry F., 231
Kroeber, A.E., 11
Ku Klux Klan, 149-152, 169, 208

L

La Escuela Mexico (creation of), 169
Landaeta, Father Martin, 35
Land Law of 1951, 63, 98-99, 128-130
La Paz, settlement of, 4
Larkin, Thomas Oliver, 55-56, 59, 61-65, 68
Lashly, William Henry, 178
Lasuen, Father Fermin Francisco de, 11, 23-24,
    28-30, 33-44
Lataillade, Caesar, 100
Leaner, Dr. Earl T., 139
Lee, Dr. Henry, 239
Lee, Kwang-son, 157
Lee, Odell, 214
Leidesdorff, William A., 66-69
Leonis, Miguel, 124
Lew Case, 219-220
Life In California (Alfred Robinson), 40-50
Light, Allen B. (first African American in
    California), 90
Lim, J., 157
Lincoln Roosevelt League, 138-139
Lindsay, Carl, 146-147
Little Chile riot of 1849, 75-76
Little Negro Hill, 81-82
Lizzarras, J.M., 146
Long, Percy, 179
Lopez, Francisco, 75-76
Los Angeles (founding of), 29-30, 36-37
Los Hermanos Banuelos, 172
Love, Harry S., 98-100
Lummis, Charles Fletcher, 175
Lumumba, Biko, 217
Lynching of Francisco Torres, 121-122

M

Maclay, Charles, 123
Mailer, Norman, 214
Malaspina, Alejandro, 33, 41
Malcolm X, 212
Malone, A.E., 138
Manifest Destiny, 59-60
Manila Galleons, 6
Mapp, Lester, 139-141
Marshall, James, 73-74, 80-81, 99
Marshall, Thurgood, 197-198, 210-211
Mason, Biddy, 95-96
Mason, Eula, 97
Matsuda, Mari, 224
McClatchy, H.J., 151
McClatchy, V.S., 147-149, 151-152, 160, 164-165,
    169
McCone, John A., 211-212
McCracklin, Jimmy, 242-245
McDougal, Governor John, 68, 109
McKinny, Laura Hart, 237-239
McPherson, Aimee Semple, 175
McWilliams, Carey, 127, 188, 190, 218, 223
Megino, Liz, 156
Menendez, Erik and Lyle, 234
Merriam, Governor Frank, 176
Mexican Americans,
    economic decline 1851 to 1880s, 128-130
    in nineteenth century California, 87-101
    in Southern California from ranchos to
        fields, 121
    in World War II, 187-192
    progress in California, 1920-1940, 167-181
Mexican California, 45-57
    economic questions and racial capitalism,
        48-49
    Spanish speaking foreigners, 59-72
Mexican gold rush in California, 75-76
Mexican repatriation and the Great Depression,
    174-175
Mexican labor in California, 1880-1910, 119-126
Mexican War and California, 59-72
Mexican War, Racism and Manifest Destiny, 65-
    66
Micheltorena, Manuel, 61
Miller and Lux, 143
Miller, Stuart Creighton, 104
Minikus, Lee W., 208-209
Miscegenation, 149-150
Mission Purisma Concepcion, 53
Mission San Gabriel, 8, 52-53
Mission San Jose, 8, 30
Mission San Luis Obispo, 22
Mission Santa Inez, 53

Rancho La Canada, 121
Rancho San Rafael, 121
Rancho Santa Margarita y Flores, 48
Randolph, A. Philip, 194-195
Randolph, T.E., 79
Rawls, James J., 21-22
Reading, Mayor John, 215
Reagan, Ronald, 206, 214-218
Reglamento of 1779, 25-26, 53-54, 69
Reiner, Ira, 230-231
Repatriation and Mexicans, 174-175
Reyes, Francisco, 42
Richardson, Friend, 163-164
Rivera, Captain Fernando, 19-20
Roberts, Frederick M., 180
Robinson, Alfred, 49-50
Robinson, Tyrone, 217
Robinson, Ruby, 150
Rodgers, Daniel, 90
Rodgers, Morses, 93
Roldan, Salvador, 150
Rolle, Andrew, 61
Rolph, Governor James, 131, 153-154, 176
Roosevelt, Franklin D., 154, 163, 176, 184-187, 197-198
Roosevelt, Theodore, 133
Ross, Dell, 214
Ross, E.A., 131
Rothmiller, Mike, 231
Rowell, Chester, 131-132, 144-145, 180
Royce, Josiah, 16
Ruby, Reuben, 79
Ruggles, David, 79
Rumford Fair Housing Act, 207-208
Rumford, W. Byron, 207-208
Russian American Company, 33-44

S

Sacred Expedition and Spanish settlement, 20-21
Sakamoto, James, 163
Salazar, Guadalupe, 171
Sanchez, Father, 52
Sanderson, Rev. Jeremiah, 91-94, 96-97
San Diego,
    discovery of, 4-5
    settlement of, 12-13
San Gabriel Mission (seizure of), 48
San Jose, establishment of, 36
Santa Barbara, 76-77
Sante Fe railroad, 124-126
Saxton, Alexander, 104
Scheck, Barry, 234-240
Scheer, Bob, 212-218
Schell, Abraham, 106

Schlatter, George, 234
Schmitz, Eugene, 129
Scott, Erven and Bernice, 195
Seale, Bobby, 212-218
Severson, W. Reed, 241
Shaler, William, 35
Serra, Junipero, 4, 12, 15-30, 35, 40
Shaman, 11
Shapiro, Robert, 234-240
Shelley, Mayor John F., 207
Sheppard, Hannibal T., 178
Shibley, George, 189
Shima, George, 131
Shoemaker, Clyde, 189-190
Shoong, Joe, 165
Sikhs, 159-163
Simi Valley trial of LAPD officers for King
    beating, 229-231
Simms, Gabriel, 83
Simpson, Sir George, 49-50
Simpson, Nicole Brown, 232-240
Simpson, O.J., 227-246
Singer, Melanie and Timothy, 228-229
Singh, Bisaka and Jawala, 161
Singh, Puna, 160
Slavery and California statehood, 90-91
Sleepy Lagoon incident, 189-190
Sloat, John Drake, 65-66
Small, Joe, 195-198
Smith, Page, 216
Smith, Robert, 95
Sola, Governor Pablo Vicente de, 54
Somerville, J. Alexander, 97
Sontag, Susan, 214
Southern Pacific railroad, 124
Spark, Anna Marie, 66, 69
Spain, seeds of racism in California, 12-13
Spanish California,
    1769-1821, 15-31
    addicted to Independence, 40-41
    black settlers, 42-43
    last days of, 33-44
Spanish conquistadors, visions of California
    Indians, 19
Spanish settlers and violent cultural conflict,
    27-28
Spencer, Glenn, 241
Stanford, Leland, 112, 114
Starkey, James R., 80
Stephens, William D., 147
Steward, McCants, 138
Stockton, Robert F., 66
Streeter, William, 77-78
Sutro, Adolph, 129
Sutter, John, 57, 61-65, 67

T

Taft, William Howard, 133, 136
Takaki, Ronald, 107, 114
Tanaka, Togo, 147
Taylor, President Zachary, 111
Tenney, Jack, 193-194
Thind Case, 160
Tholmer, Brandon, 234
Tomas (Indian accused of witchcraft), 53
Torres, Francisco (lynching of), 121-122
Toyota, Tritia., 234
Toypurina, 28
Trans-creation (theory of), 172, 188
Treaty of Cahuenga, 71
Trivors, Bob, 216
Tuoloumne anti-Chinese riot of July 4, 1849,
    105-106
Turner, Ike and Tina, 215
Two Years Before The Mast (Richard Henry
    Dana), 49-50

U

Unruh, Jesse (Big Daddy), 206-207
Urdaneta, Andres de, 6
U.S. v. Bhagat Singh, 160

V

Vallangca, Roberto, 156
Valdez, Maria Rita (founder of Rodeo Drive in
    Beverly Hills), 42
Velez, Lupe, 172
Vallejo, Dona Francisca Benicia Carrillo, 65
Vallejo, Mariano, 45-57, 60, 62-65
Vancouver, Captain George, 33, 38-39
VanPatter, Betty, 216-218
Varela, Serbullo, 69-70
Vasquez, Tiburcio, 99
Velazquez, Zeferino, 170-172
Veltmann, Gerald E., 197
Vera Cruz, Philip, 202
Verdugo, Don Julio, 121
Victoria, Manuel, 47-48
Vila, Vicente, 18, 20
Visel, Charles P., 174
Vizcaino, Sebastian, 6-7
Vosburg, Fritz, 83

W

Walker, C.J., 138
Walker, Joe, 231
Ward, Mary Francis, 96-97
Warfield, J.B., 79
Warren, Governor Earl, 184-187
War Relocation Authority, 184-187
Watson, Marvin, 211
Watsonville lettuce strike of 1930, 156
Watts riot of 1965, 206-211
Weaver, Robert C., 177
Weisberg, Judge Stanley, 230-231
Welch, Richard J., 152-153
Wheeler, B. Gordon, 43
White, Terry L., 230
Whithe, Henry, 80
Williams, Willie, 222, 237
Wilson, Governor Pete, 221-223, 230-232, 241
Wind, Timothy, 228-231
Wolfskill, William, 74
Wong, Delbert, 233-234
Wong, John, 245
Wong, Wei Ming, 241
Woods, Arthur, 174
Workingmen's Party, 117, 119
Wright, Carleton, 197

X

Xenophobia,
    directed toward the Chinese, 103-118
    directed toward the Filipino, 152-157
    directed against the Japanese American,
    183-187

Y

Yniguez, Arcadio, 171
Yoneda, Karl, 163
Yoon, Do-Yun, 157
Yorba family, 45
York, Margaret, 234, 238
Yorty, Sam, 210-211
Young, C.C., 149, 174

Z

Zambos, 12
Zoot Suit riot of 1943, 190-192